NATIONAL GEOGRAPHIC

T R A V E L E R

costa rica

NATIONAL GEOGRAPHIC

TRAVELER

costa rica

by Christopher P. Baker

National Geographic
Washington, D.C.

CONTENTS

Pages 2–3: The quintessential cone of Arenal volcano, centerpiece of a national park
Opposite: Surfers flock to Playa Samara in Guanacaste

TRAVELING WITH EYES OPEN

Alert travelers go with a purpose and leave with a benefit. If you travel responsibly, you can help support wildlife conservation, historic preservation, and cultural enrichment in the places you visit. You can enrich your own travel experience as well.

To be a geo-savvy traveler:

- Recognize that your presence has an impact on the places you visit.

- Spend your time and money in ways that sustain local character. (Besides, it's more interesting that way.)

- Value the destination's natural and cultural heritage.

- Respect the local customs and traditions.

- Express appreciation to local people about things you find interesting and unique to the place: its nature and scenery, music and food, historic villages and buildings.

- Vote with your wallet: Support the people who support the place, patronizing businesses that make an effort to celebrate and protect what's special there. Seek out local shops, restaurants, and inns. Use tour operators who love their home—who love taking care of it and showing it off. Avoid businesses that detract from the character of the place.

- Enrich yourself, taking home memories and stories to tell, knowing that you have contributed to the preservation and enhancement of the destination.

That is the type of travel now called geotourism, defined as "tourism that sustains or enhances the geographical character of a place—its environment, culture, aesthetics, heritage, and the well-being of its residents." To learn more, visit National Geographic's Center for Sustainable Destinations at *travel.nationalgeographic.com/travel/geotourism.*

TRAVELER

costa rica

ABOUT THE AUTHOR & PHOTOGRAPHER

Christopher P. Baker

After studying geography at the University of London and Latin American studies at the University of Liverpool, Christopher P. Baker settled in California and established a career as a travel writer, photographer, and lecturer. He has written four books about Costa Rica, plus the Costa Rica ¡Pura Vida! travel app. He has also authored and photographed the *National Geographic Traveler* guidebook to Colombia, and written *National Geographic Traveler* guidebooks to Cuba, Dominican Republic, and Panama, as well as *Mi Moto Fidel: Motorcycling Through Castro's Cuba* (National Geographic Adventure Press). Baker—the Lowell Thomas Award Travel Journalist of the Year 2008—also writes regularly for such publications as *Robb Report* and *National Geographic Traveler* magazine. He has spoken at the National Geographic Society (televised live from National Geographic); has been profiled in *USA Today;* and has appeared on ABC, CBS, CNN, Fox TV, MSNBC, and NPR, among other radio and TV outlets. He escorts National Geographic Expeditions tours to Costa Rica, Panama, and Cuba. He promotes his work through his website: christopherbaker.com.

Charting Your Trip

Abundantly blessed by Mother Nature, Costa Rica—a world leader in ecotourism—enthralls for its scenic beauty and tropical wildlife. Wilderness lodges throughout the country immerse you deep in the animal and avian world, placing you in close proximity to monkeys, jaguars, marine turtles, and birds by the score.

The diversity of terrains also astounds. You can explore a lowland rain forest or snorkel a coral reef in the morning and steep yourself in the mist-shrouded cloud forest or hike the rim of a steaming volcano in the afternoon. Active travelers rave about the dizzying options offered by this small-size nation. Sportfishing. Mountain biking. White-water rafting. Horseback riding. Even golf! Your options are seemingly endless.

How to Visit in One Week

Despite so many options, it's easy to plan an itinerary that condenses the crème de la crème. A week-long visit should begin in San José, the capital city, where rental cars, buses, and planes are all readily available for your touring needs. Although it lacks the colonial structures of many other Central American cities, San José's Teatro Nacional is a neoclassical gem, and several superb museums honor pre-Columbian cultures. The city's key sites can all be seen in one day.

San José makes a great base for visiting the surrounding Central Highlands, where there's plenty to keep you busy. De rigueur sights include Poás volcano, a little more than an hour by road northwest of San José, where you can drive to the summit and peer down into the steaming depths. While here, you'll want to visit La Paz Waterfall Garden, five miles (8 km) to the east, with superb exhibits on butterflies, birds, snakes, and frogs, as well as rigorous hikes to the waterfalls. The drive from San José to Poás takes you through coffee country. En route, stop at Café Britt for a fun-filled tour that explains coffee culture, from the plantation to the cup.

Pre-Columbian pottery figure

Visitor Information

For the most up-to-date information on recommended hotels, travel agencies, ecotourist hot spots, ways to get around, and awe-inspiring tours, check out the Costa Rican government's official tourism website at visitcostarica.com.

Another excellent resource is the English-language weekly *Tico Times,* available online at ticotimes.net. Once a print newspaper, the website offers an overview of the country's current events as well as travel ideas within Costa Rica and details on local restaurants and arts and cultural happenings.

Money Matters

While the national currency is the *colón*, U.S. currency is widely accepted. Most stores, shops, restaurants, and tour companies take dollars. One tip: Bring lots of single dollar bills for tips, streetside souvenirs, and other small purchases, as change for larger bills may be hard to come by. If you do use colones, know that exchange rates are notoriously fickle; check the rate before leaving for your trip, but expect some fluctuation upon arrival. Travelers checks are difficult to cash due to widespread fraud. Credit cards are widely accepted. Many banks have ATMs that work with U.S. bank cards, usually with a small usage charge.

Admission Costs

The $–$$$$$ scale used in this guidebook delineates entry fees into Costa Rica attractions:
- $ = Under $10
- $$ = $10–$15
- $$$ = $15–$20
- $$$$ = $20–$25
- $$$$$ = Over $25

Next, consider two days exploring the Monteverde region—about 100 miles (160 km) west of Poás via a cliff-hanging, potholed road—where options are boundless. Start with a hike in the world-famous Monteverde Cloud Forest Biological Reserve, considered ground zero for birders keen to spot a resplendent quetzal. A zip line ride on the Sky Tram adds an adrenaline rush to your forest exploration. And you'll want to check out the area's many fine restaurants, plus its quirky nature exhibits, including Bat Jungle, the Serpentarium, and the Jewels of the Rain Forest Bio-Art Exhibition, which displays thousands of colorful arachnids and insects.

To close out your week's adventure, drive to Volcán Arenal—Costa Rica's most active volcano—a circuitous three-hour trip from Monteverde around Laguna de Arenal. Even if the clouds dampen the view of the volcano, there's fabulous hiking on trails at the base, horseback riding, and even helicopter rides—plus steaming hot springs in which to soak.

If you're eager to visit the beach during your week's stay, bypass Arenal and head southeast from Monteverde to the coast. Any of the country's stellar Pacific beaches will beckon—fine locations include Jacó and Parque Nacional Manuel Antonio (about three and four hours southeast of Monteverde, respectively).

If You Have More Time

Costa Rica's biggest draw, undoubtedly, is wildlife viewing. You'll see monkeys, iguanas, and a rainbow of birds everywhere, but dozens of national parks and private wildlife reserves offer unparalleled opportunities for spying a Noah's Ark worth of wildlife species. Corcovado (on the Osa

NOT TO BE MISSED:

A drive up Irazú volcano **90**

White-water rafting on the Río Pacuare **96**

Hiking the cloud forest at Monteverde **108**

Bird-watching at Parque Nacional Palo Verde **112**

Riding a zip line at Arenal **115**

Steeping at the Tabacón hot springs **116**

Watching leatherback turtles lay eggs at Playa Grande **141**

A crocodile safari on the Río Tárcoles **157**

Lazing at a top wilderness lodge **186–187**

A boat tour at Tortuguero **224**

Traditional oxcarts, vestiges of a bygone era in Costa Rica, are a rare sight today.

Peninsula southeast of the capital, a nine-hour drive or a short flight away) and Tortuguero (150 miles/240 km by road and canal northeast of San José on the Caribbean), for example, both offer genuine wilderness experiences and a chance to experience Costa Rica's incredible natural diversity, while beaches up and down the Caribbean and Pacific shores promise virtually guaranteed viewing of marine turtles nesting and hatching.

Birding is also world-class throughout the country, with more than 850 species recorded to date. In addition to quetzal-spotting in Monteverde, birders flock to Caño Negro wildlife refuge (about 50 miles/80 km north of Arenal) for waterbirds by the thousands, and Carara National Park (a three-hour drive west of San José) to see rare scarlet macaws.

For exploring more off-the-beaten-path zones, the southwestern Pacific coast of Nicoya, in the western reaches of the country, offers challenges by 4WD (if fording rivers is your idea of fun). Also, remote parts of both the Northern Lowlands and the Osa Peninsula beyond Corcovado have been opened up, permitting access to pristine areas teeming with wildlife. And the

Renting a Car

Renting a car is a fabulous way to get around Costa Rica, but it comes with some warnings.

Roads throughout the country are poor. Local drivers can be reckless. Stray cattle, pedestrians in the road, and potholes are additional hazards.

Don't leave anything in your car, for fear of theft. Don't pay tickets on the spot; take care of them with the rental company.

Insurance is mandatory, and most rental companies refuse to honor insurance issued abroad. Drive the speed limit, be on your guard, and you'll be fine.

Talamanca mountains, knifing southeast from San José, are a rugged frontier where indigenous communities on both the Caribbean and Pacific sides are now opening up to tourism.

Active Pursuits

Costa Rica is also famous for surfing, and surfers come from far and wide for its diamond-dust beaches and thrilling breakers. Beaches up and down the Pacific coast (especially Jacó) have great surfing, and instruction is available everywhere. Puerto Viejo, on the Caribbean, is also a fine option.

Costa Rica has few coral reefs, but scuba diving is nonetheless superb, with large pelagics (including manta rays and sharks) being the biggest draw. Drake Bay, on the Osa Peninsula, and Playas del Coco in northern Nicoya are the main centers, but experienced divers will want to try Isla Cocos, 300 miles (485 km) off the Pacific coast.

White-water rafting in Costa Rica is also top shelf, with rivers such as the Central Highland's Pacuare and the Reventazón drawing aficionados to their rapids as they cascade Caribbean-bound.

Sportfishing gives anglers rod-bending fights to remember. Seeking tarpon or snook? Then head to Parismina or Barra del Colorado, on the Caribbean. On the Pacific, sportfishing vessels set out principally from Playas del Coco, Tamarindo, Playa Herradura (near Jacó), Quepos, and Golfito. ∎

What to Take

Costa Rica has a tropical climate, so dress accordingly. Expect hot days with warm evenings, except in mountain areas where nights can be chilly. Avoid bright colors if you want to get close to wildlife. Informal wear is fine nearly everywhere, but you might want to bring a more elegant outfit for smarter restaurants in San José.

You'll want comfortable shoes for hiking, but be prepared to get them wet (bring a spare pair). Also bring insect repellent, sunglasses, sunscreen, and a hat or cap to ward off the tropical sun.

Wet or Dry? Best Times to Visit Costa Rica

The nation has distinct wet (May–Nov.) and dry (Dec.–April) seasons, and weather is predictable throughout the year. Dry season is considered the best time for touring, as sunny skies are the norm. It's also high season, when many hotels are full, rental cars are booked, and rates for both are high. However, Costa Rica also has a dozen distinct climatic zones, with many microclimates and regional variations. Along the Caribbean and the Pacific southwest, there is a good chance of rainfall year-round. And while temperatures throughout the country vary little year-round, Guanacaste and northern Nicoya broil in spring.

The wet season sees a drop in visitors and hotel and car rental rates. The Institute of Costa Rican Tourism (ICT) promotes this time of year as "green season" with good reason: The country is lush from all the rains. In much of the country, rainfall is typically an afternoon affair, often limited to short-lived downpours. However, the Caribbean, Pacific southwest, and Northern Lowlands often see day after day of heavy rains. And exploring such off-the-beaten-path corners as southwest Nicoya and the Osa Peninsula can be tough going.

Note that Costa Ricans call the summer wet season *invierno* (winter) and the winter dry season *verano* (summer).

History & Culture

Muse in San José's Teatro Nacional de Costa Rica
Opposite: A traditional oxcart wheel at Fábrica de Carretas Eloy Alfaro, Sarchí

Costa Rica Today

Common clichés about Costa Rica paint a canvas in tropical hues. The background is of glorious emerald, teeming with colorful wildlife: rainbow-hued scarlet macaws, electric blue morpho butterflies the size of saucers, and the iridescent green holy grail of neotropical birds, the quetzal.

The settings are also familiar: sweeping rain forest, rugged mountains, fire-spitting volcanoes, and lonesome beaches stretching along jungle-lined shores. All of these images fulfill the stereotype of Costa Rica as a Lilliputian country proffering virginal nature on a Brobdingnagian scale.

These familiar impressions are real and made easier to confirm by the nation's size: about the same as West Virginia or Nova Scotia and only slightly larger than Switzerland. Costa Rica has the advantage of being small enough to explore end to end in a

The sun casts its waning rays over beachgoers outside Parque Nacional Manuel Antonio.

matter of days A more slothful pace lets you discover the full kaleidoscope of wilderness wonders. The diversity of terrain is remarkable, and the landscape changes as if on a revolving hinge.

The Central Highlands are ringed by mountains flanked by row upon row of glossy green coffee bushes. Guanacaste is cowboy country and provides a strong sense of the past, while the Nicoya Peninsula beckons with diamond-dust beaches where turtles come ashore to lay eggs. The Caribbean appeals for a distinct culture rooted in a Jamaican heritage. No less compelling is the rugged Pacific coast, popular with surfers. The lagoons of the Northern Lowlands boil with tarpon, and the remote Talamanca massif is an unexplored world where jaguars still roam free.

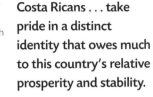

Costa Ricans . . . take pride in a distinct identity that owes much to this country's relative prosperity and stability.

Virtually everywhere you will encounter wildlife: Costa Rica boasts 5 percent of all the known species on Earth, including more butterfly species than are found in all of Africa. Seeing the wildlife is easy. About 28 percent of the country is protected in wildlife reserves or national parks. Local entrepreneurs have been inventive in finding ways to make wildlife viewing simple. The country boasts scores of serpentariums, butterfly farms, and elevated walkways through the rain forest canopy. You could spend a lifetime oohing and aahing over the exotic flora and fauna.

Costa Rica, the most homogeneous society in Central America, is set apart from its neighbors by its lack of indigenous culture. Visitors will find no Teotihuacans, Tuxmels, or Tikals, although Monumento Nacional Guayabo continues to be excavated from the jungle and promises to elevate Costa Rica's archaeological standing. As capital cities go, San José is small fry, but it boasts art museums and some phenomenal gold and jade museums. It has improved vastly in recent years, with a vibrant nightlife that makes even the most city-wise sophisticates sit up and take notice.

Costa Rica has blossomed as a popular destination for active pursuits, from angling to white-water rafting. It's also become recognized as one of the world's leading ecotourism destinations. In fact, Costa Rica helped define the notion of ecotourism due to good stewardship of the nation's 12 distinct ecological zones. Today, more than 160 national parks, wildlife refuges, and other protected entities lure nature lovers seeking a wish list of tropical treats: a birding trip in the Central Highlands, an aquatic jungle journey in Parque Nacional Tortuguero, a crocodile safari on the Tárcoles River, whale-watching south of Uvita, and perhaps even a stint volunteering to help save endangered species, such as leatherback turtles or scarlet and great green macaws.

Ticos

Costa Ricans—*los costarricenses*, or *Ticos*—are unique on the isthmus. They take pride in a distinct identity that owes much to this country's relative prosperity and stability in a region beset by poverty and turmoil. Tenaciously proud of their country, Ticos cling to tradition.

Costa Rica's original inhabitants were the roughly 100,000 indigenous peoples orga-nized in disparate tribes. Most of them rapidly succumbed to disease and the ruthless ways of 16th-century Spanish conquistadors and were reduced to subsistence status. Whereas in neighboring countries Spaniards intermixed with the native peoples, pro-ducing a large mixed-blood population, Costa Rica, largely devoid of an indigenous base, has remained primarily European.

The early Spanish colonialists came in search of gold and, frustrated in that quest, settled the Central Valley. Starting in the 18th century, they were joined by other Euro-pean immigrants, notably Germans and Swiss peasant farmers who began to arrive in larger numbers in the 19th century—along with Italians—as the boom in coffee took hold. Widely dispersed in the countryside, they were quickly assimilated into the mainstream Spanish-speaking Tico culture. On the Caribbean, African slaves had intermarried with Native Americans as early as the 16th century, result-ing in mixed-blood Moskitos. Beginning in the 1870s, about 11,000 English-speaking Jamaicans also came as contract labor; they put down roots in the Caribbean Lowlands and have managed to affirm their own colorful Afro-Caribbean identities. "White" highlanders looked down (literally and figuratively) upon their darker brethren; it was only in 1949 that blacks were granted citizenship and legally permitted to travel to and take jobs in the highlands.

> **The peaceable Costa Rican way is based on compromise and a desire to please ... using charm, humor, and avoidance of conflict.**

In recent decades, there has been a large influx of North Americans (around 50,000) seeking to retire in the sun in Costa Rica, predominantly around Escazú, Santa Ana, and Alajuela. In addition, Nicaraguans and other Central American immigrants (around 750,000, about 16 percent of Costa Rica's population of 4.8 million) have arrived in the wake of warfare in their own countries, causing some resentment among Costa Ricans. Easily recognized by their dark skin and Native American fea-tures, Nicaraguan refugees are treated with a general contempt by their color- and class-conscious host culture. Most recently, Europeans of every nationality have begun to arrive as well; these newest residents have primarily settled around the Pacific and Caribbean beaches.

What Makes Ticos Tick: The evolution of *criollo* (locally born) society differed markedly from that of neighboring lands, characterized by feudal land ownership and serfdom. In Costa Rica, the neglected settlers tilled their own lands and were equalized as peasant farmers, called *hermanticos* (little brothers), the name given to fellow citizens by the ruling cliques, who shared hardships and destitution. (In 1719, the governor of Costa Rica complained that he, too, had to till his own land.) In time, they became known by the diminutive: *Tico*. Cut off from most out-side influence by the forbidding terrain, they began to develop distinct traits—not least *ticismos*, a unique vocabulary and slang, and a profound aversion to conflict. The peaceable Costa Rican way is based on compromise and a desire to please, known as *quedar bien* (to be appealing), using charm, humor, and avoidance of conflict. These sometimes surface-thin courtesies are endearing. But the

Many Costa Ricans practice the Catholic faith.

temporizing Ticos know that promises should never be taken as such. Regional blood runs thick. Frustration and resentment get bottled up and find their outlets in this otherwise pacific society in drunkenness, lunacy on the roads, and surreptitious acts of revenge.

Although Tico society is not fraught with the tensions of neighboring nations, Costa Rica is far from egalitarian. It is riddled with elitist ways. "Whiteness" is considered an ideal, and many urbanites and members of the San José–based social elite look down on campesinos (peasants). Nonetheless, while 77 percent of the population is urban, the vast majority of Ticos retain ties to the land; Costa Rica has the highest rural population density in Latin America. The vast majority of rural folk live a simple life, tending coffee and cows in the highlands or as *sabaneros* (cowboys) in Guanacaste, where

Costa Rica—a colorful aviary of almost 900 bird species—supports 51 types of hummingbirds alone.

everyday life evokes the cowboy spirit. Tico society is far from urbane: The only true city is San José, the capital, which has burgeoned in recent years. Most other towns are regional market centers with their own subtle charm.

Standards of Living: Costa Rica's annual per capita income in 2015 was about $15,500, and its standard of living is exemplary in a region racked by destitution and disease. Both life expectancy and infant mortality are on a par with developed nations. The population enjoys free (albeit much-burdened) public education and decent (though inefficient) health care, paid for by none-too-progressive taxation. The telecommunications system is the equal of anywhere in Latin America. The average Tico lives thriftily in a modest-size home with a small garden patch. But the regional disparities are great; the average income in the Northern Lowlands is less than 20 percent of the national average. About 20 percent of the population are *marginados* (disadvantaged groups) who live in humbling poverty, usually in wood and adobe huts in the countryside or on the fringes of the towns, in slum shacks hammered together from corrugated metal sheets and refuse.

Indigenous Peoples Today: Costa Rica has around 104,000 indigenous people in a population of 4.8 million; about 2.5 percent of the total. The Indigenous Bill of 1977 guaranteed the eight indigenous tribes rights to self-government on their lands in which the government held title in trust. Today they live a reclusive, marginalized existence and are widely dispersed on 24 indigenous reserves in the Talamancas and the rugged mountains of the Pacific Southwest. Only in 1992 did the indigenous peoples receive citizenship, and they were permitted to vote for the first time only in 1994.

While the campesino views himself as a pioneer and the forest as a resource to be conquered, indigenous people see themselves as custodians of the forest and its interrelated inhabitants. Native Americans live in simple homesteads scattered around the reservations, much of it low-quality land. The men hunt in the forests; grow bananas, beans, citrus fruits, coca, and corn; and drink home-brewed *chicha* (beer made of yucca or corn). The communities struggle to preserve vital elements of their traditional culture. Most wear Western clothes and speak Spanish—few know their native languages. Alcoholism and other social problems are rife. Their cultural integrity is further eroded by the efforts of missionaries working to break down their traditional religious beliefs.

Politically disempowered, these groups are suspicious of outsiders and feel intensely dissatisfied by the National Commission for Indigenous Affairs (CONA), which has responsibility for their welfare. Despite the passage of laws intended to safeguard their heritage, the government continues to issue rights to powerful mining and logging entities that whittle away at the Native Americans' land. While not subject to the systematic persecution of Guatemala's indigenous peoples, Costa Rica's Native Americans suffer ongoing rights violations. Yet the past few decades have brought attempts to provide greater self-sufficiency, including the establishment of the first Native American bank in 1994. Acknowledgment and appreciation of indigenous cultures has grown in recent years.

> **The only true city [in Costa Rica] is San José, the capital . . . Most other towns are regional market centers with their own subtle charm.**

The Bribrí, who inhabit the mountains inland of the southern Caribbean, welcome visitors on a limited basis. Other groups are turning to tourism as interest in indigenous culture revives, although a permit is required from CONA to enter some reserves. A revival in crafts is nascent; women of the Boruca and other tribes of the Pacific Southwest still dress in traditional garments. Among the Chorotega of Nicoya, a renaissance of pride finds its outlet in faithfully reproduced ceramics made by the villagers of Guaitíl.

Government & Politics

The 1949 constitution defines Costa Rica as a democratic republic run by an elected president and a 19-member cabinet, called the Council of Government. A president must be a secular citizen and traditionally could only serve one term (as of 2003, a president may serve two terms). Power rests with the Legislative Assembly, composed of 57 elected members (*diputados*) representing the country's seven provinces. Voting is compulsory for citizens aged 18 to 70 (though there are no consequences for those who choose not to vote). Elections are held on the first Sunday in February, every four years, and are overseen by a Special Electoral Tribunal whose members are elected by Supreme Court judges and serve staggered six-year terms. Diputados are elected by proportional representation, with seats allocated according to the number of votes for each party. They serve four-year terms and may not be elected for consecutive terms. There is no higher chamber of review. The legislature's right to veto presidential decisions is a source of friction that occasionally results in rule by presidential decree. The Assembly sits in a handsome Moorish building overlooking the Plaza de la Democracia in San José.

Costa Rica is divided into seven provinces: Alajuela, Cartago, Guanacaste, Heredia, Limón, Puntarenas, and San José. Each is run by a governor appointed by the president, while municipal councils run the day-to-day affairs of 421 *distritos* (districts) that make up the province's 81 *cantones* (counties).

Parties & Personalities: Costa Rica traditionally alternates presidents every election, switching between candidates for the two great rival parties: the National Liberation Party (PLN) and the Social Christian Unity Party (PUSC); victors, however, rarely win by more than 2 or 3 percent. The left-leaning PLN inclines toward

welfare-state liberalism. The PUSC is made up of progressive conservatives who support business interests. The PLN traditionally holds a majority in the Legislative Assembly. Both parties are clannish. However, in 2014, Luis Guillermo Solís, of the newly formed Citizens Action Party, broke the mold when he won the presidency.

Costa Rica's political process is mired in cronyism, and favors and contracts are dispensed liberally by the victorious side. Bribery and corruption are rife in a country whose politics have been dominated since independence by a small number of families. The last four presidents have all been tainted by corruption scandals, and two—Miguel Ángel Rodríguez and Rafael Ángel Calderón Fournier—were jailed.

Top Ten Local Phrases

¿Al chile?	Seriously?
Con toda la pata	Perfect, fantastic
¡Guacala!	Disgusting!
¡Lo duda!	You said it!
¡Pura vida!	"Pure life," used as a greeting or as "Cool!" or "Perfect!"
¡Que polo!	Pathetic! How lame!
¡Salado!	Tough luck!
Tico/Tica	A Costa Rican male/female
Tiquicia	Costa Rica
Tuanis	A greeting meaning "fantastic" or "great"

Public employees—25 percent of the workforce—form the country's most powerful interest group; the well-paid bureaucracy is a crippling burden on the economy. Says one Ticoism, "The government is a cash cow with a thousand teats and everyone wants a teat to suck." The interminable bureaucratic process has given rise to a whole class of workers called *despachantes*, who tackle the bureaucracy on behalf of others.

Schoolchildren parade the Costa Rican flag on Independence Day.

Pride in Neutrality: Costa Rica declared neutrality in 1949 and has no armed forces. A heavily armed National Guard looks after the nation's security, backed by various specialized paramilitary police units. Pride in neutrality is reflected in the Ticos' passive psyche. They are not easily aroused to strong emotion or political passions about issues: "Don Pepe" Figueres (1906–1990), leader of the 1948 revolution, accused them of being as "domesticated as sheep." Issues either get resolved by consensus, or, frequently, get shelved to avoid conflict and thus fester unresolved. Harmony is more highly valued than discord, even at the cost of irresolution.

Post-independence politics has been marked by liberalism and stability. The country has had its fair share of *caudillos* (dictatorial leaders), but most redeemed themselves as proponents of progressive reform, and only three presidents have been military men. Ticos pride themselves on the "cleanliness" of their political process. Election day is a national holiday, which Ticos turn into a grand fiesta. Elections are not marred by the violence and mayhem that has traditionally accompanied polling in neighboring countries (during elections, control of the police force reverts to the Special Electoral Tribunal to protect constitutional guarantees). Costa Rica's mainstream media is conservative. ∎

Food & Drink

Costa Rica boasts fine dining, concentrated overwhelmingly in San José, where the restaurant scene plays all the notes on the international scale. Beyond the capital city, however, Ticos are timid diners whose affinities are closely attached to homey peasant fare.

Arroz con pollo, a traditional Latin American meal of rice and chicken with salad and plantains

The ubiquitous staple of rice and black beans—*gallo pinto*—forms the backbone of local cuisines, or *comida típica*. Even breakfast, typically gallo pinto with scrambled eggs, isn't exempt from this rule. Served with fried plantains (Costa Ricans are fond of fried foods) and a basic salad of tomatoes and cabbage, gallo pinto becomes a cheap *casado*, or set special, sometimes served with *sopa negra*, a bean broth. Roast pork is the main meat staple. Both it and chicken are often roasted over coffee wood (*a la leña*), which gives a smoky flavor. Many restaurants serve steaks (*lomito*). Chewy is the rule, and rarely do beef dishes come up to par for North American tastes, although *lomito encebollado,* steak marinated with local Linzano sauce, is often delicious. Seafoods are relatively scarce away from the coasts, though shrimp and lobster dishes are widely available. In San José the fish of choice is *corvina* (sea bass), usually fried with garlic (*ajo*). At seaside resorts you'll also find dolphin fish (*dorado*), swordfish, and snapper (*pargo*), almost always fried and served with white rice.

Corn finds its way into tortillas and corn pancakes called *chorreados*, and *tamales*, stuffed cornmeal pastries wrapped and baked in corn husks. Jalapeños and other hot spices are rarely used. Nor are vegetables, though overboiled carrots and greens are served, and other vegetables find their way into soups and stews, such as *olla de carne*, a meat and vegetable stew of potato, corn, yucca, and gourds. The favored vegetable is plantain (a relative of the banana) served fried with almost any meal.

Dragon fruit

INSIDER TIP:

The coffee served at restaurants can be weak and watery. You'll taste the most delicious cups on farm and plantation tours, offered as day trips from San José. The best ones take you to organic, fair-trade farms.

—NORIE QUINTOS
National Geographic Traveler *executive editor*

The Caribbean coast has its own unique flavor, one steeped in spices and coconut milk. Nowhere else in Costa Rica will you find salted codfish on the breakfast menu.

Everywhere, roadside stalls are cornucopias of tropical fruits: mangoes, melons, papayas, pineapples, and many you may not have heard of, such as the *carambeloa* (star fruit), *marañon* (cashew fruit), and *pejibayes* (like tiny coconuts), all of which find their way into *frescas*, fruit blended with ice, water, or milk, and sugar. Milk is used in cheeses such as the mild white *queso blanco*, which frequently finds its way into desserts. *Tres leches*, a three-layered custard flan, is the national dessert. It is best followed by espresso, drunk thick and sugared. *Café con leche* is coffee with hot milk in a 1:1 ratio.

Other dishes to try include:
Arregladas, greasy puff pastries filled with beef, chicken, or cheese.
Dulche de leche, boiled milk with sugar syrup.
Empanadas, turnovers filled with beans, meat, and potatoes.
Palmito, the soft heart of the *pejibaye* palm (not the fruit of the same name), popular in salads.

Costa Ricans are beer drinkers, and local lager-style brews (e.g., Imperial and Bavaria) are perfectly suited to the tropical climate. *Bocas*—snacks such as *ceviche* (marinated and spiced seafood) and thirst-inducing deep-fried *chicharrones* (pork rinds)—are usually served in bars. Wine is not popular, and imported wines, generally found in upscale restaurants, are expensive. The working man's drink is a potent, clear white spirit called *guaro*, worth trying once. Local liquors are best avoided, although coffee liqueurs make good souvenirs.

***Empanadas* filled with beans and meat**

Costa Rican History

When conquistadors first stepped ashore to subjugate the isthmus of Central America and claim it for Spain, the region was already a complex mosaic of cultures. The term "Costa Rica" first entered the European lexicon in 1522 when Capt. Gil González Davila (d. 1526) set out from Panama with a colonizing fleet to settle the region then known as Veragua.

González and his men found Indian dignitaries adorned with gold, for which the conquistador coined the term "Rich Coast." Compared to its northern neighbors, however, the land was relatively sparsely populated; perhaps no more than 100,000 inhabitants occupied the densely forested and mountainous region at the time of first European contact.

First Peoples

Little is known of the potpourri of indigenous peoples, who belonged to as many as 25 distinct and antagonistic groups that followed their own ways of life. The earliest occupants arrived from the north around 10,000 B.C., rather late in the day of human advancement following the first crossing by Hominoids of the Bering Strait around 60,000 B.C. Although these peoples came under the influence of the high civilizations of the Andes and Mesoamerica, the region remained a buffer zone and one whose meager population evolved neither the complex sociopolitical structures nor the monumental architecture of societies to the north and south. The peoples never unified to form a kingdom but remained under chieftains (*caciques*) who ruled over competing areas and whose names were adopted by the Spanish for each tribe.

> González and his men found Indian dignitaries adorned with gold, for which the conquistador coined the term "Rich Coast."

People of the Northwest: The most developed group were the Chorotega, who occupied today's Guanacaste following their arrival in the region around A.D. 500, displacing earlier and much simpler societies about which little is known. The Chorotega were influenced by the more advanced cultures of Mexico and Guatemala, initially the Olmec, and later by the Aztec and Maya, who dispersed south, imposing their culture on less advanced peoples. The name *chorotega* means "people who escaped." The details are shrouded in mystery.

The Chorotega lived in longhouses of wood and thatch that housed entire clans and centered on stone plazas where religious and civic ceremonies were held. The Chorotega constructed irrigation ditches and evolved into an advanced agricultural society based predominantly on corn. They also cultivated cotton that they wove and dyed for clothing. Among Costa Rica's indigenous peoples, only the Chorotega had a calendar and a written language, both of Maya origin. They spoke Nahua, an Aztec tongue, and shared in common with their northern ancestors a rigid hierarchical system that included nobility

Guayabo National Monument is the only pre-Columbian archaeological site of significance in Costa Rica.

and slavery, and a religious system based on bloodletting that included virgin sacrifice every full moon. The Chorotega were also noted for their distinctive ceramics, including phallic figurines, and anthropomorphic motifs of jaguars, frogs, and snakes in striking black, white, and red colors. They also traded for jade with their northern neighbors and worked it into exquisite figurines using a string-saw technique.

Highland Cultures: The Corobicís, who lived in small bands as hunter-gatherers and farmers, were the predominant group of the Central Highlands (Meseta Central). They traded gold with lowland tribes and became superb goldsmiths, leaving a legacy of beautiful amulets and statuettes depicting sacred idols, such as frogs. Although most groups lived in stockaded villages called *palenques,* the Corobicís built the only pre-Columbian town of note to have been discovered in Costa Rica: Guayabo, at the base of Volcán Turrialba. The settlement, which featured cobbled streets *(calzadas),* burial mounds, aqueducts, and stone cisterns, dates from around A.D. 1000 and may have had a population of 1,000 people. It was mysteriously abandoned around A.D. 1400.

The Cabécar and Guaymí inhabited the Talamancas farther south and lived primarily as hunter-gatherers. Shamans were important in these societies, which lived in harmony with their environment and revered the jaguar.

Coastal Tribes: The Boruca, Chibcha, and Diquis in the southwest, and the Bribrí, Caribes, and KéKöLdi on the Caribbean shore, drew their influences from South American cultures. They were semi-nomadic hunters and fishermen and supplemented the bounty of forest and sea with yucca, squash, and tubers. The preeminent group, the Diquis of the Pacific Southwest, shared with the Chorotega a tradition of ritual sacrifice and slavery.

About 1000 B.C., the Diquis began crafting lithic spheres called *bolas,* often of immense size, perhaps for religious purposes. A major change in the culture occurred between A.D. 500 and A.D. 800 as a result of contact with the seafaring peoples of Colombia or Peru. At about this time, the Diquis began fashioning gold figurines and soon became skilled goldsmiths, making use of gold from the Península de Osa. It appears that there was little cultural exchange between these mainly matriarchal groups, who remained in a state of internecine warfare. Both men and women of the Boruca were warriors.

Destruction of Local Culture

First Europeans: The first European to reach Costa Rica was Christopher Columbus, on September 18, 1502, on his fourth voyage to the New World. He was followed by

---

Europeans Thwarted

Christopher Columbus, the first European to reach Costa Rica, in 1502, recorded signs of vast wealth in the region he called "the Garden." The first attempt at colonization, in 1506, however, proved disastrous. Ferdinand of Spain appointed Diego de Nicuesa as governor of Veragua and financed an expedition to settle the Caribbean coast and discover the source of the Indian gold. The governor foundered off the coast of Panama, and he and his troops were forced to hack their way north through the jungle. They were soon repelled by the ferocity of local tribes, sweltering swamps, and diseases—a fate that also awaited Gil González in 1522. In 1524, Francisco Fernández de Córdoba established the first colony on the Pacific coast, at Bruselas, but its inhabitants, too, succumbed. Other attempts were made, but the arrivistes failed miserably, driven one and all to despair and decimation by the cruel hardships of the New World.

Diego de Nicuesa (see sidebar opposite), who attempted to colonize the area. Despite many further attempts, the Spaniards were never able to establish permanent settlements in eastern Costa Rica. After 1513, when Vasco Nuñez de Balboa (1475–1517) discovered the Pacific Ocean, the Spaniards focused their explorations along that shore. Pacific native populations came under Spanish control in the 1520s. The Spaniards were not on a holy mission: The conquistadors had set out in search of gold and silver. In 1532 Pizarro found it in Peru, and, a decade later, Cortes discovered the vast silver veins of Mexico. The Spanish found no source of gold in Costa Rica, so they plundered the gold reserves of the indigenous peoples, then began to enslave them to work in foreign mines. Victims of the Spaniards' ruthless forays, the once noble indigenous populations of Costa Rica began to decline.

In 1543 the Captaincy-General of Guatemala was created, incorporating all the lands from the Isthmus of Tehuantepec and the Yucatán Peninsula to the swampy lowlands of southern Panama. Most of Costa Rica's indigenous peoples had by then been conquered, though the region languished as the Spanish consolidated their hold farther north. In 1562 conquistador Juan Vásquez de Coronado (1523–1565) was appointed governor of Costa Rica. He established a settlement in the cool highlands and named it El Guarco (later Cartago)—Costa Rica's first capital. Although Coronado was a relatively benign conquistador, during ensuing decades, large land grants (encomiendas) were issued to Spanish soldiers. Thus, they received rights of vassalage over the indigenous peoples, who withered under forced labor. European diseases—smallpox, measles, tuberculosis—against which the

Vasco Nuñez de Balboa, the first European to see the Pacific

locals had no resistance, hastened their demise (the Great Pandemic of 1610–1660 cut through the population like a scythe). The survivors fled to the interior mountains.

Spanish settlers found themselves without labor to work the rich soil. Therefore, conditions were lacking for the development of the feudal system imposed by the Spaniards elsewhere in the New World, which were based on large haciendas worked by slave labor. An exception was lowland Greater Nicoya (today's Guanacaste), which was administered as part of Nicaragua and where cattle haciendas evolved, worked by enslaved Chorotega. Without gold, which had already been stolen and shipped to Spain, or other items of value for trade with the homeland, Costa Rica's settlers were forced to sow their own lands for a livelihood. The region became a backwater full of poor farmers foiled in their hopes of becoming nobles.

Settlement: Settlements were meager and modest. When Volcán Irazú erupted in 1723, destroying Cartago, the lowly capital consisted of a single church and a few score houses made of adobe.

By the early 18th century, however, Costa Rica had evolved a viable agricultural base and the population expanded. Other towns began to take shape: in 1717, Heredia; in 1737, San José; and in 1782, Alajuela. The population remained far removed from central authority and evolved free of the rigid social and color distinctions that developed in neighboring countries, where miscegenation between Spaniard and Indian produced large mixed-blood *(mestizo)* populations. In Costa Rica, intermixing of the races was limited, and this resulted in large numbers of poor white farmers and the absence of a resentful mestizo class subject to the abuses of the established white aristocracy.

In the Caribbean Lowlands, a separate cultural scene evolved. English, Dutch, and French pirates and merchantmen had for three centuries raided and traded along the shores of the "Spanish Main." Piracy had driven the Spanish to close their port at Puerto Limón in 1665, choking legal trade and fostering a rise in smuggling and the evolution of English-run ports for precious hardwoods beyond the limits of Spanish authority.

The Cinderella colony received little official attention. Never having felt the stern hand of colonial rule, its inhabitants remained aloof from the bitter independence movement sweeping through Spain's American empire by the close of the 18th century.

Independence & Wealth

When independence for Central America came on September 15, 1821, on the coattails of Mexico's, it took a full month for the news to reach Costa Rica, where a provisional council elected to accede to the new nation of Mexico.

Time of Turmoil: It was a time of confusion. Throughout the isthmus, battles raged between disparate interests competing to shape national boundaries. In 1823 the four provinces of Guatemala, El Salvador, Honduras, and Nicaragua formed a federation—the United Provinces of Central America—with its capital in Guatemala City and autonomy for individual states (Panama became a part of Colombia).

The decision sparked a brief civil war in Costa Rica: The conservative leaders of Cartago and Heredia favored maintaining alignment with Mexico; the more progressive gentry of Alajuela and San José were federalists. On April 5, 1823, tensions boiled over into a battle at Ochomongo in which the federalists were victorious. Costa Rica then joined the United Provinces.

....

By 1830 high-grade coffee . . . was already the nation's prime export.

....

It was a poor fit. Central America descended into a cycle of civil war and rule by repressive *caudillos* (strongmen leaders) representing the interests of elites. In Costa Rica, however, institutional rule had never been consolidated and the gains of economic prosperity were shared among a relatively classless society. Democratic institutions emerged that permitted resolution of social tensions through reform.

Consolidation & Coffee: In 1824 Costa Rica named teacher Juan Mora Fernández (1784–1854) its first head of state. He established a trend for progressive, liberal political leadership that would characterize the nation as it evolved apart from its reactionary neighbors. Internal rivalry resurfaced in 1835 when forces from the three subordinate towns attacked San José, which won the War of the League and consolidated its status as Costa Rica's capital city. Tensions within the United Provinces resulted in

The railroad's arrival in the 1800s boosted the fortunes of the banana industry. By the end of that century, Costa Rica produced more bananas than anyplace else in the world.

its dissolution in 1839, one year after Costa Rica's benevolent dictator Braulio Carrillo (1800–1845)—best known for establishing civil legal codes and an orderly public administration—had withdrawn from the federation and declared independence.

At the time, coffee drinking was all the rage in Europe. Costa Rica's pattern of small rural farms, combined with the climate conditions and terrain of the Meseta Central, proved conducive to coffee cultivation. Mora and Carrillo had sponsored this cultivation by issuing land grants, luring European immigrants who brought fashionable liberal ideals. By 1830 high-grade coffee—*grano de oro* (grain of gold)—was already the nation's prime export. Coffee income was used to prettify San José with neoclassical buildings. Earnings were spread throughout the farming community, but the immensely profitable coffee trade coalesced in the hands of a few coffee barons—*cafeteleros*—who began to dominate the political scene. In 1849 they ousted the nation's enlightened first president, José María Castro (1818–1892), replacing him with one of their own, Juan Rafael Mora (1814–1860).

Invasion & Militarism: Mora served two terms marked by economic prosperity. His second was highlighted by an unlikely invasion. U.S. President James Buchanan wanted to build a canal across Nicaragua, whose government was charging what to the U.S. government appeared an exorbitant fee. Backed by Buchanan, a brash Tennessean named William Walker (1824–1860) landed in Nicaragua in June 1855 with a band of mercenaries. He toppled the government, established himself as president, and in November 1856, invaded Guanacaste. President Mora was victorious over Walker's motley toughs at La Casona (in today's Parque Nacional Santa Rosa). Walker fled to Rivas in Nicaragua, where a Costa Rican drummer boy called Juan Santamaría gave his life torching the fort where Walker was hiding, earning a posthumous distinction as a national hero.

The war ushered in a period of militarism as politically ambitious cafeteleros used self-styled generals to attain power. In 1870 General Tomás Guardia (1831–1882) seized power as a reformer. He established a viable central government, tamed the cafeteleros and their military cronies, used coffee-tax revenues to fund civic construction, and promoted a railroad linking San José with the Atlantic to facilitate the transport of coffee. The railroad, built against almighty odds at the cost of 4,000 lives (mostly imported Chinese and Jamaican labor) and completed in 1890, was the accomplishment of Minor Keith (1848–1929), a determined North American who also started the United Fruit Company (see sidebar below).

Democracy Affirmed: President Bernardo Soto (1854–1931) stood for reelection in 1889. The nation's first honest election with popular participation produced an upset victory for Soto's opponent. When Soto refused to step down, the people took to the streets and enforced their decision. The democratic process was still tenuous and marred by presidents who whittled away at the constitution or exiled rivals to extend their rule. The army remained in its barracks until 1917, when President Alfredo González Flores (1877–1962) proposed a system of progressive taxation and the cafeteleros prompted Minister of War Federico Tinoco (1868–1931) to seize power. Tinoco was a bullying dictator who suspended the constitution. But Costa Rica's educated populace would no longer accept oligarchic caudillos. Tinoco was ousted peacefully by a demonstration led by women and high school students, ushering in another period of peaceful liberal leaders. Democracy had been affirmed.

United Fruit Company

Minor Keith, a North American living in Costa Rica to manage railroad construction, began in 1873 planting bananas along the train route and, later, on concessions wrangled from the government. By 1899 Costa Rica was the world's leading banana producer. That year, Keith's company merged with Boston Fruit to become the United Fruit Company. By 1930 the company was the largest employer in Central America. Company ownership has since changed, but bananas are still a major export of Costa Rica—the second-largest exporter of bananas in the world.

Civil War & Reform

Old-style paternalism had failed to alleviate the social ills of the relatively prosperous nation. Many people lived in destitution, a situation worsened by the Great Depression in the wake of the Wall Street crash of 1929, and by the stranglehold that the United Fruit Company—by now a powerful force—held over its workers, fueling a virulent four-year strike initiated in 1934 against "Big Fruit." A series of illegal labor strikes paralyzed Costa Rica. Change was needed.

Calderón Sets the Stage: It came in the 1940s, when Rafael Ángel Calderón Guardia (1900–1970) became president and promulgated a series of much needed reforms that included progressive taxation, a social security system, and a labor code that established workers' rights. Calderón, a deeply religious man, earned the ire of the rural-based upper classes, including cafeteleros of German descent who resented government seizure of their land when Costa Rica declared war on Nazi Germany. Calderón's massive public-spending programs coincided with a stymied economy that combined to produce rapid inflation, whittling away his support among the poor. When the 1944 election came around, he wed himself to an unholy alliance with the Communists and the Catholic Church. The triumvirate formed the Social Christian Unity Party (PUSC). Meanwhile, labor leaders made an unlikely pact with the business and rural elites and, joined by urban intellectuals, formed the Social Democratic Party.

Calderón's handpicked successor, Teodoro Picado (1900–1960), served an uneventful four-year term (1944–1948). In 1948 Calderón stood again for election. Tensions were rife; violence broke out on the streets. Unexpectedly, a third-party contender, Otilio Ulante (1891–1973), won the election. Calderón claimed fraud. That night, the building holding the ballots burned. The Calderonista congress annulled the election. On March 10, 1948, Costa Rica erupted in civil war. The ensuing events are mired in mythology.

War of National Liberation: José Figueres Ferrer (1906–1990), an ambitious revolutionary, later affectionately known as "Don Pepe," had been planning a coup for years. Exiled to Mexico in 1942 for his firebrand ways, he was permitted to return in 1944 and immediately launched a bid for the violent overthrow of the government. He founded a ragtag army—the National Liberation Armed Forces—that trained at his mountain farm in Santa María de Dota. The election debacle was a godsend. Figueres's insurrectionists swept down from the mountain and quickly took Cartago and Puerto Limón. The ill-trained government army of 500 men was armed by Nicaragua's right-wing Somoza regime and included machete-wielding banana workers. For 40 days the two forces skirmished, leaving more than 2,000 (mostly civilians) dead. As Figueres's forces prepared to strike at San José, the government's paltry standing army surrendered.

José "Don Pepe" Figueres, "savior of the nation," visits his lumber mill in 1980. He disbanded the army in the late 1940s.

Figueres established the grandiloquently named Founding Junta of the Second Republic. Calderón was exiled, and many of his followers were executed along with leading leftists and labor leaders. Then Figueres surprised everyone by disbanding the army and declaring neutrality. He saw himself as a crusader against communism and corruption. He banned the Communists, drew up a new constitution, and launched a whirlwind of social reform. He abrogated Costa Rica's apartheid laws, gave women the vote, nationalized the banks and insurance companies, and established presidential term limits and an independent body—the Special Electoral Tribunal—to oversee future elections. Then he handed power to Otilio Ulante as had been agreed and stepped down. "Don Pepe" was hailed as a national hero and went on to win two terms as president (1953–1957 and 1970–1974) as leader of the PLN, which he founded in 1951. Figueres earned the wrath of his longtime enemy, Nicaraguan dictator "Tacho" Somoza. Their two nations had a brief skirmish in 1955, when Nicaraguan troops attacked Guanacaste, meeting a pathetic demise at La Casona.

Modern Times

Immediate post–civil war politics were marked by political stability and economic prosperity. PLN governments followed conservative, pro-business agendas, while the welfare state was vastly expanded by the Social Democrats, until it reached every sector of society and subsidies consumed 40 percent of the national budget. By the 1970s, 25 percent of the workforce was employed by the state. Economic stagnation set in. A massive currency devaluation added to woes caused by crippling inflation and by the devastating fall in worldwide prices of coffee, bananas, and sugar, Costa Rica's three largest exports. The economic crisis was worsened by the Nicaraguan crisis, which consumed the region for one long, dark decade.

War & Peace: During the 1970s, Nicaragua's Sandinista National Liberation Front (FSLN) launched a war to topple the right-wing Somoza regime. The government of Costa Rican president Rodrigo Carazo Odio (1926–2009) permitted the Sandinistas to set up shop in Costa Rica. When Somoza's air force struck across the border, Carazo tried to close the Sandinistas' camps, but also cut diplomatic relations with Nicaragua and seized the Somoza family's estates in Guanacaste.

On July 19, 1979, the tables turned. The Sandinistas swept into Managua. Right-wing Somoza supporters flooded Costa Rica and found support with wealthy ranchers in Guanacaste. The exiles coalesced to form the Nicaraguan Democratic Front (FDN), better known as the Contras. Costa Rica's new president, Luis Alberto Monge Álvarez (1925–2016), struggled to remain neutral, but the economy was a shambles and the United States was pressuring Monge to commit to the Contras. Soon the CIA was building airstrips and supply bases close to the Nicaraguan border, and U.S. military specialists were militarizing the Costa Rican police forces. The Sandinista air force was bombing Contra bases, and paramilitary groups—supported by right-wingers in Monge's government (1982–1986)—were committing acts of domestic terrorism meant to implicate the Sandinistas. Costa Rica was edging dangerously away from neutrality.

In February 1986, a liberal economic lawyer named Oscar Arias Sánchez (b. 1940) became president. He kicked out the Contras and worked ceaselessly for peace in the

Costa Rican President Luis Guillermo Solis, and the First Lady Mercedes Peñas Domingo

isthmus (El Salvador and Guatemala were also wracked by internal strife). In February 1987, Arias presented a peace plan. The Reagan administration tried to nix it, but the five Central American presidents signed up. Arias earned the Nobel Prize.

Putting the House in Order: The war destabilized Costa Rica. Around 250,000 Nicaraguan refugees had flooded in, draining scarce resources. International confidence had also suffered, resulting in capital flight and a 60 percent drop in trade. The country was bankrupt. Throughout the 1960s, 1970s, and 1980s, Costa Rica had funded its development through massive loans. In September 1981, Costa Rica became the first country in the world to default on its loans, causing a banking crisis throughout the Americas. By 1989, with a five-billion-dollar national debt, Costa Rica had the dubious distinction of being the world's largest per capita debtor. A stiff dose of economic austerity was needed to put Costa Rica back on course.

> **"The risks we run in the struggle for peace will always be less than the irreparable cost of war."**
>
> —President Oscar Arias Sánchez, 1987

In February 1990, Rafael Ángel Calderón Fournier (b. 1949), a conservative lawyer and son of the reforming president, was inaugurated on the 50th anniversary of his father's inauguration. He initiated measures to curb Costa Rica's massive deficit and debt. Calderón was succeeded by José María Figueres (b. 1954), son of the elder Calderón's nemesis. Under pressure from the International Monetary Fund and World Bank, Figueres continued the austerity program, which was painful for a people used to handouts. With inflation rampant, 100,000 people took to the streets in 1995. Then in July 1996, Hurricane Cesar devastated the region.

A series of government scandals tainted Figueres's administration. He was replaced in February 1998 by wealthy businessman Miguel Ángel Rodríguez (b. 1940), whose bid for the presidency in 1994 unearthed his own involvement in a tainted-beef scandal. Dr. Abel Pacheco (b. 1933), of the center right Social Christian Unity Party, was elected president in 2002. His government was considered corrupt and inept and he was replaced in 2006 by Oscar Arias Sánchez, in the first ever re-election of a former president following a new constitutional ruling allowing for a second term. In 2010, Arias's vice president, Laura Chinchilla (b. 1959), was elected the first woman president of Costa Rica. Her pro-business administration, which supported building a controversial third international airport in the Golfo Dulce region, was considered underachieving. In 2014 progressive academic Luis Guillermo Solis (b. 1958), of the Citizens Action Party, succeeded Chinchilla in a record landslide victory. A migrant crisis erupted in November 2015, forcing Costa Rica to seal its borders with Nicaragua and Panama to prevent passage of thousands of undocumented immigrants (mostly Cuban) seeking passage to the United States.

Corruption, nepotism, and crime are major concerns. Burglary and petty theft are endemic, and, since Manuel Noriega's ouster in Panama in 1989, Costa Rica has developed a reputation as a drug transshipment center. Despite these problems, the country has managed to avoid sinking into the turmoil that surrounds it, drawing tourists in increasing numbers (tourism is Costa Rica's largest source of foreign income, generating 2.8 billion dollars from 2.66 million tourists in 2015). The country has also proved attractive to high-tech investors and foreign retirees, lured by clean air, relative prosperity, and the appeals of a stunningly scenic land. ∎

Land & Landscape

Mountains dominate Costa Rica, a pocket-size prodigy that packs a potpourri of other terrains, landscapes, and climates into its 19,652 square miles (50,900 sq km). Nowhere is the country more than 175 miles (280 km) wide, and nowhere is it more than 300 miles (480 km) long—totaling an area equal to three ten-thousandths of the world's land area.

Yet Costa Rica seems to contain the entire world within its small compass, whisking the surprised visitor allegorically on a world tour, from cool Swiss alpine forest to steamy Amazonian lowland jungle. A glance at a map explains why. Costa Rica lies at the thread-thin southern end of the Central American isthmus separating two dramatically disparate continents. It is also a land between seas: The Caribbean Sea and Pacific Ocean are separated by a mountain backbone that is still being heaved up by awesome tectonic forces that erupt in volcanoes and earthquakes.

A majority of the population lives in the Central Highlands, most within towns that cluster on a temperate plateau, the Meseta Central, that lies within a few hours' drive of beach and ocean. Though the country lies wholly within the tropics, vast extremes of elevation and relief spawn a profusion of climates and microclimates. The result is a spectacular amalgam of vegetation and wildlife. Costa Rica, a meeting point for the biota of North and South America, is crowded with exotic flora and fauna.

The Volatile Earth

Costa Rica lies at a critical juncture where four of the Earth's crustal plates converge and crumple. These plates, interconnected pieces resembling a cracked eggshell, are jostled by currents deep within the Earth's molten core and wrestle until one gives way. Costa Rica sits atop the Caribbean plate. Its arch contestant is the Pacific's Cocos plate, which shoves against it from the east and nosedives beneath it, sparking cataclysmic earthquakes and fueling volcanoes that spew out magma (molten rock) produced by the stupendous friction. The Costa Rican landmass is relatively young—only around three million years ago was it thrust upward from beneath the sea by the Cocos's dynamic burrowing. The tectonic movement has further fractured the Earth along fault lines. Megaquakes frequently rattle the country, such as the 6.2 shocker that struck on January 8, 2009, destroying the community of Cinchona and killing more than 30 people. In September 2012, the country experienced the worst earthquake in living memory. Amazingly, little damage was done.

Manuel Antonio, no less stunning for being one of the world's smallest national parks

---

Wilderness Guides

When it comes to spotting wildlife and learning about Costa Rica's flora and fauna, a naturalist guide is essential. Countless visitors report that touring with a naturalist was the highlight of their trip. The amazing interpretive ability of the finest guides includes an eagle-eyed ability to spot and identify wildlife that the untrained eye will surely miss. The best guides have had a lifetime of experience in the field and have built solid reputations. Many are specialists in birds, botany, or herpetology. Most are freelancers and can be hired through such companies as Costa Rica Expeditions (see Travelwise p. 260).

Volcanic Vertebrae

Costa Rica's lush green shawl drapes itself over a spine of volcanoes that march south from the Nicaraguan border, studding the landscape with perfect cones that look as if they've fallen from their own postcards. These volcanoes are part of the 9,000-mile (14,500 km) chain of mountains that runs along the western edge of the Americas from Alaska to Tierra del Fuego. Of the 42 active volcanoes in Central America, Costa Rica has seven. These are found in three distinct ranges, or *cordilleras*, arrayed northwest to southeast: the Cordillera de Guanacaste, the Cordillera de Tilarán, and the Cordillera Central, the latter a string of four volcanoes—Poás, Barva, Irazú, and Turrialba—that encircle the Meseta Central. Set between the Guanacaste and Tilarán chains is windswept Lake Arenal.

Both Poás and Irazú [volcanoes] recently awoke from their slumbers and periodically boil over.

Many of Costa Rica's threatening giants are ephemerally user-friendly: At two of them, Poás and Irazú, visitors can drive to the crater rims and peer into the bubbling bowels. Both Poás and Irazú recently awoke from their slumbers and periodically boil over in small but intense eruptions. At restless Poás, a mini-volcano birthed within a mile-wide caldera—the largest collapsed crater in the Western Hemisphere—erupted in 2017. On Rincón de la Vieja and Miravalles, in Guanacaste, steaming vents have been harnessed for geothermal electricity. Youthful Volcán Arenal, an archetypal cone (a Hollywood favorite, it starred in 1995 in Michael Crichton's *Congo*), thrilled visitors with almost daily eruptions until suddenly turning quiescent in 2010. That year, Volcán Turrialba awoke and has been sporadically erupting ever since.

Meseta Central

Around two-thirds of Costa Rica's population lives in the Meseta Central, a huge scalloped valley that basks in eternal springtime in the heart of the temperate Central Highlands at an average elevation of 5,000 feet (1,524 m) above sea level. The plateau measures 50 miles (80 km) across and 25 miles (40 km) north-south and nestles beneath the gentle volcanic slopes of the Cordillera Central to the north and the dauntingly sheer, forest-clad slopes of the Talamancas. It is divided in two by a low range of hills, the Cerros de la Carpintera. San José and its nouveau-riche suburbs dominate the larger and more populous level valley to the west of the hills, where most of the nation's major towns are found; the smaller Cartago Valley slopes gently eastward before falling steeply through the valley of the Río Reventazón—very popular with white-water rafters—to the Caribbean Lowlands.

The climate is idyllic. Sunshine pours down year-round (temperatures average a balmy 74°F/23°C), combining with reliable and modest rainfall and rich volcanic soils to metamorphose the Meseta into the rich breadbasket of the nation. Sugarcane dominates the valley floor, rippling in the constant light breeze like folds of green silk. The lower slopes are intensely farmed for coffee, with dairy farms, horticultural gardens, and strawberry patches situated on the cooler, higher slopes that gradually merge into lush montane forests where ecominded visitors can hike through cloud forests on the flanks of mist-shrouded volcanoes.

Talamanca Massif

Massive, dauntingly rugged, the Talamancas induce humility. They dominate the southern half of the country and consist of a chain of mountains extending along a northwest-southeast axis from the Meseta Central into Panama. Here are Costa Rica's highest peaks. Rising to 12,526 feet (3,818 m) atop Cerro Chirripó, the Talamancas separate the Caribbean from the Pacific. These great *cerros*, or peaks, are folded in serrated pleats with vast valleys nestling in between. Moisture-laden winds racing in from the east dump their cargo, and bruised clouds swirl ominously about windswept summits so cold that trees cower. Towering and sodden, they have been little explored although crosshatched by pathways known only to Indians who live in remote reserves on the lower slopes. A plush cloak of greenery covers the rugged peaks. Much of the velveteen jungle is protected within Parque Internacional La Amistad—a refuge for endangered wildlife. The montane forest merges with cloud forest on higher slopes, where stunted dwarf forests meld into *páramo,* high mountain grasslands.

Pacific Northwest

Costa Rica's dry quarter defies the image of Costa Rica the green. Humpbacked, floppy-eared Zebu cattle munch on savannas that shimmer gold in the searing sun, and cowboys register a poignant effect on the landscape. The region, lowland Guanacaste, averages less than 20 inches (50 cm) of rain per year—this in the lee of volcanoes whose sodden eastern slopes soak up as many feet. Rivers that form oases for wildlife spill down from the curving slopes and loop through the parched lowlands of the Tempisque Basin to merge in watery Parque Nacional Palo Verde, a spectacular haven for birdlife. Patches of rare dry forest burst into Monet-colored blossom year-round. Mere morsels of the great forests that were felled for cattle following Spanish settlement, these remnant tracts are easily explored at Parque Nacional Santa Rosa,

Though in a resting phase since 2010, Arenal volcano has been active for the past five decades.

where La Casona evokes Costa Rica's turbulent past relations with Nicaragua. A chain of sleepy and historic cowboy towns—Liberia, Cañas, and Cañas—speckle the Inter-American Highway, while Puntarenas, a motley port city extending along a thread-thin peninsula, is a gateway to the Nicoya Peninsula by ferry across the Golfo de Nicoya. The peninsula is lined on its Pacific coast with stunning beaches swept by surf and warm currents that bring ashore marine turtles. The country's only white-sand beaches are here—draws for a bevy of upscale resorts and golf courses whose emergence in recent years have lent a new cachet to the region. The warm waters of the Golfo de Papagayo teem with game fish, yet another angle on adventure, centered on the sportfishing resort of Playa Tamarindo. And spelunkers can explore the limestone caverns at Parque Nacional Barra Honda.

Pacific Southwest

This zone is made up of valley, mountain, and coast. To the east, the Río General, which is popular with white-water rafters, powers out of the Talamancas. The river has carved a broad trough—the Valle de El General—that is an important center for fruit plantations south of San Isidro. The valley was brought into the mainstream only in the 1950s, when the Inter-American Highway linked it with San José and Panama, drawing immigrants, including Italians whose influence is paramount in the hilltop town of San Vito, in the southerly Valle de Coto Brus. A thin range of mountains between valley and warm fecund sea rises precipitously in the north to create a narrow littoral quilted by palm plantations and, farther south, a coastal plain covered in bananas.

Beaches are backed by jungles where birds flash their bright colors and monkeys cavort in the trees, as at Parque Nacional Manuel Antonio, a tiny yet much-visited emerald where coral reefs and diamond-dust beaches enclose a rare swath of humid forest teeming with wildlife. Rainfall increases to the south, reaching a peak on the overwhelmingly green Osa Peninsula. Osa's Parque Nacional Corcovado is a sodden refuge for jaguars, scarlet macaws, and hardy hikers. Nutrient-rich offshore waters draw humpback whales to the Bahía de Coronado and game fish to the Golfo Dulce. Here, sportfishermen are lured to funky Golfito, an old United Fruit Company town that now attempts to attract business with its duty-free zone. Laid-back Zancudo is among the scores of beaches favored by surfers. Uninhabited Isla del Caño, 10 miles (16 km) offshore, boasts pre-Columbian remains. And Isla del Coco, about 300 miles (480 km) southwest of Costa Rica and part of the Galápagos chain, offers superb scuba diving for advanced divers.

The Northern & Caribbean Lowlands

Lush forests extend across the vast *llanuras*—flatlands—of northern and eastern Costa Rica like a damp carpet. The undulating plains are drained by countless rivers that

A sea of verdant green engulfs La Fortuna waterfall in Parque Nacional Volcán Arenal.

cascade down from the mountains and flow into the Río San Juan, forming the Nicaraguan border. Other rivers drain into Refugio Nacional de Vida Silvestre Caño Negro, teeming with feisty game fish, crocodiles, and birdlife. Much of the forest has been felled during recent decades for cattle, and international fruit companies are tightening their grip, pushing citrus and banana plantations up against the remaining forest. Tortuguero and Barra del Colorado, two ramshackle Caribbean hamlets where the Río San Juan meets the sea, are sportfishing centers. Parque Nacional Tortuguero and Refugio Nacional de Vida Silvestre Barra del Colorado are channel-laced forest reserves where wildlife is viewed from canoes. The Caribbean coast sashays south from Barra to the Río Sixaola and the Panama border, the shore lined by gray-sand beaches hemmed in by the sea and by the crowding Talamancas. Puerto Limón, a newly revived port, is the only town of significance, while the villages of Cahuita and Puerto Viejo preserve Afro-Carib culture, drawing surfers and younger counterculture vacationers. The Northern Lowlands are served by the Ciudad Quesada and by Fortuna, gateway to Parque Nacional Volcán Arenal and Tabacón hot springs. ■

A Conservation Ethic

Despite spiraling population growth and unsustainable economic practices—logging, ranching, large-scale commercial agriculture—that have diminished Costa Rica's forest cover by 60 percent during the past 400 years, the nation has set aside 28 percent of its land in national parks and reserves, a larger percentage than any other country on Earth.

More than a dozen marine turtle hatcheries nationwide help increase the survival rate of newborns such as this baby leatherback turtle.

The parks and reserves are grouped into 11 Regional Conservation Areas (RCAs) that create corridors for migratory wildlife by linking adjacent national parks. Every major ecosystem is represented, safeguarding natural treasures for ecotravelers to enjoy.

Diminishing Forests

To the casual visitor, Costa Rica looks like an endless lush swath of green. In fact, forest destruction has occurred at a frightening rate, much of it illicitly by loggers driven by immense profits in hardwoods. Where trees fall, rains cause wholesale erosion. The effect of lost forest is felt throughout the biological kingdom, where the survival of countless species (including jaguars, tapirs, and macaws) is at risk.

More than 95 percent of the lowland dry forests were felled during the colonial era to make way for cattle ranches. The 1960s and 1970s were particularly devastating to the rain forests of the Northern Lowlands, as vast tracts were felled to raise beef for the U.S.

market. Fruit companies continue to whittle away at lowland rain forests, and squatters edge up against protected forests, which they destroy with slash-and-burn agriculture. Nonetheless, the rate of deforestation has slowed in the past decade and, in fact, has been reversed.

Saving What Remains

Costa Rica is at the forefront of attempts to create sustainable revenue from tropical forests, and boasts 27 national parks and 124 wildlife refuges, biological reserves, and marine parks, grouped into the 11 RCAs. Ecotourism is a boon, and more private reserves are being opened to public visitation. A conservation ethic has taken hold among the local population, many of whom have traditionally seen the forest as an economic resource to be culled. In the modern world, Costa Rica's forests must earn their keep to survive. Harvesting ornamental plants and raising tree-dwelling iguanas for meat are among the schemes introduced by dozens of conservation organizations within Costa Rica to give local communities a vested interest in preservation. International bodies such as the Nature Conservancy, World Wide Fund for Nature, and U.S. Agency for International Development now sponsor creative forest management projects such as "debt for nature" swaps, where Costa Rica "swaps" part of its national debt (duly discounted) for a guarantee to safeguard a specific amount of forest. Scores of private reserves have been established in recent years dedicated to restoring native ecosystems, which take many hundreds of years to replenish themselves. As a result of all these efforts, the percentage of forested land had increased to 52.4 percent of the nation in 2010.

A Mixed Report Card

Protection requires a balancing act. Some national parks are being degraded by too many visitors, while hotels squeeze parks, such as Manuel Antonio, against the sea.

Although the scale has tipped toward greater integrity and enforcement in recent years, lack of funding and poor management bedevil the beleaguered National Park Service (NPS) and Forestry Department, which are tainted by corruption. In addition, entrenched political interests have a toehold in fighting conservation, and illegal logging and hunting continue with the connivance of NPS personnel.

The situation has been complicated by the emergence of large-scale luxury resorts concentrated in dry northwest Nicoya, where new golf courses are draining the aquifers. The temptation to build bigger was resisted for many years, but the Calderón administration (1990–1994) abandoned ecological principles established during preceding governments, paving the way for wanton disregard for protective laws.

Back From the Grave

It's not often that an animal that has been classified as extinct is rediscovered alive. But in 2007, the brown and metallic green tree frog, which hadn't been seen in Costa Rica's Monteverde Cloud Forest Reserve since the 1980s, when the amphibian population crashed probably due to climate change and fungal infection, was spotted high atop a moss-covered tree branch by British zoologist Andrew Gray. Taking a nocturnal hike deep in Monteverde's hinterlands, Gray, an expert in frog voices, heard the frog chirping and didn't recognize its species. Climbing the branch, he was astounded to discover a lone *Isthomhyla rivularis*. He took several photos and released the frog to the wild, with the intent of returning to set up a breeding program. This exciting discovery has given scientists hope that other species that are thought to be extinct may still survive.

The Lush Environment

Nature lovers speak in hyperbole, using terms like "nirvana" for the Garden of Eden called Costa Rica. Though it lies strictly within the tropics, between 8 and 11 degrees north of the Equator, the country claims 12 distinct ecological zones, from tidal mangroves and dry deciduous forest to tropical rain forest and even subalpine grassland, called *páramo,* atop the windswept heights of the Talamanca massif.

Costa Rica offers some surprises: Cactuses stud desert-dry pockets of the northwest, where hardy Zebu cattle range parched savanna that borders wetlands where crocodiles bask on mudbanks, motionless as logs. This is a veritable hothouse of biodiversity. Acre for acre, Costa Rica is as species rich as anywhere else on Earth. Around 5 percent of all known species on Earth slither, skip, or swoop through the varied habitats, including one-tenth of all known bird species. The extraordinary biodiversity stems from Costa Rica's position at the juncture of two major continents; over eons, life-forms from both have migrated across the narrow land bridge and adapted to constantly varied local relief and climate. In this arena of intense competition they have diversified remarkably to survive. No wonder travelers who are tired of seeing just pictures of jaguars, quetzals, and three-toed sloths flock here like migrating macaws.

Hothouse Diversity

In the tropics, temperatures are relatively constant, for the sun shines directly overhead throughout the year, while drenching downpours and an annual rainfall in excess of 100 inches (250 cm) maintain a constant high humidity that fosters the luxuriant growth. Lush to the point of saturation, Costa Rica is a botanical breeding ground of stupendous proportion. Its 800 or so species of ferns, for example, far outnumber those found in the whole of North America. Costa Rica is particularly rich in orchid species; about 1,400 have been identified so far.

> **Costa Rica is particularly rich in orchid species; about 1,400 have been identified so far.**

Orchids are found from sea level to the heights of Cerro Chirripó, with flowers ranging from less than one millimeter across to pendulous petals spanning 20 inches (50 cm). The greatest diversity is associated with rain forests, where orchids steep in year-round moisture. Around 90 percent of orchid species are epiphytes, or "air plants" (plants that root on other plants but are not parasitic), which thrive in the compost deposited on the limbs by decayed forebears and draw moisture by dangling their roots in the air. Whole colonies of epiphytes live atop the massive boughs, which often resemble vast galleries. Other epiphytes include bromeliads, which have evolved tightly wrapped leaves that act as miniature cisterns, trapping water and leaf litter that decays and donates its nutrients to the plant. Costa Rica has more than 2,000 species of bromeliads, which reach awesome sizes—some measure as much as four feet (1.2 m) across.

A red-eyed tree frog epitomizes the beauty of Costa Rica's miraculous fauna.

Ecological Zones

Costa Rica's landscapes are classified into 12 ecological "life zones," identified in 1947 by internationally renowned tropical forest biologist Leslie R. Holdridge (1907–1999). Each zone is characterized by a distinct terrain, climate, and life-forms. While the canvas is overwhelmingly green, Costa Rica's ecological zones include dry deciduous forest and subalpine grasslands. Various gradations exist in between.

Mangroves & Wetlands: Costa Rica's variegated coastline is rimmed by mangrove colonies, groups of halophytic plants (able to survive with their roots in salt water) that thrive on the land formed from silt carried by the slow-flowing rivers. Five species of mangroves grow at the juncture of land and sea, notably along the coast of Golfo de Nicoya (particularly the mouth of the Río Tempisque), the delta of the Río Terraba, the shores of Golfo Dulce, and in the lagoons of Tortuguero and Gandoca-Manzanillo, where variant mangrove ecosystems—*jollilos* and *orey*, respectively—have evolved. The trees' humble appearance disguises an intricate environment protecting vast numbers of wild creatures—not least, crocodiles—from human encroachment. Migratory waterfowl, wading birds, and small mammals abound in the shallows and tidal creeks, feeding on the amphipods, crabs, marine worms, mussels, and other organisms that thrive on the decayed vegetation amid the dense roots. Bacteria rework decaying leaf litter into detritus that feeds a legion of marine species that are consumed in turn by larger creatures.

EXPERIENCE:
Exploring the Canopy

Mistico Arenal Hanging Bridges Park
(tel 2479-8282, misticopark.com) has *colgantes* (suspension bridges) slung between treetops and across canyons, offering eye-to-eye views with the wildlife.
Hacienda Barú *(tel 2787-0003, haciendabaru.com)* lets you ascend in a harness 113 feet (35 m) into a treetop canopy, where you sit on a branch and watch wildlife one-on-one in the rain forest.
Rainforest Adventures Aerial Tram *(tel 2257-5961, rainforestadventure.com)* slices silently through the forest canopy. You ride in an open-air gondola, accompanied by your own guide, on a 1.6-mile (2.6 km) circuit.

Inland, Costa Rica's two prime wetland ecosystems are Caño Negro, in the Northern Lowlands, and Palo Verde, at the mouth of the Río Tempisque. Both are congenial to aquatic birds and shelter a variety of migratory birds and other creatures—crocodiles, monkeys, deer, peccaries, coatis, ocelots—that is the equal of any other environment in Costa Rica. The wetlands flood in the rainy season and contract to mudflats in the dry season. Streams and rivers wind among these vast aquatic systems, connecting channels and broad lagoons that draw tens of thousands of waterfowl and other exotic birds.

Rain Forests: Rain forests are among the most complex ecosystems on Earth. More than 50 percent of *all* known living species on the planet can be found in tropical rain forests, in a band 10 degrees north and south of the Equator. Biologists recognize at least 13 distinct types of rain forest, based on differences in altitude, rainfall, and soil conditions. Thus, the same latitude in Costa Rica may be marked by tropical evergreen rain forest on the Caribbean coast and seasonally dry evergreen forest on the Pacific shore, though both share near-constant, stifling humidity and heat, and a profusion of plant life. All rain forests receive more than 100 inches (250 cm) of rainfall per year; lowland rain forests may receive up to 300 inches (750 cm)! Premontane wet forest is found at higher elevations, as in rain-soaked Braulio Carrillo and Tapantí National Parks, where conditions are cooler. Pockets of mist-soaked tropical montane rain forest, or cloud forest, swathe the mountains at elevations around 4,000 feet (1,220 m), where branches drip with mosses and epiphytes thrive in the humidity. At the highest elevations, as atop Poás and Irazú volcanoes, stunted trees cower before wind-driven rains.

The true lowland rain forests that smother the *llanuras*—flatlands—of the Atlantic lowlands, the Osa Peninsula, and the eastern flanks of the Talamancas are of Gothic proportion, with trees soaring 100 feet (30 m) or more before merging like a crowd of giant umbrellas. Their mushroom-shaped crowns form a green canopy so dense that you might imagine yourself able to walk across it. The canopy is shaded by mammoth trees—emergents, such as the kapok (*Ceiba pentandra*)—that soar past their neighbors like great Corinthian columns. Height is paramount in the competitive search for light. Most trees have long, straight limbless trunks with branching not occurring until 60 or more feet (18 m) aboveground. These branches

Water and detritus trapped in their tightly whorled leaves nourish bromeliads.

form an understory. Some emergents tower as much as 100 feet (30 m) above the canopy. The lowland rain forest is a multilayered labyrinth (see pp. 179–181).

The canopy is subject to the passage of clouds, wind, and storms and has a separate climate than the forest understory and the shrub-covered floor below. Rainfall may take many minutes to reach the ground, if at all. Similarly, only about 10 percent of sunlight reaches the ground, where the vegetation is consequently sparse. Saplings of many high canopy species stop growing once they reach about 10 feet (30 m) in height, then wait until a tree falls before erupting into explosive growth with the sudden burst of sunlight. Forest floor species have adapted crafty techniques to make the most of the subaqueous light. In clearings, plants put out broad leaves to soak up the sun, such as the "poor man's umbrella" (*sombrilla de pobre*), whose leaves like elephant ears make perfect cover in downpours.

Whereas in temperate zones, forests may have "neighborhoods" of one or two tree species, in rain forests hundreds of species intermingle—from cecropia trees favored by sloths to towering mahoganies favored by loggers. One tree may host around one hundred other species of smaller plants, such as ferns, vines, and bromeliads. In the hot and humid tropics, plants grow and reproduce year-round. Dead leaves decompose and nutrients are quickly recycled and sucked back up to the forest canopy and reabsorbed, unlike in temperate zones where tissue breakdown is slow and nutrient-rich humus builds up a thick layer of soil. Since tropical soils are thin, most tree species have adapted and spread their roots wide for balance and maximum nutrient uptake; the emergents, unsecured by the intertwined canopy, have evolved great flanges, like rocket fins, to overcome their inherent instability. Vines twine up their hosts, often reaching several hundred feet in length as they coil along branches and between trees, knitting the canopy together. The strangler fig, however, germinates in the canopy and sends down tendril roots, which anchor to the forest floor and send up nutrients. As the roots envelop the host tree, they suffocate it until it dies and decomposes, providing sustenance and leaving a cylindrical, freestanding fig tree.

Wildlife Viewing

Most wildlife in Costa Rica is well camouflaged or shy, and viewing it usually requires great patience. Often animals and birds may be present, but the untrained eye can't see them. The more still and quiet you are, the more species will reveal themselves. Wear khakis and colors that blend with the background. Binoculars are essential. It pays to educate yourself about local ecology and the particular species you're eager to see. Bring a good field guide to identify individual species or tracks. Above all, hire a reputable guide (see sidebar p. 34).

Dry Forests: On the eve of Columbus's landfall, the lowlands of the Pacific Northwest were swathed in dry deciduous forest, which covered a greater expanse than did Central America's rain forests. These forests evolved in the five-month seasonal drought that befalls Guanacaste in November, when the trees shed their leaves to conserve water. Trees in dry forest rarely rise more than 40 feet (12 m) and are relatively sparsely distributed, making wildlife viewing easy; anteaters, monkeys, and scarlet macaws are numerous. The open-crowned canopy rises above a secondary layer of trees with smaller crowns, and thorny scrub and grass at ground level. Often all the members of a single species burst into bloom on the same day before dropping their petals like colored confetti: jacaranda in purple, the *poró* in bright orange, and the *corteza amarillo*—Guanacaste's state flower—in yellow. Trees blossom one after another in a strict cycle: the rose pink *pouí* in January, for example, followed by the pastel pink *tabebuia rosea* in March and the vermilion *malinche* in April. When the rains return in April or May, the dry forest buds afresh.

During the colonial era, the Spanish destroyed vast areas of forest for cattle, decimating dry forests from Panama to Mexico. In Costa Rica, only some 200 square miles (520 sq km)—about 2 percent—of the original dry forest cover remains in a threadbare patchwork in Guanacaste and Santa Rosa National Parks and the Tempisque Basin. Reforestation projects have begun to reverse the decline.

Tropical Menagerie

Costa Rica is a cornucopia of botanical and zoological treasures. The National Institute of Biodiversity, which is attempting to identify every plant and animal species in the country, estimates there are at least one million species. Anteaters, coatis, iguanas, monkeys, birds by the hundreds, and insects in tens of thousands, are as colorful as creatures in a Rousseau painting and often can be seen within an arm's length. Yet only the rare visitor is fortunate enough to see an elusive jaguar on the prowl.

Mammals: Costa Rica claims only around 200 species of mammals, of which half are bats—including vampire bats and a giant fishing bat that scoops up fish with its claws while on the wing. Most mammal species are shy and rarely seen by the casual visitor. The cats are well represented, notably by jaguars, ocelots, pumas, and extremely rare margays and oncillas—both spotted like cheetahs—and dark brown

The harmless rhinoceros beetle can reach six inches (15 cm) long.

jaguarundis. Superb climbers, cats can sometimes be seen racing up tree trunks to chase down rodents and monkeys scampering along the high branches. All six cat species are both endangered and elusive.

Far more easily seen are the four species of neotropical monkeys found in all lowland and mid-elevation habitats. Descendants of Old World monkeys that migrated across the Bering land bridge eons ago, the New World species are noted for their long prehensile tails. The large, leaf-eating black howler monkey is the most common species—and the most noticeable: The males frighten tourists with their loud roars, announcing their territorial fiefdoms, particularly at dawn and dusk. The small, omnivorous, black- and white-faced capuchin monkeys are also easily spotted playing among the branches, notably at Parque Nacional Manuel Antonio, where their presence is guaranteed. The diminutive, orange-hued squirrel monkey (titi), though endangered, is gregarious, and groups of 40 or so family members are not unusual. By contrast, the long-limbed, copper-colored spider monkey is a solitary critter that faces severe deprivations from loss of habitat.

Sloths abound throughout the country (see sidebar p. 49). They live high up in the treetops and are perhaps the slowest animal of the forest.

Two species of raccoon (mapache) are found in Costa Rica: The white-faced northern raccoon is found throughout the lowlands, while its dark-faced, crab-eating cousin confines itself to habitats along the Pacific coast. One of the most frequently seen mammals is the coati (pizote), which can be easily identified by its panda-like ringed eyes, brown coat, and ringed tail, which the animal craftily uses to thwart predators: When attacked, it rears up, stuffs its tail between its legs and waves it in front of its face, so that predators will attack the tail and get slashed in the eyes in return. Smaller, nocturnal, tree-climbing cousins in the raccoon family are the olingo, cacomistle, and kinkajou.

In addition to two squirrel species and around 40 species of rats and mice, Costa Rica claims two neotropical rodents of note. The brown agouti (guatusa) is a dainty forest-dwelling creature that resembles a large tailless squirrel with long, slender legs. Different subspecies have evolved with both darker and lighter coloration as adaptations to either wet or dry forest habitats. The agouti and its nocturnal cousin, the paca *(tepezcuintle)*, which resembles a large guinea pig, are traditionally hunted by campesinos for meat and are now endangered. The timid tapir *(danta)*, a distant relative of the elephant, also once roamed far and wide but has been brought to the point of extinction by hunting. Intrepid hikers may find these trunk-snouted animals high in the mountains, drinking at volcanic lakes, and in remote sections of Corcovado and the Talamancas.

Other mammals include Costa Rica's three species of anteaters—which subsist solely on a diet of ants, scooped up with a long sticky tongue—and two species of armor-plated armadillos. Coyotes and foxes abound, as do rabbits, and two species of opossums represent the marsupials (mammals whose embryonic offspring are reared in an external pouch). Peccaries *(sainos)*, fearsome wild pigs, roam in herds and grub up roots and other foods from beneath the topsoil. Although normally shy around humans, aggressive males

Sloths have evolved for a life spent upside down.

have been known to attack people. Several other creatures are also common, including the fierce badger-like grison and the sleek, chocolate brown tayra, a 3-foot-long (0.9 m) giant that hunts rodents and small deer and can be found in both lowland and highland habitats.

Manatees—endangered marine herbivores that resemble tuskless walruses and have a spatulate tail in lieu of flippers—inhabit the watery recluses of Parque Nacional Tortuguero and Refugio Nacional de Vida Silvestre Gandoca-Manzanillo, where a rare dolphin endemic to the region, the *tucuxí*, inhabits the lagoons. Otters are commonly seen in lowland rivers, notably in the waterways of Tortuguero and the adjacent Refugio Nacional de Vida Silvestre Barra del Colorado.

Amphibians & Reptiles: Amphibians and reptiles thrive in the hot, damp tropics. Costa Rica claims around 160 species of the former and 220 or so of the latter, of which 162 are snakes, though only 22 species are venomous.

Frogs abound, including gaily colored poison dart frogs (dendrobatids) hopping among the forest litter in their fluorescent livery—red as lipstick and blue as the morning sky—meant to scare predators. About 20 species of Costa Rican frogs produce deadly toxins. Frog and toad populations have declined precipitously in recent years. The golden toad, a diminutive wonder discovered at Monteverde only in 1964, is already considered extinct. Many frogs have adapted to life away from large bodies of water; some have evolved suction-cup feet and taken to a life in the trees, where they lay their eggs in the cisterns of bromeliads.

While snakes are ubiquitous, most are fairly small, like the chunk-headed snake, and feed on birds, small rodents, and lizards. Others, such as the commonly seen boas, can grow up to 10 feet (3 m) in length. Pythons are often spotted along riverbanks, glowing yellow or iridescent green, snoozing in sensuous coils on branches. The viper family includes the burnished brown fer-de-lance (terciopelo), waiting with jaws of death for passing fodder. This aggressive giant accounts for three-quarters of all snakebites in Costa Rica, and almost all snakebite deaths. Most other fatalities are credited to the brightly banded coral snake, which has a distinct venom (all other snakes produce the same venom).

Costa Rica's river estuaries and lowland waterways are favored by American crocodiles (cocodrilos), which reach lengths of up to 15 feet (4.5 m). Their diminutive cousins, caimans, rarely grow beyond 6 feet (1.8 m). Crocodiles have suffered mightily from hunting during four centuries. Protected since the 1970s, they are making a comeback, particularly in the Río Tárcoles and Refugio Nacional de Vida Silvestre Caño Negro.

Sloths

Sloths (perozosos) are commonly seen moving in treetops at a pace close to rigor mortis using their powerful arms and curved claws. Costa Rica has two species: the three-toed sloth and the smaller, nocturnal Hoffman's two-toed sloth. These leaf-eaters have huge stomachs to process large quantities of near-indigestible food, which can remain in their belly for up to one week. Their metabolic rate is correspondingly slow; the animal even garners energy from direct sunlight, much like cold-blooded reptiles. Sloths typically spend 18 hours a day sleeping and digesting their meals. They do not wash much, and their shaggy fur is tinted green by algae and inhabited by bugs.

The tree-dwelling iguana inhabits both wet and dry lowland forest and can grow to 3 feet (0.9 m) in length. Cloaked in scaly armor, it presents a fearsome appearance but is quite harmless to humans. The spiny-tailed iguana is green, though males turn orange during the November–December mating season; the smaller ctenosaur is dun colored. The dozens of smaller lizard species include the Jesus Christ lizard, a resident of the Pacific Lowlands, named for its ability to run across water on its hind legs.

Many visitors come to Costa Rica hoping to see marine turtles laying their eggs, which is easily done at beaches on both the Caribbean and Pacific coasts. The females of five species of turtle come ashore here at various times throughout the year. The green turtle is most easily seen at Tortuguero. Leatherback turtles, the largest reptiles on Earth (they can weigh up to a ton/907 kg), nest at Playa Grande in Nicoya. Most exhilarating are the synchronized nestings (arribadas) at Refugio Nacional de Vida Silvestre Ostional, where tens of thousands of olive Ridley turtles swarm ashore during full moons from July to December.

Insects: Costa Rica's insect fauna is incalculably rich—from the microscopic flower mite, which hitches a ride inside the hummingbird's nostril, to giants such as the 3-inch-long (7.5 cm) rhinoceros beetle, so named for its horn. Tens of thousands of species await identification. The kingdom comes into its own at night, when moths and beetles take wing and the forests resound with a cacophonous chirruping and croaking. Guanacaste is particularly rich; when seasonal rains strike, the insect fauna explodes. More than one thousand species of butterflies—one-quarter of the world's total—flit about the country. The undisputed king is the saucer-size, electric blue morpho. Subspecies differ in coloration according to locale; one rain-forest-canopy species is iridescent red. When threatened, the 6-inch (15 cm) owl butterfly (*Caligo memnon*) flashes its underwing coloration, which resembles a pair of owl eyes.

> **Leaf-cutters [ants] . . . farm mushrooms underground using mulch chewed from leaves.**

Of the thousands of species of ants, the most intriguing are the leaf-cutters that farm mushrooms underground using mulch chewed from leaves stripped from trees. Costa Rica even has army ants, fearsome colonies that number in the millions and sweep through the countryside, terrorizing and devouring any living thing in their path.

Birds, Birds, Birds!: Remarkably, one-tenth of all known bird species in the world inhabit this little patch of land. Of the 850 or so species found here, at least 600 are permanent residents, including 51 species of hummingbirds found throughout the nation in cloaks of shimmering cerulean blue, green, purple, and red.

Costa Rica has 16 species of parrots, from diminutive green parakeets to giant scarlet macaws, which are easily seen at Corcovado, Palo Verde, and Carara National Parks. The smaller, predominantly green Buffon's macaw is found only around Tortuguero and the Northeastern Lowlands. Both species are endangered due to habitat loss. Several private institutions have active breeding programs that release macaws back into the wild.

Another dazzler is the quetzal, the crown jewel of the cloud forest and the sole reason that many visitors flock to Costa Rica. This pigeon-size beauty—one of ten species of trogons in Costa Rica—boasts iridescent emerald feathers. The male woos potential mates with a bloodred chest and a sweeping, forked tail up to 24 inches (60 cm) long. At Monteverde in the spring, the birds descend to lower altitudes and perform acrobatic midair mating displays. Visitors should listen for their mournful two-note whistle. That eerie metallic *bonk* resounding through the cloud forests is the call of the three-wattled bellbird.

Keel-billed and chestnut-mandibled toucans, with banana-like beaks, are common. Their sharp-beaked cousins, the toucanets and aracaris, are no less flamboyant. A favorite of birders is the motmot, which has a racquet-like tail and lives in a hole in the ground. Tanagers, exotically colored in flame reds and sky blues, are represented by 50 species. There are 78 species of flycatchers, 52 species of warblers, and 22 species of wrens. Some 50 species of raptors feed on everything from crabs and fish to monkeys—a favorite of the harpy eagle, reduced to remote parts of Corcovado and the Talamancas. Four species of vultures (*zopilotes*) pick at carrion; count yourself lucky to spot the mighty king vulture.

White cattle egrets are seen in pastures and along riverbanks. The remaining 25 species of waders include herons; three species of ibis; storks, such as the massive jabiru; and the roseate spoonbill, now confined to the safety of Caño Negro and Palo Verde. Costa Rica's wetlands, directly beneath the Pacific migratory flyway, attract water-fowl—coots, ducks, grebes, teal—in such numbers that their wings sometimes mimic the roar of a jet engine. Marine birds include cormorants, anhingas, and boobies. In Bahía Salinas and Golfo de Nicoya, the mangroves prove ideal nesting sites for frigate birds. Ironically, the national bird of Costa Rica is the somewhat drab robin, locally known as the *yiquirro*. When the male sings during the spring mating season, local lore says he is calling the rains.

Marine Life: The tropical waters of both of Costa Rica's coasts allow scuba divers to swim with whale sharks, manta rays, and groupers, and anglers can cast lures for the billfish that cruise the offshore waters. The Golfo de Papagayo and Golfo Dulce are particularly rich in game fish, such as dolphinfish, marlin, tuna, and wahoo. The top draw for experienced divers is Isla del Coco, where hammerhead sharks school in unsurpassed numbers. Off Manuel Antonio and in Bahía Ballena, an extravaganza of fish play amid the coral, while stingrays flap over the ocean bottom. Smaller coral reefs exist off Gandoca-Manzanillo and Cahuita in the Caribbean, and off Isla del Caño. Humpback whales gather seasonally to feed and mate in the warm, nutrient-rich waters of Bahía Ballena, providing exhilarating encounters for whale-watchers. ■

EXPERIENCE: Birding at Its Best

Wherever you are in the country, the birding is sure to astound. With so many dedicated wilderness lodges, and so many distinct ecological zones, you have many choices. Still, some specific locales offer birding par excellence. Here are a few of the best places to find some of the more than 850 species found in Costa Rica.

Bosque de Paz (*tel 2234-6676, bosquedepaz.com;* see p. 77), in the northern foothills of the Cordillera Central, boasts at least 330 species in its 988-acre (400 ha) cloud-forest reserve. Tours offer a chance to see the black guan, resplendent quetzal, and three-wattled bellbird. **Mirador de Quetzales** (*tel 8381-8456, quetzalesde costarica.com*), off the Pan-American Highway south of Cartago, is perhaps the best site in Costa Rica for viewing quetzals. Self-guided and guided hikes are offered.

Parque Nacional Palo Verde (*tel 2200-0125;* see p. 112) protects the floodplains and marshes of the Río Tempisque estuary, plus 15 distinct habitats, including dry forest. Roseate spoonbills and scarlet macaws are among the highlights. **Parque Nacional Tortu-guero** (*tel 2709-8086;* see p. 223) grants a unique perspective as you cruise the waterways in search of toucans and green macaws. Forest walls lining the open waterways are like a gallery for 300 bird species. For additional insight, Karla

Taylor is recommended for guided tours (see Travel-wise p. 260). **Selva Verde** (*tel 2761-1800, selvaverde.com;* see p. 211), a private reserve protecting 474 acres (192 ha) of northern lowland rain forest, abounds in birdlife. It specializes in guided birding trips, offered from the lodge. Companies specializing in birding tours include **Cheesemans' Ecology Safaris** (*tel 800/527-5330, cheesemans.com*) and **Field Guides** (*tel 512/263-7295, fieldguides.com*).

The Arts

Costa Rica's modern National Symphony Orchestra rises to the standard of its stunning venue: the Teatro Nacional (National Theater) in San José. But otherwise, Costa Rica is culturally underdeveloped, and the nation has searched in vain for a pre-Columbian legacy to stimulate a modern renaissance.

The sterility can be explained by Costa Rica's relatively benign colonial history, because social tensions have always been a spark for vibrant cultural expression. This peaceful nation thereafter suffered from a creative paucity, excepting a few native crafts.

Costa Rica has long been dismissed as a cultural backwater. The entire cultural scene, including dance and theater, was for a long time moved by the national sense of a brotherhood of lowly, country-based Ticos. For example, visual art struggled to break out of the traditional confines of portraying idyllic rural scenes.

In recent years, however, Costa Rica has developed a new confidence as artists have cast aside rigid norms. The nation's young, up-and-coming artists and wood-carvers are following the examples of American artists-in-residence, whose success owes much to their freedom from the constraints of a campesino-based national identity and spirit.

In the performing arts, too, dance and theater companies have broken away from their traditional bonds, especially in the realm of contemporary dance.

Traditional bucolic scenes are a quintessential theme of Costa Rican art.

Visual Arts

Until recently, there was little energy to Costa Rican art, which lacked the passionate, socially engaged formats of other Latin nations. Artists struggled for decades to escape the straitjacket of stylized Costa Rican landscapes that developed in the late 1920s based on depictions of campesino life. The so-called Group of New Sensibility was influenced by the French Impressionists and headed by Teodorico Quirós (1897–1977). The movement's legacy remains preeminent today in naive paintings, including miniatures, showing adobe dwellings and cobbled rural villages, usually with a volcano for a backdrop. The school evolved in Escazú and neighboring Santa Ana, southwest of San José, which remain informal artists' enclaves.

This art of *casitas* (little houses) was derided by the next generation of artists, who by the 1950s were experimenting in abstract styles. Modernist and en vogue contemporary styles have since found their way into a more mature artistic expression, and today, Costa Rican artists display an eclectic world vision. In recent years, artists such as Isidro Con Wong (b. 1931) have won international acclaim. Wong's works—described as "magic realism"—fetch up to $35,000 on the world market. Rafa Fernández (b. 1935) is another magic realist, specializing in erotic female images. Rolando Castellón (b. 1937) is renowned for his sensual acrylics, and Felix Murillo (b. 1971) is acclaimed for his flamboyant evocations of nature.

Three-dimensional Arts

Tourism has sparked a revolution in crafts, notably in wood carving.

Sculpture has never been a strong suit in Costa Rica, although the pre-Columbian influence can be seen in a tradition of jewelry work and an outpouring of splendid gold and silver adornment. Contemporary jewelry styles owe much to traditional indigenous forms, such as animist figurines.

The nation's most famous sculptural piece dates back to 1936, when sculptor Francisco Zuñiga (1912–1998) unveiled a stone carving of a mother suckling her child. The piece, called *Maternity,* can be seen today outside San José's Maternidad Caritas maternity clinic. It was ridiculed by local critics who derided it as looking more like a cow than a woman, causing Zuñiga to leave for Mexico. His *Evelia con Batan* stands at the entrance to San José's Centro Nacional de Artes y Cultura, and the modernist sculpture garden at the Museo de Arte Contemporaneo has several of his works.

Tourism has sparked a revolution in crafts, notably in wood carvings inspired primarily by Escazú's Barry Biesanz (b. 1948). Sarchí, however, is the undisputed center of crafts. Here, Costa Rica's traditional wooden oxcarts, called *carretas,* are still made and decorated in floral motifs, including miniatures intended as garden ornaments or as domestic liquor carts for the home. Traditional wooden furniture hewn from hardwoods, including mahogany, lignum vitae, and rosewood, can also be found in Sarchí.

Santa Ana is famed for its earthenware. And at Guaitíl, in Nicoya, a renaissance in Chorotega pride finds its outlet in much-sought-after pottery. Members of the Boruca tribe make traditional musical instruments, wooden masks, and handwoven textiles.

Literature

Unlike other Latin American cultures, the dispassionate Ticos are not a particularly literate people, despite a high literacy level. Only a fistful of writers make a living from the profession, which is dominated by parochial themes, and Costa Rica has yet to produce a writer of international note.

Injustice and social turmoil are the grist for great literature and Costa Rica has lacked both; the singular literary work to gain broad recognition is *Mamita Yunai*, a story decrying the injustices wrought by the United Fruit Company upon Costa Rica's banana workers, by Carlos Luis Fallas (1912–1996). Likewise, the acclaimed *El Eco de los Pasos* by Julieta Pinto (b. 1922) had the 1948 civil war as its theme. The works represented in a lone anthology of literary works by 20th-century Costa Rican authors, *Costa Rica: A Traveler's Literary Companion*, are prosaic. Cocorí, a little cartoon character by José Joaquín Gutiérrez (1918–2000), played on the stereotypical idiosyncrasies of Ticos.

Music & Dance

Costa Rica is the southernmost of the marimba countries—those owing much to the Africa-derived xylophone that forms the base of native music throughout Central America. It is no surprise then that Guanacaste, where the native tradition remains strongest, provides the impetus for traditional music and dance, typified by the national dance: the *punto guanacasteco*, a toe-and-heel stomp for couples. Pre-Columbian instruments, such as the *quijongo* (a gourd amplifier attached to a string bow) are still used to accompany the Spanish guitar. Traditional dancing is based on the stylized Spanish *paseo*, with men and women alternately circling each other, accompanied by much *"yip-yipping"* and tossing of hats and scarves. It is now mostly performed at tourist venues by such groups as Fantasía Folklórica.

The traditional Latin *peña*, where intellectuals gather and share poems and music, is strong among the educated middle class. On the classical music front, however, Costa Rica has been neither an inspirational locale nor a breeding ground for composers and instrumentalists. The Teatro Nacional hosts the National Symphony Orchestra, formed in 1970, which draws middle-class *Josefinos* (residents of San José) during the April–November season. Several minor classical and choral groups also perform.

Younger Ticos have forsaken traditional music and dance for the modern dance hall. Latin rhythms draw them to clubs featuring hip-swiveling merengue, cumbia, and salsa. On the Caribbean coast, where musical influences derive from Jamaica, Bob Marley is king. Reggae, a modern phenomenon, has displaced traditional musical forms such as the *sinkit* and *cuadrille*, colonial island carryovers based on the banjo and drum.

Jazz has gained in popularity in recent years and finds its major outlet in the annual Costa Rica Music Festival each August. A national style has emerged—a bravura, macho style with trumpeters playing the highest possible notes and pianists going as fast as they can go. The Envision Festival in February offers New Age side by side with an eclectic musical range from harp to flamenco. ∎

Theater

Ticos enjoy theater so much that the country boasts more theaters per capita than any other country in the world. This enthusiasm dates from the turn of the 20th century, when drama became part of the school curriculum and an influx of South American playwrights boosted theatrical fortunes. San José's tiny theaters offer a mix of comedy, mime, and avant-garde, drawing an audience every night except Mondays. The nation's oldest theatrical group, the Little Theater Group, performs in English.

A capital city with a provincial feel, plenty of small museums, pocket-size plazas, and intriguing edifices from the halcyon days of coffee

San José

The Museo Nacional de Costa Rica overlooks Plaza de la Democracia, San José's largest open square.

San José

Perched among a crescent of mountains, San José enjoys an enviable setting in the heart of the Meseta Central at 3,773 feet (1,150 m). The compact city of around 300,000 enjoys what *National Geographic* dubbed one of the three best climates in the world, with temperatures that hover around 70°F (21°C) year-round.

Rainfall is mostly short-lived showers and occasional downpours, May to October. Pleasantly small-scale as Central American capitals go, San José clings to a provincial feel despite sprawling suburbs that now claim 1.2 million residents—one-quarter of the nation's total. San José can never be called colonial quaint. The city was founded as late as 1737 and has relatively few colonial architectural glories. The main commercial boulevards are little strips of America, with neon signs blaring the offerings of fast-food outlets, car dealerships, strip clubs, and shopping malls. The city—which is made up of a set of distinct districts called *barrios* —has not entirely shaken off its village feel, however. In many ways it remains a working-class town where social life is based around the local *pulpería*, or corner store.

Coffee Culture

Throughout its first century of existence, San José endured as a humble village of simple adobe structures. But its position in the heart of the fertile valley was advantageous, and by the 1820s it had grown to equal the then capital Cartago in size. In 1823 the city seized the standard after a brief civil war and became the capital. San José prospered as coffee took hold on the surrounding slopes; plazas, parks, and fine public buildings rose up. The city's nouveau-riche *cafeteleros* (coffee-trading barons), who looked to Europe for inspiration, adopted the French-inspired New Orleans and Port-au-Prince (Haiti) style for their new homes.

The years following World War II saw rapid growth, and the city's infrastructure has been hard-pressed ever since to keep pace

with the changes. Beyond the touristed core, central San José is a chaos of ugly modern buildings, decrepit sidewalks, open sewers, and potholed streets. Crowds elbow their way along streets that teem with overflowing markets, lottery sellers, and sidewalk vendors. Pedestrians are forced to fend off a noisily honking armada of buses, trucks, motorcycles, and taxis that belch out fumes. Friendly, efficient tourist police patrol the city center, although petty theft is still common and muggings occur; visitors are advised to leave valuables in their hotel safe.

NOT TO BE MISSED:

Architectural Renewal

Nonetheless, San José has an undeniable charm, and many visitors grow fond of *chepe,* as the city is colloquially known. Most sites of interest lie within a few blocks of the Plaza de la Cultura. On weekends the heavy traffic thins and Josefinos, the residents of San José, stroll the pedestrian-only Avenida Central and the half dozen plazas shaded by mauve jacarandas. In recent years, the Ministry of Culture has put a polish on the previously run-down plazas and the fistful of notable edifices, such as the Catedral Metrópolitano.

Most tourists find that San José can be fully explored in two days, after which you will be ready to escape to the country. Coffee fields edge up against the city, so the countryside is close at hand. San José provides a splendid base for day-trips throughout the Central Highlands, either by rental car or organized excursion.

Popular destinations from the capital include the Butterfly Farm, the Café Britt coffee plantation tour, Poás volcano, Orosí, the Rainforest Adventures Aerial Tram, La Paz Waterfall Gardens, and the artisans' center, Sarchí. ■

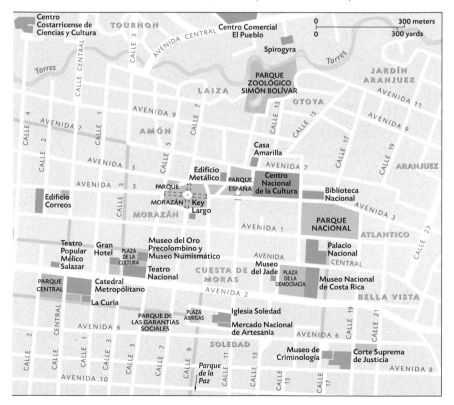

The City Core

Although San José offers suburban temptations, the city's main sites of interest are concentrated in a compact core laid out in a grid, which makes exploring easy. Use Avenida Central as an axis to find major nodes of interest sprinkled handily along its route. A good place to start is Plaza de la Cultura, not least for the sensational Museo del Oro Precolombino, glittering with pre-Columbian gold.

San José's streets hum with the clamor and activity of street vendors and crowds.

San José
* Map pp. 56–57

Visitor Information
* Aeropuerto Juan Santamaría
* 2299-5800

Museo del Oro Precolombino
* Map p. 57
* Calle 5, Ave. Central
* 2243-4202
* $$

museosdel bancocentral.org

Plaza de la Cultura

The nondescript Plaza de la Cultura is the center around which life in San José whirls. Hemmed by Calles 3 and 5, it lies at the heart of a pedestrian-only shopping zone extending seven blocks along Avenida Central. The plaza is a gathering spot for young people, and jugglers and musicians entertain the crowds who gather here on weekends. A clock tower and fountain stand at the junction of Avenida Central and Calle 3.

On the east side of the plaza, on Calle 5, steps lead to the subterranean **Museo del Oro Precolombino,** the gold museum, which is best explored using the audio-taped self-guided tour. Some 2,000 pieces of pre-Columbian gold jewelry, as well as life-size figures adorned in gold, glitter under spotlights. The collections of the adjoining **Museo Numismático** *(for visitor information, see Museo del Oro Precolombino),* include coinage dating back three centuries.

On the south side is the neoclassical **Teatro Nacional,** the jewel in Costa Rica's architectural crown. It owes its origins to a fit of local pique when operatic prima donna Adelina Patti (1843–1919) bypassed Costa Rica during a Central American tour in 1890. The ruling clique promptly voted a tax on coffee exports to pay for the construction of a theater in the style of the Paris Opera House. The resulting edifice was sumptuous enough to tempt the Paris Opera to perform *Faust* at the inauguration in October 1897. Statues of the Muses of Dance, Music, and Fame decorate the Renaissance facade. Beyond the pink marble foyer, the intermezzo has a colorful mural of an idyllic coffee harvest, while in the lavish triple-tiered auditorium nude deities prance across the ceiling.

The theater and the landmark **Gran Hotel** (see Travelwise p. 242) open onto tiny **Plaza Mora Fernández,** where marimba bands frequently perform. The hotel lobby has a 24-hour casino fronted by the balcony of **Café 1830,** a popular spot for people-watching.

Parque Central

This bustling plaza draws Ticos to converse and flirt beneath the guanacaste trees and bandstand, where concerts are given on Sundays. The city's blue-domed **Catedral Metropóli-tano,** erected in 1871 in an austere Greek Orthodox style, looms to the east. The cathedral replaces an original structure toppled by an earthquake in 1821 and boasts an ornate altarpiece. Attached is the rugged and mellowed **La Curia** *(closed to the public),* the Archbishop's Palace, built in 1887. To the left of the cathedral entrance stands a marble modernist monument, *Homenaje a Juan Pablo II* (Homage to John Paul II), erected in September 2006.

Teatro Nacional
- Map p. 57
- Ave. 2, Calle 3
- 2010-1100
- Closed Sun.
- $

teatro
nacional.go.cr

A pre-Columbian gold figurine from the Museo del Oro Precolombino

EXPERIENCE: Where the Music's At

San José has a nightlife hot enough to boil a pot of *gallo pinto*. Whether you're seeking mellow jazz or sizzling salsa, there's a wide choice of venues. Here are some of the best:

El Cuartel de la Boca del Monte *(Ave. 1, Calles 21/23, Barrio La California, tel 2221-0327)* This dressy, bohemian, brick-lined nightspot is a popular venue for both students and the well-heeled alike. It particularly packs in the crowds for live music on Monday, Wednesday, and Friday. Also a late-night venue, it proudly offers a vast cocktail list and serves meals, too. It remains the place to be seen in San José.

Jazz Café *(Ave. Central, San Pedro, tel 2253-8933, jazzcafecostarica.com)* Though it is small, this redbrick building is Costa Rica's premier jazz venue. International stars such as Chucho Valdés and The Yellowjackets often perform alongside the nation's own accomplished musicians. **Rapsodia Lounge & Night Club** *(Paseo Colón & Calle 40, tel 2248-1720, rapsodiacr.com)* One of the

trendiest nightspots in San José, this stylish bar has multiple rooms, from lounges to dance and live music venues, and it also has outdoor patios. **Castro's** *(Ave. 13, Calle 22, Barrio Mexico, tel 2256-8769)* This popular bar and dance club spans the spectrum from electronic trance to reggae, but one of the two rooms usually has Latin tunes. Check online or call for special promotions and parties.

Parque Central's north fringe is Avenida 2, the city's busy main thoroughfare, dominated by the neoclassical facade of the **Teatro Popular Mélico Salazar** *(tel 2295-6000, teatromelico.go.cr),* built in the 1920s and named for Costa Rican tenor Mélico Salazar (1887–1950). The marble lobby is supported by Corinthian columns that extend into the delightful café. The theater is occasionally used for classical and folklore-related concerts.

Parque Morazán

Situated between Avenidas 3 and 5 and Calles 5 and 9, this small park is highlighted by the domed Temple of Music and makes a quiet retreat. Named for Central American federalist Francisco Morazán (1800–1845), the park features statues and busts of Latin American notables, including the South

American liberator Simón Bolívar (1783–1830).

The area to the south forms a mini red-light district serving the tourist trade. Many visitors choose to pop into **Key Largo** to sample the bordello flavor that belies the beauty of the turn-of-the-20th-century mansion, which features exquisite stained-glass work as well as a metal crest crowning the roof.

Parque Morazán is bordered to the east by tree-shaded **Parque España,** featuring busts of conquistador Juan Vásquez de Coronado and Queen Isabella of Spain (1830–1904). Songbirds roost in the densely packed trees. To the northwest is the green **Edificio Metálico** *(private),* made in Belgium of prefabricated metal and shipped to Costa Rica in 1892. Now a school, it took four years to weld together.

To the north is the glass-fronted National Insurance Company (INS) Building.

Plaza de la Democracia

San José's largest square, 400 yards (365 m) east of Plaza de la Cultura, was laid out in 1989 for the Hemispheric Summit. Recently restored, it is centered around a small waterfall and a bronze statue of "Don Pepe" Figueres (see p. 31), inscribed: "He defended the freedom and protected the arts." The large, terraced plaza also hosts concerts and other gatherings.

On the west side, opened in 2014 in a custom-designed five-story building, is the **Museo del Jade** (Calles 13, Ave. Central/2, tel 2521-6610, www.museodeljade ins.com, $$). Here you'll find the

INSIDER TIP:

Nature in the heart of the city? The Museo Nacional has a walk-through butterfly garden under shrouds.

—CHRISTOPHER P. BAKER
National Geographic author

Americas' largest collection of pre-Columbian jade—superbly backlit—from adzes to jewelry and carvings. It also has gold miniatures, plus ceramics and stone *metates,* stools used for grinding corn with a pestle.

To the east, the castle-like, ocher-colored Bellavista Fortress overshadows the plaza. Riddled

with bullet holes from the 1948 civil war, it is like a vision from *Beau Geste.* Today the fortress is home to the **Museo Nacional de Costa Rica,** which traces the nation's historical and cultural development using exhibits illustrating topics that range from religion to geology and archaeology. A room dedicated to pre-Columbian gold and jade is the highlight.

Museo Nacional de Costa Rica

🗺 Map p. 57
✉ Bellavista Fortress, Calle 17, Ave. Central/2
☎ 2257-1433
🕐 Closed Mon.
💲 $

museocostarica .go.cr

Museo Nacional, originally built as a military barracks

The seat of Costa Rica's government is a handsome whitewashed building off the plaza, on Calle 15. The Moorish-style **Palacio Nacional,** which houses the Legislative Assembly, began life in 1912 as the would-be home of presidential candidate Máximo Fernández (1858–1933). He lost the election, but then magnanimously offered his house to the victor, Alfredo González Flores.

Parque Nacional

All levels of society take to San José's largest inner-city park—at the east side of downtown—at lunchtime and on weekends, when it is pleasant to stroll beneath shade trees and palms that vibrate with birdsong.

The white marble **Monumento Nacional** proclaims the victory of the Central American nations in 1856 over William Walker and his *filibusteros* (mercenaries). It was cast in the Rodin studios in Paris and stands atop a granite pedestal with bas-reliefs. Costa Rica's national hero, the drummer boy Juan Santamaría, stands in effigy at the park's southwest corner. Go during the day; it is best to avoid the park at night.

The **Biblioteca Nacional** *(tel 2221-2436, closed Sat. & Sun.)*, the nation's main library, lords over the park to the northwest, on Avenida 3.

Across the street is the Centro Nacional de la Cultura, containing the **Museo de Arte y Diseño Contemporáneo** *(Ave. 3, Calle 15, tel 2257-7202, madc.cr).* This museum features collections of art from throughout Latin America. The gallery is housed in a former liquor factory dating from 1887, which is also home to two theaters and the office of the Ministerio de Cultura.

INSIDER TIP:

When leaving your car unattended, look for a "watchman" wearing a reflective vest. For a few hundred colones, he'll keep an eye on it.

—ELLIANA SPIEGEL
National Geographic contributor

Plaza Abrigas

This tiny plaza, two blocks southeast of Plaza de la Cultura at Avenida 4 and Calle 9, is dominated by a charming church: **Iglesia Soledad.** The plaza's west side is studded with sculptures, including one of John Lennon by Cuban artist José Ramón Villa. The life-size bronze figure shows Lennon cross-legged, left arm casually draped over a bench, and at his feet is the inscription, "Imagine all the people living life in peace." ■

Beating Pickpockets at Their Game

Thieves seek easy targets. Here are a few commonsense precautions that can help you avoid becoming a victim.

- Wear your shirt over your fanny pack; make sure the clasp isn't exposed.
- Use a zippable purse; keep it locked, and wear it around your neck.
- Carry money and documents in a money belt worn inside the waistband of your skirt or pants.

- Make photocopies of your important documents. Leave the originals in the hotel safe.
- Don't carry your camera loosely on your shoulder; sling it around your neck.
- Leave your jewelry at home and your valuables in the hotel safe.
- Stick to well-lit main streets, especially after dark.
- Educate yourself on problem areas, and avoid them.

Parque Sábana & Nearby

West of downtown, Avenida Central opens up into a wide boulevard, Paseo Colón, sloping gently uphill to Parque Sábana de Metropólitano. Paseo Colón epitomizes the modern mayhem of San José with its billboards, supercharged neon advertisements, and pandemonium of honking traffic, culminating, eventually, in the pacific counterpoint of leafy Sábana.

Parque Sábana acts as both an active retreat and a leafy asylum from the chaos of the city center.

A stroll along Paseo Colón puts you in touch with San José's busy main artery. Step south along Calle 24, where after 440 yards (400 m) you will arrive at the **Cementerio de Obreros,** on the south side of Avenida 10. This exercise in pious excess makes for intriguing browsing among the flamboyant mausoleums, vaults, and tombs.

The west end of Paseo Colón bumps up against **Parque Sábana de Metropólitano,** with grassy expanses, tree-lined jogging trails, and a miscellany of sports facilities. The bucolic, yet dishevcled, retreat overlays the old airport, and the former terminal is today the **Museo de Arte Costarricense,** displaying many of the nation's finest artworks, ranging from pre-Columbian artifacts through robust contemporary pieces, including a superb collection of wooden sculptures and woodcuts. To the rear, the **Jardín de Esculturas** displays pre-Columbian and contemporary sculptures, including those by such leading artists as Francisco Zuñiga. Soaring over the west end of the park, the 35,000-seat **Estadio Nacional** opened in March 2011 as the nation's foremost sports stadium.

Tucked off the southwest corner of Parque Sábana is the **Museo de Ciencias Naturales La Salle,** which spans the natural-science world with more than 22,500 exhibits. A dinosaur exhibit in the foyer features a life-size *T. rex, Torosaurus,* and *Utahraptor.* ∎

Museo de Arte Costarricense
- Map inside back cover
- Calle 42, Paseo Colón
- 2256-1281
- Closed Mon.

musarco.go.cr

Museo de Ciencias Naturales La Salle
- Map inside back cover
- 100 yards (91 m) W of Colegio La Salle, Calle Lang
- 2232-1306
- $

museolasalle.ed.cr

A Walk Around Barrios Otoya & Amón

This walk explores two contiguous barrios—Barrio Otoya to the east and Amón to the west—that form the city's historic district, replete with Victorian-era mansions squeezed into narrow one-way streets in a hilly area north of Avenida 7.

Face-painting, a novelty for children at the Parque Zoológico Simón Bolívar

The neighborhood contains much of the city's finest domestic architecture, built by *cafeteleros* (coffee barons) inspired by the French style of New Orleans and Martinique. Many of these mansions once faced demolition. The area has been popularized in recent years by the wealthy class, including hotel owners, who have conjured beautiful mansions into homey inns. A few of the streets are steep, but the ambling is peacefully pleasant.

Begin at the **Legación de México ❶**, a splendidly restored neoclassical stone gem 50 yards (45 m) northeast of Parque España, on the edge of Barrio Otoya. Immediately west, pause to admire the stuccoed facade of the **Casa Amarilla ❷**, the Yellow House (closed to the public), an 18th-century neobaroque edifice bequeathed to Costa Rica by Andrew Carnegie to serve as the Pan-American Court of Justice. Later the Residencia Presidencial and then the Asemblia Legislativa, it now houses the Ministry of Foreign Affairs.

NOT TO BE MISSED:

Casa Amarilla • Hotel Don Carlos

Walk to the northeast corner of the ministry to view a large section of the **Berlin Wall** *(Calle 13, Avenida 9)*.

Turn left and walk along Avenida 9 two blocks past the **Hemingway Inn** to Calle 9, then peek inside the **Hotel Don Carlos ❸** (see Travelwise p. 242), an exemplary wooden home, blending art deco and neoclassical elements with colonial-style grillwork. Built as the residence of President Tomás Guardia, it is run by art connoisseur Don Carlos Balser and brims with pre-Columbian treasures and Sarchí oxcarts. An exquisite ceramic in the lobby shows a quintessential bucolic scene—a theme that continues along Avenida 7 as you go downhill past walls inlaid with hand-painted tiles depicting coffee pickers and the like.

One block west, to your right at the corner of Calle 7, in Barrio Amón, is the former **La Casa Verde de Amón ➍**, a stately mansion made of red pine imported from New Orleans in exchange for a shipment of coffee. It received a UNESCO award in 1994 for restoration and today forms part of the Instituto Tecnológico de Costa Rica.

Victorian Flavor

Continue west along Avenida 9, lined with low-slung aristocratic wooden houses in Caribbean Victorian vernacular, with detailed wainscoting and extensive decorative touches. At Calle 5, to your right, note **Le Chambord,** another splendid home, and farther along Avenida 9, **Casa Morisca,** with Moorish influences. Turn right at Calle 3 and right again onto Avenida 11. At the corner of Calle 3 on the west side of the street, you will pass the **Castillo del Moro ➎**, colloquially called the Bishop's Castle after Archbishop Don Carlos Humberto Rodríguez, for whom it was built in 1925. The crenelated structure was inspired by Moorish design, with such extravagant touches as hand-painted tiles adorning a dome, keyhole windows, and intricate plaster decoration. It houses the charming Cafe

Moro restaurant *(tel 2223-3116)*. On the east side is the **Britannia Hotel ➏**, built in 1910 and one of several neo-Victorian mansions hereabouts to metamorphose into hotels.

Follow Avenida 11 east one block to **Galería Talentum ➐** *(tel 2256-6346, galeriatalentum.com, closed Sun.)*, an impressive art space that hosts events, offers art classes, and has a colorful gourmet café. A stone's throw east, stop at the recently opened **Casa de la Cultura Amón** *(cnr. Calle 5, tel 2550-9449)*, a similarly bohemian cultural center. Now follow Avenida 11 east to the entrance to **Parque Zoológico Simón Bolívar ➑** *(tel 2256-0012, $)*, just east of Calle 7. The zoo, with many of its tiny cages dating from 1916, is appalling by contemporary standards. You will get a good sense of Costa Rica's wildlife though.

Return to Avenida 9 via Calle 7, stopping at **TeoréTica,** an avant-garde art space in a restored mansion. To end your walk, return to the Hotel Don Carlos, where **Café Amon** *(tel 2221-6707)* serves delicious local Costa Rican fare.

- 🅰 Also see area map pp. 56–57
- ▶ Legación de México
- 🕐 90 minutes
- ↔ 1.25 miles (2 km)
- ▶ Hotel Don Carlos

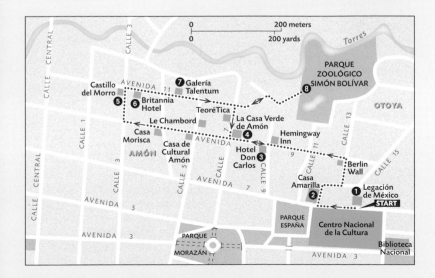

More Places to Visit in San José

Centro Costarricense de Ciencias y Cultura

The turreted "castle," a former penitentiary, is now the Costa Rican Science and Cultural Center. The **Galería Nacional** displays avant-garde works of art in the converted jail cells. Its **Museo de Niños,** Children's Museum, spans themes ranging from astronomy to communication. A state-of-the-art theater, the **Auditorio Nacional,** has performances. *museocr.org* 🅐 Map p. 56 ✉ Calle 4, 100 yards (90 m) N of Ave. 9 ☎ 2258-4929 🕓 Closed Mon. 💲 $

Edificio Correos

Built in 1917 with an ornate green facade, the Postal Building is one of San José's most dramatic structures. It functions as the nation's central post office and as the **Museo Postal, Telegráfico y Filatélico** (second floor). This museum has a collection of early telegraphic and telephonic equipment, as well as a philatelic display. The Edificio Correos faces a plaza with a statue of Juan Mora Fernández, the nation's first president (1824–1828). 🅐 Map p. 57 ✉ Calle 2, Ave. 1/3 ☎ 2223-6918 🕓 Closed Sat. & Sun. 💲 $

Mercado Central

There is no more truly Costa Rican experience in San José than visiting this market built in 1880. Crowds maneuver through alleyways lined with artisans' stalls, cobblers, fishmongers, florists, fruit sellers, and trinket sellers. Dine at one of the tiny *sodas* (snack bars), which offer traditional meals for a pittance. 🅐 Map p. 56 ✉ Ave. Central, Calles 6/8 ☎ 2547-6104 🕓 Closed Sun.

Pueblo Antiguo

This theme park, a mixture of Colonial Williamsburg and Disney World, re-creates an idyllic past, with urban, rural, and coastal sections staffed by Ticos in period costume. Children can help milkmaids fill their pails. Horse-drawn carriages ply the streets of the make-believe village. Marimba bands perform, and folk troupes re-create historical scenes. Craft shops and restaurants complete the experience. Pueblo Antiguo is part of Parque Diversiones, a fairground with roller coasters, bumper cars, waterslides, and other rides. *puebloantiguo.co.cr* 🅐 Map pp. 56 ✉ 1.2 miles (2 km) NW of Hospital México ☎ 2242-9240 💲 $$$$$ (4-hr. tour)

Spirogyra

Immerse yourself in a lepidopteran world in this 420-square-yard (350 sq m) netted butterfly garden, home to more than 30 species. *butterflygardencr.com* 🅐 Map p. 57 ✉ 100 yards (91 m) E & 150 yards (137 m) S of Centro Comercial El Pueblo ☎ 2222-2937 💲 $

EXPERIENCE: Fun With the Family

To keep the kids happy in San José:

Fossil Land *(1.2 miles/2 km E of Patarrá, on SE outskirts of San José, tel 2276-6060, fossillandcr.com)* **This adventure park thrills adolescents with paintball, ATV rides, and mountain cycling. Younger kids can enjoy a fossil trail, horseback rides, and confidence-building hikes with waterfall scrambles.**

Museo de Niños *(Calle 4, Ave. 9, tel 2258-4929; see this page)* **The Children's Museum offers all manner of educational, interactive exhibits covering sciences, technology, the natural world, and human society.**

Pueblo Antiguo *(1.2 miles/2 km NW of Hospital México, La Uruca, tel 2242-9240; see this page)* **Re-creations of a 19th-century farmstead, town plaza, and coastal port provide a fun-filled educational experience.**

A mountain-rimmed region with colonial antiquities, butterfly farms, bubbling volcanoes, and cloud forests roamed by wildlife

Central Highlands

A banded peacock butterfly, *Anartia fatima,* feeds on a flower.

Central Highlands

Beauty lies around every bend in the sublime, temperate Central Highlands, a region of forest- and coffee-cloaked mountains cradling a broad fertile valley—the Meseta Central—some 40 miles (64 km) long by 20 miles (32 km) wide.

Touring is facilitated by roads that span the Inter-American Highway and spiderweb even the highest slope. No place is too remote to find lodgings ranging from rustic mountain hostelries to modern architectural stunners.

Many visitors explore the Central Highlands for the sheer pleasure of varying vistas, which grow more dramatic with altitude. You have no need for your own wheels—organized excursions are offered from San José—but a rental

car provides the flexibility to stop for snapshots and serendipitous treats. Everything of interest is within a three-hour drive of San José, although many of the narrow roads are appallingly potholed and deteriorate in places into rutted tracks that your vehicle ascends only with wheezing difficulty.

The intermontane Meseta Central—central plateau—is roughly wedge-shaped: broad to the west and narrower to the east, averaging

Costa Rica
Area of map detail

in elevation around 3,000 feet (914 m). The Meseta Central is bisected by the Cerros de la Carpintera, a relatively low, north-south mountain range rising immediately east of the capital city. To the south are the Talamancas, dauntingly rugged and cut through with valleys that invite exploration. To the north, a series of volcanoes—notably Poás, Barva, Irazú, and Turrialba—form the Cordillera Central. The range reaches its apex at 11,260 feet (3,432 m) atop Irazú, which still fumes, although most days you can drive to the top to look into the burbling bowels.

You can also thrill to the sparkling highland sunshine and crystal clear air. The lower flanks are cloaked in coffee bushes—the sine qua non of the highland economy—shaded by *erythrina* trees and aligned in trim rows. At cooler heights, coffee gives way to dairy farms, strawberry patches, and *viveros* (flower farms) where tropical flowers grow under black cloth. To the east, Irazú's lower slopes are quilted in "market gardens" growing potatoes and carrots. Corn, sugarcane, coffee, and macadamia plantations dominate the fertile valley floors. On the upper slopes, mists swirl through pines and oaks festooned with mosses and epiphytes typical of conditions atop the continental divide—perfect for spotting quetzals and three-wattled bellbirds.

NOT TO BE MISSED:

A walk through La Paz Waterfall Gardens 73

Bird-watching at Zoo Ave Wildlife Conservation Park 73

Viewing wildlife at Bosque de Paz 77

The topiary park at Zarcero 79

Learning about coffee culture at Café Britt 81

A trip to Volcán Poás 84

Cartago's Basílica de Nuestra Señora de los Ángeles 88–89

The region has always been a breadbasket. Pre-Columbian people tilled the soil and thrived. Although they were swiftly decimated following the arrival of the Spanish, their legacy remains in stone at Monumento Nacional Guayabo. The broad-leaved forests that originally covered the land were cleared during colonial times by yeoman farmers. The quintessential highland vignette remains the farmer wearing rubber boots carrying a machete, leading an ox-drawn cart or a herd of cows down the road. Church spires pinpoint scores of rural villages lined with colorful wood-and-adobe houses with neat trimmed lawns. The plateau shelters about 70 percent of Costa Rica's population, concentrated in three historic cities—Alajuela, Heredia, and San José (see pp. 55–66).

To the east sits Cartago, the original capital city, commanding the Reventazón Valley at a lower elevation than the main valley, which narrows eastward and falls ever more steeply as the Cordillera Central and Talamancas crimp together. The eastern, windward slopes of the mountains are rain sodden. Tapantí and Braulio Carrillo National Parks are lush forests echoing with birdsong; hikers might even spot pumas and tapirs. La Paz Waterfall Gardens, Zoo Ave Wildlife Conservation Park, and a dozen other venues offer wildlife viewing for less intrepid souls. Cloud forests close to the mountain crests prove exhilarating for hikers hoping to glimpse quetzals. ■

Escazú & Santa Ana

The soaring hills southwest of San José are a dramatic setting for hip Escazú, which combines Old World charm and contemporary chic. This bewitching town is beloved by expatriates and wealthy Ticos alike for its luxury living, trendy restaurants and nightclubs, and well-stocked shopping plazas. Escazú is only 3 miles (4.8 km) west of Parque Sábana and central San José.

Iglesia Jiménez y Tandi graces San Rafael de Escazú plaza.

Escazú
🅰 Map p. 68

Biesanz Woodworks
✉ Bello Horizonte, 2 blocks S of Bello Horizonte school (business sign reads "Obras de Madera Design")
☎ 2289-4337
🕐 Closed Sun.

biesanz.com

Though Escazú is linked to the capital by the Próspero Fernández Expressway, it retains a beguiling campesino spirit and has an array of B&Bs. Santa Ana, 5 miles (8 km) west, has a more reclusive, old-fashioned appeal.

Triptych Town

Escazú sprawls haphazardly up the northern slopes of its namesake mountain, **Cerro Escazú.** At the base of the hills, near the freeway, is trendy, modern **San Rafael de Escazú,** with deluxe villas and condominiums, restaurants, the **Costa Rica Country Club** (members only), and upscale shopping areas such as the **Multiplaza** (see Travelwise p. 258), Costa Rica's largest mall. Incongruously in San Rafael's midst is a grassy plaza with a gleaming white colonial-style church built in the 1930s. The hip restaurants and nightclubs draw crowds at night. The tony suburb of **Bello Horizonte,** northwest of San Rafael, is a center for charming country inns plus **Biesanz Woodworks,** where carvers conjure masterly hardwood bowls and boxes under the genius-level guidance of Barry Biesanz.

Nearby, a venue not to be missed is **Butterfly Kingdom** (Calle Travesia, Bello Horizote, tel 2288-6667, butterflykingdom.net, closed Sun., $$), which breeds pupae for export to zoos around the world—the offspring of some 60 native species of butterflies that flap freely through a lush environment secured by netting. Here a video and erudite guides enlighten visitors about the complex relationships between the insects and their host plants, and about butterfly life cycles from egg to adult. You can witness metamorphosis as a butterfly wriggles free of its chrysalis.

Calle León Cortes, the main road, leads a mile (1.6 km) uphill to **San Miguel de Escazú,** the tranquil heart of Escazú laid out around its own colonial-era square. This is the original town and one of the oldest settlements in the nation, dating back to at least 1711, when a chapel was built as a nucleus for an adobe hamlet. Many of the red-tile-roofed homes are extant; likewise the red-domed 1799 church commanding the square and fringed at its base by a strip of blue to ward off witches. Don't be surprised to see cattle or ox-drawn carts laden with coffee beans being led through the streets.

Calle 1 snakes sharply upward 2 miles (3.2 km) to the smaller community of **San Antonio de Escazú,** where rolling clouds swirl around the church. Every second Sunday in March, the square is the focus for an annual fiesta, the **Día de Boyeros,** when traditional gaily colored oxcarts (carretas) parade in honor of the boyeros (oxcart drivers), and young girls and women put on traditional garb.

INSIDER TIP:

Tipping in Costa Rica is at your own discretion. Waiters earn a wage. Many people in touristy areas do tip, so waiters there have learned to expect one—but don't feel obligated.

—BEN HORTON
National Geographic field researcher

Santa Ana

The Carretera Próspero Fernández sweeps west beyond Escazú and drops to Santa Ana, in a vale whose warm microclimate has fostered flower farms and apiaries. This town of simple adobe-and-wooden homes is also a center for ceramics.

Just three miles (5 km) southwest of Cuidad Colón,

Of Brooms & Brujas

Some 60 witches are said to live in Escazú, the *bruja* (witch) capital of Costa Rica. "Any woman who lives in Escazú long enough eventually becomes a bruja," claims Doña Estrella, matriarch and self-proclaimed, kindhearted witch in a town where they are openly accepted.

Yet evil spirits are said to abound here, too. Among them is La Zegua, a maiden whose enchanting beauty belies her true nature: Men who make love to her discover that she has turned into a horse. And many older residents still believe that the Río Tiribí is haunted and that the evil monkey Mico Malo attacks those who dare to cross the Los Anonos bridge at night.

Local musician Lencho Salazar relates the legends of the brujas.

Hacienda el Rodeo (tel 2249-1013, haciendaelrodeo.com) offers equestrian tours and mountain biking. It also hosts restaurants and now doubles as a delux hotel. Trails lead to the forest adjoining the **Universidad de Paz** (tel 2205-9000, upeace.org), dedicated to world harmony. Statues of famous pacifists fill its inviting botanical garden. An adjoining park hosts the **Monument for Disarmament, Work & Peace.** ∎

Alajuela & Around

Alajuela, a small regional town founded in 1676, lies at the base of Volcán Poás a mile (1.6 km) north of Juan Santamaría International Airport and 13 miles (21 km) northwest of San José. Although hardly a calling card in its own right, it is a splendid base for exploring Poás, and there are several key sites tucked amid the waves of coffee that wash against the town on all sides.

Rancho San Miguel provides a chance to ride Andalusian horses.

Alajuela

🅰 Map p. 68

Museo Histórico Cultural Juan Santamaría

☎ 2441-4775

🕐 Closed Mon.

💲 $

museojuansanta maria.go.cr

Alajuela, Costa Rica's second city, is colloquially called the City of the Mangoes for the trees that shade **Parque Central.** It's officially the Plaza de General Tomás Guardia; local wags call it Park of the Dead Doves for the old men who gather to gossip and watch pretty girls pass by.

The body of former president Guardia is buried in the simple metal-domed cathedral, dating from 1863, on the park's east side. The main attraction is the **Museo Histórico Cultural Juan Santamaría,** to the northwest in the old city jail. Its meager collection relates the William Walker saga in 1856 in which Juan Santamaría, Alajuela's drummer-boy hero, gave his life (see p. 29). Cultural programs are offered in a screening room; you can request an English-language video about the story. A statue of the young hero stands in **Parque Juan Santamaría** at the corner of Calle 2 and Avenida 2.

The town bustles on Saturday; this is when you should visit the compact **Mercado Central,** where all manner of produce is sold within the tight, shaded warren. On the west side of town, a factory tour at **Señor y Señora Ese** (tel 2441-8333, srysraese.com), at Villa Bonita de Alajuela, is a fun and fascinating experience as you watch skilled workers hew hardwoods into crafts.

The soccer team, La Liga, is a source of local pride. You can catch a match on weekends at Avenida 7 and Calle 13.

Toward Volcán Poás

North of Alajuela, the land rises incrementally toward the forested summit of Volcán Poás. The drive is superbly scenic as you wend up through coffee fields hugging the convex slope. Higher up, the coffee fields are replaced by strawberries and

EXPERIENCE: Saving Macaws

Once abundant in Costa Rica's lowland tropical forests, green macaw and scarlet macaw populations have been reduced by deforestation and poaching for the pet trade. Two decades ago, only two areas on the Pacific side of the country had viable populations of scarlet macaws. Since then, efforts by private foundations to breed and reestablish macaw populations in the wild have had tremendous success.

The Ara Project (tel 8389-5811, thearaproject.org) breeds scarlet and green macaws for release into the wild. Volunteers are needed to help care for the vibrantly colored birds. **Tiskita Scarlet Macaw**

Restoration Project (tel 2296-8125, tiskita.com), near Pavones, releases scarlet macaws into primary forest and has established a free-flying flock of more than 30 birds. Volunteers observe their progress and gather

seeds to feed caged birds. **Zoo Ave** (tel 2433-8989, rescateanimalzooave.org; see below) hires volunteers for its Centro de Reproducción de Animales, where macaws are bred for release.

---

ornamental plants grown under black shade nets, while Holstein dairy cattle munch contentedly on green pastures. Log fires scent the crisp air, drawing you to eat at rustic restaurants that serve traditional peasant fare, such as roast pork or chicken. At **Poasito** you can continue north to Parque Nacional Volcán Poás (see p. 84) or east to Vara Blanca and the Catarata La Paz.

Animal Worlds

You'll be enthralled by **La Paz Waterfall Gardens,** a private nature reserve named for the Catarata La Paz (Peace Waterfall), accessed by steep stairs that cling to the cliffside. The falls are a series of cascades that tumble for some 3,000 feet (915 m) down the eastern flank of Poás Volcano. A visitor center and local nature guides explain rain forest and cloud forest ecology. A serpentarium (snakes), ranarium (frogs), giant butterfly garden, hummingbird garden, vast aviary, and wild cat and

monkey exhibits all entertain. You can also sense what life was like one hundred years ago at the Casita de la Paz, a re-creation of a traditional farmstead. A restaurant serves *típica* (traditional) fare, and accommodations are offered at the one-of-a-kind Peace Lodge (see Travelwise pp. 244–245).

Zoo Ave Wildlife Conservation Park, situated in La Garita, west of Alajuela., is a 142-acre (57 ha) haven for more than one hundred species of birds, including quetzals, curassows, cranes, and toucans. Re-creations of natural habitats are home to all four species of native monkeys, as well as crocodiles and other beasts. Injured and confiscated wildlife are tended at a rescue center (closed to the public).

Two miles (3.2 km) north of La Guácima, **Rancho San Miguel** (tel 2439-0003, e-mail: ranchosanmiguel@ice.go.cr) offers a chance to ride Andalusian horses. The highlight is the thrice-weekly show, when the beautiful horses perform. ■

La Paz Waterfall Gardens

⬛ Map p. 68

✉ Hwy. 126, 5 miles (8 km) N of Vara Blanca

☎ 2482-2720

$ $$$$$

waterfallgardens.com

Zoo Ave Wildlife Conservation Park

⬛ Map p. 68

✉ Dulce Nombre, 2 miles (3.2 km) E of the Inter-American Hwy.

☎ 2433-8989

$ $$

rescateanimalzooave.org

A World of Butterflies

At times the Costa Rican countryside resembles a storm of sweetpeas, as butterflies float by in endlessly colorful streams. The nation has around 1,250 species, more than the whole of Africa and one in ten of all known species worldwide. Most of these winged insects are as beautiful as the denizens of an exotic harem—from *Riondinidae* with metallic gold wings to the electric blue morphos, the neon narcissi of the butterfly world.

Blue morpho butterflies often descend to the ground to lick salts and other minerals.

Color With a Purpose

There is nothing common about the morpho, colloquially called *celeste común*, which ranges from sea level to 4,500 feet (1,370 m) and zigzags through the forest with a great loping gait along flyways that follow the route of others, like cars on a highway. The 50 or so species range from satiny red to the teals of a Maxfield Parrish sea. The bluest of all morpho species are found on the Caribbean coast.

Unlike most butterflies, the morpho does not owe its coloration to pigmentation. Morphos are brown, but their scales have a complex structure that absorbs all colors of the spectrum except blue, making them appear that color. The morpho's dun-colored underwings are uninspired, but when it takes off it displays its iridescent upper wings like a flashing sign. The exotic flash serves as a dinner bell to flycatchers and jacamars, for whom the morpho is a favored tidbit.

There are also other purposes to bright coloration. Take the Heliconids, a family whose chromatic schemata—normally black speckled in red, white, and yellow—advertise their foul taste: As caterpillars, they gorge on leaves containing cyanide. The strategy works so well that edible species mimic Heliconids by adopting their liveries. Slight variations in coloration serve as flags so that potential suitors can distinguish their perfect partners from among the subspecies. The females of some Heliconid subspecies release pheromones while in the

Exhibits at butterfly farms let you watch as butterflies emerge from their chrysalises.

chrysalis, drawing male butterflies to mate with them before they emerge.

Many species of Lepidoptera migrate to mate. With the onset of rainy season around May, the countryside is a never-ending ballet as millions of insects flutter from lowland to highland. The iridescent green-and-black *Uranidae* flaps its way between Mexico and Bolivia, a distance of 34 degrees latitude. The *Uranidae* is often mistaken for the swallowtail butterfly, which it mimics. Butterflies are experts at guile. One species of moth even imitates a wasp! Even caterpillars are expert tacticians. The larvae of the giant swallowtail *(Papilio cresphontes)* appear to be bird droppings and give off an appropriate stench. Another resembles the head of a viper.

A Mime Troupe

Some species blend with their backgrounds, such as the cream owl butterfly *(Caligo memnon)*, whose wings of up to 6 inches (15 cm) wide provide superb camouflage. While the upper wings are an attractive blue-gray, the undersides are mottled brown and gray and have yellow "eyes" complete with black pupils and white spots resembling reflected sunlight, so realistic that when opened they look like the face of a wide-eyed owl. They are relatively static by day, but with dusk they take to the air and flit about the forest in search of rotting fruit. The cream owl butterfly is found at elevations up to 3,500 feet (1,070 m), especially on the Pacific side.

The devilish *caligo* caterpillar can grow to 5 inches (13 cm) long; it has horns on its head and a forked tail. Caterpillars exist to eat and grow. "Butterfly larvae are a mouth with chewing mandibles and a long body to house a long gut," says P. J. DeVries, author of *Butterflies of Costa Rica.* Lacking jaws, butterflies use a proboscis to feed on juices—nectar, decaying fruit, or decomposed carrion.

Population densities vary by habitat and seasonality, but all habitats have significant increases in populations in June and July. In general, you will see more butterflies on sunny days. At least one species of butterfly is nocturnal, though most are diurnal and more active by morning.

To learn about butterfly ecology, visit a butterfly "farm," most of which are live exhibits. There are more than a dozen in the country. Butterfly Kingdom (see p. 70), in Escazú, near San José, is a butterfly breeding center that offers insightful tours.

The Heliconid family's chromatic schemata—black speckled in red, white, and yellow—advertises their foul taste.

The Western Slopes

The classic touring circuit takes in the Western Highlands, coffee and dairy country par excellence laced with small artisan and market towns lining the Inter-American Highway and Highway 3. Those two parallel routes weave through the region, ascending gradually toward the western rim before beginning their plummeting descents to the Pacific and the Northern Lowlands. The vistas over the Central Valley are stupendous.

Dairy cattle roam the heights of Costa Rica's Western Highlands.

Grecia

⚠ Map p. 68

Sarchí

⚠ Map p. 68

Grecia

This compact market center, founded only in 1864, is known for its twin-spired **metal church,** which was imported from Belgium in 1897 and now commands the palm-shaded main plaza. The somewhat dour rust red exterior of the edifice belies the handsome wooden interior, which features pendulous glass chandeliers and a soaring marble altar—a fanciful confection in stone.

Sarchí

A staple on the beaten tourist path, this agricultural town— divided into Sarchí Norte (the main town) and Sarchí Sur (the

artisan center) about 0.6 mile (1 km) farther east—is also renowned as Costa Rica's center of crafts and fine furniture, despite being firmly in the grip of commercialism. The main road is lined with souvenir stores selling leather and wooden items—from handsome bowls of lignum vitae (wood of life) and classic wood-and-leather rockers to miniature hand-painted oxcarts, Sarchí's hallmark and also a national symbol.

You can see oxcarts being made and adorned at **Fábrica de Carretas Eloy Alfaro** (tel 2454-4131, souvenirscostarica.com) in

Sarchí Norte. The only workshop in Costa Rica still making traditional oxcarts is powered by an old waterwheel. Nearby, the **Else Kientzler Botanical Gardens** *(tel 2454-2070, elsegarden.com, $$)* spans 7 acres (2.8 ha); trails— including one for the blind—wind through specialty gardens displaying more than 2,000 species of plants. Kids will love the maze.

INSIDER TIP:

Driving the narrow, steep, and snaking mountain roads that lead to Bosque de Paz is not for the faint of heart, especially when the clouds swirl in. If in doubt, hire a driver.

—CHRISTOPHER BAKER
National Geographic author

The rambling town is cusped by coffee-clad vales. The photogenic appeal of this magnificent setting is enhanced by the town's quintessential floral motif adorning whitewashed adobe buildings and the blush pink **church** in the main square of Sarchí Norte. The church has an impressive vaulted ceiling.

Try to visit Sarchí during the first week of February for the town's lively fiesta.

Bosque de Paz & Around

North of Sarchí is a narrow winding road that climbs up the western flank of Volcán Poás and, beyond the cloud-shrouded saddle between Poás and Volcán

Platanar (7,162 feet/2,183 m), plummets precariously down to **Bajos del Toro,** a scenic Shangri-la secreted in its own valley. This remote farming community provides access to 960-acre (390 ha) **Bosque de Paz,** a private nature reserve whose mountainous rain-soaked terrain is a veritable Noah's Ark of safeguarded wildlife. Trails offer an opportunity to spot scores of rare birds such as curassows and black guans. Big cats, which give people a wide berth, prowl through the lush forests in search of brocket deer and primates, including howler monkeys, capuchins, and the endangered spider monkeys.

The reserve lies at the foot of **Parque Nacional Juan Castro Blanco,** a 35,230-acre (14,260 ha) swath created in 1995 to protect the precious montane rain forest and cloud forests of Volcán Platanar.

Shopping With a Conscience

Be aware that many craft and souvenir items sold in Costa Rica are made from endangered flora or fauna. Buying such items contributes to their demise. Trade in endangered products is illegal, and such items may be confiscated by U.S. Customs. Avoid jewelry made from turtle shell or coral, furs of ocelots or other animals, and items made from macaw or quetzal feathers. Only buy tropical hardwood products if they are made from fallen timber.

Else Kientzler Botanical Gardens
- Map p. 68
- 0.6 mile (1 km) N of Sarchí
- 2454-2070
- $$

elsegarden.com

Bosque de Paz
- Map p. 68
- Bajos del Toro, 7 miles (11 km) N of Sarchí
- 2234-6676
- By appt.
- Call for details

bosquedepaz.com

Parque Nacional Juan Castro Blanco
- Map p. 68
- Bajos del Toro, 8 miles (13 km) N of Sarchí
- 8815-7094
- $$

San Ramón

🅐 Map p. 68

Jardín de las Guarias

🅐 Map p. 68

✉ Cocaleca, 1 mile (1.6 km) S of Palmares

☎ 2452-0091

🕐 Call for details

💲 $

Nectandra Cloud Forest Garden

🅐 Map p. 68

✉ 9 miles (15 km) N of San Ramón

☎ 2445-4642

🕐 Closed Mon.

💲 $$$$$

nectandra.org

The park is cut through by trails perfect for hardy hikers. These begin at Bajo del Toro, but the main entrance—with new visitor center—is at El Sucre, three miles (5 km) south of Ciudad Quesada (see p. 212).

Naranjo & Around

The countryside west of Sarchí appeals mainly for its uplifting vistas. Three miles (4.8 km) west of Sarchí is Naranjo, an important market town sitting astride Highway 3 and alluring for its comely church supported by Corinthian columns. Next comes the regional center of **San Ramón,** 7 miles (11.2 km) farther, on the western rim of the Meseta Central and gateway to Puntarenas and Guanacaste. The town's Saturday **farmers market** *(feria de agricultor)* is well worth a stop. So, too, is the

The whimsical creatures of Zarcero's famous topiary park stand guard before the quaint village church.

centenarian metal church, which was made in Germany, shipped to Costa Rica, and welded together in situ.

The Inter-American Highway skirts San Ramón, which sits immediately to the north, and **Palmares,** a mile (1.6 km) to the south. Palmares is renowned for its colorful mid-January fiesta, which features rodeo-style bull-fights and all the fun of the fair. The largest orchid collection in the country, consisting of some 40,000 blooms, can be enjoyed at **Jardín de las Guarias,** the private garden of Javier Solórzaro Murillo, at Cocaleca, a mile (1.6 km) south of Palmares.

From San Ramón, lonesome Highway 702 climbs north up the mountain slopes and 12 miles (19 km) above the town, where it begins its looping drop to the Northern Lowlands. You'll want to stop at the **San Lorenzo Canopy Tour** *(tel 2447-9331, arenalcanopy .com, $$$$$)* for a thrilling zip line ride across a canyon. Nearby, **Nectandra Cloud Forest Garden** invites visitors keen to explore its landscaped garden displaying plants native to the 321-acre (130 ha) cloud forest reserve (a small area is accessible by reservation).

For a fuller immersion, detour to the private **El Silencio de los Angeles Reserve,** where more than 200 bird species, plus three species of monkeys and elusive cats such as ocelots, await visitors on guided hikes from the enchanting **Villablanca Cloud Forest Hotel & Spa** (see Travelwise p. 244), perched on the very edge of the continental divide. The National Biodiversity Institute has a research center here open to visitors, and the hotel's organic greenhouses can be toured.

Atop the Cordillera

You could be forgiven for imagining that you are in Switzerland as you drive along Highway 141 between Naranjo and **Ciudad Quesada** (see p. 212), a center of the local dairy industry that clings to the mountainside. The mountains fall away to the Northern Lowlands via a breathtaking switchback.

Midway between Naranjo and Ciudad Quesada is **Zarcero,** a pretty village whose simple church is fronted by a leafy arbor running through a **topiary park** that resembles a circus. The gardener responsible, Evangelisto Blanco, wields his pruning shears like an artist's paintbrush, conjuring up such smile-inducing spectacles as an elephant with light bulbs for eyes and a cat riding a motorcycle atop a hedge. All around the area, black-and-white Holstein cattle chomp on emerald green alpine meadows and even many of the farmsteads hint at Swiss provenance.

Atenas & Around

The charming town of Atenas on Highway 3, 8 miles (13 km) south of Palmares, has a truly sublime climate. The town plaza boasts an exquisite church and is surrounded by wooden homes. The **Monumento a Los Boyeros,** on the east side of town, commemorates the days when Atenas was a major stop on the *camino de carretas,* the old coffee route to Puntarenas.

Cultural Faux Pas to Avoid

- Don't grip too tightly when shaking hands.
- Don't insult Costa Rican culture. Ticos are proud of their country.
- Don't behave like a know-it-all. Modesty is appreciated.
- Do maintain personal hygiene. Ticos appreciate cleanliness.
- Don't use *piropos,* impolite "compliments" meant to woo women.
- Don't attempt to draw the easygoing Ticos into arguments.

East of Atenas, the **Botanical Orchid Garden** has more than 150 orchid species, plus bamboo, heliconia, and palm gardens. Guided tours are offered, and there is a superb open-air café. Adrenalin junkies flock to a bridge spanning the Río Colorado off the Pan-Am Highway near Rosario, 5 miles (8 km) northeast of Atenas. **Tropical Bungee** *(tel 2248-2212, bungee.co.cr)* offers hair-raising jumps into the canyon. ■

El Silencio de los Angeles Reserve

- ✉ Off Hwy. 142, 6 miles (9.7 km) N of San Ramón
- ☎ 2461-0300
- 💲 $$$

villablanca -costarica.com

Botanical Orchid Garden

- 🅰 Map p. 68
- ✉ 3 miles (5 km) E of Atenas
- ☎ 2487-8095
- 🕐 Closed Mon.
- 💲 $$

orchidgarden cr.com

Grano de Oro

Costa Ricans call coffee *grano de oro*—the grain of gold—with good reason. The humble bean lifted the nation out of obscurity two centuries ago, bringing wealth to countless subsistence farmers and to the country as a whole. The slopes and steep vales of the Meseta Central are patterned in endless rows of dark green corduroy.

Coffee cherries turn bloodred when mature.

Coffee bushes, native to Ethiopia, came to Costa Rica from Jamaica in 1779; they turned out to be Costa Rica's economic salvation. The rise of coffee in Central America coincided with the demise of slavery in the Caribbean, which threw the islands' industry into chaos. Jamaica—at that time the world's largest coffee producer—was quickly displaced by Costa Rica, whose climate and rich volcanic soils proved perfect for coffee cultivation.

Ideal Conditions

The coffee plant grows best in well-drained soils at elevations of 2,500 to 3,500 feet (760–1,070 m), with nearly constant temperatures between 59 and 82°F (15–28°C) and a distinct wet and dry season. The Meseta Central met these conditions as well as anywhere in the world. On the Central Highlands a particular combination of aspect, slope, soil type, and climactic conditions combined to produce a distinctly flavored coffee—mellow and aromatic, with a hint of acidity—that international coffee connoisseurs soon acclaimed as one of the best in the world. Economically, a dry season aided the Costa Rican harvest; it was also propitious for the transportation of the beans down the mountains via mule train to the port of Puntarenas, whence a three-month journey via Cape Horn delivered the beans to java-thirsty Europe.

For Costa Rica's subsistence farmers, the coffee was a commercial godsend—and one on which no taxes were levied. Soon everyone was growing the grano de oro (in the early 1800s there was even a law that required every Tico household to grow coffee bushes in its yard), which by 1829 had established itself as the nation's numero uno income earner.

Small farmers dominated production and took their fair share of wealth. But the real profits lay in the processing and trade, which quickly coalesced into relatively few hands. Costa Rica gained its first social and political elite—the *cafeteleros* (coffee barons). Even today there are only 95 coffee mills *(beneficios)* in the country, although some 80,000 producers grow coffee on approximately 270,000 acres (110,000 ha).

From Seed to Bean

The seeds are planted in nurseries and nourished until, as yearlings, they are planted in rows that follow the contours of the mountain slopes under shade trees or tousled bananas, which fix nitrogen in the soil. Shaded coffee bushes are more productive. The glossy green bushes will begin fruiting by their fourth year (carefully tended, a coffee bush will bear fruit for up to 40 years). At the onset of the rainy season, their tiny white blossoms scent the air with a jasmine-like fragrance. The beans are surrounded by lush green berries that turn bloodred by the seasonal harvest in November.

The handpicked beans are shipped to beneficios, where the fleshy outer layers are removed to expose the beans, which are blow-dried or spread out in the sun in the traditional manner. The leathery skins are then stripped away; the beans are roasted, sorted, vacuum sealed, and finally shipped to market.

Coffee remained the nation's prime source of income until 1991, when world coffee prices plummeted and the grano de oro was toppled from its pedestal by both bananas and tourism, causing economic distress in the industry. Coffee's fortunes have continued to decline; production has fallen from 2.5 million bags in 1997 to 1.45 million in 2010. Still, coffee producers attain higher productivity per acre in Costa Rica than anywhere else in the world. Ideal conditions are enhanced by the propagation of high-yielding plants and intensive production techniques. The highest-quality coffee grows at higher elevations, where beans take longer to mature and are more robust and aromatic, with less caffeine.

EXPERIENCE: Learn About Coffee Culture

Coffee isn't simply an agricultural product of economic importance to Costa Rica. Its importance to the historical evolution of the modern nation is such that traditions associated with coffee production are the sine qua non of Tico culture. The following venues will help you appreciate the intricacies of coffee production and its hallowed place in the national psyche.

Beneficio Coopedota *(tel 2541-2828, coopedota .com)*, near San José, roasts the beans grown by scores of small-scale producers in the Tarrazú district. Tours are given during harvest.
Beneficio Tierra Madre *(tel 2277-1600, beneficiotierramadre.com;* see p. 83), in San Rafael, Heredia, a historic high-mountain coffee farm and mill, still processes coffee beans in age-old fashion and welcomes visitors by appointment.
Café Britt *(tel 2277-1600, coffeetour.com;* see p. 83) near Barva, Heredia, is renowned for amusing multimedia tours, led by guides in period costume, that educate about the importance of coffee in Costa Rican culture.
Doka Estate *(tel 7300-* 7158, dokaestate.com; see p. 98), on the slopes of Volcán Poás, offers organized tours with folkloric shows to teach about coffee production, roasting, and culture.
Finca Rosa Blanca *(tel 2269-9392, fincarosa blanca.com)*, at Santa Barbara de Heredia, offers tours of the coffee plantation and is a deluxe boutique hotel.

Heredia & Volcán Barva

The pull of Heredia and its beautiful surroundings defies gravity, luring you inexorably up the slopes of Volcán Barva, where emerald pastures give way to pine and merge into the mystical cloud forests that shroud the uppermost slopes of Parque Nacional Braulio Carrillo. On weekends, Josefinos also head north, seeking cozy cottages warmed by log-burning hearths and rustic restaurants where simple fare is cooked over coffee-wood fires.

Basílica de la Immaculada Concepción dominates Heredia's Parque Central.

Heredia
◪ Map p. 68

**Casa de la
Cultura**
✉ Ave. Central,
Calle Central,
Heredia
☎ 2260-1619

Heredia

This former coffee capital of Costa Rica, 7 miles (11.2 km) northwest of San José, dates from 1706 and is affectionately called City of the Flowers. At its core is the **Parque Central** dominated by the venerable **Basílica de la Immaculada Concepción,** erected in 1797 and featuring bells imported from Cusco, Peru. The handsome tree-shaded plaza proffers a panoply of historic attractions, including the circular brick fortress, **El Fortín,** erected by president Alfredo González Flores (1914–1917). Note how the gun slits open outward, so that bullets ricochet into the

fortress—a military heresy that speaks volumes for Costa Rica's innocence in such matters. Flores lived across Calle Central in what is now the **Casa de la Cultura,** a small museum and art gallery.

On the east side of town is the **Universidad Nacional,** with its surrounding area bustling with coffee shops. West of town, the bougainvillea-lined suburb of **San Joaquín de las Flores** is famous for its traditional Easter Parade.

Near **Santo Domingo de Heredia,** southeast of town, is **INBioparque** *(tel 2507-8100, inbio .ac.cr),* the headquarters of the National Biodiversity Institute. Housing millions of species of flora and fauna, this educational facility also has opportunities for volunteer internships.

Barva

Exquisite and endearing, this historic village 1.5 miles (2.4 km) north of Heredia lures visitors to its narrow streets lined with old adobe homes adorned with grill windows and terra-cotta roofs. At its heart is the **Iglesia de San Bartolomé de Barva,** built in 1867.

About 3 miles (4.8 km) northwest, outside Santa Barbara de Heredia, **Costa Rica Meadery & Ark Herb Farm** (tel 8718-4090, www.costaricameadery.com) spreads over 20 acres (8 ha) with hundreds of species of medicinal and culinary herbs raised for export. Trails weave among the herb beds, shrubbery, and fruit orchards.

INSIDER TIP:

For a wide range of generous *bocas*—Costa Rican tapas—try Bar y Marisquería El Róbalo, in Heredia's southeastern suburb of Santo Domingo.

—MICHAEL H. GRAYUM
National Geographic field researcher

Guided tours are offered, including of the apiary and meadery, offering a fascinating look into the world of bees and mead production.

To see an example of adobe construction and learn about campesino culture at the turn of the 19th century, pop into the **Museo de la Cultura Popular,** housed in the former home of

Alfredo González Flores at **Santa Lucía de Barva,** midway between Heredia and Barva.

Barva is surrounded by coffee, much of it belonging to the estates of **Café Britt,** which offers a highly recommended tour. This features a multimedia presentation and includes the roasting plant and tasting room where visitors learn the fine art of coffee discernment. Actors in traditional garb blend the tale of a love story, the nation's development, and the evolution of coffee. Café Britt's **Beneficio Tierra Madre** coffee farm and mill, at San Rafael de Heredia, is adorned with murals celebrating the "golden bean."

Volcán Barva

On weekends and holidays, Josefinos hit the slopes of Volcán Barva, where exclusive mountain regions such as **San José de la Montaña** and the **Reserva Monte de la Cruz** offer cabins amid the pines. Temperatures grow chillier as roads climb past alpine meadows and forests draped with orchids, ferns, and Spanish moss. It is easy to imagine yourself in the Tyrol.

The finest example of the transplanted Alps is above **San Rafael de Heredia** at the **Hotel Chalet Tirol** (see Travelwise p. 244), which looks like a set from *The Sound of Music*. In summer the hotel hosts the **International Music Festival,** with classical concerts in the Salzburg Theater.

Hiking at these upper heights is stupendous. Trails lead through cloud forest reserves such as that of **Cerro Dantas Wildlife Biological Center** (tel 2274-1997), which has an ecological center, educational trails, and guided hikes. ∎

Barva
⚠ Map p. 68

Museo de la Cultura Popular
✉ Carretera 126, 1.5 miles (2.4 km) NW of Heredia
☎ 2260-1619
$ $

musco.una.ac.cr

Café Britt
⚠ Map p. 68
✉ Carretera 126, 1.25 miles (2 km) NW of Heredia
☎ 2277-1600
$ $$$$

coffeetour.com

Beneficio Tierra Madre
⚠ Map p. 68
✉ San Rafael de Heredia
☎ 2277-1600
$ $$

beneficiotierramadre.com

Parque Nacional Volcán Poás

The most developed of the country's national parks protects the most dramatic of the region's volcanoes, which rises above the northwest Meseta Central. On clear days you can see both the Caribbean Sea and the Pacific Ocean from its summit. Poás awakened in 2017 with a series of violent eruptions leading to the closure of the park as part of an "exclusion zone" around the crater.

A view of Poás's crater prior to the 2017 eruptions

Parque Nacional Volcán Poás

🗺 Map p. 68

☎ 2482-2424

💲 $$

www.sinac.go.cr

The 13,838-acre (5,600 ha) Parque Nacional Volcán Poás is centered on the eponymous 8,871-foot-high (2,704 m) volcano, whose main crater collapsed eons ago to form a mile-wide (1.6 km) caldera. Prior to the 2017 eruptions, you could drive all the way to Poás's summit. A 300-yard (275 m) walk from the parking lot leads to a viewing terrace 600 feet (183 m) above the cauldron, where fumaroles hiss, a sulfurous pool bubbles, and smoke is disgorged. At times, the sulfur fumes become so acidic that the park must close.

The feisty giant, still intermittently active, entered its most recent volatile phase in April 2017. The main crater, which had burbled and belched persistently since the 1990s, began a series of violent eruptions that led to the park being closed to visitors. Phone the regional office *(tel 2268-8091)* for an update on current conditions before your visit, or check online *(costa-rica-guide.com/nature/volcano -tourism-in-costa-rica)*.

Poás also has two minor craters, both extinct, snoozing beneath lush green blankets. One, **Botos,** has a jade-colored lake reached via the **Botos Trail,** which leads through an eerie cloud forest with trees bowing together to form an arch. The forests resound with the songs of sooty robins and toucanets, as well as the two-note whistle of resplendent quetzals. Fiery-throated hummingbirds flit past, and you'll also see the endemic Poás squirrel.

Arrive early to beat the clouds that blanket the chilly heights by midmorning. Bring warm clothing to shield yourself from the wind whistling over the Continental Divide. Traditionally the most visited park in the country, Poás is popular on weekends with Ticos who disdain the wondrous silence. If possible, visit midweek, once the park reopens.

The 23-mile (37 km) drive from Alajuela, featuring a summit road that winds like a coiled python, is half the fun; for those without transportation, excursions leave daily from San José. ■

Parque Nacional Braulio Carrillo

Rugged to the point of being almost impenetrable, Parque Nacional Braulio Carrillo protects a precious watershed on the windward side of the Cordillera Central—a massive tract of pristine wilderness spanning five life zones, less than a 40-minute drive from the metropolis of San José.

Braulio Carrillo is a 108,970-acre (44,100 ha) swath of endless dark green cloaking the flanks of **Volcán Barva** (9,534 feet/2,906 m) and **Volcán Cacho Negro** (7,053 feet/2,150 m). It ranges from windswept cloud forest at higher elevations to lowland rain forest in the soggy Northern Lowlands barely 100 feet (30 m) above sea level. Given the park's size and elevation range, temperatures differ markedly, though rainfall is a near constant and nowhere less than 10 feet (3 m) per year.

INSIDER TIP:

Be sure to stop at the bridge over Río Sucio in Braulio Carrillo and see where a bright red river (caused by weird geology off the northern flanks of Volcán Irazú) joins a clear water river.

—JOHN LONGINO
National Geographic field researcher

Hiking the rugged trails guarantees seeing wildlife, including more than 500 species of birds, from quetzals to toucans, and almost 150 mammal species, including jaguars, monkeys, peccaries, pumas,

Rain Forest Aerial Tram

Few rain forest experiences are as immersive as the 90-minute, mile-long (1.6 km) excursion through the forest canopy aboard this open-air aerial tram, in a private tropical wet forest reserve abutting Braulio Carrillo. The trip reveals details of everyday life in the treetops, where 75 percent of all rain forest species dwell. You can view monkeys eye-to-eye suspended 200 feet (60 m) above the forest floor.

and *tepezcuintles* (or pacas)—a giant rodent that's the park mascot. Permission is required for camping.

The park is easily accessed by Highway 32, the Guápiles Highway, whose construction in 1978 led to the park's creation. **Zurquí Ranger Station,** on the highway 13 miles (21 km) northeast of San José, has an information center, but the trails here are closed. The main access is from the lowlands at the **Puesto Carrillo Ranger Station,** on the Guápiles Highway. You can also access with a rugged four-wheel drive from the west, and from the south via the **Puesto Brava Ranger Station,** above Sacramento. ∎

Parque Nacional Braulio Carrillo

🄽 Map p. 68
✉ Hwy. 32, 14 miles (22.5 km) NE of San José
☎ 2257-0922 or 2266-1883
💲 $$

Rain Forest Aerial Tram

✉ Rainforest Adventures, Rara Avis, Hwy. 32, 30 miles (48.3 km) NE of San José
☎ 2257-5961
💲 $$$$$

rainforestadventure .com

Orosí Valley Drive

Southeast of Paraíso, 5 miles (8 km) east of Cartago, Highway 224 drops sharply into a Shangri-la canyon edged to the south by the dauntingly forested flanks of the Talamanca mountains. The rivers that drain the vale have been dammed to form Lago de Cachí, around which the road loops. This tour makes a circle that begins and ends in Paraíso, passing two precious colonial churches and many intriguing stops en route.

Carving a coffee-tree stump at Casa del Soñador

NOT TO BE MISSED:
Iglesia de San José de Orosí
• Casa del Soñador • Ruins
at Ujarrás

At the main square in **Paraíso,** turn south off the main highway—Highway 10—and follow the looping road 1.5 miles (2.4 km) to the **Mirador Orosí ❶** (tel 2574-4688), offering views over the valley and set in a park run by the ICT (Institute of Costa Rican Tourism). Shortly beyond, the road begins to slalom the ski-ramp route into the canyon. At the foot you're instantly immersed in coffee, with shiny-leaved bushes to all sides.

The road wends through the coffee fields and, beyond the **Río Aguacaliente,** deposits you in the picturesque village of **Orosí ❷** (Orosí Tourist Info & Art Café, tel 2533-3640), backed by forested hills. On your right is the **Iglesia de San José de Orosí,** a charming little church built in 1743 whose thick adobe walls and beamed roof have withstood many an earthquake. Its ascetic interior, with a terra-cotta floor and wooden gilt altar, was recently restored. Adjoining is the small **Museo de Arte Religioso** (tel 2533-3051, closed Mon., $, no photography), containing religious art, chalices, and other ecclesiastical icons plus

colonial furniture. Continue four blocks south and one east to the hillside **Balnearios de Aguas Termales Orosí** (tel 2533-2156, balnearioaguastermales orosi.com, closed Tues.), offering relaxing bathing in well-maintained thermal mineral pools. Just south of the village you'll pass the **Beneficio Orlich** coffee-processing plant. The plant sits at a junction for Parque Nacional Tapantí—Macizo de la Muerte (see p. 98). Turn left and cross the **Río Grande de Orosí** via a narrow suspension bridge.

Turn left immediately beyond the river and trace its course to pass through the heart of coffee country. After about 4 miles (6.4 km) pick up the pavement again as the road swings along the southern shore of **Lago de Cachí ❸,** which attracts waterfowl. The lake was created in the 1960s when the Río Reventazón was dammed for hydroelectricity. It is becoming popular for fishing and boating, offered at **La Casona del Cafetal** (tel 2577-1414, lacasonadelcafetal.com), a lakeside coffee farm that also offers hiking and horseback riding and a hotel and restaurant with marvelous views.

Continue east less than 1 mile (1.6 km) to the rough-hewn **Casa del Soñador ❹** (House of the Dreamer; tel 2577-1186), a wooden-and-bamboo structure adorned with primitivist carvings—the whimsical creations of the late Macedonio Quesada, whose sons continue the tradition of conjuring twisted coffee-tree stumps into carvings. Two miles (3.2 km) farther, the road turns west and crosses the **Presa de Cachí ❺** (Cachí Dam),

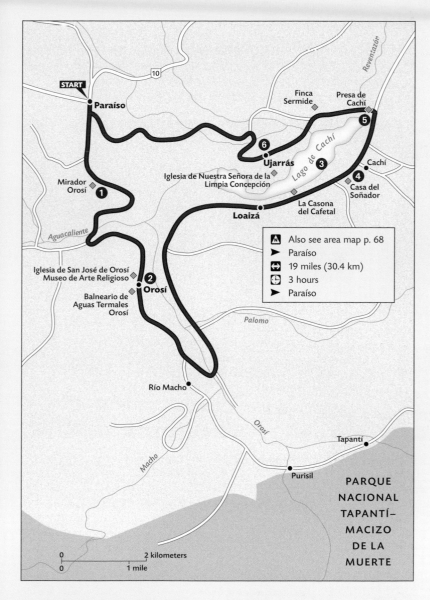

START

Paraíso

10

Finca Sermide

Presa de Cachí

5

6

Ujarrás

Lago de Cachí

Reventazón

3

Cachí

Iglesia de Nuestra Señora de la Limpia Concepción

4

Casa del Soñador

Mirador Orosí

1

La Casona del Cafetal

Aguacaliente

Loaizá

Also see area map p. 68

Paraíso

Iglesia de San José de Orosí Museo de Arte Religioso

2 **Orosí**

19 miles (30.4 km)

3 hours

Paraíso

Balneario de Aguas Termales Orosí

Palomo

Río Macho

Orosí

Tapantí

Macho

Purisil

PARQUE NACIONAL TAPANTÍ– MACIZO DE LA MUERTE

0   2 kilometers
0   1 mile

pointing you back to Paraíso. After about 1,000 yards (1 km), turn right to **Finca Sermide** *(tel 2574-2027, fincasermide.com)*, an eco-sustainable farm that offers tours and lodging. Return to the main road. After about 5 miles (8 km) you'll see signs for **Ujarrás 6**, renowned for its ruined church—**Iglesia de Nuestra Señora**

de la Limpia Concepción—on the fringe of the lake. The church dates from 1681 but was abandoned in 1833 when the valley flooded. Today it sits amid lawns fronted by giddily colorful flowers. It is the setting every third Sunday in April for a pilgrimage from Paraíso, which awaits at the top of a scenic climb.

Cartago

Although Cartago, the nation's erstwhile capital and today its second-largest city, offers meager attractions, a fistful of first-class sites lie nearby, the surrounding countryside is enrichingly scenic, and the city is a starting point for stupendous drives up Volcán Irazú, through the Orosí Valley, and along the mountain ridge that leads south to Cerro de la Muerte.

Hardwood columns and exquisite stained glass adorn the Basílica de Nuestra Señora de los Ángeles.

Cartago
- Map p. 68

Visitor Information
- ✉ Cartago Chamber of Commerce, 30 yards (27 m) E of Las Ruinas de Cartago
- ☎ 2551-0396
- 🕐 Closed Sun.

camaracomercio
cartago.com

Cartago, Costa Rica's oldest settlement, was founded in 1563 by conquistador Juan Vásquez de Coronado and remained the nation's capital until 1823, when it lost the Battle of Ochomongo to San José. It is hardly a beautiful city and long ago ceased to wear its history on its sleeve. Most of the colonial edifices have literally fallen victim to earthquakes (most recently in 1910), and nearby Volcán Irazú frequently spews ash on the city.

The parochial city, at the eastern base of the Cerros de la Carpintera, 16 miles (26 km) east of San José, retains its role as religious capital, symbolically represented by the ruins of **Iglesia de la Parroquia,** in a tree-shaded plaza at Avenida 2 and Calle 2. The nation's preeminent church, the gray-and-white **Basílica de Nuestra Señora de los Ángeles** (tel 2551-0465), stands foursquare in the main square at Avenida 2 and Calle 14. It was built of steel with a concrete stucco surface in 1929 in Byzantine style following the collapse of its precursor in 1926. The stunning interior of glistening hardwood boasts exquisite stained glass. Supplicants kneel and pray to **La Negrita,** the nation's *mulatta* (mixed-blood) patron saint to whom local superstition ascribes miraculous cures. She resides in an 8-inch-high (20 cm) effigy set in a gold-encrusted shrine above the main altar. In the basement, to the rear, the **Cripta de la Piedra** shrine is a veritable mini-museum of *promesas,* or votive offerings.

The town's history is on display at the excellent **Museo Municipal de Cartago,** in the fortress-like former army barracks. It also hosts concerts and special events.

INSIDER TIP:

Learn from the locals; many times the little *sodas* on the side of the road are the best spots to grab a cheap bite to eat.

—BEN HORTON
National Geographic field researcher

El Jardín Botánico Lankester

This 27-acre (11 ha) garden at **Paraíso,** 5 miles (8 km) east of Cartago, protects an invaluable collection of neotropical flora that is one of the largest in the Americas, including its pride and joy—more than 700 species of orchids. The gardens also abound with palms and bromeliads, effusive as a Pisarro painting, drawing butterflies and birds by the thousands. Peak blooming is in springtime.

La Negrita Pilgrimage

Pilgrims from Costa Rica and Central America descend on Cartago and the Basílica de Nuestra Señora de los Ángeles each August 2 for the Procesión de los Milagros (Procession of the Miracles). Penitents set out at dawn from San José to pray to La Negrita. Some carry large wooden crosses on their backs; others crawl on their knees. Lepers and mendicants plead for charitable donations while the townsfolk do a thriving business selling votive candles and flowers. The occasion is both colorful and emotional.

Established in the 1940s, the gardens are named for their founder, Charles H. Lankester (1879–1969), an English orchiddologist and naturalist who worked to collate a representative corpus of Central American flora. Through the joint efforts of the American Orchid Society and the Stanley Smith Horticultural Trust, the garden was donated to the University of Costa Rica in 1973. ∎

Museo Municipal de Cartago

⊠ Ave. 6, Calle 2
☎ 2591-1050
🕑 Closed Mon.
**muni-carta.go.cr
/museo-municipal-de
-cartago**

El Jardín Botánico Lankester

🅰 Map p. 68
⊠ Hwy. 1, Paraíso
☎ 2552-3247
🆂 $$
jbl.ucr.ac.cr

Parque Nacional Volcán Irazú

Volcán Irazú looms over both Cartago and the Reventazón Valley, rising to the north as steadily as the line created by a logarithmic equation. For anyone with a head for heights, a drive to the top offers sublime rewards. On clear days, the view takes in the shimmering waters of both the Caribbean and the Pacific.

The mineral-rich lake in Volcán Irazú's crater shifts between jade green and bloodred.

Parque Nacional Volcán Irazú

- Map p. 68
- 22 miles (35 km) NE of Cartago
- 2200-5025
- $$

www.sinac.go.cr

Volcán Irazú (11,260 feet/ 3,432 m) is an active volcano that made international news on March 13, 1963, when it erupted the day that President John F. Kennedy arrived in Costa Rica for an official visit. A resulting mudslide left highland dwellers ankle-deep in volcanic mud, obliterating the coffee crop but enriching the countryside for years to come. Irazú's last major hiccup was in 1996. In more benign moods, the giant welcomes visitors.

The volcano is the centerpiece of its namesake national park, created in 1955 and encompassing 5,705 acres (2,300 ha) of primary forest, including cloud forest. A 22-mile (35 km) drive from Cartago leads to the barren, windswept summit. As you climb upward, the views grow ever more panoramic until it is all you can do to keep your eye on the serpentine road. On the lower flanks you'll pass through trim little farming communities, like colorful pointillist dots on the emerald green canvas. Although dairy farming is predominant, the area is Costa Rica's main center for market gardening: The indecently rich slopes are a patchwork of fields growing vegetables such as carrots, potatoes, and legumes.

The volcano has twin craters. The smaller of the two, the 300-foot (91 m) deep **Diego de la Haya Crater,** cradles a mineral-rich lake that changes hue from jade green to bloodred. Fumaroles steam in the larger crater, which yawns 900 feet (275 m) deep.

It is foggy and chilly up here most of the time. Bring a sweater and jacket to brave the wind that beats down the vegetation, such as stunted dwarf oaks that cling low to the ground. Don't be put off from below by the clouds swirling near the summit, for it is quite possible to climb above the clouds and emerge in the sunlight, giving you views of the crater with the clouds far below.

INSIDER TIP:

Because the clouds normally thicken as the day progresses, early mornings are usually the best time to visit Volcán Irazú.

—CHRISTOPHER P. BAKER
National Geographic author

For your own safety, stick to the marked trails. Out of respect for the fragile ecosystems, refrain from following the illicit paths that have been trampled by visitors who chose to ignore the signs warning not to approach the dangerously unstable rims of the craters.

Mountain rabbits, squirrels, and even armadillos and coyotes can be seen scurrying across the ashy plains, while birds such as the ruddy nuthatch, night sparrow, and masked woodpecker swoop by within arm's length.

The ranger station is 1.25 miles (2 km) below the summit, where facilities include picnic benches and a café that serves snacks. Take warm, rainproof clothing to guard against inclement weather. Also, plan on stopping at the **Restaurante Nochebuena** *(tel 2530-8013, nochebuenacr.com, $)* for hearty fare. Here, the **Museo Vulcanológico** *($)* provides a fascinating educational overview of vulcanism and Irazú. ∎

Volcano Safety

Volcanoes are unpredictable and potentially lethal. A few precautions are in order when exploring. First, sign in with the rangers before setting off. Stay on assigned trails, and heed all warning signs. Do not venture into restricted areas or get too close to fumaroles, mud pools, or vents; they can explode without warning, and the ground around them is often just a thin crust that can easily give way. Volcán Arenal is highly active, and hiking is restricted to designated "safety zones" around the base. On Irazú and other volcanoes, trails lead into the active craters; resist any temptation to stroll off the trails to peer over the unstable rims. Take sturdy shoes and a rainproof jacket, plus a flashlight and sufficient water and food for longer hikes in case you get lost.

Valle de Reventazón

Draining Lake Cachí, the Río Reventazón falls through a narrow valley, tumbling ever more steeply to the east as the land steps down toward the Caribbean Lowlands. Hemmed between the Talamancas and the slopes of Volcán Turrialba, the area's charms are often overlooked.

Turrialba volcano dominates the lower Valle de Reventazón.

Turrialba
 Map p. 69

CATIE
 Map p. 69
✉ Hwy. 10,
   2.5 miles
   (4 km) E of
   Turrialba
☎ 2558-2000

catie.ac.cr

At its heart lies **Turrialba,** a somewhat nondescript town in a broad valley swaddled in citrus, macadamia, and sugarcane plantations. Once a major waystation on the old highway between San José and the Caribbean, it has been left high and dry since the completion of the Guápiles Highway in 1987 and the subsequent demise of the Atlantic Railroad in 1991. It's now best known as the launching point for white-water rafting trips.

CATIE (Centro Agronómico Tropical de Investigación y Enseñanza) is a 2,150-acre (870 ha) research center devoted to the investigation of tropical agriculture and husbandry. A highlight is the botanical garden, with plants from around the globe. Visitors can witness breeding experiments with both animals and crops. Trails offer superb birding. Weekend visits are by prior arrangement, but tour operators offer excursions from San José.

Nearby is **Hacienda Atirro,** a coffee, macadamia, and sugarcane farm that can be explored on horseback. Tours can be arranged from **Casa Turire** (see Travelwise p. 246), a sublime hotel that also serves as a water-sports center for **Lago Angostura.** This 633-acre (256 ha) lake was created by Proyecto Hidroeléctrico Angostura, a controversial project completed in 2000 that tapped the Río Reventazón (Exploding River) for energy by building the country's largest dam and hydroelectric plant. The lake now draws waterfowl, and much of the surrounding land is being rehabilitated to create wildlife habitats and natural forest, providing an ecological link with the forests of the Talamancas.

INSIDER TIP:

Because of Costa Rica's proximity to the Equator, the sun sets at roughly 6 p.m. year-round and the sky grows dark at a fast rate. Don't get stuck in the dark.

—ELLIANA SPIEGEL
National Geographic contributor

Turrialba is a base for rafting on the **Río Reventazón,** which plunges through a remote canyon and is considered a classic whitewater run. It is also the place to arrange excursions to **Volcán Turrialba** (10,919 feet/3,328 m), reached with four-wheel drive via Santa Cruz or Santa Teresa.

In 2010, this slumbering giant awoke and has continued to spew ash ever since, and the park has been intermittently closed. When open, you can hike up to the summit, which boasts three craters and cloud forest; stay at the rustic **Volcán Turrialba Lodge** *(tel 2273-4335).*

EXPERIENCE:
The Fun of 4WD

If the Indiana Jones within you is hankering to explore Costa Rica, a four-wheel-drive (4WD) vehicle is a must. They can be rented at almost any rental car agency. Access to much of the country is via badly potholed, rock-strewn, and/or unpaved roads. Dusty in dry season, they turn to a bouillabaisse in the wet season, when fording rivers can add to the challenge. Even paved roads quickly wash out in the rainy season. In some areas, landslides are common.

Exploration by 4WD can be fun, turning touring into a true adventure. You get to explore remote parts of the country totally inaccessible by sedan, test your driving skills under conditions that would challenge a goat, and enjoy the thrill of feeling like a true pioneer. Even in 4WD vehicles, however, you have to know when to quit.

Monumento Nacional Guayabo

The nation's most important archaeological site pales beside the great Mexican and Guatemalan ruins, yet nonetheless is impressive for its setting amid the jungle at the base of Volcán Turrialba.

The settlement, which may have housed up to a thousand people, was occupied between

(continued on p. 96)

Casa Turire
✉ Hwy. 225, 8 miles (13 km) SE of Turrialba
☎ 2531-1111
hotelcasaturire.com

Mountain Ridge Drive

To travel this 45-mile (72 km) route between Cartago and the Cerro de la Muerte opens up some of the most spectacular vistas in the entire country. The rich profusion of scenic views—not to mention a chance to escape the heat of the lowlands atop the Talamancas—makes amends for the poorly engineered road.

Linking the valleys of the Meseta Central and El General, this section of the Inter-American Highway (Hwy. 2) exposes visitors to the highest mountains accessible by road, to dwarf forests, and to cloud forest reserves where a quetzal sighting is nearly guaranteed.

The Inter-American Highway was built in the 1950s to link the nations of the Central American isthmus. Remarkably, for most of its length the nation's main artery is an unlighted, shoulderless, narrow two-laner. Exercise extreme caution: Grades are steep, and the twisting road is subject to fog. Slide areas, potholes, and big-rig trucks are common. Three-lane passing zones may allow uphill traffic to pass slower vehicles. Pass with care, though, as downhill traffic often rips down this lane. Set out early in the morning to beat the clouds and to ensure that you'll be safely back in the valley before dusk. Note: In the rainy season *(May–Nov.)* clouds settle over the mountains, obscuring the beautiful panoramas.

Two miles (3.2 km) south of Cartago at **San Isidro ❶**, you begin to climb. The winding road rises to **Vara de Roble ❷**, where Highway 222 falls south to Santa María de Dota. The views down the mountain are sublime—and they grow more so as you ascend another 2 miles (3.2 km), to **Empalme ❸**, your last chance to buy gas. Orchards and lime green pastures cling to the slopes, forested with pines and oaks. Roadside trout farms offer fishing and horseback rides.

Continue to the Km 58 marker, where the yellow church of **Cañón ❹** is a good place to admire the breathtaking vista. You are now atop the crest of the Continental Divide. Settlements thin as you continue up through **Parque Nacional Los Quetzales** (the ranger station is at Km 76.5), which protects rare, 500-year-old cipresillo oaks and aguacatillos, a favorite food of quetzals.

NOT TO BE MISSED:

Cañón church • Mirador de Quetzales • Dantica Cloud Forest Lodge & Gallery

At the Km 70 marker, you'll pass the turnoff for **Mirador de Quetzales ❺** (see Travelwise p. 245), a mountainside lodge that welcomes day visitors for hiking and viewing quetzals.

The road levels out near the Km 80 marker, where a side road spirals sharply westward into the valley of the **Río Savegre.** The road drops 2,100 feet (640 m) in 9 miles (14.5 km), depositing you in **San Gerardo de Dota ❻**, tucked into a valley fulsome with orchards, trout-filled streams, and a large quetzal population. The **Savegre Natural Reserve** *(tel 2740-1028, savegre .com)* welcomes visitors curious about these elusive birds; it also offers a spa, accommodations, hikes, and horseback riding and hosts the **Quetzal Education Research Center** *(tel 2740-1010, qerc.org).* Midway between the highway and San Gerardo de Dota, stop at **Dantica Cloud Forest Lodge & Gallery** (see Travelwise p. 245). This modernist lodge is a good access point for a brief hike in Parque Nacional Los Quetzales.

Return to the main road and continue south to Km 85, where a 1-mile (1.6 km) path leads to the windswept summit of **Cerro de la Muerte** (11,450 feet/3,491 m) ❼. The Mountain of Death is named for the many campesinos who froze to death hauling produce over it to San José. Above the tree line, shrubs skulk close to the ground; the peak is covered by bogs and *páramo* grasses. The road continues 2 miles (3.2 km) to a truck stop, **Las Torres ❽**, whence it begins its dizzying descent into the Valle de El General.

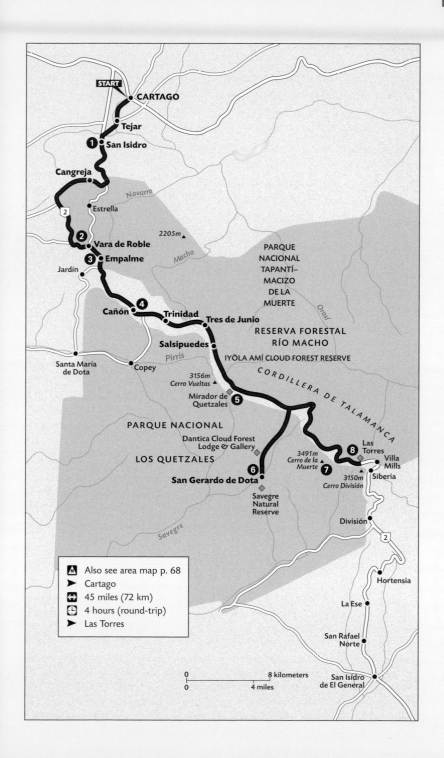

START

CARTAGO

Tejar

1 San Isidro

Cangreja

Navarro

2 Estrella

2205m ▲

2 **Vara de Roble**

3 **Empalme**

Jardín

Macho

PARQUE
NACIONAL
TAPANTÍ–
MACIZO
DE LA
MUERTE

4 **Trinidad**

Cañón **Tres de Junio**

Orosí

RESERVA FORESTAL
RÍO MACHO

Salsipuedes

Pirris

IYÖLA AMÍ CLOUD FOREST RESERVE

Santa María
de Dota

Copey

CORDILLERA DE TALAMANCA

3156m ▲
Cerro Vueltas

Mirador de
Quetzales **5**

PARQUE NACIONAL

Dantica Cloud Forest
Lodge & Gallery

3491m ▲
Cerro de la
Muerte

Las
Torres **8**

7 Villa
Mills

LOS QUETZALES

6

San Gerardo de Dota

Savegre
Natural
Reserve

3150m ▲
Cerro División

Siberia

División

2

Savegre

Hortensia

🅰 Also see area map p. 68

▶ Cartago

⬌ 45 miles (72 km)

🕐 4 hours (round-trip)

▶ Las Torres

La Ese

San Rafael
Norte

0 _____ 8 kilometers
0 _____ 4 miles

San Isidro
de El General

Monumento Nacional Guayabo

◭ Map p. 69

✉ 12 miles (19.3 km) N of Turrialba

☎ 2559-0117

§ $

www.sinac.go.cr

1000 B.C. and A.D. 1400, when it was mysteriously abandoned. The monument covers 540 acres (218 ha), mostly tropical wet forest, which is gradually being peeled back to reveal a vast cobbled pavement (calzada). Trails lead to a

INSIDER TIP:

Go out in the forest at night; it's a whole different world. Use a headlamp, not a flashlight. You see eyeshine better with a headlamp, and it frees your hands to slap mosquitoes.

—JOHN LONGINO
National Geographic field researcher

lookout point above the excavated village, featuring stone cisterns, working aqueducts, and circular terraces (montículos) on which conical bamboo structures were built. A self-guided walk leads down from the ranger station past petroglyphs and around the montículos, where lizards scuttle amid bleached ruins.

The surrounding forests are rich in fauna and superb for birding: Oropendolas and aricaris are particularly numerous.

Into the Talamancas

East of the Río Reventazón, Highway 232 cuts into the flanks of the Talamanca mountains, deteriorating until about 20 miles (32 km) east of Turrialba. Beyond the hamlet of **Moravia del Chirripó,** you arrive at the threshold of **Reserva Indígena**

Chirripó, a remote indigenous reserve that makes a good base for expeditions into the rugged **Parque Internacional La Amistad** (see pp. 200–201), a haven for wildlife extending south into Panama. The reserve receives few visitors, and it is a good idea to go with a guide, who can be hired in Moravia del Chirripó.

Quetzals

The resplendent trogon, better known as the quetzal, is an exotic and elusive species that draws many birders to Costa Rica. Its iridescent emerald plumage is so luxuriant that the Maya worshipped it as a god called Quetzalcoatl, or the Plumed Serpent. The endangered pigeon-size bird is common at elevations of 3,500 feet (1,070 m) associated with cloud forests. The male boasts a chest of brilliant crimson and trailing tail feathers, put to good use in its mating displays. The quetzal prefers the avocado-like fruit of the *aguacatillo,* which it plucks from below in mid-flight.

At **Tuís,** midway between Turrialba and Moravia, a dirt road leads north 10 miles (16 km) to the remote hamlet of **Bajo Pacuare,** the traditional starting point for rafting trips on the **Río Pacuare.** Reservations should be made in advance with a tour company such as Costa Rica Expeditions or Ríos Tropicales (see Travelwise p. 260). ■

Route of the Saints

Named for the villages that speckle the ridges south of San José, this off-the-beaten-path region offers superlative vistas as the roads rise and dip over forested highlands. It makes a fabulous day-long trip as you savor the calm poetry of green glens and felicitous silence broken only by the braying of a mule or the distant chiming of a church bell.

Situated on the northern face of the **Cerro de Escazú** mountains, **Aserrí,** 7 miles (11.2 km) south of San José on Highway 209, has a fine church, but it is better known for its rustic roadside restaurants that serve campesino fare and offer mesmerizing views across the Meseta Central toward the distant volcanoes. Beyond **Tarbaca,** Highway 222 drops eastward toward the whitewashed village of **San Gabriel;** at dusk it glistens like hammered gold from the sunlight slanting in from the west.

East of **San Cristóbal Sur** is **La Lucha Sin Fin** (The Endless Struggle; *closed to the public*), the farm where "Don Pepe" Figueres trained his army for the 1948 revolution. The **Fila de Bustamente** rises south of San Cristóbal, and the slopes green with coffee surround the pretty villages of **San Pablo de León Cortés** and **San Marcos de Tarrazú,** which has a domed hilltop church. Finally you reach **Santa María de Dota,** where the road swings north up the mountain to the Inter-American Highway, offering stupendous views. The town boasts the **Monumento Liberación Nacional,** commemorating the 1948 revolution, plus **Beneficio Coopedota** (see p. 81), a cooperative coffee mill that offers tours during the winter harvest. ■

The quetzal, the holy grail of neotropical birds, frequents the highlands along the Route of the Saints.

More Places to Visit in the Central Highlands

Doka Estate

For an authentic "Coffee 101" experience, head to this working coffee farm and *beneficio* (coffee-processing mill) on the slopes of Volcán Poás. Guided educational tours, taking place several times a day, take visitors into the fields and roasting facilities to learn about harvesting, processing, and roasting of coffee. The tour ends in the tasting rooms with a sampling of the estate's eight different roasts of coffee. The Vargas family has owned the 4,000-acre (1,600 ha) estate since 1929, although the beneficio dates from 1893. It is the oldest working water-powered mill in the entire country. *dokaestate.com*

▲ Map p. 68 ✉ San Luis de Sabanilla de Alajuela, 7 miles (11.3 km) N of Alajuela ☎ 7300-7158 💲 $$$$

Parque Nacional Tapantí– Macizo de la Muerte

This 15,024-acre (6,080 ha) national park covers mountainous territory ranging from 3,600 feet to 8,832 feet (1,100 m–2,692 m) and protects the pre-montane and montane rain forest blanketing the precipitous northern slopes of the Talamancas. Trees such as giant mahoganies, Spanish cedar, and ficus thrive in the persistent rains, which average 300 inches (75 cm) a year, feeding numerous pummeling waterfalls. The park teems with wildlife, including anteaters, jaguars, monkeys, ocelots, otters, poison dart frogs, tapirs, and almost 300 bird species, including quetzals, which are often seen near the ranger station. The park is easily accessed using well-marked trails. *www.sinac.go.cr*

▲ Map p. 68 ✉ 23 miles (37 km) SE of Cartago ☎ 2206-5651 💲 $$

Serpentario Vibarona

Giant boas hiss like teakettles as you pass their cages at this family-run serpentarium.

More snakes, some of them deadly venomous, reside in glass cages. You can see the snakes being fed live tidbits. Trails lead into the adjacent pre-montane wet forest.

▲ Map p. 69 ✉ Hwy. 10, at Chitaría, 15 miles (24 km) E of Turrialba ☎ 2538-1510 💲 $

Sibú Chocolate

Anyone within a day's drive of this fabulous venue should make a beeline to savor both the sublime artisanal chocolates made here and the fascinating tasting tour, courtesy of owners and master chocolatiers George Soriano and Julio Fernández. Their presentations span themes such as the ecology of cacao and the history of chocolate making (which began in pre-Columbian Mesoamerica). Then to the gustatory delight of various types of beautifully prepared Sibú chocolates, truffles, and caramels—all made from organically grown cacao and adorned with pre-Columbian indigenous motifs. Tours by reservation only. It has a café and store. *sibuchocolate.com*

✉ Calle Bomcacho, off Hwy. 32, San Isidro de Heredia, 9 miles (15 km) N of San José ☎ 2268-1335 🕐 Closed Mon 💲 $$$$$

Toucan Rescue Ranch

At San Isidro de Heredia, on the southern slope of Braulio Carrillo volcano, this wild animal rescue center is run by a *gringa*-Tico couple who take in sloths, toucans, parrots, macaws, and other creatures rescued by MINAE, the Ministry of Energy & Environment. A favorite with visitors is Emma the otter. The owners also have a breeding program for various toucan (and other bird) species, to be released to the wild. The old farmhouse has accommodations and magnificent views.

toucanrescueranch.com

✉ San Isidro de Heredia ☎ 2268-4041 💲 Donation

Cowboy country with dramatic landscapes—from dry deciduous woodlands to mist-shrouded cloud forests—and a unique culture derived from its Chorotega heritage

Guanacaste

The elusive tree-dwelling margay rarely sets foot on the ground.

Guanacaste

Guanacaste is one of the country's premier attractions, drawing visitors to its untamed splendors. It is bounded on the east by volcanoes forming the Cordillera de Guanacaste and Cordillera de Tilarán. The vast alluvial plain below the mountains' steep flanks is drained into the Golfo de Nicoya by the Río Tempisque—the nation's longest river.

The province is named for the *guanacaste* tree—the national tree—also called the ear pod tree. This unmistakable giant is as broad as it is high; branches spread low to the ground, providing a shady retreat for all manner of creatures. Guanacaste is Costa Rica's dry quarter. During summer (Nov.–April), the sun beats down relentlessly and no rain falls. The lowlands' dry deciduous forests and savannas bring forth bright blooms beloved by insects.

Historically the region developed apart from the rest of the nation, as befits its distinct physical nature. As part of Nicaragua, a province within the Captaincy General of Guatemala during the Spanish colonial era, the land was cleared at an early stage and developed into huge cattle haciendas worked by enslaved Chorotega, the most vibrant indigenous tribe of its day. A cowboy culture still clings to the reins and although the Chorotega culture was virtually annihilated, the Native American influence is clearly seen in the broad, bronze-skinned faces of Guanacastecans. The region was legally united with the rest of Costa Rica only in 1858 and has always felt strong affinities with Nicaragua.

You can savor the magnificent scenery without leaving the Inter-American Highway; national parks and wildlife reserves line the north-south route. Branch roads, many unpaved, probe east and west, leading to such varied treats as the misty Monteverde Cloud Forest Biological Reserve; bubbling mud pools on Volcán Miravalles; the wetlands of Palo Verde, where you can hunt crocodiles and roseate spoonbills from a boat with a camera; and fish-filled Laguna de Arenal, set like a jewel between the two cordilleras.

Cattle ranches invite visitors to saddle up. Mountain biking is popular. And hiking—be it backpacking into the upland wilds or tamer tramping on wildlife trails at Monteverde and Santa Rosa—truly puts you in the landscape.

NOT TO BE MISSED:

Waterborne options range from windsurfing on Laguna de Arenal and Bahía Salinas to river rafting trips.

The highway threads its way from one dusty colonial town to another, where *sabaneros* (cowboys) gather for annual fiestas held in *retornos de toros* (bullrings). Horsemen preen and show off their steeds' fancy footwork at *topes*–lively horse parades–while every macho male leaps into the bullring to play tag with a snorting *toro*.

The national costume, music, dance, and fare originate in Guanacaste, where Costa Rica's cultural traditions are kept alive. The nation's second international airport, west of Liberia, today receives one-fifth of international flights arriving in Costa Rica. ■

Costa Rica
Area of map detail

NORTHERN LOWLANDS
p. 205

NICARAGUA

Santa Cecilia
Haciendas
Brasília
▲ 1487m
Volcán Orosí
▲ 1659m
Volcán Cacao
Pizote
San José
164
Dos Ríos
1806m
*Volcán Rincón
de la Vieja*
▲ 1916m
▲ *Volcán S. María*
Quebrada
Grande
Pital
PARQUE NACIONAL
RINCÓN DE LA VIEJA
Santa María
Curubandé
Cañas
Dulces
San
Jorge
Liberia
Cereceda
Liberia
**La Ponderosa
Adventure
Park**
Pijije
RESERVA BIOLÓGICA
LOMAS DE BARBUDAL
Montenegro
REFUGIO DE VIDA
SILVESTRE DR. RAFAEL LUCAS
RODRÍGUEZ CABALLERO
**Hacienda
Palo Verde**
Bebedero
PARQUE
NACIONAL
PALO
VERDE
NICOYA
p. 129
Solimar
San
Buenaventura
Abangaritos
**Refugio Nacional
de Vida Silvestre
La Enseñada**
Isla Pájaros

Guayabo
ZONA
PROTECTORA
MIRAVALLES
La Fortuna
**Río Perdido
Activity Center**
Salitral
Bagaces
6
Canalete
Aguas
Claras
2028m
*Volcán
Miravalles*
Bijagua
1916m
Volcán Tenorio
PARQUE NACIONAL
VOLCÁN TENORIO
L. de Coter
**Las
Hornillas
Volcano
Activity
Center**
Tierras
Morenas
**Planta
Eólica
Tilarán**
142
Tilarán
**Sky Adventures
Arenal Park**
Nuevo Arenal
Laguna de Arenal
Presa Sangregado
Arenal Observatory Lodge
El Castillo
Arenal Eco Zoo
**Mistico
Arenal
Hanging
Bridges
Park**
**Club Río
Outdoor
Center**
Tabacón Resort
▲ 1643m
Volcán Arenal
▲ 1100m
Volcán Chato
Rancho Margot
PARQUE NACIONAL
VOLCÁN ARENAL
**Centro de
Rescate
Las Pumas**
San Miguel
**Reserva
Bosque Nuboso
Santa Elena**
Santa
Elena
MONTEVERDE
CLOUD
FOREST
BIOLOGICAL
RESERVE
**BOSQUE
ETERNO
DE LOS
NIÑOS**
Cañas
145
Las Juntas
de Abangares
Palma
Limonal
18
Pueblo Nuevo
Colorado
Arizona
Guacimal
Lagarto
1
**Ecolodge San Luis
& Research Station**
Tilarán
Aranjuez
**Finca Daniel
Adventure Park**
Unión
San
Gerardo
Manzanillo
Pájaros
Peñas Blancas
San
Rancho
Grande
Miramar
R.N.
DE VIDA
SILVESTRE
PEÑAS
BLANCAS
CENTRAL HIGHLANDS
p. 67
**Santuario de
Lapas
Natuwa**
Chomes
Pitahaya
Santa Rosa
San Isidro
144
Esparza
Barranca
Jesús
María
Puntarenas
Barranca
Caldera
San Mateo
Orotina
**Mahogany
Park**
San Pablo de
Turrubares
Golfo de Nicoya
Punta
Caldera
Z.P.
TIVIVES
Tárcoles
PARQUE
TROPICAL
TURUBARI

0 ————— 30 kilometers
0 ————— 15 miles

CENTRAL
PACIFIC
p. 153

Puntarenas & Costa Pájaros

Three miles (5 km) long but barely five blocks wide, the anomalous sea-girt city of Puntarenas is somewhat of an ugly duckling. Jutting into the Golfo de Nicoya at the tip of a pencil-thin peninsula, it makes an ideal springboard for maritime leaps to Nicoya by ferry or for day-long forays to Isla Tortuga. The mangrove-rimmed gulf shores lure binocular-laden birders, while inland the grasslands and tropical moist forest can be explored via canopy tours and even an aerial tram.

Pelicans await tidbits at a fisher's wharf in Puntarenas.

Puntarenas

[M] Map p. 101

Visitor Information

[✉] Puntarenas Chamber of Commerce, 1st floor, Oficina INC, Blvd. Casa de la Cultura

[☎] 2661-0407

puntarenas.com/catup

Puntarenas, 75 miles (120 km) west of San José, traces its lineage to 1524, when conquistador Francisco Fernández de Córdoba (1490–1526) founded an ill-fated settlement here. It grew to be the nation's major port for coffee export, but a gradual demise set in after the completion of the Atlantic Railroad in 1890. For a while, the town had a viable conch-pearl fleet and drew Josefinos to bathe at its *balnearios* (swimming pools).

Josefinos of modest means still flock to the brown-sand beach that runs unbroken for 7 miles (11 km) from **Boca de Barranca** to the tip of the spit.

Cruise ships call at Puntarenas, but most passengers bypass the town. Still, you'll find a funky charm in the weathered wooden homes and in decrepit fishing boats tethered to equally decrepit piers. Ongoing development is gradually beautifying the city. The small **Museo Histórico Maritino,** in the

19th-century jail, traces the city's history with displays spanning pre-Columbian times to the building of the Atlantic Railroad, as well as the coffee industry. The jail was a family residence and later served as the military command post and Casa de la Cultura. The **Paseo de las Turistas** boulevard makes an intriguing walk along the gulf shore. The north of the spit faces a mangrove-lined estuary that is a great spot to see roseate spoonbills.

Ferries operate between Puntarenas and Playa Naranjo and Parquera, providing quick access to southern Península de Nicoya.

Costa Pájaros

Pelicans, herons, frigate birds, ibises. Bird-watching is the name of the game along the "bird coast," the inner gulf shoreline stretching north from Puntarenas up to the mouth of the Río Tempisque. Caimans also lurk in the dense reeds and mangroves. To see them, head to **Refugio Nacional de Vida Silvestre La Enseñada,** which encompasses 940 acres (380 ha) of lagoons, creeks, and forest in the midst of a cattle and salt farm. A short way offshore, brown pelicans and other seabirds have colonized a rocky islet protected as **Reserva Biológica Isla Pájaros.** Only biologists may go ashore, but you can view it from a boat.

Farther north, **Santuario de Lapas Natuwa** breeds macaws to release to the wild, plus acts as a refuge for animals—sloths, tapirs, monkeys, big cats—saved from illegal pet trade or death in the wild.

The **Puente de Amistad con Taiwan bridge** spans the wide mouth of the Río Tempisque, linking Highway 1 and the Costa de Pájaros with the Península de Nicoya.

The Hinterland

Inland from Puntarenas lies **Orotina,** a town known for its ceramics and fruit stalls lining Highway 3. Orotina is gripped in a pincer by the **Río Jesús María** and **Río Cuarros,** which spill into the Golfo de Tivives. This wetland

Chorotega Pottery

In towns like Orotina and in every gift shop, pottery is sold with geometric and animal motifs emblematic of Costa Rica. Most of it comes from the village of Guaitíl, in Nicoya, where Chorotega indigenous people make vases, plates, and pots in traditional fashion by hand. Most pieces are ocher-colored, with motifs in black, white, and orange. Three-legged vases in the stylized form of cows are popular.

ecosystem supports crocodiles, monkeys, and all sorts of fabulous birds. Farther south, **Ecojungle Cruises** (tel 2582-0181, ecojunglecruises .com, $$$$$) will take you by canopy boat in search of crocodiles and the distinctive scarlet macaw on the Río Guacalillo estuary. ■

Museo Histórico Maritino
- ✉ Ave. Central, Calles 5/7, Puntarenas
- ☎ 2661-5036
- 🕐 Closed Mon.

Refugio Nacional de Vida Silvestre La Enseñada
- 🅰 Map p. 101
- ✉ 1.5 miles (2.4 km) S of Abangaritos, off Hwy. 132, 11 miles (17.7 km) W of Hwy. 1
- ☎ 2289-6655
- 💲 $$$$$ (tours)

laensenada.net

Santuario de Lapas Natuwa
- ☎ 8823-2460
- 🕐 By reservation only
- 💲 $$$

natuwa.com

Inter-American Highway Drive

Highway 1, Costa Rica's umbilical cord to its neighboring states, sweeps through Guanacaste like a Roman imperial highway, linking historic cowboy towns. This section of the Inter-American Highway is magnificent, with the scenery gathering northward like a series of Hollywood stage sets making irresistible compositions for your camera.

Linking San José with Nicaragua, the road leads to sublime vistas of savanna ranged by *sabaneros* (cowboys), with cattle against a backdrop of cloud-crowned volcanoes to the east. Side roads lead to national parks and wildlife reserves, but the beauty of the surrounding countryside—and the ugly quality of the road—may make you miss your turnoff.

The route described is a 128-mile (205 km) journey with only a handful of traffic lights. The highway is mostly a fast two-laner; arrow-straight stretches unwind for miles, tempting motorists to speed. Don't do it! Traffic cops sit beneath shade trees, training their radar guns on unwary speedsters. Other caveats: Some potholes are big enough to swallow a cow; oncoming cars tend to swerve into your lane at inopportune moments; and behemoth, hell-bent trucks hurtle up and down the highway.

Begin in **Barranca ❶**, at the interchange of Highway 1 and Highway 27, the junction for Puntarenas (west), Jacó (south), and San José (east). This heavily trafficked southern section is a bit of a roller coaster and gives a foretaste of the beauty that lies ahead, with the western slopes of the Cordillera Tilarán pressing upon the road. After 4 miles (6.4 km), at **Santa Rosa ❷**, you will pass the turnoff for Miramar and Refugio Nacional de Vida Silvestre Peñas Blancas. The road continues to dip and rise beyond

San Gerardo ❸, where it becomes pinched between the hillsides of the **Río Lagarto Valley,** with long glades of trees leaning over the road like kissing lovers. The long grade descends to an iron-framed bridge over the river, 16 miles (26 km) north of Barranca. The turnoff for Monteverde is here, 100 yards (90 m) south of the bridge, poorly marked and well hidden. Slow down well before the bridge in either direction: *Túmulos*—road bumps—lie across the road and should *not* be hit at high speed.

Eight miles (13 km) farther along turn off for **Las Juntas de Abangares ❹**, a somewhat self-consciously attractive

NOT TO BE MISSED:

Centro de Rescate Las Pumas
• Liberia • Parque Nacional
Santa Rosa

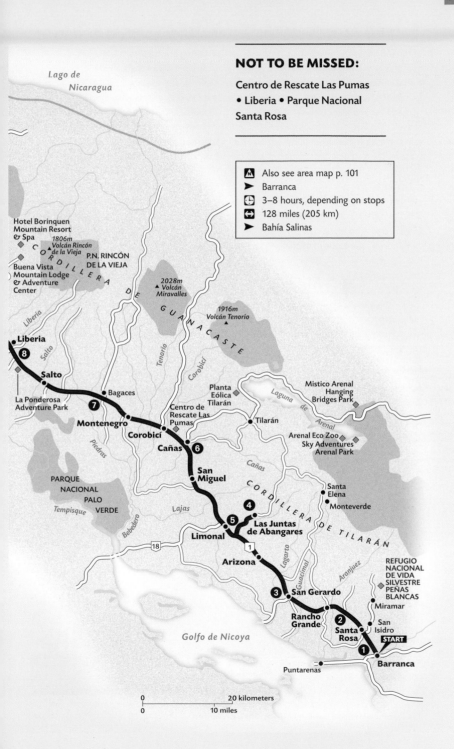

Also see area map p. 101

Barranca

3–8 hours, depending on stops

128 miles (205 km)

Bahía Salinas

Lago de Nicaragua

Hotel Borinquen Mountain Resort & Spa

1806m Volcán Rincón de la Vieja

P.N. RINCÓN DE LA VIEJA

CORDILLERA

Buena Vista Mountain Lodge & Adventure Center

2028m Volcán Miravalles

1916m Volcán Tenorio

DE GUANACASTE

Liberia

Salto

Liberia
8

La Ponderosa Adventure Park

Bagaces

Montenegro
7

Planta Eólica Tilarán

Centro de Rescate Las Pumas

Mistico Arenal Hanging Bridges Park

Laguna de Arenal

Corobicí

Cañas
6

Tilarán

Arenal Eco Zoo Sky Adventures Arenal Park

San Miguel

Cañas

PARQUE NACIONAL PALO VERDE

Tempisque

Lajas

CORDILLERA DE TILARÁN

Santa Elena

Monteverde

Las Juntas de Abangares

Limonal

4

5

18

1

Arizona

Lagarto

Bebedero

REFUGIO NACIONAL DE VIDA SILVESTRE PEÑAS BLANCAS

Miramar

3

San Gerardo

Guacimal

Aranjuez

Golfo de Nicoya

Rancho Grande

Santa Rosa
2

San Isidro

START

1

Barranca

Puntarenas

0   20 kilometers
0   10 miles

village strong on history tucked into the folds of the mountains, 4 miles (6.5 km) northeast of Highway 1. The town is famed for a gold rush that began in 1884 when nuggets were found in these hills, and *oreros*—miners—flocked from the four corners of the world to seek their fortunes. A patined bronze statue in their honor stands in a triangular plaza on the northeast side of town. A pint-size old steam train, *María Cristina*, sits in the main plaza.

Highway 1 edges north along the foothills, with the parched golden grasslands of the **Llanos San Pedro** to the west grazed by hardy humped cattle, ashen colored and well muscled, standing fixedly in the magnesium light like bovine figures on a Cretan urn. Rounded hillocks dot the plain. Deciduous trees speckle the scene in a palette of pastels: yellow *cortexa amarilla*, scarlet *poró*, and bright orange *spathodea*, locally known as the Jesús Cristo tree because it blooms bloodred at Easter. You will notice the heat building as you move north,

with the warm air parting ahead of you like an unfolding blanket.

Beyond **Limonal** ❺, where Highway 18 peels off westward for the Río Tempisque ferry and the Península de Nicoya, continue straight 13 miles (21 km) to whitewashed **Cañas** ❻ *(tel 2669-0042)*, a cowboy town par excellence and the gateway to Parque Nacional Palo Verde, Tilarán, and Laguna de Arenal. On the far side of town is **Centro de Rescate Las Pumas** *(tel 2669-6044, centrorescatelaspumas .org, $$)*, where Costa Rica's six species of cats—cougars, jaguars, jaguarundis, margays, ocelots, and "tiger" cats—prowl safely behind chain-link fences. The zoo takes in orphaned and injured cats and others confiscated from private owners and hunters. A stone's throw north, the highway crosses the 25-mile-long (40 km) **Río Corobicí**. Fed by dam-controlled runoff from Laguna de Arenal, it flows even in the midst of drought and is popular for float trips—which are good for birding and for seeing howlers in the branches of stately mahoganies and ceiba trees.

The Parroquia de Cañas, an icon of the art deco movement

You can watch rafters on the river from the veranda of the roadside **Restaurante Rincón Corobicí** (see Travelwise p. 246), where **Ríos Tropicales** *(tel 2233-6455, riostropicales.com)* has an office offering half-day rafting trips.

Beyond Cañas the road opens up, swinging northwest and gaining distance from the **Cordillera de Guanacaste** so that three volcanoes—Tenorio, Miravalles, and Rincón de la Vieja—are in glorious view. The sky is usually an exhilarating clear, deep blue; clouds pour up over the mountains from the Caribbean before burning off under the searing heat of the sun.

Continue north to **Bagaces ❼**, where Parque Nacional Palo Verde is signed to the west. The park is administered along with other regional parks and reserves as the **Area Conservación Arenal Tempisque** (see p. 112) whose administrative office *(tel 2671-1290)* is beside Highway 1, opposite the Palo Verde junction. Bagaces, which is also the gateway to Zona Protectora Miravalles, is intriguing for its old adobe houses. More appealing by far is **Liberia ❽**, 15 miles (24 km) farther north, the capital city of Guanacaste and another cowboy town known as the Ciudad Blanca (White City) for its dazzling white buildings. If low on gas, you should fill up at one of the gas stations at the junction with Highway 21 (which takes you to the airport and Nicoya).

Into Cattle Country

The final 33 miles (53 km) steal the show, with breathtaking landscapes seen fleetingly through gaps in the deciduous trees that flare with seasonal blooms. You are now in the heart of cattle country, hot as Hades in summer when a searing breeze rustles the grasslands that carpet the billowing flatlands, like a gently undulating sea of chartreuse. **Volcán Rincón de la Vieja** (5,925 feet/1,806 m) looms massively to the east, tempting you to tackle the blindingly white roads of exposed ignimbrite that lead to cattle haciendas where horseback rides are offered and to the ranger stations that are gateways for hiking in Parque Nacional Rincón de la Vieja.

For an intriguing side trip, 11 miles (17.7 km) north of Liberia turn northeast from the highway. After 8 miles (13 km), you'll arrive at **Hotel Borinquen Mountain Resort & Spa** (see Travelwise p. 247), a spa facility built around bubbling mud ponds good for rejuvenating thermal treatments. Monkeys abound in the surrounding forest. Nearby, the **Buena Vista Lodge & Adventure Center** (see Travelwise p. 248), is a ranch that offers horseback rides, a 0.6-mile-long (1 km) canopy tour, and a 1,312-foot (400 m) waterslide, plus occasional rodeos. Rustic yet charming cabins are available, and *típico* meals can be savored.

Farther north are the steep spires of **Cerro Cacao** (5,443 feet/1,659 m) and **Volcán Orosí** (4,879 feet/1,487 m) piercing the eastern sky. They both are accessed from **Potrerillos,** 15 miles (24 km) north of Liberia, with a police checkpoint at the junction. The two volcanoes are encompassed within **Parque Nacional Guanacaste** (see p. 126), a 208,800-acre (84,500 ha) expanse that spans the highway and tethers several disparate ecologically independent parks and reserves, including **Parque Nacional Santa Rosa** (see p. 127), accessed from Highway 1 about 5 miles (8 km) farther north and a must-see on any tourist's list. Wildlife viewing in Santa Rosa is staggering; more than one hundred mammal species include coatis, jaguars, ocelots, tamanduas, and three species of monkeys, plus a rainbow assortment of birds, all easily seen in the sparse dry forests. The park wears Costa Rica's history on its sleeve, too, at an old farmstead called **La Casona,** now a museum dedicated to the battle fought here in 1856.

From here, the traffic thins and it is a joy to zip along with the sun mantling low-slung guanacaste trees in pools of light and shadow. At last you reach **La Cruz ❾**, a sleepy town 14 miles (22 km) from the Nicaraguan border. A left turn at the town plaza in La Cruz leads 100 yards (91.4 m) to the **Centro Cultural y Turístico El Mirador** *(tel 2679-9058)*, offering staggering views over **Bahía Salinas**.

Monteverde

The jewel in the crown of cloud forest reserves, the Monteverde Cloud Forest Biological Reserve is generously blessed with bucolic beauty. Its immense popularity has spawned contiguous forest reserves and a gamut of nature attractions that combine with Monteverde's world renown to draw tens of thousands of visitors annually.

Zip-lining through the treetops of a cloud forest reserve is a thrilling way to channel Tarzan.

Monteverde
🗺 Map p. 101

Monteverde Institute
✉ Monteverde
☎ 2645-5053

monteverde -institute.org

The community that translates as "green mountain" squats upon a plateau 3,500 feet (1,065 m) above sea level near the crest of the Cordillera de Tilarán; a vertiginous, bone-shaking road leads up to it from the Inter-American Highway. The setting is idyllically pastoral, with incandescent light intensifying the emerald greens of the mountain pastures grazed by black-and-white Holstein cattle. Ethereal mists swirl overhead and the crisp alpine climate is a constant interplay of drizzle and warming sunshine.

The heart of things is the village of **Santa Elena.** There is no village of Monteverde as such. Instead, this community of farmsteads sprawls upon the hillside that rises east of Santa Elena, accessed by paths that branch off the steep road leading to Monteverde's cloud forest reserve. The community was founded in 1951 by Quakers who fled the draft in the United States and chose Costa Rica because it was neutral. *Cuaquerismo* (Quakerism) is still the bedrock of the local culture in Monteverde, but commercialism rules in and around the urban center of Santa Elena.

The Quaker settlers have been at the forefront of conservation since Monteverde's inception: The kernel of today's world-famous cloud forest reserve was founded in 1972 jointly by the community and by scientists seeking to protect the watershed and the unique species it shelters. The contiguous communities have also been leaders in efforts to educate local children. The **Cloud Forest School** *(tel 2645-5161, cloudforestschool.org)* and the **Monteverde Conservation League** *(tel 2645-5003, acmcr .org)* work to educate youngsters in ecology and train youths as naturalist guides to help move Tico families away from destructive practices and toward tourism-related income derived from conserving their green heritage.

Art is also vibrant here. Venues such as **Bromelia's** *(tel 2645-6272)* put on live musical performances. The **Monteverde Institute** has workshops with themes from basketry to wood turning from January through August with local craftspersons. Similarly, the **Monteverde Art House** *(tel 2645-5275, monteverde arthouse.com)* displays works by local artists; it also has gardens and an auditorium for events.

The Long &
Winding Road

A narrow, serpentine road leads 3 miles (4.8 km) uphill, eastward from Santa Elena to the entrance to the Monteverde Cloud Forest Biological Reserve (see pp. 110–111). The route—a quagmire in the wet season and cloudy with dust during rare dry spells—is lined with attractions, plus roughly 20 wooden mountain lodges with roaring log fires to add to the alpine ambience.

To learn about amphibians and reptiles that can be encountered in the reserves, visit **Herpetarium Adventures Monteverde** *(tel 2479-4100, skyadventures.travel /herpetarium)* to see chameleons, poison-arrow frogs, and more than 20 species of snakes, including the fearsome fer-de-lance—safely behind glass. More than 500 orchid species are displayed at **Monteverde Orchid Garden,** an exquisite garden specializing in miniatures such as *Playstele jungermanniodes,* the world's smallest flower, best seen with the aid of a magnifying glass (thoughtfully supplied). And the **Monteverde Theme Park** has a herpetarium displaying frogs and other amphibians, plus an *insectario* (insects) and *mariposario* (butterflies).

La Lechería

Monteverde's original Quaker settlers established "the cheese factory" in 1953 to produce Gouda cheese. Twenty types of cheeses are now made, including Monte Rico, the local best seller. The original herd of 50 Jersey cows is today supplemented by milk from local farmers.

More than 500 species of butterflies flit about these hillsides and forests. More than 40 species are at **Monteverde Butterfly Gardens,** where North American biologist Jim Wolfe oversees a huge netted garden and two greenhouses that re-create three distinct natural habitats. The "Garden of the Butterflies" features an educational nature center, library, and weather center as well as

Monteverde Orchid Garden

✉ 100 yards (90 m) S of Santa Elena bus station

☎ 2645-5308

$ $$

monteverdeorchid garden.net

Monteverde Theme Park

✉ 100 yards (90 m) N of Monteverde Lodge

☎ 2645-6320

$ $$

Monteverde Butterfly Gardens

✉ 400 yards (360 m) W of Heliconia Ecolodge, Santa Elena

☎ 2645-5512

$ $$

monteverde butterflygarden.com

Bat Jungle

- ✉ In front of Hotel El Bosque, Santa Elena
- ☎ 2645-7701
- 💲 $$

batjungle.com

Monteverde Cloud Forest Biological Reserve

- 🗺 Map p. 101
- ✉ 6 miles (10 km) E of Santa Elena
- ☎ 2645-5122
- 💲 $$$$

cloudforest monteverde.com

exhibits of other colorful insects. Visit early- to mid-morning.

Bat Jungle dispels common fearful notions about bats with exciting interactive exhibits that educate visitors about the mammals' ecology and their critical importance to local ecosystems. Live bats swoop about behind a glass wall in a recreated nocturnal habitat.

covering eight distinct life zones on both the Caribbean and Pacific slopes. The diversity of flora is astounding—from dwarf cloud forest atop the mountains to bamboo forests and even swamp forest in poorly drained areas. Zoological treasures include more than one hundred mammal species, all five species

Surveying the verdant cloud forest canopy from a high *puente colgante* (hanging bridge)

You can admire and purchase fine artwork at the **Hummingbird Gallery** (see Travelwise p. 258), named for the hummingbirds that zip in to feed on the patio of the gallery, where nature slide shows are given.

Monteverde Cloud Forest Biological Reserve

This internationally acclaimed reserve straddles the Continental Divide. Its upper-elevation forests are cloaked year-round in swirling mists formed by humid Caribbean trade winds condensing as they are forced up and over the ridge crest. The reserve encompasses 25,730 acres (10,400 ha),

of cats, plus howler and capuchin monkeys, deer, and sloths. The 400 species of birds here include 30 species of hummingbirds and the endangered three-wattled bellbird (named for the worm-like wattles that hang from its beak). About one hundred breeding pairs of quetzals also nest within the reserve, migrating to lower levels during the spring mating season.

The reserve is run by the Tropical Science Center of Costa Rica, which regulates visitor numbers and maintains the boardwalks that lead into the reserve. More rugged trails punch down the Caribbean slopes into true wilderness, spilling out in the Northern Lowlands. You can rent rubber boots to ease exploration. Guided nature hikes are offered, and well-versed nature guides can be hired.

Other Reserves

The **Reserva Bosque Nuboso Santa Elena,** which is owned and administered by the Santa Elena community, protects 1,440 acres (580 ha) abutting the Monteverde Cloud Forest Biological Reserve to the northwest. It has most of the same species as the larger reserve, plus endangered spider monkeys, absent at the Monteverde reserve.

You can hike well-maintained trails or take to the air on a **Sky Walk** and follow half a mile (0.8 km) of "pathways" and suspension bridges through the treetops. At **Monteverde Xtremo Park** (tel 2645-6058, monteverde extremopark.com) you can glide through the treetops in a harness, or bungee jump, or even thrill to a muddy ATV adventure.

The **Bosque Eterno de los Niños,** to the east and south of the Monteverde reserve, has grown to more than 50,000 acres (20,200 ha). Funded by children around the world and administered by the Monteverde Conservation League, it encompasses a similar range of terrain and flora and fauna to Santa Elena. Trails and facilities for visitors are minimal.

Sendero Bajo del Tigre (Jaguar Canyon Trail) grants access to a 44-acre (18 ha) portion of the reserve and features a forest habitat that's distinct in the region. It is especially good for seeing quetzals in springtime.

There is an arboretum and self-guided interpretive trail, and kids will enjoy the **Children's Nature Center,** with interesting exhibits.

Nearby, the **Monteverde Ecological Sanctuary** is a 40-acre (16 ha) private reserve where trails grant access to montane moist forest and where coatis, capuchin monkeys, sloths, and countless bird species are easily seen with a guide.

Selvatura Park, abutting the Reserva Bosque Nuboso Santa Elena, grants a similar entrée to a wildlife-rich world with treetop walkways, a zip line canopy tour, and guided nature hikes. In the education center, the **Jewels of the Rain Forest Bio-Art Exhibition** features dramatic displays of arachnids and insects, the largest such private collection in the world.

Golden Toads

In 1967, an endemic species of vermilion toad was discovered in the Monteverde cloud forest, helping to spark the preserve's creation. Only the inch-long (2.5 cm) males are gold; the much larger females are black, speckled with vermilion and yellow. The last sighting was in 1988. This sudden demise has struck amphibious species worldwide.

Farm Tours

Monterverde remains at heart an agricultural community. Small-scale coffee farms abound; the **Don Juan Coffee Tour** (tel 2645-7100, donjuancr.com, $$$$$) offers a fascinating insight. ∎

Reserva Bosque Nuboso Santa Elena
🅜 Map p. 101
✉ 4.5 miles (7 km) NE of Santa Elena
☎ 2645-5390
💲 $$
reservasantaelena.org

Sky Walk
✉ 1 mile (1.6 km) NE of Santa Elena
☎ 2479-4100
💲 $$$$$
skyadventures.travel /skywalk

Bosque Eterno de los Niños
🅜 Map p. 101
✉ 2 miles (3.2 km) E of Santa Elena
☎ 2645-5200
💲 $$
acmcr.org

Monteverde Ecological Sanctuary
✉ 300 yards (274 m) W of Heliconia Ecolodge
☎ 2645-5869
💲 $$$$$
santuarioecologico .com

Selvatura Park
✉ 4 miles (6.4 km) NE of Santa Elena
☎ 2645-5929
💲 $$$–$$$$$
selvatura.com

Parque Nacional Palo Verde

Birders flock to rugged and remote Palo Verde, a marvelous repository of avian fauna at the mouth of the Río Tempisque, named for the green-barked *palo verde,* or horseshoe bean tree. Combining wet and dry ecosystems, it supports not only vast flocks of waterfowl but crocodiles and mammals that are easily seen in the sparse vegetation.

Parque Nacional Palo Verde
- Map p. 101
- 18 miles (29 km) SW of Bagaces
- 2524-0607
- $$

Area Conservación Arenal Tempisque
- 2659-5180
- $
www.sinac.go.cr

Organization for Tropical Studies
- 2524-0607
- Tours from $$$$
ots.ac.cr

The 32,266-acre (13,057 ha) park encompasses 15 distinct habitats, from mangroves, grassland, and scrubland to tropical dry forest. Along with the Refugio de Vida Silvestre Dr. Rafael Lucas Rodríguez Caballero and the Reserva Biológica Lomas de Barbudal, which abut it to the north, and Parque Nacional Barra Honda to the southwest, it forms the **Area Conservación Arenal Tempisque.**

A jabiru stork

This vast arena of limestone ridges, marshes, and seasonally wet floodplains is best explored in the dry season (Nov.–April), when the drought-resistant trees shed their leaves and thirsty wildlife congregates at water holes, especially at dawn and dusk. The park adjoins **Refugio de Vida Silvestre Cipanci,** created in 2001 to protect mangroves and wetlands north of Palo Verde. Fed by the Río Tempisque and its mangrove-lined tributaries, this oasis in the heart of the Tempisque Basin forms an aquatic haven for birds—more than 300 species of neotropical birds roost or nest here. After the rainy season, the alluvial plains flood, and roughly 250,000 migratory ducks, geese, and other waterfowl winter alongside their native cousins.

Isla Pájaros has particularly prolific and unusual birdlife, including great curassows. You also might see anhingas, white ibises, and the world's largest stork, the jabiru, plus the only permanent colony of scarlet macaws to inhabit a dry environment.

The park headquarters is situated in the old **Hacienda Palo Verde,** surrounded by mango trees that draw coatis, monkeys, peccaries, and white-tailed deer. Anteaters and armadillos abound. Crocodiles—motionless as logs—rest on the muddy banks. There are modest archaeological sites within the park, some in caverns gouged from limestone cliffs. Local companies arrange guided natural history tours, as does the **Organization for Tropical Studies,** which maintains a biological field station here. It's impossible to explore in the wet season other than by boat. **Palo Verde Boat Tours** *(tel 2651-8001, paloverdeboattours.com)* has boat trips from Bolson, in Nicoya, and other companies operate from Puerto Humo, 17 miles (27 km) east of Nicoya township. ∎

Dry Forest Reserves

Costa Rican naturalists have worked hard to preserve the last vestiges of the dry forests that were so much a part of the environment in pre-Columbian days. Their chief early success has been the establishment and maintenance of the Reserva Biológica Lomas de Barbudal, where the native woodland habitat supports a thriving range of wildlife.

Palo Verde adjoins two contiguous wilderness regions. To the north is the remote, infrequently visited 18,172-acre (7,353 ha) **Refugio de Vida Silvestre Dr. Rafael Lucas Rodríguez Caballero** (administered jointly with Lomas de Barbudal), which offers the same array of wetland and dry habitats and their associated wildlife. The refuge extends north to **Reserva Biológica Lomas de Barbudal,** enshrining 5,631 acres (2,279 ha) and protecting precious remnants of the dry deciduous forest that once encompassed most of the Tempisque Basin. The Río Cabuyo flows through the "bearded hills" reserve, named for the mosses that drape from tree branches, feeding lush riparian forest and drawing wildlife to its banks. There is a small **information center** and **museum** at the entrance beside the river. Nature trails lead from here to swimming holes.

Many endangered tropical hardwoods thrive here: the cannonball tree, mahogany, Panama redwood, rosewood, and sandbox, whose tart fruit is favored by scarlet macaws visiting from Palo Verde. Yellow-naped parrots and chicken-like great curassows, popularly hunted by campesinos for food, are among the many other bird species commonly seen, as are monkeys and a host of other mammalian frugivores that gorge on the seasonal fruits. The

Capuchin monkeys play a vital role in rain forest pollination.

three parks form a vital migratory route for wildlife and are renowned for their huge insect populations, including hundreds of moth species and more than 250 bee species, pollinators for the flowering trees, which burst into often synchronized blooms in the midst of drought. ∎

INSIDER TIP:

The Lomas de Barbudal reserve is best known for its long-term studies of bees and capuchin monkeys, but it is also an excellent place to observe birds and other animals, particularly in the dry season.

—SUSAN PERRY
National Geographic field researcher

Reserva Biológica Lomas de Barbudal

🅰 Map p. 101

✉ 4 miles (6.4 km) SW of Pijije (Km 221) on Inter-American Hwy.

☎ 2671-1290 (Bagaces office)

💲 $

Around Laguna de Arenal

Fringed by emerald mountains, Laguna de Arenal is a svelte platinum gem of entrancing beauty, enticing camera-toting visitors seeking pleasure in its picture-postcard appeal and proving the adage that a fine jewel is made complete by its setting.

Lake Arenal's consistent winds are heaven for kitesurfers.

Costa Rica's largest inland body of water occupies a depression that forms a gap between the Cordillera de Guanacaste and Cordillera de Tilarán. The lake, which covers 48 square miles (124 sq km), lies to the east of the Continental Divide at an elevation of 1,798 feet (548 m) above sea level. It is topped by mountains shimmering every shade of green in the clear light. To the south and west, carpets of green pasture unfurl down to the cobalt waters. To the north, primary tropical wet forest clambers up the steep slopes, dark and foreboding and raucous with the screeching of monkeys and birds. To the east, reflected in the silvery lake is the black, smoking peak of Volcán Arenal, brooding ominously between fits of pique.

Although the natural depression dates back about two million years, the lake was created by engineers in 1973 when **Presa Sangregado,** a 290-foot-long, 190-foot-high dam (88 m by 58 m), was built at the eastern egress, where the Río Arenal begins its cascade through a narrow gorge dropping down to the Northern Lowlands. The 20-mile-long, 3-mile-wide (32 km by 5 km) lake inundated several pre-Columbian sites plus the sole settlement in the valley. It is caressed by near-constant winds that whip up from the Caribbean and become compressed as they push through the gap. The howling winds, which can reach 60 miles an hour (96 kph) in winter are beloved by windsurfers. They also drive the wind turbines of Planta Eólica Tilarán that have been erected atop the Continental Divide. Anglers, too, find their lures in *machaca*, mojarra, feisty *guapote*, or rainbow bass that give a good run on the end of a line.

Laguna de Arenal lies 18 miles (29 km) east of Highway 1 on well-paved Highway 142, which leads via the trim agricultural town of **Tilarán** (on the western flank of the Continental Divide) to the lake around which it curls clockwise. The windswept western shore makes a perfect venue for **Tico Wind Surf Center** (see Travelwise p. 262), from which active outdoorsy types set out to skim over the waves on their boards.

Capping the north shore is the small town of **Nuevo Arenal,** created in 1973 when its precursor was drowned with the lake's creation. This side of the lake is otherwise uninhabited except by the lakeside lodges spawned by the tourism boom. Immediately east of the town, the forested slopes crowd in with a murky closeness and the pavement is often washed out by mud that sluices down from the rain-sodden hillsides. However, some stupendous vistas are thrown in as a reward for perseverance.

Immediately northeast of Presa Sangregado, a road winds up to **Mistico Arenal Hanging Bridges Park,** *(tel 2479-8282, misticopark .com, $$$$),* where a 2-mile-long

(3 km) rain forest trail includes 16 suspension bridges, each offering stupendous lake and volcano views.

To catch your breath, stop for a bite to eat at **Tom's Pan** *(tel 2694-4547, tom.cmxworker.de, closed Sun.),* a German restaurant in Nuevo Arenal serving scrumptious international fare. Or head over to **Restaurant Caballo Negro** (see Travelwise p. 247), which also has an art gallery. Here you can enjoy divine meals on a veranda overlooking a lake. ∎

A Tropical Eden

Explore nature's Eden via **Sky Adventures Arenal Park** on the forested slopes southeast of the lake. A tram brings vistors to a mountainside platform for stunning views of the volcano and lake; for a thrilling return, try a zip line tour across the canyon or an adrenaline-packed mountain biking or multi-activity challenge.

Nearby, El Castillo hosts the **Butterfly Conservatory** *(tel 2479-1149, butter flyconservatory.org, $$),* with a netted butterfly garden and fascinating insect displays, and the **Arenal Eco Zoo** *(tel 2479-1058, arenalecozoo.com, $$),* displaying snakes, lizards, and poison-arrow frogs. **Rancho Margot** is an organic farm that doubles as an animal rescue center and eco-friendly all-inclusive hotel with its own rain forest reserve.

Sky Adventures Arenal Park
- Map p. 101
- ✉ 14 miles (22 km) SE of La Fortuna
- ☎ 2479-4100

skyadventures .travel

Rancho Margot
- Map p. 101
- ✉ 1 mile (1.6 km) W of El Castillo
- ☎ 2302-7318
- 💲 $$$$$

ranchomargot.com

Parque Nacional Volcán Arenal

Costa Rica's most dramatic attraction is known for its occasional sensational eruptions, providing grand views of its fiery fury. The surrounding area offers soothing hot springs and fabulous hiking and a medley of other activities.

Parque Nacional Volcán Arenal

⚠ Map p. 101

✉ Hwy. 142,
   10 miles (16 km)
   W of La Fortuna

☎ 2479-8811

💲 $$

arenal.net

The quintessential cone of Volcán Arenal (5,389 feet/1,643 m) is the focus of this national park, one of 16 protected reserves that make up the Arenal Conservation Area, which spans 12 life zones (see p. 44). The 26,690-acre (10,800 ha) park boasts two volcanoes; Volcán Arenal's minor sibling is **Volcán Chato** (3,609 feet/1,100 m), a dormant cone with a pea green lagoon within its collapsed crater.

Arenal began to emerge about seven thousand years ago, pushing up like a great molehill. Understandably, pre-Columbian Indians considered it to be sacred. It barely hiccuped during the colonial era, then on July 29, 1968, a fateful earthquake awakened the slumbering giant, which exploded, decimating the nearby hamlet of Tabacón. The volcano simmered for 42 years, with barely a day passing without a minor eruption; there were usually smoking rocks rolling down the slopes. At night the pyrotechnics would appear like giant fireworks as red-hot lava oozed down the steep slopes. Since September 2010, the volcano has been quiescent. There is still much to see, though, and experts are keeping a watchful eye for resumed activity.

You can buy an interpretive map-guide at the ranger station, which lies 1 mile (1.6 km) south of Highway 142, 2 miles (3.2 km) east of Laguna de Arenal and 10 miles (16 km) west of La Fortuna (see p. 213), in the Northern Lowlands. Five separate trails lead to washes of lava fossilized by the sun. **Arenal Observatory Lodge,** on the slopes of Volcán Chato, offers spectacular views, plus a museum on volcanology. You can also stay here (see Travelwise p. 247).

The waters of **Río Tabacón** provide hot springs best enjoyed at **Tabacón Resort** *(tel 2479-2000, tabacon.com),* 1.5 miles (2.4 km) east of the park entrance, where mineral pools and a warm waterfall have been laid out amid gardens. Adjacent to the park entrance, **Arenal 1968** *(tel 2462-1212, arenal1968.com, $$)* has trails atop the 1968 lava flow. ∎

Arenal volcano has recently grown dormant.

Volcán Tenorio & Zona Protectora Miravalles

The twin volcanoes Tenorio and Miravalles lie within a few minutes drive of the Inter-American Highway, yet are a world away in their brawny, thick-forested, aloof appeal.

Mantled in savanna on the lower western slopes, montane rain forest at mid-elevations, and by cloud forest above, these contiguous volcanoes offer a pristine, wildlife-rich world seen by few tourists. Arrive prepared for the steep trails and you will be rewarded. Monkeys—howlers and white-faced capuchins—abound,

Bubbling mud pots at Las Hornillas Volcano Activity Center

INSIDER TIP:

The Llanos de Cortes waterfall on the Río Portrero makes for great swimming. Follow signs on the left of the road, beginning ten minutes past Bagaces as you drive from Cañas to Liberia.

—SUSAN PERRY
National Geographic field researcher

as do agoutis, pacas, and sloths. Visitors are as likely to see ocelots, cougars, or jaguars here as anywhere else in the country.

You'll reach **Parque Nacional Volcán Tenorio** from the Inter-American Highway north of Cañas via Highway 6, which dips and rises for 21 miles (34 km) northeastward to Bijagua, nestled between the volcanoes. **Heliconias Lodge** *(tel 2466-8483, hotelheliconias.co.cr)* is a perfect base for exploring

Volcán Tenorio. The trail leads to a waterfall of the **Río Celeste** and on to mud pools and fumaroles.

The best way to reach the **Zona Protectora Miravalles** is from Bagaces by Highway 164, arching over the volcano's western haunch. Miravalles (6,653 feet/ 2,028 m) is known for its fumaroles, sulfur springs, and mud pots, easily seen at **Las Hornillas,** where the Costa Rican Institute of Electricity harnesses superheated vapor for geothermal energy.

Las Hornillas Volcano Activity Center *(tel 8839-9769, hornillas.com)* offers visitors trails through an active crater, plus therapeutic mud baths. Nearby, the **Río Perdido** resort also has thermal springs and a sensational upscale restaurant and spa. Mountain bike trails snake through the center's 500-acre (202 ha) dry forest reserve. ∎

Parque Nacional Volcán Tenorio
- Map p. 101
- 21 miles (34 km) NE of Inter-American Hwy. off Hwy. 6
- 2206-5369 or 2695-5180
- $$

Río Perdido
- San Bernardo de Bagaces, 19 miles (30 km) NE of Bagaces
- 2673-3600
- rioperdido.com

Volcanoes

Volcanoes are the primary vents in the Earth's crust through which hot molten rock—magma—wells up from the mantle of liquid rock beneath the crust. There are more than 600 active volcanoes in the world today. Costa Rica has 7—another 60 are dormant or extinct—making it one of the most volcanically active areas of the world.

Volcanoes are associated with the movement of rigid sections of the Earth's crust, or lithospheric plates, that ride atop the asthenosphere (mantle) made of hot, plastic rock—a process called plate tectonics, proposed by German geophysicist Alfred Wegener in 1915 and adopted by earth scientists in the 1960s. The major and minor plates pull apart or press against each other. Convection currents rise from deep within the Earth's interior, much like a pot of boiling water, to fuel the process, bringing molten material to

Cocos plate

the surface and forming necklaces of fire along the fractured joint lines.

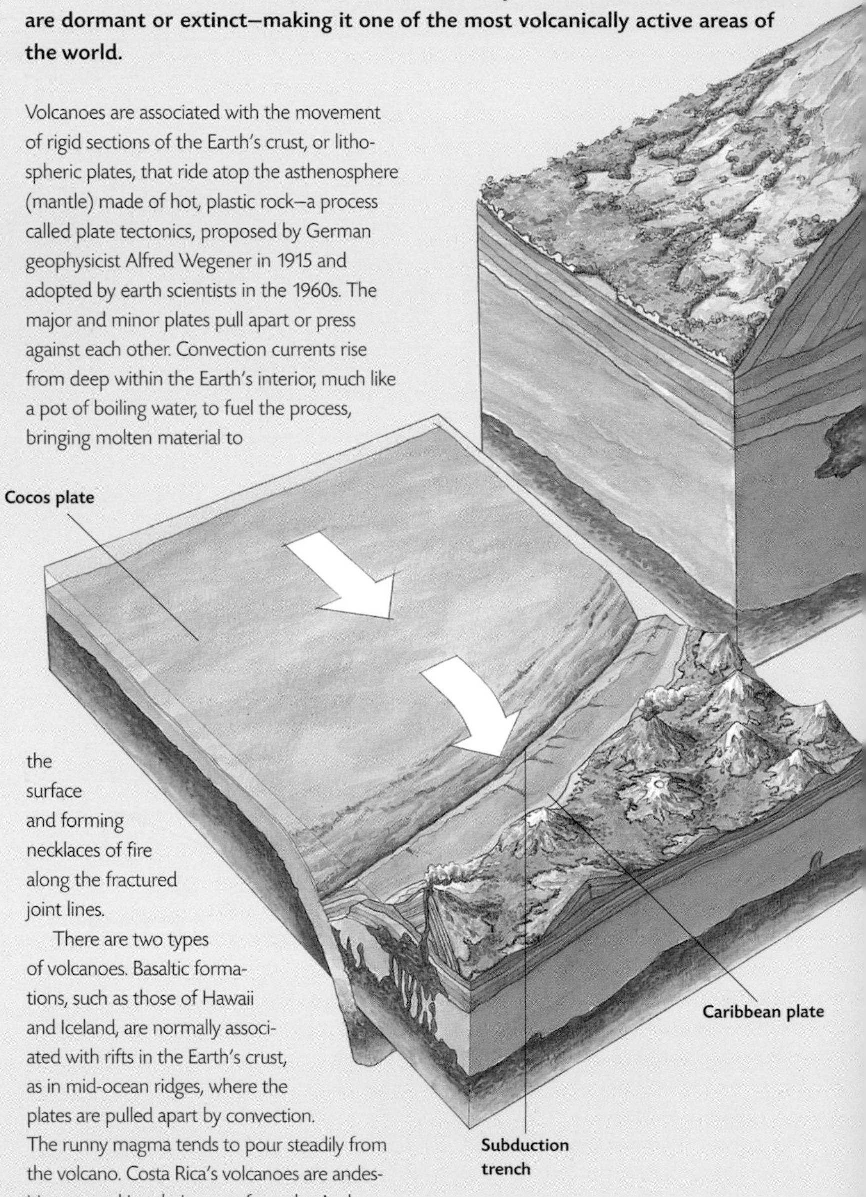

There are two types of volcanoes. Basaltic formations, such as those of Hawaii and Iceland, are normally associated with rifts in the Earth's crust, as in mid-ocean ridges, where the plates are pulled apart by convection. The runny magma tends to pour steadily from the volcano. Costa Rica's volcanoes are andesitic types, taking their name from the Andes

Caribbean plate

Subduction trench

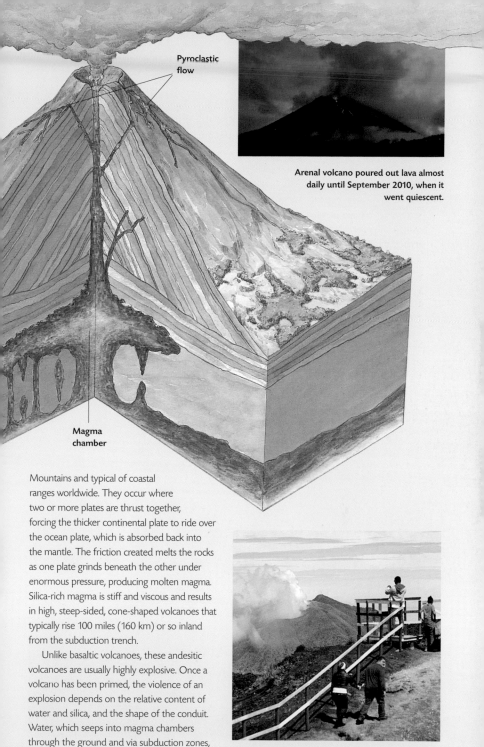

Pyroclastic flow

Arenal volcano poured out lava almost daily until September 2010, when it went quiescent.

Magma chamber

Mountains and typical of coastal ranges worldwide. They occur where two or more plates are thrust together, forcing the thicker continental plate to ride over the ocean plate, which is absorbed back into the mantle. The friction created melts the rocks as one plate grinds beneath the other under enormous pressure, producing molten magma. Silica-rich magma is stiff and viscous and results in high, steep-sided, cone-shaped volcanoes that typically rise 100 miles (160 km) or so inland from the subduction trench.

Unlike basaltic volcanoes, these andesitic volcanoes are usually highly explosive. Once a volcano has been primed, the violence of an explosion depends on the relative content of water and silica, and the shape of the conduit. Water, which seeps into magma chambers through the ground and via subduction zones, provides the explosive potential of steam.

Turrialba volcano entered an active phase in 2009.

Viscous, silica-rich magma prevents the steam from rising to the surface so that the pressure builds like a pressure cooker. Silica-rich magma also tends to clog quickly, plugging the vent like a cork in a champagne bottle. When a dome is plugged by solidified lava, the magma becomes supersaturated with pressurized steam until the volcano is at a breaking point; it then ruptures explosively at its weakest spot. Sometimes the explosion may occur via a fissure to the side. When blasted laterally from the volcano, the lava appears as a *nouée ardente* (glowing cloud), a superheated avalanche of steam, red-hot ash, and poison gases that can roar downhill with the force of a thermonuclear explosion.

Vegetation for many miles around is often bowed down by blankets of hot mineral-rich ashes that eventually are transformed into fertile soils. The vast quantities of dust and energy released sometimes spawn great clouds above the volcano charged with lightning and triggering tremendous storms that dump torrential rain.

At other times, the walls protecting a crater lake may rupture and the waters cascade down-hill, turning into a *lahore*—a massive avalanche of mud up to 100 feet (30 m) deep and laden with trees, boulders, and other debris, as destructive in its power as a runaway locomotive.

Volcanoes can lie dormant for centuries before awakening with a series of mutterings that grow gradually stronger and more ominous. There may initially be emissions of sulfurous gas, followed by puffs of steam, a series of small earth tremors, and clouds of ash. Then—*BOOM!* The mountain detonates either all at once or in an ongoing series of thunderous explosions that may end in a cataclysmic detonation. In lush tropical settings such as Costa Rica, such pronounced eruptions often set off stampedes of wildlife, so that any settlements in their path of flight become overrun with ants, centipedes, and a variety of venomous snakes.

Several volcanoes, such as Miravalles and Rincón de la Vieja, are associated with features such as the fumaroles and boiling mud pools that occur where rainwater seeps into the porous ground above the volcano's magma chambers. The water in the permeable ground thus becomes superheated from below like a giant boiler, with water temperatures reaching 5,000°F (2,760°C). Rising back to the surface, the water begins to boil as pressure is released, emerging in great vents of steam or bubbling mud pools, or mingling with cool groundwater to form hot springs, like those at Tabacón on the flanks of Volcán Arenal.

Clouds frequently shroud the summit of Arenal volcano.

Liberia

Striking for its simple adobe architecture, this whitewashed provincial capital astride the Inter-American Highway resounds to the clip-clop of hooves, providing an intriguing sun-bleached way station beneath the gaze of Volcán Rincón de la Vieja and handily situated as a springboard for Parque Nacional Santa Rosa and the Península de Nicoya.

Liberia is without a doubt the most colonial of Costa Rican cities, redolent with its own unique charm that owes much to its historic core of red-tile-roofed buildings made of ignimbrite, a diatomaceous rock as white as burning magnesium. Liberia is known colloquially as the Ciudad Blanca, or White City. Many venerable old homes feature *puertas del sol,* corner entranceways with doors on two sides that work as an effective air-vent system.

A saddlemaker's colorful storefront attracts shoppers in Liberia.

Situated at the heart of Guanacaste and cattle country, Liberia is wholeheartedly a cowboy town and plays host to several lively fiestas, when townsfolk dress up in traditional garb for the parades, mariachis serenade, and rodeos provide entertainment. The liveliest fiesta is the **Día de Guanacaste,** on July 25, which is a celebration of Guanacaste's independence from Nicaragua in 1812. The festive spirit is resurrected in early September for **Semana Cultural.**

The town sprawls eastward from the Inter-American Highway and is accessed along a broad tree-shaded boulevard, Avenida Central, which features a life-size bronze cowboy statue, the **Monumento Sabanero** *(Calle 10).* The avenue slopes gently past the peaceful tree-shaded main plaza *(bet. Calles 2 & Real),* which features

---

EXPERIENCE:
Local Fiestas

Costa Rica's annual calendar is a whirligig of fiestas. Almost every town has its *fiestas patronales* (patron saints' days), typically featuring a traditional rodeo and *tope* (display of horse-riding skills), fireworks, a beauty pageant, and traditional music and dance. Religious *feriados* (holidays) and processions are held during Easter Holy Week *(Holy Thurs.–Easter Sun.).* And the nation's indigenous communities hold their own unique and colorful festivals that incorporate Catholic and pre-Columbian traditions. The **Costa Rica Tourism Board** website *(visitcostarica.com)* has a complete listing of events.

A fiesta worth catching takes place in Liberia every July 25, when Día de Guanacaste celebrates Guanacaste's independence from Nicaragua with a rodeo, bullfights, and folkloric dancing.

Liberia

 Map p. 101

Visitor Information

✉ Aeropuerto Internacional Daniel Oduber

☎ 2668-0095

the **Iglesia Immaculada Concepción de María**—a church in dramatic modernist style. The old town hall, or *ayuntamiento*, locally called the **Antigua Gobernación** *(tel 2665-7114)*, is topped by a fluttering Guanacastecan flag. The plaza ends at the **Iglesia La Agonía** *(Calle 11, tel 2666-1506)*, an enchanting church dating from 1854, which is simply adorned and has a small religious art museum. Time your visit for mid-afternoon —the only time the church is open— when women gather daily for the rosary. To learn about local history, stop in at the nearby **Museo de Sabaneros** *(Ave. 6, Calle 1, no tel)*, displaying weathered saddles and other memorabilia paying homage to local cowboy culture. It's housed in a charming example of typical Guanacastecan architecture.

On the plaza's northwest corner, the old city jail and former police station boasts crenellated towers and today houses the **Museo de Guanacaste** *(Ave. 1, Calle 2, tel 2665-7114, closed Sun.)*.

Iglesia La Agonía, one of the oldest structures in Costa Rica

Rodeo

Costa Rica's cowboy *(sabanero)* culture has been part of the traditional Guanacastecan way of life for centuries. Just as in North America's Wild West, breaking wild broncos was a part of the daily routine, while riding bulls served to prove a sabanero's manhood—a tradition kept alive at *fiestas cívicas*, where *recorridos de toros* (bull rodeos) are everyone's favorite part of the entertainment. The sabaneros ride the enraged bulls bareback and display their rope-handling skills, accompanied by much whooping and hollering.

Opened in 2012 with a striking contemporary redesign, it features art galleries and live event venues.

Calle Central, east of the plaza, has been renamed **Calle Real** and boasts many fine colonial structures, many of them converted to budget hotels. Most remarkable is **Posada de la Calle Real** *(Calle Real, Ave. 4)*, with exterior walls entirely covered in murals depicting newspapers. The two blocks that run south from the plaza display typical Liberian architecture at its finest, with old wrought-iron lanterns and creaky nail-studded wooden doors.

Liberia has taken on an increasingly important role in recent years, following the 2002 opening of the Daniel Oduber International Airport, 7 miles (11 km) west of town. ■

Parque Nacional Rincón de la Vieja

The velveteen cone of Rincón de la Vieja (meaning "old woman's corner") makes a theatrical backdrop that dominates the landscape of northern Guanacaste and offers active travelers a variety of invigorating attractions within the 34,800-acre (14,080 ha) park.

This volcano is the grandest of the fiery giants that make up the Cordillera de Guanacaste. The park spans an elevation range of 5,000 feet (1,525 m) and protects markedly different vegetation on its rain-soaked Caribbean and

INSIDER TIP:

The Rincón Corobicí restaurant, 10 minutes past Cañas on the Inter-American Highway to Liberia, offers excellent ambience, particularly in the evening when flocks of egrets come to roost outside.

—SUSAN PERRY
National Geographic field researcher

seasonally parched Pacific sides— from savanna to montane rain forest to upper-level dwarf cloud forest. Rain clouds cloak its summit, spawning swift rivers that radiate in every direction, gouging deep ravines into its concave sides.
The volcano has two peaks— **Rincón de la Vieja** (5,925 feet/ 1,806 m) and **Santa María** (6,256 feet/1,916 m). The nine craters include the Rincón peak's bowl-shaped, gently steaming **Von Seebach Crater**—a reminder that

Hacienda Guachipelín serves as a working cattle ranch and activity center.

this is an active volcano. **Casona Santa María,** a farmstead, houses the park headquarters and an exhibition. The hacienda was purchased by Costa Rica's national park service from former U.S. President Lyndon Johnson.
The main access point is at **Estación Las Pailas** *(tel 2200-0399),* to the northwest, reached from Highway 1 by dirt road via Curubandé. The volcano's lower western slopes are mostly occupied by working cattle haciendas, which provide lodging and horseback riding. Key among them are **Hotel Borinquen Mountain Resort & Spa** (see Travelwise p. 247), and **Hacienda Lodge Guachipelín** (see Travelwise p. 248), offering myriad activities. Mammals here include tapirs, seen at higher elevations. ∎

Parque Nacional Rincón de la Vieja

🅐 Map p. 101
✉ 16 miles (26 km) NE of Liberia
☎ 2666-5051
🅢 $$

www.sinac.go.cr

A Hike to the Top of Rincón

The soaring mass of Rincón de la Vieja draws hardy hikers up its jungle green sides in search of rare wildlife and the satisfaction of ascending the summit. Hot springs, mud pools, and "ovens"—evidence of vibrant geothermal activity—make diverting landmarks along this rewarding two-day walk. Note that increased volcanic activity has led to the sporadic closure of some trails. Check ahead for current restrictions.

It is a straightforward hike, beginning at the **Casona Santa María Ranger Station ❶** on the southwestern side of the volcano. There is a basic campsite 400 yards (365 m) from the hacienda, or you can sleep in dormitory-style accommodations in the ranger's *cabina* by prior arrangement *(tel 2200-0399 or 2666-5051)*. You will need to bring your own sleeping bag and blanket. The hike to the summit covers 8.3 miles (13.3 km), with an elevation gain of 3,614 feet (1,100 m).

Head out along the old roadway that leads west from the ranger station. After half a mile (0.8 km) you pass the **Sendero Bosque Encantado ❷** ("enchanted forest trail") on your left, making an interesting side excursion into old growth forest that abounds with orchids, including *guaría morada,* the national flower. The main trail continues 0.6 mile (1 km) to another side trail marked **Aguas Termales ❸** ("hot springs"); you should save your visit for the return journey (when you will be better able to appreciate a soothing celebratory soak). About 2.5 miles (4 km) farther along take the right-hand trail, uphill, at the Y-junction. The landscape opens up at the top and you can make a short detour—marked as **Pilas de Barro ❹** ("mud pots")—to where boiling mud explodes in great belching bubbles and the superheated mineral-rich pools are tinged with a rainbow of colors. Stay away from the overhanging edges of the pools; they are often insecure underfoot.

Continuing along the main path, you will pass through former cattle pasture that is being slowly regenerated with native forest. Steam rises mystically over the treetops, luring you along another short trail to your right that deposits you at **Las Hornillas ❺** ("ovens"), also

NOT TO BE MISSED:

Aguas Termales • Pilas de Barro • Von Seebach Crater

known as Lagunas Fumarólico, where fumaroles (vapor geysers) hiss like teakettles, spitting up odoriferous steam and gases—hydrogen sulfide and sulfur dioxide. Again, use caution when walking around the "stove pipes." Continue half a mile (0.8 km) on the steep main trail to the **Río Colorado ❻**, where there is a basic campsite on the riverbank. Just beyond that is the **Las Palilas Ranger Station ❼**, *(tel 2200-0399 or 2661-8139)*, 4 miles (6.4 km) from Santa María and accessible by car via Curubandé. You can pitch a tent here. Plan on getting up before sunrise and ascending to the summit in time to beat the clouds, which tend to form in mid-morning. Or begin your hike here.

It is a 6-mile (10 km) ascent through premontane and montane rain forest festooned with bromeliads and epiphytes, including hundreds of the park's renowned orchid species. The forests vibrate with birdsong; look for the turkey-like black guan, a raucous bird that hops about in the branches. The trail snakes upward through bamboo, then through stunted dwarf forest near the edge of the tree line. About 3 miles (5 km) above Las Pailas, you pass through gnarly copey clusia, a cloud forest species with waxy leaves that perfume the air. You are now only a few hundred yards below the ridge, attained by a scramble up loose lava scree. **Von Seebach Crater ❽** is a half mile (0.8 km) away. The way is marked by cairns, but it is easy to lose the trail when the clouds set in, whipped up by a cold wet wind swirling about the summit. Volcanic eruptions occasionally obliterate the summit trails.

With luck, the sky will be scintillating blue overhead and the last 1.5 miles (2.5 km) across the lava-strewn saddle to the smoking summit of **Volcán Rincón de la Vieja** will be clear. You can revel in the vast views, which are phantasmagoric in their expanse, with the Pacific and Caribbean shimmering on hazy horizons. With proper planning, you might have time to hike to **Laguna Los Jilgueros ❾**, which is 1.5 miles (2 km) from the Von Seebach Crater and surrounded by a ravaged moonscape like a scene from Dante's *Inferno*. There is a chance at both dawn and dusk to watch super-shy tapirs drink at the pea green lake that sits in the saddle between the Von Seebach and Rincón craters.

This hike is best tackled in the dry season (*Nov.–April*), with January to April being the best months. Ticks and other biting insects inhabit the thick elephant grass. Long pants tucked into socks are recommended, especially around campsites. Take insect repellent and warm, water-repellent clothing—as much as 200 inches (500 cm) of rainfall douses upper elevations each year. Remember overnight camping on the mountain is no longer permitted; you must return to Las Palilas before day two of your hike.

▲	Also see area map p. 101
►	Casona Santa María Ranger Station
◷	2 days
↔	17 miles (28 km)
►	Laguna Los Jilgueros

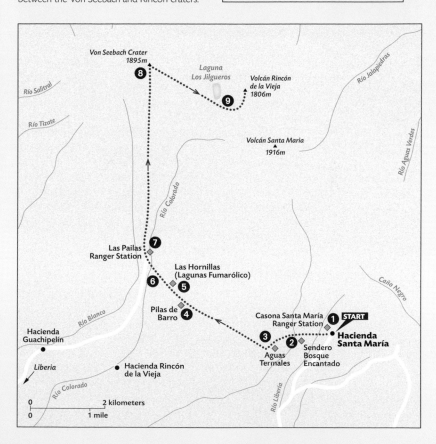

Parque Nacional Guanacaste

Wellspring of the Río Tempisque, the watershed of the Orosí and Cacao volcanoes was protected in 1989 and enshrined in this national park, a rugged, rarely visited world devoid of tourist services and appealing to those with a spirit of adventure.

The greater anteater—*oso hormiguero* to locals—is endangered and rarely seen.

Parque Nacional Guanacaste
🅰 Map p. 100
☎ 2666-5051
💲 $$
www.sinac.go.cr

The 207,560-acre (84,000 ha) Parque Nacional Guanacaste is the keystone in the 2,742,810-acre (1,110,000 ha) **Guanacaste Conservation Area** *(acguanacaste .ac.cr)*–an amalgam of contiguous parks and reserves. The park is a mosaic extending from lowland savanna to cloud forest atop its two volcanoes: **Orosí** (4,879 feet/ 1,487 m) and **Cacao** (5,443 feet/ 1,659 m). Much of the former cattle ranges at their western bases is being returned to dry deciduous forest in an effort to fuse the disparate native habitats and create migratory corridors for the profusion of wildlife found here.

The main entrance to the park is via **Quebrada Grande,** accessed from Highway 1 at Potrerillos via a 6-mile (10 km) dirt track. Beyond **Gangora,** hike 3 miles (5 km) to the **Cacao Field Station** on the south side of Cacao at 3,350 feet (1,021 m). From here, you can hike through cloud forest, watching for wildlife as you head for the summit, 1.5 miles (2.5 km) beyond Cacao. Another trail slopes down through montane moist forest and seasonally dry moist forest to the spot where **Maritza Field Station** is linked to Highway 1 by a trail from the Cuajiniquil turnoff. Maritza, the main ranger station, has basic dormitories. You can hike to the summit of Orosí via **El Pedregal,** an archaeological site where pre-Columbian petroglyphs peer through mosses on the **Llanos de los Indios** (the plain of the Indians).

On the Caribbean side, the **Pitilla Field Station**, set in premontane rain forest (good for birding) is reached via a dirt track from **Santa Cecilia,** 18 miles (29 km) east of Highway 1. ■

Parque Nacional Santa Rosa

This national park, the first to be established in Costa Rica, boasts an abundance of human and natural history. Sea-girt on two sides, Santa Rosa has fine beaches washed by rugged surf. Good camping facilities help make this one of the country's most appealing wildland attractions.

Its 122,350 acres (49,512 ha) enfold ten distinct habitats, home to about 115 mammal species and more than 250 species of birds—all easily seen amid the predominant landscape of dry deciduous forest, where anteaters, deer, iguanas, and howler, spider, and white-faced monkeys are preyed upon by five species of cats, including rarely seen jaguars. In the scorching heat of the dry season, the forests explode in vibrant color, birds and beasts gather at precious watering holes, and wildlife viewing is easy for patient and silent visitors.

The park is divided into two sections. To the south is the larger **Santa Rosa sector,** where armored vehicles rust amid tall grass west of the entrance gate, marking an ill-fated invasion by Nicaraguan troops in 1955. The park headquarters, which houses a museum, is a replica of **La Casona** (acguanacaste.ac.cr), where in 1856 Costa Rica's ragtag army of peasant soldiers routed William Walker and his mercenaries (see p. 29). The original hacienda was destroyed by arsonists in 2001.

Numerous trails branch out from La Casona through the dry forest. The **Naked Indian Trail,** named for the gumbo-limbo trees whose peeling bark exposes a red trunk, makes an easy loop; the **Los Patos Trail** is good for spotting rare mammals. Visitors with rugged four-wheel-drive vehicles can descend the 8-mile (13 km) track to **Playa Naranjo,** which is flanked by headlands and beloved by surfers for its tubular waves. Nearby **Playa Nancite** is off-limits to visitors, for here one of nature's miracles plays out each summer as Ridley turtles swarm ashore to lay eggs. Crocodiles lurk in the mangrove swamps that back the shore.

INSIDER TIP:

Swimmers and even waders should avoid estuaries and the mouths of rivers, particularly at Playa Naranjo and Playa Potrero Grande, where crocodiles are a real and present danger.

—MICHAEL H. GRAYUM
National Geographic field researcher

To the north is the **Murciélago sector,** which extends along the Santa Elena peninsula. Rarely visited white-sand beaches sparkle like diamonds. Bring camping gear. Pelicans and frigate birds wheel overhead. **Hacienda Murciélago,** once owned by the Nicaraguan Somoza family, was the site for Oliver North's secret airstrip during the Contra era. Fishermen will take you to the **Islas Murciélagos** (Bat Islands), renowned for their superb diving. ■

Parque Nacional Santa Rosa

🗺 Map p. 100
✉ 4 miles (6.4 km) W of Hwy. 1, 20 miles N of Liberia
☎ 2666-5051
$ $$$
www.sinac.go.cr

More Places to Visit in Guanacaste

Bahía Salinas

Several fine beaches line this flask-shaped bay, including the sugar white Playa Pochotes, which is backed by glistening salt pans picked upon by wading birds and mangroves where crocodiles lurk. The bay is enfolded to the south by Punta Descartes, which opens to the northwest and garners winds off the open sea. It is a nirvana for windsurfers, who are served by the Kite Surf Center *(tel 8826-5221, bluedreamhotel.com)*, or hire an experienced instructor *(kitecostarica.net/kite surfing-schools-instructors)*. A few rustic fishing hamlets remain, tethered to a hard life at sea. A craggy isle covered with drought-resistant

INSIDER TIP:

In season (mainly June to September), restaurants in La Cruz offer a delicious *refresco* **(drink) made from the fruits of** *pitahaya,* **a cactus native to the region.**

—MICHAEL H. GRAYUM
National Geographic field researcher

shrubs—**Refugio Nacional de Vida Silvestre Isla Bolaños**—studs the bay. This island is a protected nesting site for frigate birds, American oystercatchers, brown pelicans, and boobies. The island is off-limits to visitors. ⚑ Map p. 100 ✉ 4 miles (6.4 km) W of La Cruz

Club Río Outdoor Center

Adults and children will enjoy this riverside activity center at The Springs Resort & Spa, midway between Arenal volcano and La Fortuna. Activities include kayaking and tubing on the Río Arenal, hiking and horseback riding, and soaking in thermal springs that pour up from "Calcium Canyon." A

highlight is the wildlife reserve, where pumas, jaguarundis, ocelots, margays, and oncillas are displayed in large cages, alongside other mammal species. Tours of the center—which takes in rescued animals—are offered five times daily. Guided night tours into the forest are also offered. *thespringscostarica.com* ⚑ Map p. 101 ✉ 3 miles (5 km) W of La Fortuna. ☎ 2401-3313 💲 $$$$$

Ecolodge San Luís & Research Station

This private research center of the University of Georgia welcomes tourists to its 165-acre (67 ha) reserve and working farm in the small hamlet of San Luís, which is being integrated into a project to develop a model for sustainable development. Montane wet forest and cloud forest provide opportunities for birding and viewing wildlife on foot or horseback, and visitors are welcome at the research facilities for lectures and classes on local ecology, or to help out in the fields. Participatory educational workshops and cultural activities are offered for both resident students and ecotourists. Accommodation is available in comfortable *cabinas. dar.uga.edu/costa_rica* ⚑ Map p. 101 ✉ 5.5 miles (9 km) SE of Santa Elena ☎ 2645-7363

La Ponderosa Adventure Park

One senses that this wildlife park's giraffes, ostrich, and zebras feel at home in the grasslands of Guanacaste, which closely replicate the African savannas. La Ponderosa Adventure Park hosts a panoply of creatures. Giraffes stretch their necks to nibble thorny acacias as antelope, eland, gemsbok, and warthog trot past. The park also has camels, watusi cattle, and peacocks, as well as monkeys and other animals endemic to Costa Rica. Guided tours are offered aboard open safari vehicles. *ponderosaadventurepark.com* ⚑ Map p. 101 ✉ 5 miles (8 km) S of Liberia ☎ 2105-7181 🕐 Guided tours 💲 $$$

Diamond-dust beaches, emerald golf courses, superb sportfishing, scuba diving, and surfing in an otherwise sleepy region

Nicoya

Nicoya's famous surfing beaches draw experienced and novice surfers alike.

Nicoya

Sand and sea are the names of the game in Nicoya, a mountainous crab-claw peninsula that hooks around the Golfo de Nicoya. Visitors love its white-sand beaches, unique in the nation, and enjoy a six-month dry season, when the sun dances incandescently on the sea beneath a virtually ever blue sky.

Northeastern Nicoya is an undulating plain fringed by wetlands fed by the Río Tempisque—fabulous for birding—that open into the Golfo de Nicoya. The region's few towns speckle well-paved Highway 21, which runs north to south down the plain, east of the low-slung mountain range. Much of the land has been denuded for cattle ranching, the predominant industry since colonial days. Prior to the depredations of the Spanish, the peninsula was the home of the Chorotega, whose legacy can be seen in distinctive pottery. Tiny Guaitíl is at the center of a Chorotega cultural rebirth.

Local life still revolves around fishing and ranching, and Nicoya moves at a sleepy bucolic

pace. A half dozen burgeoning resorts dot the rugged shoreline, though Tamarindo is the only coastal town of significant size or sophistication. While all of San José seems to descend on weekends and holidays, Josefinos tend to flock to a fistful of beaches, and visitors find it relatively easy to escape the madding crowd despite the fact that three-quarters of the nation's hotel rooms are along Nicoya's sugar white northern beaches. Two experiences stand out: watching leatherback turtles nesting at Playa Grande, and witnessing the awesome spectacle of the *arribadas*—synchronized nesting of Ridley turtles at Playa Ostional that occurs at predictable times every year. Parque Nacional Marino Las Baulas and Refugio Nacional de Vida Silvestre Ostional protect these precious havens.

In southern Nicoya, the lush tropical moist forests of Reserva Natural Absoluta Cabo Blanco and Refugio Nacional de Vida Silvestre Curú protect their own wildlife wonders.

Recent years have brought an explosion of construction. Due to a contentious decision during the Rafael Calderón administration (1990–1994) to target the untapped deluxe vacation market, Bahía Culebra is shaping up to become a mini-Cancún. The Gulf of Papagayo Project stalled in the mid-1990s under charges of corruption and environmental abuse; it is now moving ahead under more careful surveillance. The nation's second airport—Daniel Oduber International Airport—opened near Liberia, fostering a huge boost to the region.

Golf courses offer relaxed pleasures, though they are draining the drought-stricken region's aquifers. Waves pump ashore, providing thrills for surfers. Despite low visibility, scuba divers rave about eye-to-eye encounters with giant groupers and other fish. And sportfishing is world-class, centered on the Golfo de Papagayo, where marlin run thick and fast. Ashore, cavers can escape the searing summer heat in the cool caverns at Parque Nacional Barra Honda.

Most roads linking coastal hamlets are unpaved and covered with fine dust in the dry season and are hard to access in the rainy season except in a four-wheel-drive vehicle. Some rivers still need to be forded—adding to the adventure of exploring—and due care should be taken. ∎

Costa Rica
Area of map detail

0   20 kilometers
0   10 miles

Golfo de Nicoya

The isle-studded, mangrove-fringed Golfo de Nicoya is a slender sleeve of shallow water separating the Península de Nicoya from mainland Guanacaste, revealing mudbanks during low tide and forming an aquatic haven for crocodiles and profuse birdlife.

Seabirds race the ferry from Puntarenas.

Golfo de Nicoya

⬚ Map p. 131

Visitor Information

☎ 2685-5417

⛴ Coonatramar R.L. (Naranjo): 2661-1069; Ferry Peninsular (Paquera): 2661-2084

$ $ for ferry (passenger), $$ for ferry (car)

coonatramar.com
navieratambor.com

El Viejo Wildland Refuge & Wetlands

✉ 10 miles (17 km) SE of Filadelfia

☎ 2296-0966

$ $$$

elviejowetlands.com

Settlements are few along the banks of the gulf, where mangroves envelop vast acres fed by the Río Tempisque's sediment-laden waters. The hamlet of **Puerto Humo,** 16 miles (26 km) east of Nicoya (see p. 136), on the west bank of the river, offers plentiful options for wildlife viewing. **Humedal Palustrino Corral de Piedra** (tel 2659-8190, actempisque.org) protects a wetland habitat of jabiru storks and other wading birds. Nearby, **Rancho Humo** (tel 2105-5400, ranchohumo.com) has a wetland viewing area with restaurant, plus guided hikes and tours along 8 miles (14 km) of trails using golf carts. A working cattle ranch, it also offers farm tours.

Farther north, **El Viejo Wildland Refuge & Wetlands** is centered on a still-functioning sugar estate. This 5,000-acre (2,023 ha) reserve borders Parque Nacional Palo Verde (see p. 112) and offers boat trips on the Río Tempisque, mountain bike rides, and a lagoon hike through the reserve—a chance to spot crocodiles, monkeys, white-tailed deer, and Costa Rica's largest bird, the jabiru stork.

The largest of the gulf isles is **Isla Chira,** a favored nesting site for frigate birds, which hang in the sky like kites. Roseate spoonbills grub about in the mudflats and salt pans—salinas—from which a few hardy inhabitants eke a living extracting salt. Precious nesting sites of brown boobies, frigate birds, and other seabirds are also protected on scrub-covered **Isla Guayabo** and **Isla Negritos,** two tiny isles at the mouth of the gulf. Guayabo, uniquely, is a winter nesting site for peregrine falcons. Both isles are off-limits to visitors. Dolphins and whales cavort in the open waters.

Isla San Lucas, off the southeast tip of Nicoya, was a sacred burial place for pre-Columbian Indians. In the 19th century its barren wastes were turned into a hellish prison. Ghosts seem to haunt the forlorn isle, a national wildlife refuge and cultural heritage site recovered from the jungle this past decade for tourism, with cells, a cemetery, and a church to visit. **Bay Islands Cruises** (tel 2258-3536, bayislandcruises.com) offers excursions from Puntarenas. ∎

Parque Nacional Barra Honda

Riddled with stygian chambers like holes in Swiss cheese, Barra Honda—unique in the nation—offers cavers an exciting challenge. Not all of its appeals are subterranean, however; aboveground, its hiking trails thread a wonderful, wildlife-rich world of dry forests.

Barra Honda comprises a 5,670-acre (2,295 ha) wilderness of pitted limestone uplands that rise west of the Río Tempisque floodplain, from which eons of weathering have carved out caverns. Of the 42 known caverns, only 19 have been explored. The deepest, **Caverna Santa Ana**, extends to almost 800 feet (240 m) underground.

INSIDER TIP:

Drink the water in Nicoya—it has off-the-charts levels of calcium, and if you drink enough, it amounts to taking a supplement.

—DAN BUETTNER
National Geographic author

The only cavern open to the public in Parque Nacional Barra Honda is the **Caverna Terciopelo,** accessed by a ladder that descends 100 feet (30 m). The cavern boasts spectacular dripstone formations, including one known as "the Organ" that fills the cave with haunting chimes when struck. Terciopelo's three distinct chambers are named for the formations within, with the most obvious being **Mushroom Hall.** In the **Hall of the Caves,** it's fun to exercise your imagination with the crystal

structures—a lion's head? entwined lovers? And **Caverna Nicoya** contains pre-Columbian remains dating back two millennia.

The caves have "homegrown" species; among them are endemic blind fish and salamanders that have adapted to absolute darkness. The bats here have deposited so much guano that one cave is called **Pozo Hediondo**—"fetid pit."

Barra Honda also is ideal for terrestrial exploration—convoluted trails stipple the hilly, scrub-covered landscape. Pick up trail maps and hire a guide at the ranger station. **Cerro Barra Honda** (1,459 feet/445 m) offers a tremendous vantage over the country below. Take plenty of water, plus a camera to capture anteaters, monkeys, scarlet macaws, or other exotic denizens of the relatively open dry forest. ∎

Parque Nacional Barra Honda

🅜 Map p. 131

✉ Hwy. 18, 10 miles (16 km) E of Nicoya

☎ 2659-1551; or guided tours c/o Asociación de Guías Especializados de Barra Honda

🕐 Closed Easter week

💲 $$$

actempisque.org

Limestone massifs rise from the floodplain of the Río Tempisque.

Mangroves

Mangroves are a distinctive tropical habitat with halophytes—plants that exist in salty conditions—although they also thrive in freshwater. Five species—black mangrove, buttonwood mangrove, red mangrove, tea mangrove, and white mangrove—are found in Costa Rica, and each has evolved its own unique method for ridding itself of salt—from secreting it through leaf glands to preventing it from being taken up by the roots.

The glutinous mud that mangroves call home is so dense that it contains almost no oxygen. The mud is also acidic, and the nutrients upon which mangroves feed lie not deep down but near the surface, where decomposing organic debris drops from above or is deposited by the receding tides. Thus, most mangroves form aerial roots, drawing oxygen in through spongy bark and giving the appearance that the mangroves are walking on water. Black mangroves differ, preferring to send forth underground roots that sprout long lines of offshoots, called pneumatophores, that stick up from the ground like upturned nails.

The tangled spiderweb of interlocking roots helps stabilize land, protecting it against erosion by waves while acting as a pioneer land builder by filtering out the silt brought down to the sea by Costa Rica's turbulent rivers. The nutrient-rich muds foster the growth of microorganisms that form a food source for larger species, such as shrimps and snails. Many creatures live on the buffet, including stilt-legged wading birds that pick tiny, shrimp-like amphipods from the glistening mud. The redolent mangroves are also important nesting sites for cormorants, pelicans, kingfishers, and frigate birds that deposit their guano atop the

Crab

Kingfisher

Red mangrove

Frigate birds

mud, fertilizing the mangroves and speeding their growth.

Mangroves also serve as aquatic nurseries for creatures such as crustaceans, fish, oysters, sponges, and even stingrays and baby sharks. These habitats are so important to marine species that the destruction of mangroves has an inordinately harmful effect on the entire marine ecosystem.

Raccoons, lizards, and snakes abound, too, as do insects, including a species of mangrove ant that is only found here. Many animal species are unique to mangroves, such as the yellow mangrove warbler *(Dendroica petechia)*, an insectivorous migrant that's present from August to May; and the arboreal mangrove tree crab *(Aratus pisonii)*, a leaf-eater that is stalked by another arboreal crab species, *Goniopsis pulchra*, and is thereby forced to spend a life away from water in the crowns of the mangroves.

Mangrove Proliferation

Mangroves propagate swiftly and often establish new colonies far removed from the parent plants—this is thanks to a splendid reproductive system. The mangrove blooms briefly in spring, then produces a fruit from which sprouts a fleshy seedling shaped like a plumb bob. This pendulous seed, which can grow to a foot (30 cm) in length, germinates on the branch then drops like a dart. At low tide, they stick upright in the mud and instantly send out roots. Seeds that hit water float on the tides like half-filled bottles. They are astoundingly hardy and can survive sea journeys of several hundred miles, often traveling for a year or more before touching a muddy shore, where they anchor themselves and begin a new colony.

A seedling can grow 2 feet (60 cm) or more within its first year. By its third year it has become a mature bush and begins sprouting seeds that establish themselves around the parent's prop roots. Within a decade a mangrove colony has been formed and the process of silting is well under way as the colony creeps farther and farther out to sea. As the land builds up in their lee, they may eventually strand themselves high and dry and die on land of their own making.

Anhinga

Raccoons

Black mangrove

White mangrove

Black mangrove

Yellow mangrove warbler

Fer-de-lance

Mangrove fern

Button-wood or gray mangrove

Heartland of the Chorotega

Nicoya's heartland maintains a regional pride as the wellspring of a newly resurgent Chorotega heritage. The countryside is still worked in the traditional manner: Ox-drawn plows and carts, familiar icons, are tended by campesinos in soiled cotton linens and straw hats, each with a machete and a gourd canteen by his side.

The Festival of La Virgén de Guadalupe honors the mythical Virgin in a parade every December.

Nicoya

🅐 Map p. 131

Visitor Information

✉ Hwy. 21, 1 mile (1.5 km) S of Nicoya, opposite Universidad Nacional

☎ 2685-3260

By some accounts the oldest town in the country, **Nicoya,** administrative capital of the region, serves agricultural communities for miles around. A settlement existed here and served the same purpose prior to the arrival of Spanish conquistador Gil González Dávila (d. 1526), who named his colony for the local Chorotega Indian chief. Nicoya was the center of the Chorotega culture, and well-defined trade routes radiated as

far as Nicaragua. The nation's oldest extant church—**Iglesia de San Blas**—is here, a squat 16th-century adobe affair on the tree-shaded main plaza. The town comes alive each December 12 for the **Festival of La Virgén de Guadalupe,** a celebration that combines Catholic beliefs with the Chorotega legend of La Yequita, which tells of two brothers spared by a mare from killing each other over a Native American princess. There are no other attractions, but the town has several banks, a hospital, and other key services.

Santa Cruz, situated 12 miles (19 km) north of Nicoya astride Highway 21, is renowned as the "folkloric city" for its civic fiestas. Each January 15 and June 25, beer and *chicha* (corn liquor) flow freely, citizens kick up their heels by dancing the Punto Guanacasteco, and the bullring resounds with the cheers of spectators. **Plaza Bernabela Ramos** has some notable statues plus a ruined colonial church and the modern building that has replaced it.

Guaitíl

There is a splendid charm and vitality to this hamlet, 7 miles (11 km) east of Santa Cruz. Guaitíl

marks the heart of the renaissance of Chorotega cultural pride, and local residents carry proudly the dark, robust facial features of their Indian forebears. The village, which squats amid parched cattle country, is lined with stalls of pottery made in the traditional

INSIDER TIP:

In Nicoya, many people reach a healthy age of 90. In fact, this piece of real estate has one of the highest rates of centenarians in the world. So if someone you meet looks like they are a hundred, they probably are.

—DAN BUETTNER
National Geographic author

manner: turned by hand on wheels and fired in wood-fueled, open-hearth kilns, finished with jade grinding stones that local matriarchs believe have magical powers, and then painted with animal motifs.

The artists are organized in cooperatives. Visitors are welcome to stop at family workshops where the homespun craft is performed in front yards beneath spreading shade trees. The **Eco-Museo de la Cerámica Chorotega** *(tel 2681-1563, ecomuseosanvicente.org),* in the adjoining village of San Vicente, honors the cultural traditions and is a center for several annual fiestas. ∎

Santa Cruz
 Map p. 131

Visitor Information

✉ MINAE
Hwy. 21, 200 yards (180 m) N of Plaza de Buenos Aires

☎ 2680-1820

Jade

The pre-Columbian Chorotega were masters at crafting jade. They used the string-saw carving technique, in which a hole is drilled and a string is inserted through it, then repeatedly drawn back and forth like a saw. This enabled them to create detailed figures of frogs, crocodiles, eagles, jaguars, and humans; the last were often shown engaging in the most worldly of pleasures. Archaeologists have found no local source for the semiprecious stones, which more advanced northern cultures introduced to the Chorotega around 400 B.C.

The Northern Beaches

Cupped by bays and coves gilded with a dusting of sugary beaches, northern Nicoya's rugged shoreline—the nation's laid-back "riviera"—provides a variety of choices for vacationers seeking sun, sand, and sea. All of Costa Rica's ubiquitous nature highlights are on hand.

The road to Playa Pan de Azúcar offers superb coastal vistas.

The Northern Beaches
☒ Map p. 130

Easily accessed from Liberia along well-paved Highway 21, Nicoya's northern beaches extend southward from Bahía Culebra to Bahía Tamarindo in scalloped relief, set in deep basins which are separated by scrub-covered headlands. The nation's major resort developments are concentrated here. Playa Flamingo, Playa Hermosa, Playa Tamarindo, and the all-important Bahía Culebra are nodes for the burgeoning flock of self-contained upscale resort complexes that have reshaped the face of the region. Between them are lesser resorts where local fishing communities cling to a simple life by the sea. Sportfishing, scuba diving, and surfing are favorite pastimes. And golfing is now established— a contentious use of precious water and a source of growing conflict between government and local communities concerned about the effects of tourism on their lives.

Weekends and holidays get crowded, when Josefinos flood lemming-like from the capital to sun themselves and swim in the surf conjured by the breeze from the warm Prussian blue sea. Be warned, because the most popular beaches get terribly littered in the wake of these weekend invasions.

Bahía Culebra

This massive horseshoe-shaped, cliff-rimmed amphitheater is held in the pincers of **Punta Ballena** to the south and **Península de Nacascolo**—an archaeologically precious region of pre-Columbian sites—hooking around to the north. Its setting is dramatic, and the sublime vistas across its aquamarine waters are made more so by the dramatic backdrop of Rincón de la Vieja volcano looming to the east.

The previously uninhabited Bahía Culebra is at the center of the largest development project attempted in this part of the Central American isthmus. The Gulf of Papagayo Project, named for the vast gulf into which the bay opens, was initiated in 1993 by the Rafael Calderón administration with ambitions to push Costa Rica into the big league of resort tourism—with 15,000 hotel rooms, two golf courses, self-contained residential communities, a massive marina, and other resort facilities. Most of the score of beaches that nestle in coves between rocky headlands along the bay have been earmarked for development.

Take your pick from several completed resort hotels at **Playa Arenilla** and **Playa Buena** to the south, and **Playa Manzanillo** and **Playa Nacascolo** to the north. The 2003 opening of the **Four Seasons Resort at Papagayo Peninsula** (see Travelwise p. 248) brought new panache to the project, along with a championship golf course that was created by visionary designer Robert Trent Jones, Jr. The **Marina Papagayo** *(tel 2690-3600)* opened here, followed by deluxe hotels, with more planned. Nearby, the **Witch's Rock Canopy Tour** offers a zip line jaunt through the forest.

Around Playas del Coco

A real estate boom in recent years has catapulted Playas del Coco from a small fishing village to a major resort destination. It is popular, not least, with Tico youth who pack in as tightly

INSIDER TIP:

Many of the beaches that are frequented by tourists are also frequented by thieves. Leave all of your valuables at home or bring them with you to the beach, keeping the car empty.

—BEN HORTON
National Geographic field researcher

as sardines on weekends and holidays to tan their bodies, play volleyball, and flirt beneath the palms. Pelicans perch on the fishing boats anchored in the mile-wide (1.6 km) horseshoe-shaped bay. The noisy partying climaxes in January with the civic fiesta's beauty contests, rodeos, and over-the-top revelry.

To the north lies **Playa Hermosa**, a gray-sand beach with tide pools at the northern end. The beach is in the throes of

Witch's Rock Canopy Tour

✉ 22 miles (35.4 km) W of Liberia

☎ 2696-7101

$ $$$$

witchsrockcanopy.com

development yet manages to retain its laid-back appeal. This is enhanced toward its southern end by nets that drape old fishing shacks drawn up on the sands. Farther north, on the southern cusp of Bahía Culebra, lies **Playa Panamá,** offering grand views and a choice of moderately priced to deluxe accommodations. You can hike inland 600 yards (550 m) to the community of **Panamá** along a paved road that is good for spotting wildlife.

A paved road leads 2 miles (3.2 km) south from Playa del Coco to **Playa Ocotal,** a secluded beach with tide pools that is known as a base for sportfishing and scuba diving excursions in the Golfo de Papagayo. The snorkeling is good, particularly at Las Corridas, where sea horses float among soft corals.

Around Playa Flamingo

No, there are no flamingoes in Costa Rica, and this beach resort is also called **Playa Blanca**—White Beach—particularly by promoters. In combination, its sparkling sands and setting are as alluring as any other beach in the nation. The stunning mile-long (1.6 km) scimitar of silver lamé unspools within the cusp of rocky headlands speckled with the luxurious villas of wealthy Ticos and gringos.

Despite a few modest resort hotels, the colloquial title of the "Acapulco of Costa Rica" belies the paucity of nightlife and other tourist facilities. Playa Flamingo was once Nicoya's major sportfishing center; the marina closed in 2005.

The commercial development extends along Bahía Potrero, whose gray sands sweep north to the rustic fishing hamlet of **Potrero**

and, beyond a rocky headland, to the white sands of **Playa La Penca,** backed by a vital mangrove estuary good for spotting coatis, iguanas, monkeys, parrots, and roseate spoonbills amid the rare saltwater forest. The dirt road dips and rises, eventually depositing you at **Playa Pan de Azúcar,** a splendid cove. **Isla Santa Catalina,** a precious nesting site for seabirds such as bridled terns, is just offshore. Northeast of Portrero, the **Congo Trail Canopy Tour** *(tel 2666-4422, congocanopy .com)* offers zip line thrills, plus snake and butterfly exhibits.

The explosion that has come to Nicoya's beaches has hit the funky fishing hamlet of **Brasilito,** a mile (1.6 km) south of Playa Flamingo, with megaton force. This community has been forced into the modern era by the construction of the **Westin Golf Resort & Spa** (see Travelwise p. 249), set south of the village at **Playa Conchal.** The half-mile-long (0.8 km) beach of powdered sugar—actually pulverized seashells—drops into warm turquoise waters, ideal for snorkeling. Water sports are available. The spectacular 18-hole golf course is studded with lagoons. The resort adjoins the recently created **Refugio Nacional de Visa Silvestre Mixto Conchal** *(tel 2654-3067, reservacon chal.com),* a forest reserve with trails.

From **Huacas,** 4 miles (6.4 km) south of Brasilito, a dirt road leads west via **Matapalo** to **Playa Real,** a secluded gem of a beach hidden within the cusp of headlands. You can wade in tidal pools, and a rugged islet attached to the shore by a short isthmus provides a nesting site for pelicans that perch on rustic fishing boats that bob in the bay. ■

Parque Nacional Marino Las Baulas

This marine national park encompasses a stunning long beach white as flaming magnesium and known as the nation's preeminent nesting site for leatherback turtles. Waves pound ashore all year, drawing the surfing cognoscenti.

Parque Nacional Marino Las Baulas protects 1,100 acres (445 ha) of Pacific shoreline and an additional 54,000 acres (21,850 ha) out to sea, safeguarding environments vital to the endangered leatherback turtle, whose females lay their eggs on **Playa Grande.** The females come ashore to lay during the cool nights, October through April. They prefer a full moon—a boon to tourists who can watch the awe-inspiring spectacle under the scrutiny of local guides. This magnificent white beach unfurls along the north shore of **Bahía Tamarindo** and suits the leatherback's need for a deep-water approach that minimizes the distance it has to crawl to nest.

The park's creation in 1990 is seen as a victory over commercial egg poachers, including members of the local community who today derive their livelihood from eco-tourism and protecting the turtles.

Evening shadows shroud the white beaches of Playa Grande.

Although visitation is regulated., developers have nonetheless been permitted to erect hotels abutting the beach, boosting the numbers of trampling feet.. The government is considering downgrading the park to permit further development projects to be built.

Dry forest and mangroves behind the beach are laced by trails good for spotting birds, crocodiles, and monkeys. ■

Parque Nacional Marino Las Baulas

- Map p. 130
- 5 miles (8 km) W of Huacas & 35 miles (56.3 km) W of Liberia
- 2653-0470
- Turtle watching Oct.–April
- $

actempisque.org

Leatherback Turtles

The world's largest reptile traces its lineage back to the antediluvian dawn. Males can grow to 10 feet (3 m) in length and weigh 2,000 pounds (900 kg)—yet their brains weigh less than an ounce (28 g)! The leatherback has an internal skeleton and a leathery exterior of thick, cartilaginous skin, and is insulated from extreme cold by a thick layer of fat. This turtle is powered by huge flippers and tapered for streamlined motion. It can dive to 4,000 feet (1,220 m) in pursuit of jellyfish—its favorite food.

Marine Turtles

Seven species of fast, graceful marine turtles *(Chelonidae)* roam the world's oceans, from the diminutive Ridley, which rarely grows to more than 30 inches (75 cm) long, to the Cadillac-size leatherback. The turtle, which boasts a remarkable physiology that includes an external skeleton and a toothless jaw that acts like a paper cutter, dates back 200 million years, proving an incredible ability to adapt and endure.

An olive Ridley turtle hauls back to sea after nesting at Playa Ostional.

Turtle populations are endangered worldwide, and several species are nearly extinct. After the discovery of the New World, turtle meat became a staple of seamen cruising these waters. Turtles also were harvested to indulge Europe's taste for turtle soup. In Costa Rica, the green turtle population has been reduced to only three remaining major nesting sites.

Turtle populations continue to face domestic pressures, although all of the nation's major nesting sites are now protected. Raw eggs, valued for their reputed aphrodisiac properties, are imbibed in local cantinas, and nest poaching still goes on despite laws against it. Natural predators also snatch up hatchlings as they flail their way to the sea. Adult turtles face capture in shrimpers' nets or by commercial pirates. And turtles nest on the same beaches beloved by developers.

Nature's Miracle

Adults navigate vast distances, often crossing oceans, on foraging forays. Males spend their entire lives—up to half a century—at sea; only females return to land. Each female returns to shore every two or three years during high tide, usually by night, and often under the full moon to ease her climb up the beach.

After finding a spot above the high-tide mark, she uses her front flippers to scoop a hollow and digs a pit with her back flippers. In this she lays an average of 107 spherical, golf-ball-size eggs. "There is a great deal of biology packed into that figure," said turtle expert Dr. Archie Carr (1909–1987). "The whole race and destiny of the creature are probably balanced at the edge of limbo by the delicate weight of that magic number." Any fewer and predators prevail and the species wanes.

Once the first egg drops, the turtle will proceed with egg laying oblivious to any intrusion. After shoveling the sand back into place and thumping it down with her body, she flings sand about to hide her nest, then heads back to sea. If no longer producing eggs, she swims off. If the turtle is still receptive, she will remain near shore where the males take turns mounting her. Females often nest several times in one season.

Whither the Youth?

After incubating in the warm sand for around seven weeks, the eggs hatch. Hatchlings are usually the same gender in each nest, due to the temperature of the sand (cooler for males), with 2 to 3°F (1°C) making the difference. They emerge from their eggs together, dig their way up to the surface, and wait until night to make their mad dash to the sea.

Baby turtles are programmed to head for the ocean horizon and are easily disoriented by other lights. Hotel guests who leave their lights on often find baby turtles at their door. Once at sea, hatchlings paddle maniacally for several days. Then they are rarely seen until some come back as big as a chest of drawers. Recent genetic evidence bears out the long-held belief that turtles return to their natal beaches. How they accomplish this navigational feat is unclear.

Turtle Viewing

Five species of turtles lay their eggs on Costa Rica's beaches and can be seen nesting at any time of year. Leatherback turtles (see sidebar p. 141) come ashore from October through April at Playa Grande in Nicoya and at Refugio Nacional de Vida Silvestre Gandoca-Manzanillo on the southern Caribbean shores. Green turtles can be seen at Gandoca-Manzanillo and Parque Nacional Tortuguero, where as many as 35,000 turtles come ashore between June and November. The most awe-inspiring site is the *arribada* (see p. 144), or mass nesting, of olive Ridley turtles occurring principally at Playa Ostional and Playa Nancite (*off-limits*) in Nicoya, where tens of thousands of turtles swarm ashore during full moons between July and December. Hawksbill turtles nest singly and in far smaller numbers at select beaches throughout the nation, and loggerheads are found on the Caribbean shore.

Leatherback
74 inches
(188 cm)

Olive Ridley
30 inches (76 cm)

Green
49 inches (124 cm)

Loggerhead
47 inches (119 cm)

Hawksbill
35 inches
(89 cm)

EXPERIENCE: Saving the Turtles

Marine turtles have lived in the oceans for more than 100 million years. Today, the world's six marine turtle species are endangered. Tens of thousands of turtles are killed every year by fishing gear and ocean pollution. Others are illegally killed for food or commercial reasons, while poaching of eggs, destruction of nesting sites, and climate change are among a panoply of actions that threaten to reduce the populations beyond the point of no return. The turtles' future existence could depend on human efforts to safeguard their precious nesting sites.

Newly hatched leatherback turtles strike out for the sea.

Costa Rica is a world-leader in efforts to protect marine turtles. As part of a plan designed to help save the Ridley, for example, the residents of Ostional hold a unique license to harvest the turtles' eggs and sell them. Because so many turtles pack the beach during the *arribada* (or egg-laying) season, eggs laid on the first few nights are often destroyed by turtles on subsequent nights. At the same time, incubating eggs are often dug up and destroyed when another arribada occurs before the first batch has hatched. By allowing local residents to legally harvest a quota of eggs—those that would likely be destroyed anyway—during the first 36 hours of each arribada, bacterial infections have been reduced and significantly more eggs are hatching.

Similarly striving to help save marine turtles, several conservation organizations run programs in Costa Rica that are always seeking volunteers.

Sea Turtle Conservancy: The largest and oldest of the entities active in Costa Rica, the Conservancy focuses its efforts at Tortuguero, one of the world's oldest and largest green turtle nesting sites. Volunteers are needed to assist with turtle tagging and monitoring. (4424 NW 13th St., Ste. B-11, Gainesville, FL 32609, tel 2297-6576 or 352/373-6441, conserveturtles.org)

Earthwatch: Working at the stunning beaches of Playa Grande (see p. 141), Costa Rica's principal leatherback nesting site, volunteers count eggs; protect hatchlings; monitor, measure, and tag nesting turtles; and perhaps even help attach transmitters to adults to monitor their migration. (114 Western Ave., Boston, MA 02134, tel 978/461-0081 or 800/776-0188, earthwatch.org)

La Tortuga Feliz: This organization focuses its marine conservation efforts along the Caribbean coast between the mouth of the Río Parismina and Tortuguero. You'll patrol beaches to keep poachers away, collect research data, and give a helping nudge to newborn hatchlings flailing to reach the sea. The zone is a major leatherback nesting site, but volunteers also work to save green turtles. (latortugafeliz.com.)

Tamarindo

This once sleepy fishing village has been catapulted from obscurity to become Costa Rica's most sophisticated and popular beach resort, offering a base for exploring Parque Nacional Marino Las Baulas and the wildlife-rich ecosystems adjoining it.

Tamarindo looks west over a deep bay and the long silver sweep of Playa Grande, which is separated from the village by the Río Matapalo unfurling majestically to the northeast. The beach is lackluster, though tide pools offer interest at low tide. **Isla Capitán** beckons a short distance offshore, and pelicans perch on fishing boats at anchor.

Surfers come here for the waves. Several local tour operators run surf trips to more remote spots, including the unspoiled **Playa Langosta.** Sportfishing and scuba diving trips are also available.

Surfers in search of the perfect wave

Arenas Adventures *(tel 2653-0108, aa.arenascr.com)* offers ATV and other adventures. And party and sunset cruises are popular.

Tamarindo adjoins the **Refugio Nacional de Vida Silvestre Tamarindo,** protecting 1,000 acres (400 ha) of mangrove-riddled wetlands and dry forests at the estuary of the Río Matapalo, which extends inland from Parque Nacional Marino Las Baulas, of which the reserve forms a part. Crocodiles lurk in the brackish waters. Monkeys can sometimes be seen cavorting on the edge of Playa Grande. And ocelots, deer, and several other endangered species have reappeared in recent years. You can rent canoes or take organized boat excursions.

Tamarindo's growing popularity has spawned chic cafés and upscale hotels under the aegis of European and North American proprietors. ∎

Watch Out!

Try to avoid becoming one of the many victims of scams and petty crimes:
- Keep your credit card in sight during transactions, and make sure the imprints are destroyed.
- If you get a flat tire, be wary of "good Samaritans" offering to help but who may try to rob you.
- Never accept unsolicited help with your luggage, as you may never see it again.
- Watch merchants when you pay with a large bill. They may switch it with a counterfeit and try to unload the bogus bill back on you, claiming it's a fake.

Refugio Nacional de Vida Silvestre Tamarindo

- 🅰 Map p. 130
- ✉ Tamarindo
- ☎ 2296-7074
- 🕐 Call for details
- 💲 $$

Refugio Nacional de Vida Silvestre Ostional

Around Ostional there are almost always turtles in the water, particularly during the July to December nesting season, when battalions of helmeted Ridley turtles storm ashore in an astonishing example of synchronized reproduction.

Refugio Nacional de Vida Silvestre Ostional

🅰 Map p. 130

✉ 3 miles (5 km) W of Nosara

☎ 2682-0400

💲 $$$

This 613-acre (248 ha) reserve protects three critical nesting sites for olive Ridley turtles—Playa Ostional, Playa Nosara, and Playa Guiones—extending along 9 miles (15 km) of shoreline between **Punta India** and **Punta Guiones.** The refuge centers on

the coastal hamlet of **Ostional** midway down a gray-sand beach that is one of the world's most important turtle hatcheries. The Ridley, known as the *lora,* has hit on a clever idea to ensure its survival: an occurrence known locally as an *arribada.* Playa Ostional is one of two principal arribada sites in Costa Rica.

During full-moon periods, tens of thousands of turtles congregate offshore, then surge ashore like armored battalions. Each arribada can occupy an entire week as wave after wave of turtles come ashore: often as many as 150,000! Stragglers come ashore at other times of year, as do leatherbacks between October and January.

All beach-going visitors must report to the **ranger station** *(tel 2682-0400)* in the village center. Guides from the Asociación de Guias Locales *(tel 2682-0428, $$)* are compulsory for visits, and a video is shown prior to stepping onto the beach.

Southward Playa Ostional melds into **Playa Nosara,** which had its first arribada in 1997. The recovery of the turtle population at Playa Ostional has been such a success that overpopulation has resulted in spillover onto adjacent beaches. The beaches are backed by steep forest-clad hills that are good for hiking. The **Río Montaña** and

The refuge encompasses several beautiful beaches.

EXPERIENCE: Learn Yoga in Costa Rica

Seeking to balance mind, body, and spirit in an environment of natural beauty and tranquility? Costa Rica has evolved as one of the world's premier destinations for yoga vacations. Barely a year goes by without a half dozen new venues being added to the roster. A handful are dedicated yoga facilities. Others range from wilderness lodges or deluxe beachfront hotels with yoga dojos where you can harmonize the rhythms of your inner self to those of Mother Nature. Here are a few key venues.

Luna Lodge *(tel 4070-0010, lunalodge.com)*, within minutes of Parque Nacional Corcovado on the Osa Peninsula, has an open-air dojo overhanging the rain forest hillside with a view of the Pacific Ocean. Week-long yoga retreats are offered by nonresident masters. Programs in tai chi and tantric intimacy are also given. Wildlife abounds on the property. Sleep in a bungalow or the lodge.

Nosara Yoga Institute *(tel 2682-0071, nosarayoga .com)* in Nicoya, run by renowned yoga masters Amba and Don Stapleton, is the largest and most respected of Costa Rica's dedicated yoga facilities. Surrounded by rain forest in the hills above the Nosara beaches, it's a magnificent venue that specializes in advanced techniques geared to training for yoga professionals.

Río Chirripó Yoga Retreat *(tel 2742-5109, riochirripo .com)*, in the Chirripó Valley (see p. 196), is a lovely mountainside eco-resort specializing in yoga. It offers daily classes, ongoing week-long retreats, and training for yoga professionals. The restaurant serves gourmet, health-conscious cuisine, and the resort is a great base for hiking Cerro Chirripó (see pp. 194–195).

Río Nosara tumble down from the hills and snake across the coastal plain, forming a tangled estuary of mangroves and forests full of play-acting monkeys, coatis, iguanas, and more than 190 species of birds, including parrots. You can take boat trips locally.

Nosara

The Río Nosara is hemmed by a craggy headland, **Punta Nosara,** in whose lee a cove with a blowhole and cave full of bats lies cupped by **Punta Pelada.** Punta Pelada offers stupendous views over **Playa Guiones,** a wide coral-colored beach arcing 2 miles (3.2 km) south. Tidal pools tempt you to wade the knee-deep shallows, and rollers crash ashore, luring the many surfers.

Behind Playa Guiones is Beaches of Nosara, a residential area for North Americans and Europeans. A few cafés and small hotels, plus the **Nosara Yoga Institute** (see sidebar this page), nestle amid the foliage, connected by a maze of dirt roads. Howler monkeys are often seen by the beach. Crocodiles, monkeys, and a wealth of other creatures are easily seen in **Reserva Biológica Nosara** *(tel 2682-0035, lagarta.com)*, at the river estuary. Tours by reservation are offered at **Sibu Sanctuary** *(tel 8413-8889, sibusanctuary.org)*, which takes in injured and orphaned animals.

An airstrip is located in the middle of the main village, **Bocas de Nosara,** a hamlet redolent of campesino life, 3 miles (5 km) inland of Playa Guiones. ∎

Sámara to Malpaís by 4WD

There is no shortage of adventure in Costa Rica, where one of the best to be had is this 57-mile (91 km) drive along the rugged southwestern shore of Nicoya. You will need a sturdy four-wheel-drive vehicle and an Indiana Jones spirit to tackle the rough dirt track that turns travel into a minor expedition, especially in the wet season when fording swollen rivers (see sidebar p. 151) can add to the adrenaline rush.

This rutted dirt road clambers over mountainous headlands and down to hidden beaches passing forlorn fishing villages and farming communities separated by long stretches of jungle green shoreline. There are no road signs, and the roads have many deceptive forks in them. Fill up before setting off: There are no gas stations. Don't attempt this drive late in the day.

Begin your journey in **Sámara ❶**, reached from Nicoya township via Highway 150, a well-paved road. This offbeat funky fishing hamlet and resort is popular with budget-conscious European travelers and young Ticos. It has gained a few upscale touches of late but nonetheless retains its slightly raffish, impecunious charm, assisted by vultures hopping about the sand-blown streets. Sámara is set in a deep basin and faces a handsome horseshoe bay where pelicans dive for fish and surf rolls in, bringing the surfing crowd to town.

Immediately south of town, the dirt road narrows and begins to dip and rise before spilling you onto **Playa Carrillo ❷**, a sliver of white sand with an eponymous fishing hamlet—a base for sportfishing sorties—tucked into the cove at the southern end of the beach. Additional beaches lie hidden along the shore as the road—now dirt—runs inland, parallel to the coast, deteriorating all the while. Ridley turtles nest all along the jungle shore, including at **Playa Islita ❸**, beyond which the track begins a stiff climb that would challenge a goat. The hilltop **Hotel Punta Islita** (see Travelwise p. 249) makes a perfect break point thanks to the magnificent vistas to be enjoyed from the bar and excellent restaurant. The hotel hosts **The Ara Project** (tel 8389-5811,

theáraproject.org), a macaw breeding center open to visits.

You then spiral down to the hamlet of **Islita ❹**—with trees and public structures that make up the **Museo de Arte Contemporáneo al Aire Libre**—and ascend again over **Punta Barranquilla**, with the narrow dirt road clinging magically to the mountainside. The road disgorges you at **Playa Corazalito ❺**. Farther south come **Playa Bejuco ❻** and **Playa Coyote ❼**, both good for turtle spotting, with the road running inland parallel to a shore backed by thick wetland swamp teeming with wildlife. Along this itinerary you will also pass the hamlet of **Pueblo Nuevo** and inland of **Playa San Miguel,** en route to the crossroads of **San Francisco de Coyote ❽**, where the going begins to get tricky. Unpaved Highway 162 links San Francisco to Highway 21 and continues southwest along the **Río Jabillo,** which you must ford. The road is subject to flooding. The river winds through mangroves that form a haven for egrets, snakes, turtles, and other wildlife. Don't be surprised to see a crocodile padding across the road. Locals with tractors are usually on hand to assist drivers who misjudge their fordings.

After twisting for 4 miles (6.4 km), the road makes a sharp left beside **Cantina El Bongo** ❾ and leads inland to the hamlet of **Río Frío** ❿, reached via a bridge over the **Río Bongo**; the hamlet is signed. Continue straight through the hamlet and turn left at the T-junction. Continue downhill to the Río Bongo, which after a downpour, the mud can be deep. The surf that pounds the beaches that line the jungle green shore draws surfers. Rustic hotels and surf camps announce your arrival in the offbeat surfers' resort of **Malpaís** ⓬, where you can pick up the paved road that links to Highway 160.

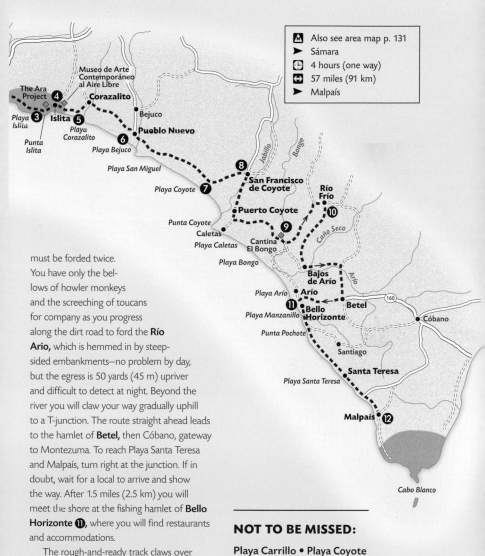

must be forded twice. You have only the bellows of howler monkeys and the screeching of toucans for company as you progress along the dirt road to ford the **Río Ario,** which is hemmed in by steep-sided embankments—no problem by day, but the egress is 50 yards (45 m) upriver and difficult to detect at night. Beyond the river you will claw your way gradually uphill to a T-junction. The route straight ahead leads to the hamlet of **Betel,** then Cóbano, gateway to Montezuma. To reach Playa Santa Teresa and Malpaís, turn right at the junction. If in doubt, wait for a local to arrive and show the way. After 1.5 miles (2.5 km) you will meet the shore at the fishing hamlet of **Bello Horizonte** ⓫, where you will find restaurants and accommodations.

The rough-and-ready track claws over **Punta Pochote** and follows surf-washed **Playa Santa Teresa.** In the wet season, or

NOT TO BE MISSED:

Playa Carrillo • Playa Coyote • Playa Bongo

The Eastern Shore

Nicoya's serrated eastern shore runs southwest like a great saw, deeply indented with swampy coves and beach-lined bays in the lee of sheer cliffs. Tropical dry deciduous forest merges into moister jungle replete with wildlife, protected in several prime retreats including Costa Rica's most exquisite island.

Rocky outcrops and tidal pools give Playa Montezuma a distinctive rugged coastal terrain.

Refugio Nacional de Vida Silvestre Curú

🗺 Map p. 131

✉ Hwy. 160, 2 miles (3.2 km) S of Paquera

☎ 2641-0590

💲 $$

curuwildliferefuge .com

From **Paquera,** Highway 160 writhes over rugged headlands. The road is mostly unpaved and badly deteriorated, but grand coastal vistas make amends for this. The largest indentation is **Bahía Ballena,** named for the whales that sometimes visit the bay. Travelers can choose from several resort hotels around **Tambor,** a small fishing village. Caimans and waterfowl are among the wildlife to be seen in the mangrove swamps to the northeast at the estuary of the **Río Pánica.** The **Tango Mar** hotel, 3 miles (4.8 km) south of Tambor (see Travelwise p. 249), offers a nine-hole golf course and sits over its own splendid beach.

Highway 160 runs to **Cóbano,** a crossroads gateway to Malpaís (see p. 149) and to Reserva Natural Absoluta Cabo Blanco (see p. 152). The latter is reached via **Montezuma,** a quintessential laid-back retreat with coral-colored beaches featuring rocky outcrops and tidal pools. The village has a reputation for attracting New Age types with its inexpensive accommodations and health-food cafés; a local citizens' association tends it conscientiously. You can cool off in the waterfalls that cascade down from the forest-clad hills where monkeys cavort in open view.

The dusty coast road continues west to the hamlet of **Cabuya,** which provides access to Cabo

Blanco. At low tide you can cross the causeway to **Isla Muertos** ("Isle of the Dead"), which has served as a cemetery since pre-Columbian times.

Between Cóbano and Montezuma, the **Montezuma Canopy Tour** (tel 2642-0808, montezumatraveladventures.com) lets you whiz through treetops that are full of various wildlife species.

Refugio Nacional de Vida Silvestre Curú

Tucked within the shore of Golfo Curú, this 208-acre (84 ha) jewel forms the nucleus of a 3,000-acre (1,214 ha) private cattle hacienda. Two-thirds of the ranch is smothered in primary forest that extends along 3 miles (5 km) of shore and into the hills behind. Its Lilliputian scale notwithstanding, Curú's habitats range from mangrove swamps along the banks of the Río Curú to deciduous forest atop the hills. You can expect to see caimans and howler and capuchin monkeys. Agoutis, ocelots, pumas, sloths, endangered spider monkeys, and white-tailed deer are also present, along with more than 150 species of birds. Both hawksbill and olive Ridley turtles lay eggs at **Playa Curú, Playa Colorado,** and **Playa Quesara.** A boggy trail leads to a spider monkey enclosure.

Isla Tortuga

This emerald jewel in a sea of aquamarine 2 miles (3.2 km) offshore of Curú is everything you hope a tropical isle will be—white-rimmed, shaded by palms, lapped by waves washing lazily onto the beach. Tortuga's 770 acres (312 ha) of forested hills rise steeply from the shore.

This idyll draws day-trippers on cruise tours from Puntarenas, who come to snorkel, tour in glass-bottom boats, and paddle kayaks and water bicycles. Others flock here simply to laze about in a

---

EXPERIENCE: Fording Rivers the Right Way

Fording unbridged rivers is part of the fun of off-road driving in Costa Rica. The dry season normally poses few problems; the wet season, however, requires more caution, as rivers swell and may be impassable.

Before attempting to cross, assess the current and riverbed. Scout on foot for deep channels that may be hidden in murky water. If it's too deep to wade, it's too deep to drive. And don't forget to calculate the height of your doorsills to avoid a flooded compartment. Open your windows and door locks beforehand (in case the engine stalls). Enter the river slowly. Rushing in will create a wave that washes over the hood. You don't want to swamp the engine and stall and risk getting washed downriver. Stay in low gear and keep a heavy foot on the accelerator. Sometimes the best route isn't always a straight line across. If the river looks dangerous to cross, it probably is.

---

hammock and soak up the sun with a *coco loco* (rum, coconut milk, and coconut liqueur served in a husk) in hand. **Calypso Cruises** (see Travelwise p. 262) was the company that pioneered the cruises and they still lead the way, whisking guests from Puntarenas aboard a state-of-the-art catamaran, *Manta Ray.* It is best to avoid the weekend crowds. ∎

Reserva Natural Absoluta Cabo Blanco

Dangling off the tip of the Nicoya Peninsula, this 2,896-acre (1,172 ha) reserve lies at the boundary between tropical dry and tropical wet ecosystems and is known for its rich biodiversity, including Pacific tropical lowland forest unique to southwest Nicoya. For hardy hikers (with a trail guide and plenty of water) the rewards are enriching.

Sloths inhabit the transitional forest of Cabo.

Reserva Natural Absoluta Cabo Blanco

- 🅰 Map p. 131
- ✉ 10 miles (16 km) SW of Cóbano
- ☎ 2642-0093
- 🕐 Closed Mon. & Tues.
- 💲 $$

actempisque.org

The reserve wraps around the southwestern shores of Nicoya, protecting precious mountain forests. In 1963, Costa Rica's national park system was born here—the culmination of the remarkable dedication shown by Olof Wessberg, a Swedish immigrant who arrived to find the lush wilderness under siege. Ultimately, this ceaseless campaigner paid with his life—he was murdered in 1975—for the wilderness he managed to save. A plaque at the **ranger station** at the end of the road 5 miles (8 km) west of Montezuma commemorates his work. From here a trail leads into the park.

Sendero Sueco is a stiff climb over steep ridges before dropping down to lonesome **Playa Balsita** and **Playa Cabo Blanco,** separated by a great headland. The crushed-diamond beaches have tidal pools good for spotting sea urchins and starfish. From Balsita, **Sendero El Barco** follows the coast west before climbing inland and looping north. Don't try walking the shoreline trail except at low tide—you might get cut off! Rising out of the ocean about a mile (1.6 km) offshore is **Isla Cabo Blanco,** strung like a pearl off the southern tip. It gains its white hue from guano deposited by a large colony of brown boobies and other seabirds.

The park was initially off-limits, but visitors have been permitted entry since 1989; the trail system remains limited, however, making most of the park inaccessible. Species you might spot include anteaters, coatis, sloths, and boa constrictors and other snakes, plus howler, capuchin, and spider monkeys. Tepezcuintles or agoutis might run across your path, chased by an ocelot or puma (if you're lucky). Peccaries are also abundant and not to be trifled with. Sulfur-winged parakeets chatter in treetops that soar to 150 feet (45 m), and crested caracaras, elegant trogons, and herons are among the scores of other rainbow-hued birds.

Be aware that the park is now under threat from too many visitors, and wildlife species have increasingly retreated to the park interior, bringing calls for renewed restrictions. ∎

A coastal strip of surf-pounded shore walled by jungle-clad mountains, offering adventure, fantastic wildlife, and splendid accommodations

Central Pacific

Cataratas Nauyuca, the waterfalls near Dominical

Central Pacific

It is not hard to see why the Central Pacific region has become one of the country's most visited areas, attracting travelers seeking a medley of treats from easygoing immersions in nature to wild white-water rides on mountain rivers.

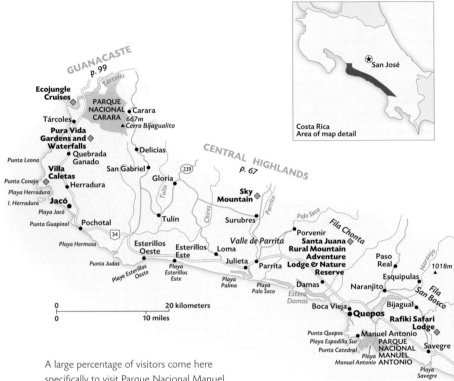

A large percentage of visitors come here specifically to visit Parque Nacional Manuel Antonio, a shining star in the park system, within walking distance of more than 60 fine hotels. Backed by kelly green mountains, the surf-washed beaches offer something for everyone, whether they are surfers in search of the ultimate wave or sybarites seeking a poolside retreat at Playa Jacó, Costa Rica's party-hearty resort town that is the yang to Manuel Antonio's yin.

Everything happens down on the coastal plain. To the north, rugged spurs of the Talamancas curl around the plain and crash to the coast, dramatically marking the transition from dry to wet life zones. South of Jacó the mountains recede and the plains open out,

dominated by cattle farms and, farther south, row upon row of sturdy palms grown for palm oil and centered on the town of Parrita. Still farther south, the plain is crimped by a range of coastal mountains—the Fila Costeña—that seem to rise straight up from the sea.

A single highway—Highway 34—runs parallel to the coast, with peekaboo views of the blue Pacific. Follow the posted speed limits; police prey on visitors. Between Parrita and Dominical forges a path through a string of tidy little villages set amid a sea of African date palm plantations. It was as late as 1996 before the highway pushed beyond Punta

Uvita, providing a link with Golfo Dulce and the Inter-American Highway via the rugged rain forest of the Brunca Coast. In 2010, Highway 34 was finally widened and paved to become the new Inter-American Highway.

Lonesome gray-sand beaches stretch for miles in a long daisy chain, one after the other, separated by rugged headlands. Many beaches are hidden from the main highway by thick stands of forest. The wide-open coastline receives waves head-on and offers fantastic surfing, though swimming is dangerous everywhere due to strong riptides.

Several beaches, including Playa Herradura, have long been popular weekend destinations for Josefinos. Today this once languid hamlet is the setting of a golf course and the nation's largest marina. Nearby Jacó has traditionally served a budget-minded Canadian market, plus surfers drawn to the endless swells. The resort has gained a modicum of sophistication in recent years, as has Quepos, a sportfishing center that now boasts a lively restaurant and night scene. A recently completed mega-marina has added new luster.

The forested mountains are popular for both hiking and horseback riding—activities offered at mountain retreats such as Escaleras and the Santa Juana Rural Mountain Adventure Lodge & Nature Reserve. The rivers that tumble out of the mountains provide enthralling white-water rafting. Below, the rivers meander lugubriously through swathes of mangroves and riparian forest that provide vital habitats for a Noah's Ark of wildlife. Crocodiles are numerous, notably in the estuary of the Río Tárcoles. And Parque Nacional Carara and Parque Nacional Manuel Antonio offer even the least intrepid souls the opportunity of coming face-to-face with wildlife. Manuel Antonio has a coral reef and picturesque beaches. ■

NOT TO BE MISSED:

A crocodile safari on the Río Tárcoles   157

The cliff-top ocean views from the restaurants at Villa Caletas   158

Sportfishing from Quepos   160

Snorkeling at Parque Nacional Manuel Antonio   162–163

Surfing at Dominical   166

Canopy tours at Refugio Nacional de Vida Silvestre Hacienda Barú   167

p. 189

ZONA SUR
p. 171

Parque Nacional Carara & Río Tárcoles

Though small, Carara—a Huetar Native American name meaning "crocodile"—is astoundingly rich. This seminally important national park lies at the meeting point of the dry and wet climatic zones, marking the shift from predominantly Mesoamerican to Amazonian influences.

The bridge over the Río Tárcoles offers a bird's-eye view of crocodiles.

Parque Nacional Carara
- 🄰 Map p. 154
- ✉ Hwy. 34, 14 miles (22.5 km) S of Orotina
- ☎ 2637-1080 or 2637-1054
- 🅢 $$

Carara protects the last major stand of transitional forest on the isthmus; representative species from both ecosystems abound within its 11,613 acres (4,700 ha). A broad river flows to a sweeping mangrove and wetland system teeming with birdlife.

Parque Nacional Carara

A one-hour drive from San José, Carara shrouds the westernmost foothills of the Talamancas.

The profusion of tree species belies Carara's scale. Hardwoods soar over the evergreen forests that cloak **Cerro Bijagualito** (2,188 feet/ 667 m). Access is via a mile-long (1.6 km) loop trail—**Sendero Las Araceas**—from the **Quebrada Bonita Ranger Station** beside Highway 34, 2 miles (3.2 km)

south of the **Río Tárcoles,** which forms the reserve's northern boundary. Just south of the bridge over the Río Tárcoles, a second trail—**Sendero Sura**—follows the river inland for 3 miles (5 km). The terrain is fairly flat, making access easy for everyone, including via a new riverside wheelchair-friendly interpretive trail.

You are almost assured of seeing capuchin monkeys. Endangered spider monkeys are also present, plus howler monkeys, coatis, great anteaters, ocelots, peccaries, and, in moister sections, poison dart frogs hopping on the forest floor. Birding is especially rewarding: The riverbanks are good places to spot kingfishers, parrots abound, and toucans are everywhere, as are their cousins the fiery-billed aracari. The most colorful denizen, and reason enough to visit, is the endangered scarlet macaw. At least 100 pairs breed in Carara, where their nests are guarded against poachers. Time your arrival for dawn or dusk and you can see the flock migrating between Carara's tropical wet forest interior and the mangrove forest at the mouth of the Río Tárcoles, where they roost.

To minimize human impact, visits are limited to 60 people at a time, to a small lowland section of the park. Numerous archaeological sites have been excavated,

What a Croc

Despite their rather fearsome reputation, crocodiles are good parents. Female crocs build nests of compost above the high-water mark, in which they lay 30 to 70 eggs. They tend their nests assiduously; then, when they hear the first squeaks of hatchlings, they carefully dig open the nests and take the little ones into their mouths to carry them to the water. The male croc helps guard the nursery.

INSIDER TIP:

If you encounter a band of monkeys moving through the treetops, stay still and silent after they've passed. All manner of exotic mammals may emerge to forage on fruits the monkeys drop.

—CHRISTOPHER P. BAKER
National Geographic author

though none are open to visitors. Insects abound, so bring repellent. Carara's weather is seasonal: March and April are the driest months. Guides can be hired through the **Asociación de Guías del Pacifico Central** *(tel 8723-3008).*

Río Tárcoles

Highway 34 crosses the **Río Tárcoles,** where crocodiles are almost always present, basking motionless as logs on the banks.

You have a grandstand view from the bridge on the main highway. Close-up views of these monsters can be arranged through **Ecojungle Cruises** *(tel 2582-0181, ecojunglecruises.com),* at miles-long gray-sand Playa Guacalillo, on the northern side of the river estuary. Unlike other tour operators, this more responsible company does not feed the crocodiles, dozens of which gather near the mangrove-lined rivermouth.

The estuarine mangroves also form one of the richest repositories of avian fauna in Central America. More than 400 species have been recorded—an astonishing number that includes roseate spoonbills, a significant breeding population of scarlet macaws, and boat-billed herons, named for their broad keel-shaped beaks. Near Bijagual, in the coastal mountains inland of Tárcoles, **Pura Vida Gardens and Waterfalls** *(tel 2645-1001, puravidagarden.com, $$$)* is ablaze with tropical blossoms enjoyed along well-groomed trails. ∎

Jacó

The nation's most popular resort has been drawing visitors for more than two decades. Though its own appeal seems limited, its proximity to San José assures a regular local clientele. Jacó also remains steadfastly popular with Canadian charter tourists—so much so, in fact, that the maple-leaf flag flutters above the town.

Jacó, the most popular and developed of Costa Rica's resorts

Rainforest Adventures

✉ 2.5 miles (4 km) E of Jacó

☎ 2257-5961

💲 $$$$$

rainforest adventure.com

Jacó, 9 miles (15 km) south of Parque Nacional Carara, remains Costa Rica's most developed retreat. Hotels, restaurants, surf shops, and travel services line the sole drag, which runs parallel to Highway 34. Jacó's unpretentious character appeals to party-loving Josefinos and to the young, carefree surf crowd who lend the town an irrepressibly offbeat edge. It is gaining sophistication, however, helped by the deluxe **Los Sueños Resort & Marina** (*tel 2630-4000, lossuenos.com /marina; see Travelwise p. 252*), north of town at Playa Herradura, incorporating a mega-marina, and by **Villa Caletas** (*tel 2630-3000, hotelvillacaletas.com*), a stunning cliff-top resort hotel featuring fine dining and classical concerts. And the town hosts the **Jungle Jam** (*junglejam.com*) music festival each March.

Flanked by headlands, the palm-fringed beach of gray sand extends for 2 miles (3.2 km). Tidal pools beneath the headlands can be tempting, but beware of the strong riptides. Offshore, **Isla Herradura** is an important nesting site for seabirds. To view wildlife amid native forest, ride the **Rainforest Adventures Aerial Tram** into the coastal mountains, where it offers eye-level encounters with monkeys and other canopy dwellers. Or take to the hills in a saddle with **Discovery Horseback Tours** (*tel 8838-7550, horseridecostarica.com*) or **AXR Tours** (see Travelwise p. 263). ∎

Lonesome Beaches

The long, linear coast south of Jacó is a necklace of surf-pounded beaches that are divided by estuaries where silt-laden rivers snake through swamps and mangrove. These beaches offer a rare chance to play Robinson Crusoe, although the tourist industry has begun to stir.

South of Jacó, Highway 34 crests a steep headland—**Punta Guapinol**—where you have your first magnificent view of the beaches, beginning with **Playa Hermosa** rolling southward for 6 miles (9.6 km) like a ribbon of silver lamé, with tiny surfers like ants rolling in on the waves. Don't get too close

INSIDER TIP:

Walking the beaches at night with a flashlight can sometimes afford a glimpse of sea turtles that have come ashore to lay eggs.

—BEN HORTON
National Geographic field researcher

to the cliff edge, as it is unstable in places. An international surfing championship is held here annually. The beach has its share of modest accommodations catering to the laid-back surf crowd.

The central and southern parts of the beach are backed by a wetland area populated by stilt-legged waders, kingfishers, parrots, and other exotic species. The wetland forms part of **Refugio de Vida Silvestre Playa Hermosa y Punta Mala** *(tel 2643-1066)*, incorporating a turtle hatchery to protect the

four species of marine turtles that nest on these beaches.

Punta Judas separates Playa Hermosa from **Playa Esterillos Oeste, Playa Esterillos Central,** and **Playa Esterillos Este,** three ruler-straight beaches backed by palms and thick tropical forest, and kept clean by pounding surf. Playa Esterillos Oeste is intriguing for the fossils that can be seen in the rocks at the northern end of the beach. Horseback rides are offered at **Savegre Rancho Monterey** *(tel 6080-0501, ranchosavegre.com)*.

Farther south are the **Río Palma** and **Río Parrita,** which feed the vast wetland systems that back **Playa Palma** and **Playa Palo Seco.** ∎

Coconut palms line the shores of the Esterillos beaches.

Quepos

Quepos is known as a sportfishing center whose fortunes were boosted by Parque Nacional Manuel Antonio (see pp. 162–163), 4 miles (6.4 km) away. It is a service-and-entertainment center for the hotels that line the hilly road between the town and the park.

Smiling children play among boats docked for the night in the fishing village of Boca Vieja.

Quepos

🅰 Map p. 154

Visitor Information

✉ Edificio Copaza, Camino al Muelle

☎ 2777-4221

Quepos nestles at the foot of a bay 2 miles (3.2 km) southwest of Highway 34. In the 1930s, banana plantations were established here and Quepos became a key shipping port. Alas, banana blight swept through the hills in the 1950s, and the Standard Fruit Company switched its interest to African palms.

Today, Quepos's fortunes rest on tourism. Small hotels, hip restaurants, and nightclubs have proliferated. The town hosts a Carnival each February that attracts visitors. And the 196-slip **Pez Vela Marina** *(tel 2774-9000, marinapezvela.com),* which opened in 2010, hosts the colorful Festival del Agua, the

Pelagic Rockstar! Offshore Tournament, and the Quepos Billfish Cup sportfishing tournament.

The compact town center melds northward into the fishing village of **Boca Vieja;** its ramshackle wooden houses perch rather precariously on stilts over the mangrove-lined **Estero Boca Vieja.** More handsome clapboard homes hide in the hills south of town, where the Standard Fruit Company once had its residential compound. Do not swim off the gray-sand beach that fronts the town; the bay is polluted. Nearby is the **Río Naranjo,** which spills down the flanks of the **Fila San Bosco** mountains and is popular for white-water rafting excursions. Horseback rides are available at several nearby estates. And ATV tours, offered by **FourTrax Adventures** *(tel 8731-5284, fourtraxadventuretours.com)*, are a popular local activity. But by far the biggest activity is sportfishing—with marlin the main lure in the December to April peak season. Several outfitters berth their sportfishing vessels at Pez Vela Marina (see p. 160).

Greentique Wildlife Refuge & Butterfly Atrium, south of Quepos on the road to Manuel Antonio, provides an immersion in lepidopteran lore. This 30-acre (12 ha) "living laboratory of nature conservancy" features trails, netted flyways, and butterfly exhibits. The facility is operated by Hotel Si Como No, which also offers the **Santa Juana Rural Mountain Adventure Lodge & Nature Reserve** (see p. 170).

Damas Estuary

This vast wetland system extends northwest of Quepos for 12 miles (19 km). The **Río Palo Seco** and **Río Damas** wash large volumes of silt down from the mountains to make the estuary a Minotaur's maze of interconnected channels, some of which open into broad lagoons while others peter out in narrow cul-de-sacs.

Boat and sea-kayaking trips depart from **Damas wharf** for "mangrove safaris"; **Iguana Tours** *(tel 2777-2052, iguanatours.com)*, in Quepos, also offers tours. You are sure to see crocodiles, monkeys, and wading birds, and you might spot raccoons and their native cousins, coatis.

Isla Damas pins the main estuary and is good for walks. Its attractions consist of a small zoo and a floating restaurant. ∎

Greentique Wildlife Refuge & Butterfly Atrium

- ✉ 2.5 miles (4 km) S of Quepos
- ☎ 2777-0777
- 💲 $$$

sicomono.com/tours

EXPERIENCE: Dining & Cooking Like a Local

There's no shortage of impressive restaurants in Costa Rica serving international cuisines. The tourism industry has brought professionally trained chefs whose menus have little in common with native traditions, nor a particular attachment to Costa Rica. But you'll come to appreciate the country more, and save money, if you adopt local habits when dining.

Look for *bocas*, savory snacks served at most self-respecting bars. *Sodas* are small family-run roadside eateries. Distinctly no-frills, they serve simple local fare, including *casados*: inexpensive set meals served on one plate, consisting of a salad, a starch, and a main course. Casados have either beef, chicken, or fish with beans and rice or potatoes, plus vegetables, fried yucca, and salad.

Costa Rica Culinary Tours *(tel 510-473-5989, costaricaculinarytours.com)* owners Chef Gilad Chutner, a local food guru, and San Francisco culinary whiz Mike C show off the best of Tico tradition and contemporary flair in six itineraries, with visits to chocalatiers, craft brewers, organic farmers, and private pairing dinners. Venues include the Costa Rica Meadery & Ark Herb Farm (see p. 83), Finca

Rosa Blanca coffee plantation (see p. 81), and Sibú Chocolate (see p. 98). At Chimirol de Rivas, **Monte Azul** (see Travelwise p. 254) offers "Food & Nature" packages with classes in making local cheeses, tapas, and the chef's gourmet dishes. Guayabo Lodge *(Santa Cruz de Turrialba, tel 2538-8400, guayabolodge.co.cr)* offers a **Tropical Cooking School** for students and professionals.

Parque Nacional Manuel Antonio

Tucked into a rugged cranny midway down the Pacific coast, pocket-size Parque Nacional Manuel Antonio embodies many of the diverse attributes that visitors hope to see in Costa Rica. The popular park offers white-sand beaches, a coral reef, and rain forest teeming with wildlife that loves to put on a song and dance.

Parque Nacional Manuel Antonio, a peninsula of beaches, rain forests, and reefs

Parque Nacional Manuel Antonio

- Map p. 154
- 4 miles (6.4 km) S of Quepos
- 2777-2100
- Closed Mon.
- $$

manuelantonio park.com

The 1,685-acre (682 ha) park is set on a blunt-nosed peninsula backed by forested hills; it also includes the waters of the Pacific on three sides. The peninsula is in fact a tombolo: a slender, low-slung sand spit connecting two larger sections of land—in this case, a former island called **Punta Catedral,** which seems to hang on the map like a pearl. You can hike to its summit via a steep trail at the end of **Playa Espadilla Sur,** a quarter-mile (400 m) scimitar that forms the tombolo's west side, one of four white beaches in the park.

On the east side, the smaller **Playa Manuel Antonio** is the prettiest of the bunch, curling around its deep flask-shaped bay like a shepherd's crook. A small coral reef a short distance offshore is perfect for snorkeling; the water clarity is best during the dry season (Nov.–April). There are plenty of tidal pools, too, good for wading out into the crystal clear shallows to spot sea stars and crayfish. And Pacific green and olive Ridley turtles come ashore to lay eggs. Pre-Columbian Native Americans captured them; you can still see traps hollowed into the rocks and exposed at low tide. The turtles swam in at high tide and got caught in the scalloped basins when, exhausted after their exertions ashore, they tried to struggle back to sea with the receding tide.

The main park entrance is 600 yards (550 m) inland of Manuel Antonio hamlet. You can also wade across the mouth of the **Río Camaronera,** at the south end of Playa Espadilla; a boatman will ferry you across at high tide. Wide, well-maintained trails perfect for wildlife viewing lead into tropical forest. Sightings of certain species are virtually guaranteed by following the easy **Sendero Perezoso** (Sloth Trail). Cheeky capuchin monkeys chatter within arm's length in the trees that shade the beaches (best not to get too close; they can be aggressive). You can also see howler monkeys, iguanas, and sloths high up in the trees, while many a hiker sees a coati or crab-eating raccoon scamper across the path. Toucans and parrots are commonly seen.

A more adventurous hike along the **Sendero Mirador** (Mirador Trail) leads into the farther reaches of the forest, where with luck you might encounter spider monkeys; Manuel Antonio is home to a population of more than 350 of this endangered species. The steep trail, which is muddy in the wet season, leads to a mirador offering fabulous views over the park and out to sea.

The park has proved so popular in recent years that it has begun to feel the adverse effects of all those trampling feet. A daily quota of 600 persons seems not to be honored, and at peak hours Sendero Perezoso can seem as crowded as Grand Central Station.

The Road to Manuel Antonio

Manuel Antonio's umbilical cord is a narrow serpentine highway that connects it to Quepos, some 4 miles (6.4 km) to the north. The forest-fringed road clambers over a steep headland and wriggles along the ridgetop, offering teasing views best enjoyed from one of the scores of hotels and restaurants that command grandstand seats.

Zapped by Sap

Poisonous manchineel trees *(Hippomane mancinella),* colloquially called "beach apple" or *manzanillo,* shade the beaches of Manuel Antonio. Make sure to avoid sitting underneath them; the sap is caustic. The fruits are poisonous, and simply touching the bark causes severe skin irritation. If you are camping, do not burn the wood, which gives off a poisonous smoke.

A **Fairchild C-123 airplane,** formerly used by the CIA—now converted to a bar and restaurant—stands by the road on top of a hill that is midway between Quepos and Manuel Antonio.

Dirt trails lead down through the forests that cascade into carefully secreted coves. The road drops down to the bustling hamlet of Manuel Antonio, which clings to the edge of Playa Espadilla and then dead-ends at the national park entrance. ■

Sportfishing

The waters off Costa Rica have far more fish than fishhooks, making the country one place from which you can return home with tales of the one that didn't get away. The angling on the Pacific coast differs markedly from that on the Caribbean; in either case, however, feisty game fish are guaranteed to give anglers a rod-bending fight to remember.

The author with a hard-won catch of yellowfin tuna

Every season you can be sure that at least one International Game Fishing Association (IGFA) record will be broken in Costa Rica. The nation has held the world record for sailfish and marlin catches in international tournament history. It has also posted more "grand slam" records—all three species of marlin and one or more sailfish caught the same day—than anywhere else in the world.

More than a dozen dedicated sportfishing lodges cater to serious anglers with package programs. Most are operated by North Americans and follow a similar regimen, using top-rated boats and equipment plus skilled guides. Scores of smaller outfitters also offer half- and full-day sportfishing trips from beach resorts up and down the Pacific coast. Most operate a catch-and-release policy to ensure the continued health of the game fish population. Four people can expect to pay from $750 for half a day fishing and from $1,000 for a full day.

The Pacific

On the Pacific side, game fish run offshore year-round and snagging the big one comes really easy. In good years the big fish seem to be jostling for space and the Pacific Ocean seems to boil with marlin, tuna, and wahoo fighting to get a bite on your hook. Seasons vary, however. Sportfishing often slumps as a response to the climatic changes caused in El Niño years, when fish seem to disappear. Then they come back with a vengeance, with big marlin streaming through the Pacific waters like salmon following the urge to spawn.

The big draw is the blue marlin—the "bull of the ocean." They are present year-round, though the big run begins each year in May, with June and July being the prime months. Then, too, tuna school close to shore and the dorado begins to peak. In general, the fish move

INSIDER TIP:

Even if you aren't a sport-fisherman, it's well worth getting your snorkeling gear and having a boat take you off the coast to see spinner dolphins. They can school by the hundreds and give a great show with their aquatic acrobatics.

—BEN HORTON
National Geographic field researcher

seasonally, with summer months offering the best catches in the **Golfo de Papagayo,** while winter months are best in southern waters centered on the **Golfo Dulce. Tamarindo, Quepos,** and **Golfito,** respectively, are the main sportfishing centers. High winds during the winter in the Golfo de Papagayo make fishing dangerous, and many operators move their fleets south for the season.

The Caribbean & Lowlands

The Caribbean side is different, with offshore fishing limited. Here anglers cast their light-tackle lures in river estuaries, backwater lagoons, and wide rivers that extend inland from **Tortuguero** and **Barra del Colorado,** the two sportfishing centers. The fish of choice is tarpon, a tempestuous "silver bullet" that can weigh up to 150 pounds (68 kg). Unsurprisingly, Costa Rica is the world's premier site for tarpon, which puts up a fight like no other.

Large trophy-winning snook, a smaller yet aggressive adversary weighing up to 30 pounds (14 kg), can also wear you out. Costa Rica has held the all-tackle IGFA world record for this fish. They return from the Caribbean Sea to spawn in the calm river mouths from August to January, when anglers stand knee-deep in the estuaries, or in the surf where the best catches are reeled in. *Calba,* or smaller snook, also run in midwinter, providing good sport on lighter tackle. And in the ocean, large jacks and barracudas can be caught year-round. Both are voracious; barracuda is so rapacious that it will even go for a shoestring.

The granddaddy of the Caribbean rivers is the **Río Colorado,** fed by the Río San Juan, which can both be fished far inland from Tortuga Lodge (see Travelwise p. 256) in Tortuguero, a fistful of lodges at Barra del Colorado, or aboard dedicated sportfishing houseboats that offer three- to seven-day packages (see Travelwise p. 265). Inland, the waters of Lago Caño Negro also offer superb opportunities for tarpon and snook, while **Laguna de Arenal** is renowned for its *guapote* (rainbow bass).

The big draw of the Pacific coast is the blue marlin—the "bull of the ocean."

Dominical

Well on its way to becoming the Pacific coast capital of cool, Dominical is synonymous with surfers and a laid-back lifestyle. This former fishing village situated beside the estuary of the Río Barú also makes an excellent jumping-off point for hiking and horseback riding in the surrounding mountains.

Young surfers strum a tune at Playa Dominical.

Dominical

 Map p. 155

Dominical's barefoot, casual dress code appeals to vacationers seeking a refuge that shuns pretension. The college crowd joins middle-aged misfits with sun-bleached hair and ankle beads to make waves by day and party by night at colorful bars and cafés run by transplanted gringos.

The hamlet backs a 2-mile-long (3.2 km) gray-sand beach that runs south from the mouth of the **Río Barú,** along whose banks hundreds of roosting egrets gather at dusk. You can walk along the beach to the hamlet of **Dominicalito** beneath the rugged headland of

Punta Dominical. Surfers rave about Dominical's beach breaks, but the riptides are a danger to swimmers. Both whales and dolphins can sometimes be seen from the shore.

Between Quepos and the village of Dominical, a distance of some 30 miles (48 km), rugged ranges push up hard against the coast and the narrow Highway 34—the Costera Sur—is pinned between forested mountain and mangrove-lined shore. Though Highway 34 passes through long stretches of almost uninhabited forest, it still offers attractions for the adventurous, including surfing from the beautiful and usually almost deserted beaches at **Playa Guapil** and **Playa Matapalo.**

Inland, the mountains are renowned for waterfalls, notably **Cataratas Nauyaca** (tel 2787-0541, cataratasnauyaca.com), tumbling more than 200 feet (60 m). Also known as "Don Lulo's," these cascades are a popular excursion, offered by tour companies in Dominical. Horseback trips to the falls depart Don Lulo's at 8 a.m. and 2 p.m.; reservations are essential. Nearby, at **Platanillo**, high above Dominical in the valley of the Río Barú, **Parque Reptilandia** has one of the country's largest snake exhibits, with dozens of species, plus poison dart frogs, crocodiles, and other reptiles.

Refugio Nacional de Vida Silvestre Hacienda Barú

This private reserve, on former farmland at Hacienda Barú, offers an array of natural treats on trails through cocoa plantation and pasture and into the thick of forest and mangrove backing a beautiful beach—**Playa Barú**—cleansed by surf that brings ashore hawksbill and olive Ridley turtles. Anteaters, iguanas, monkeys, ocelots, and even rare tayras and jaguarundis are among the mammal species here. And on top of all that, the birding is fabulous, with more than 300 species from roseate spoonbills to anhingas. For the curious, the local ecology is explained in exhibits at an **interpretive center.**

The property also features pre-Columbian archaeological sites, as well as an intriguing canopy tour and jungle tent camp. Kayaking and horseback rides are also offered for an even more active experience.

Riptide Dangers

By far the greatest danger facing visitors to Costa Rica is that of being caught in a riptide. These ferocious ocean currents occur when the volume of incoming water is so great that the waves form a dam preventing the water's retreat. Swimmers caught in the current will be dragged out to sea. The natural instinct is to strike for shore—a big mistake. Riptides are so powerful that even the strongest swimmer can quickly tire and drown. The key to escaping is to swim parallel to shore (i.e., perpendicular to the current). Riptides migrate along the beach, and can form and dissipate quickly. Their presence is often betrayed by a still, glassy surface in the midst of waves.

Escaleras

Escaleras ("staircase") refers to the mountain range that steps steeply inland of Dominicalito, accessed by dirt roads that clamber up from the main coast highway. The forested mountains provide rewarding hiking and horseback riding along sometimes daunting trails. One leads to the **Pozo Azul** ("blue hole"), where you can take a shower in the chill waters of a thunderous cascade.

Escaleras is blessed with a variety of accommodations, each as distinct as a thumbprint, including luxurious villas with their own swimming pools inset like sparkling jewels in the green hillside. ∎

Parque Reptilandia
- Map p. 155
- Hwy. 243, 7 miles (11 km) E of Dominical
- 2787-0343
- $$

crreptiles.com

Refugio Nacional de Vida Silvestre Hacienda Barú
- Map p. 155
- Hwy. 34, 1 mile (1.6 km) N of Dominical
- 2787-0003
- $$ (guided tours)

haciendabaru.com

The Brunca Coast

Development is still relatively nascent on the Brunca Coast, one of the last ocean stretches to be placed within easy reach of tourists following the completion of the Costera Sur Highway. Nonetheless, a prime wildlife refuge and a marine refuge grant potentially thrilling encounters, while mountain farms offer forays far from the madding crowd.

Rain forest sweeps down to the shore along the rocky Brunca Coast.

Brunca Coast

Visitor Information

⚠ Map p. 155

✉ Uvita Information Center, Uvita

☎ 2743-8072

marinoballena.org

The Brunca Coast, named for a local Indian group, extends south from **Punta Uvita,** 9 miles (15 km) south of Dominical, to the mouth of the **Río Terraba** and the **Bahía de Coronado.** A range of mountains—the **Fila Costeña**—runs parallel to the thread-thin coastal plain. Pleated in folds of velveteen foliage, the mountains are good for hiking

and horseback rides and is the setting for one of Costa Rica's most remarkable deluxe hotels: Kurà Design Villas (see Travelwise p. 252).

Down by the shore, **Refugio Nacional de Vida Silvestre Rancho Merced,** situated on the north side of Punta Uvita, protects a vital mangrove ecosystem and patches of primary forest on a 3,130-acre (1,267 ha) privately owned cattle farm that offers horseback rides, birding, and "cowboy experience" tours.

Highway 34—wide and fast—hugs the shore south of Punta Uvita, tracing a series of lonesome, miles-long, palm-shaded beaches. Sea kayaking is a popular activity; the caves on the south side of **Punta Piñuela** are a favorite destination. Note that the seas are rough and the journey is not for the faint of heart.

The plain fans out to the south, where the Río Terraba spills into the ocean through a vast swampland—the **Delta del Terraba.** This labyrinthine delta makes up Costa Rica's most extensive mangrove system, providing an invaluable home for crocodiles, caimans, and innumerable waders and waterfowl. You can explore this rich and redolent world by boat or kayak, easily arranged from any of the fistful of ecologically focused hotels, centered on the inland community of Ojochal. This once sleepy village is now booming and boasts a large French-Canadian community, plus a selection of gourmet restaurants.

Parque Nacional Marino Ballena

The 9 miles (15 km) of shoreline from Punta Uvita to Punta Piñuela is protected within Parque Nacional Marino Ballena. The park forms a quadrant that extends 10 miles (16 km) out to sea, encompassing 11,120 acres (4,500 ha) of inshore ocean. It is named after the Pacific humpback whales that gather here at predictable times each year to mate and give birth. Bottlenose and common dolphins can be seen frolicking offshore year-round; they weave their way through the bow waves of boats like ribbons of silver.

The nation's largest coral reef is within the park, surrounding a small island that is connected to Punta Uvita by a tapering tombolo. The reef also extends in patches southward toward **Isla Ballena.** Between, rising from the sea like witches' fingers, are **Las Tres Hermanas** ("the Three Sisters"), rock formations atop which boobies, frigate birds, and pelicans all maintain nesting sites.

The undersea world here is enthralling. Plentiful hard corals, sponges, and sea anemones sway to the rhythm of the ocean currents. Snorkeling and scuba diving are offered by **Mystic Dive Center,** in Ojochal, but snorkelers should beware the rough seas. At low tide, try wading in the tidal pools at the tip of Punta Uvita. With good timing, you may

even be blessed with the sight of female marine turtles coming ashore to lay their eggs, notably at the namesake **Playa Tortuga** (*Sept. and Oct. are the best months to visit*). Both olive Ridley and hawksbill turtles are a frequent sight. **Reserva Playa Tortuga** (*tel 2786-5200, reservaplayatortuga.org*) welcomes volunteers to assist with its conservation projects.

For the Love of Pod

You can depend on seeing humpback whales close to Costa Rica's shores. Two populations migrate from colder Californian (July–Oct.) and Antarctic (Dec.–March) waters to court and calve. These gentle giants reach lengths of 50 feet (15 m), weigh up to 40 tons (36.3 tonnes), and wear their fingerprints on their tails; each animal has its own distinctive markings. Individuals sighted in Costa Rica have been seen as far north as Alaska. Watch for their explosive exhalations of breath. With luck, you may witness a Herculean leap called breaching.

Though this is a national park, camping is allowed. A small donation is suggested for both daily and overnight use. There is no centralized park entrance, but ranger stations are located in the tiny community of Bahía, at Piñuela, and at the park headquarters at Playa Ballena. ∎

Refugio Nacional de Vida Silvestre Rancho Merced

- ⚠ Map p. 155
- ✉ 9 miles (14.5 km) SE of Dominical
- ☎ 2743-8032
- $ $$$$$ (tours)

rancholamerced.com

Parque Nacional Marino Ballena

- ⚠ Map p. 155
- ✉ 12 miles (19 km) S of Dominical
- ☎ Playa Ballena: 2786-5392 Palmar Norte: 2786-7161
- $ $ (parking)

Mystic Dive Center

- ✉ Centro Comercial Los Ventanas
- ☎ 2786-5217

mysticdive.com

More Places to Visit in the Central Pacific

Rafiki Safari Lodge

Inspired by the classic lodges of Africa, this thatched mountainside nature lodge overlooks the raging Río Savegre in the thickly forested upper Savegre Valley. Deluxe tents even have flush toilets. White-water rafting and kayaking are offered. In the dry season, visitors can cast for mojarra, snook, and other fish. A 328-foot-long (100 m) waterslide whisks you into a freshwater pool. Using techniques from their homeland, the South African owners have initiated a tapir breeding and reintroduction program in the 700-acre (28,111 ha) rain forest reserve. *rafikisafari.com* ■ Map p. 154 ✉ 6 miles (10 km) E of El Silencio, 12 miles (19 km) E of Hwy. 34 ☎ 8368-9944 ⑤ $

Santa Juana Rural Mountain Adventure Lodge & Nature Reserve

This ambitious ecological project, deep in the Fila Chonta mountains, was initiated to involve impoverished communities in sustainable ecotourism. At its heart is a 2,470-acre (1,000 ha) nature reserve with trails and natural swimming pools fed by cascades. The project is affiliated with the Hotel Si Como No (see p. 251), in Manuel Antonio; the on-site Santa Juana Lodge *(santajuanalodge .com)* permits community immersion. Also offered: horseback riding, zip-lining, hiking tours, and a farm experience, with traditional campesino lunch. Or plant a tree as part of a carbon-offset program. ■ Map p. 154 ☎ 2777-0777 ⑤ $$$$$

EXPERIENCE: Contributing to Community & Environment

Nothing is as satisfying as knowing you have contributed to the local community and wildlife welfare of a place you visit at a grassroots level. You can give your time by acting as a role model for children, learning about traditional customs, and contributing to the care, education, and development of vulnerable local communities and their environments. Here are some key organizations.

ATEC *(tel 2750-0398, ateccr .org)* promotes cultural and ecological tourism by helping local groups and families derive economic benefits from their natural resources. ATEC offers excursions to indigenous reserves.

Costa Rica Animal Rescue Center *(San Miguel de Turrucares, tel 8892-6771, costaricaanimalrescuecenter .org)* works with injured, abandoned, or confiscated wildlife with the aim of rehabilitation and release. Volunteers care for animals and maintain the facility.

Costa Rican Association of Community-Based Rural Tourism *(tel 2234-6851, actuarcostarica.com)* is a network of rural cooperatives that foster local tourism, educating visitors on the way of life of local fishermen, peasants, and indigenous families.

SIBU Sanctuary *(Nosara, tel 8413-8889, sibusanctuary .org)* also rescues injured, orphaned, or displaced animals. It focuses on efforts to save monkeys hurt by electrocution. It seeks volunteers to care for the animals and sanctuary.

Tiskita Foundation *(tel 2296-8125, tiskita.com)* fosters community development around Pavones and Punta Banco, with education, health, environmental, and engineering projects.

uVolunteer *(tel 877-549-8368, uvolunteer.net)* places volunteers on a two-week to six-month basis. They facilitate entry into a wide range of projects throughout Costa Rica, ranging from working on reforestation to helping out in an orphanage.

A vast swath of wet and wild rain forest abutting Panama at Costa Rica's remote southeast corner

Zona Sur

Bananas, the sine qua non of the Zona Sur economy

Zona Sur

Known for lush forests and abundant wildlife, this rainy southeastern quarter of the country's nether-reaches is epitomized by a remote national park protecting the largest extant primeval rain forest along the Pacific coast of Central America.

The region is hemmed inland by the soaring Fila Costeña mountains, along whose base the Inter-American Highway (Highway 2) runs ruler straight to the Panamanian border. To the northwest lies a broad plain—the Valle de Diquís—drained by rivers that flow north and braid the mangrove estuaries of the Delta del Terraba. To the southeast is the Valle de Coto Colorado, drained by an eponymous river and its tributaries, which flow westward into the shallow Golfo Dulce.

The banana plantations blanketing the two major valleys are the economic mainstay of the sleepy towns of Palmar Norte and Ciudad Neily. Golfito, the somewhat forlorn capital of the region, has a lassitude typical of tropical ports and derives much of its income from a duty-free zone and sportfishing. Paso Canoas, at the Panama border, is also a duty-free zone.

Costa Rica and Panama share the Península de Burica, which tapers at the country's southernmost tip, with nothing but the blue expanse of the Pacific beyond. Most of the peninsula is protected as tribal land of the Burica Indians. Many of the beaches are prized nesting sites for marine turtles. Whales frequent the warm waters, and the open ocean and Golfo Dulce draw anglers seeking to snag blue marlin, or other big-game fish.

CENTRAL PACIFIC p. 153

NOT TO BE MISSED:

Hooking around the gulf to the north is the Península de Osa, a rugged region still mostly covered in primary rain forest. Wildlife viewing is stellar, reaching its zenith in Parque Nacional Corcovado. Scarlet macaws are particularly numerous here, and many of the rarest animals— such as tapirs and jaguars—still thrive, albeit rarely seen. The Osa is ravaged by loggers (often illicit), and *oreros* (gold hunters) still sluice the rivers

ing crocodiles and waterfowl, which you can see in the deltas of the Río Coto and Río Terraba. Several reserves occupy a small mountain range separated from the Fila Costeña by the valley of the Río Esquinas. Plans to build a new international airport at Sierpe have stalled due to opposition from environmental groups. ∎

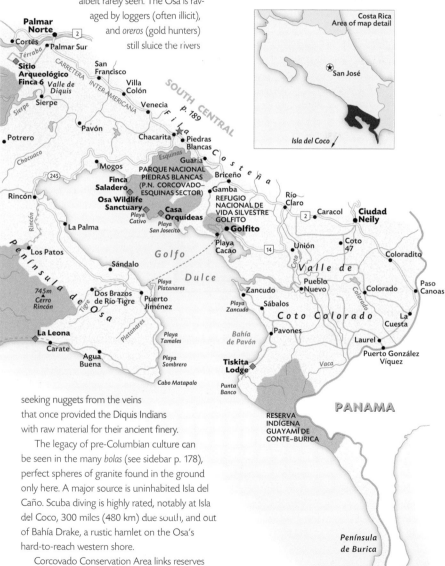

seeking nuggets from the veins that once provided the Diquís Indians with raw material for their ancient finery.

The legacy of pre-Columbian culture can be seen in the many *bolas* (see sidebar p. 178), perfect spheres of granite found in the ground only here. A major source is uninhabited Isla del Caño. Scuba diving is highly rated, notably at Isla del Coco, 300 miles (480 km) due south, and out of Bahía Drake, a rustic hamlet on the Osa's hard-to-reach western shore.

Corcovado Conservation Area links reserves and protected areas, such as wetlands support-

Península de Osa & Isla del Caño

Acclaimed for its astonishing biodiversity, the Península de Osa is swaddled in the largest expanse of tropical rain forest along the Pacific coast of the isthmus. Beach lovers can choose from a panoply of endearing beaches, where the surfing is fabulous and a bevy of top-ranked eco-lodges belie the "final frontier" feel.

Dolphin-viewing trips attract visitors to Bahía Drake.

Península de Osa & Isla del Caño
[Map] Map pp. 172–173

Osa Conservation
[✉] 100 yards (91 m) W of the gas station, Puerto Jiménez
[☎] 2735-5756

osaconservation.org

The Península de Osa receives more than 200 inches (500 cm) of rain annually, mostly from April to December. Much of its jungle-cloaked interior is banked within **Parque Nacional Corcovado** (see pp. 182–183), created in the 1970s to guard against human encroachment. However, much of the Osa is owned by logging companies that still fell hardwoods. *Precaristas* (squatters) continue homesteading by clearing forest, and the rivers here bear gold that in past decades has brought would-be millionaires with chain saws and shovels in hand.

The former gold-mining villages of **Los Patos** and **Dos Brazos de Río Tigre** now cater to ecotourism, offering horseback riding and guided hikes into Corcovado.

Puerto Jiménez

Tiny Puerto Jiménez, on the peninsula's east side and reached from the Inter-American Highway via Carretera 245, is the Osa's sole town. It attracts the college and counterculture crowd, and travelers seeking sea kayaking, surfing, and other adventures. Beside the airstrip is the administrative office for Parque Nacional Corcovado.

Osa Conservation accepts volunteers to assist with turtle conservation programs on the Osa Peninsula, including at Playa Platanares, where Iguana Lodge (see Travelwise p. 253) operates the Save the Osa Turtle Project (ASOT).

A dun-colored beach offers views across the gulf. Eastward, in the mangrove estuary of the **Río Platanares,** crocodiles and caimans cool off in brackish waters, white-faced monkeys cavort in the branches, and scarlet macaws fly overhead. Beyond is **Playa Platanares,** a major turtle nesting site.

Northwest Shore

On Osa's remote northwest side, popular with yachters, is **Bahía**

INSIDER TIP:

Kayak up the small river (Río Agujitas) at Aguila de Osa lodge at high tide. It is a short trip through a pleasant forest with some nice swimming holes.

—JOHN CALAMBOKIDIS
National Geographic field researcher

Drake (Drake Bay). At **Agujitas,** the **Corcovado Canopy Tour** *(tel 8810-8908, corcovadocanopytour.com, $$$$$)* offers treetop adventure by suspended walkway and zip line, and **Costa Rica Adventure Divers** *(tel 2231-5806, www.costaricadiving .com)* organizes scuba trips.

Getting to Bahía Drake can be half the fun—it is a two-hour boat trip down the Río Sierpe or a bumpy drive from Rincón along a rough dirt road that requires fordings. SANSA and Nature Air also serve Drake Bay airstrip. Bahía Drake may strike you as having changed little from the day in March 1579 when Sir Francis Drake deliberately beached his *Golden Hind* here.

To the south is **Río Agujitas,** flowing down a canyon that is good for kayaking. Whale-watching trips take visitors to see the humpback whales. Hikers can reach Parque Nacional Corcovado (beware of riptides; see sidebar p. 167) via 8 miles (13 km) of coastal trail.

On the hillsides above **Playa Caletas** is the 1,235-acre (500 ha) **Refugio Nacional de Vida Silvestre Punta Río Claro,** which abuts Corcovado and protects wildlife. Scarlet macaws squawk noisily, as do toucans, parrots, and monkeys; self-guided trails provide access. Nearby, **Reserva Biológica Campanario** offers simple accommodations and a field station where ex–Peace Corps volunteers lead treks.

Reserva Biológica Isla del Caño

On the horizon 10 miles (16 km) west of Osa, Isla del Caño hovers tantalizingly. Local lodges offer day excursions *(overnight stays not permitted).* The 740-acre (300 ha) island was a sacred burial site for pre-Columbian Indians; many *bolas* and archaeological sites have been excavated and can be seen beside forest trails. Olive Ridley turtles skim reefs to nest on coral-sand beaches. Snorkeling is enthralling, and whales and dolphins gather in the warm waters farther out. ■

Refugio Nacional de Vida Silvestre Punta Río Claro
- Map p. 172
- ✉ 5 miles (8 km) S of Bahía Drake
- ☎ 8877-3535
- $ $$

Reserva Biológica Campanario
- Map p. 172
- ✉ 8 miles (13 km) S of Bahía Drake
- ☎ 2289-8694
- $ $$$$$

campanario.org

Gold

In the streams of the Osa, the Diquis Indians found gold flecks, which they melted down to create their fine pre-Columbian jewelry. Later, Spanish conquistadors searched in vain for the fabled gold mines of Veragua. In the 1980s, when the United Fruit Company pulled out of Zona Sur, unemployed workers poured into Corcovado, destroying countless acres in a fit of gold fever that ended with their violent ouster in 1986. A few *oreros* (prospectors) still work the streams seeking the eternally elusive nugget that will land them on Easy Street.

A Drive Along the Osa

A single road—Highway 245—probes the peninsula and snakes along the western shore of the Golfo Dulce, curls around Cabo Matapalo, and peters out at Carate, midway along the southern coast.

It's only 73 miles (117 km) from the Inter-American Highway to Carate, but don't let that distance mislead you. Although the road is paved and in relatively good condition between Chacarita and Puerto Jiménez, conditions deteriorate thereafter; beyond Puerto Jiménez, the journey becomes an adventure. You will need a four-wheel-drive vehicle to make a fun trip of what could otherwise be an ordeal.

Highway 245 begins at **Chacarita ❶**, a trucker's stop at the junction with the Inter-American Highway. From here the well-paved road sweeps southwest, undulating like a roller coaster, with giant hardwoods—mahogany, kapok, and strangler figs—framing your passage in shades of lustrous green. After 10 miles (16 km) you get your first dramatic view of the sea. You will pass cattle ranches freshly hewn from the lush green forest, and huge logging trucks may thunder past in the other direction, hauling loads of precious hardwoods. After 25 miles (40 km) you arrive at the hamlet of **Rincón ❷**, the junction for Agujitas (see p. 175). Here the views open up like fanciful Hollywood creations, with an endless vista sweeping eastward across the length of the Golfo Dulce all the way down to Panama and southward across the immensity of the Península de Osa, swollen with billowing greenery like a violent sea.

The road, paved yet potholed beyond Rincón as far as Puerto Jiménez, drops down to **La Palma ❸**, 7 miles (11 km) south of Rincón. Turn left at the T-junction for Puerto Jiménez, 18 miles (29 km) southeast. The road parallels the shore inland, offering occasional tantalizing glimpses north toward the Fila Golfito mountains. Just before Puerto Jiménez, you might detour through the valley of the Río Tigre to the community of **Dos Brazos,** where

NOT TO BE MISSED:

Dos Brazos • Cabo Matapalo
• Lapa Ríos

the former gold-mining community operates a cooperative that leads gold-panning tours.

If you are low on gas, you should fill your tank up at **Puerto Jiménez ❹**, as there is none to be had farther along. The road is mostly level for the 10 miles (16 km) to **Cabo Matapalo,** the snub-nosed southeasterly tip of Osa. Your route is lined with ranches on one side and numerous handsome beaches on the other, notably **Playa Tamales** and **Playa Sombrero,** beloved of surfers for the terrific swells that peak in midsummer. For the best view around, stop at **Lapa Ríos ❺** (see Travelwise p. 253), a cliff-top ecolodge surrounded by greenery, with a soaring mirador—lookout tower—offering spectacular views over the coastline and, inland, a 1,000-acre (400 ha) private rain forest reserve accessed by trails.

From here, the going begins to get fun. You will ford a few streams (the mightier flows that once might have set your heart racing—particularly after torrential rains—are now bridged), and in places the gradient grows acute enough to challenge a goat. In really wet weather you will need a low gear to call on as you walk your vehicle up and over hills that can have you slithering back 2 feet for every 3 that you gain. In some places the foliage closes in on the road, brushing against you. Beyond Lapa Ríos, signs of human habitation gradually peter out and you begin to feel that you are all alone in the world. But no: 27 miles (44 km) from Puerto Jiménez, you arrive at **Carate ❻**, where the road comes to a stop beside an airstrip next to a brown-sand beach that

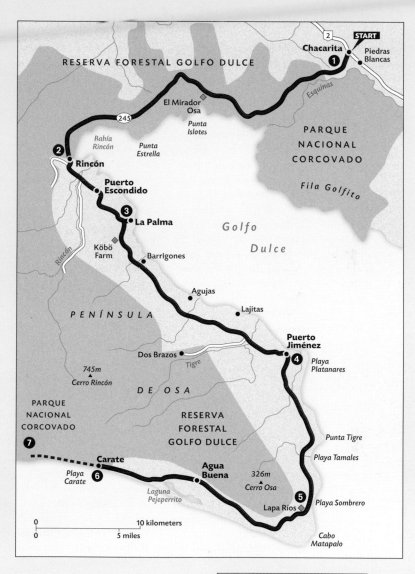

RESERVA FORESTAL GOLFO DULCE

START
Chacarita ❶
Piedras Blancas

El Mirador Osa

Punta Islotes

245

Bahía Rincón

Punta Estrella

❷ Rincón

Puerto Escondido

❸ La Palma

Köbö Farm

Barrigones

PARQUE NACIONAL CORCOVADO

Fila Golfito

Golfo Dulce

Agujas

Lajitas

PENÍNSULA

Dos Brazos

Tigre

745m Cerro Rincón

DE OSA

Puerto Jiménez ❹
Playa Platanares

PARQUE NACIONAL CORCOVADO

❼

RESERVA FORESTAL GOLFO DULCE

Punta Tigre

Playa Tamales

Carate

Playa Carate ❻

Agua Buena

326m Cerro Osa

Laguna Pejeperrito

Lapa Ríos ❺
Playa Sombrero

Cabo Matapalo

0 ——— 10 kilometers
0 ——— 5 miles

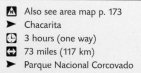

- ⚑ Also see area map p. 173
- ► Chacarita
- ⏱ 3 hours (one way)
- ↔ 73 miles (117 km)
- ► Parque Nacional Corcovado

stretches endlessly westward and is backed by the teeming jungle of Parque Nacional Corcovado (see pp. 182–183).

Plan in advance and book accommodation at Lapa Ríos or another lodge near the edge of **Parque Nacional Corcovado ❼**, 1 mile (1.6 km) west of Carate. You can drive along the beach at low tide, but make sure

you don't get stuck on the way back! Scarlet macaws fly overhead squawking mightily—a fitting finale to an adventure drive.

Río Sierpe & Valle de Diquis

Emerald points of land and the sea green of mangroves paint the view across the slate-smooth Valle de Diquis. The birding is fabulous along the banks of the Río Sierpe and Delta del Terraba.

**Río Sierpe &
Valle de Diquis**

🗺 Map
pp. 172–173

**Sitio
Arqueológico
Finca 6**

✉ 4 miles (6 km)
SE of Palmar
Norte

☎ 2100-6000

💲 $

At the north end of the Valle de Diquis is the broad **Río Terraba,** which flows down from the Valle de El General and pours out of a canyon to begin its meandering route to the sea through a vast mangrove system. **Palmar Norte,** the only town of significance, spans the banks of the silt-laden river.

The town's fortunes rise and fall with those of the banana crop. Land south of the river is swathed in banana plantations penetrated by a grid of dirt service roads that after 9 miles (15 km) will deposit you in the funky riverside hamlet of **Sierpe.** The village, which sits on a great loop of the **Río Sierpe,** is surrounded by swamps and *manglares*

Bolas

Pre-Columbian *bolas*— man-made granite balls with the perfect sphericity of glass beads—litter the Zona Sur, where they lie deep in luxuriant undergrowth. They measure from a few inches to 10 feet (3 m) wide and weigh up to 15 tons (14 tonnes). Some are found singly; others occur in groups of 20 or more. Were they religious totems? No one knows. How were they made? No one seems to know that either—though one plausible theory suggests that boulders were tumbled like ball bearings at the base of mighty waterfalls.

(mangroves) that form the **Reserva Forestal del Humedad Internacional Terraba-Sierpe,** which runs along the 25-mile (40 km) shoreline between the mouths of the Sierpe and Terraba Rivers. The waterways form a convoluted lacework that

INSIDER TIP:

Mosquito nets pack easily and only cost about 15 dollars at a sporting goods store. Buy the biggest one you can; it's best to have a net that drapes all the way to the floor.

—BEN HORTON
National Geographic field researcher

opens into a series of wide tidal *esteros* (estuaries) and isles. Nature lodges here offer guided wilderness excursions. Dug-out canoes and motorboats also depart Sierpe's dock for close-up encounters with crocodiles, caimans, and scores of exotic bird species. **Tour Gaviotas de Osa** *(tel 2788-1212, tourgaviotas deosa.com)* is recommended. Between Palmar Norte and Sierpe divert to **Sitio Arqueológico Finca 6,** part of a UNESCO World Heritage site, to view huge pre-Columbian stone spheres *(bolas)* in original astronomical alignment. The visitor center's excellent museum is dedicated to the Diquis culture, dating back almost 2,000 years. ∎

Life in the Lowland Rain Forest

The lushest environments on Earth, lowland rain forests teem with animal life. Of the world's estimated five million plant and animal species, as many as two-thirds inhabit this sodden world of throttling green, each species interdependent on other species in a complex web of unseen creatures on the move.

Within the dense lowland rain forest the air is cool and dank and underwater green, heavy with a silence that seems to ignore the crushing intensity of the sun dancing on the vast green ocean of the forest canopy above. What first seems to be silence and stillness is actually alive with liquid, musical calls and the whistles, squawks, and raucous screeches of parrots squabbling among the high branches. Peccaries and jaguars roam unseen in the cobalt shadows, while bats roost in the towering grottos of hollow trees. A brilliant blue tanager flashes by, its short stubby wings specially adapted to maneuver between densely packed branches, followed by an enormous turquoise morpho butterfly that floats by like a flashing neon sign. High in the canopy, silhouettes move slowly in the shadows. Perhaps a band of spider monkeys swinging hand over hand, foraging for fruiting trees, while eagles soar high above the canopy, hoping to snatch up an iguana innocently crawling along a branch.

Squirrel monkeys hang out in groups of up to 40 members.

A Complex Ecosystem

At first glance, the overwhelming riot of greenery might suggest that the rain forest is a place of disorganized chaos. In fact, it has a well-evolved structure. Although difficult to appreciate from the ground, the rain forest is actually built up of layer upon layer of overlapping habitats, like a Russian doll, each with its own characteristic amalgam of flora and fauna interrelated in a unique dynamic. As biologist Paul W. Richards, the father of modern rain forest science, has noted: "Tall trees, short trees, vines and epiphytes each have a specific role in the general scheme of things. And animal life in turn is well fitted into the overall architecture of the rain forest. In the jungle, in short, there is a place for everything—and everything remains pretty much in its place."

An "Undiscovered Continent"

The abundance is truly prodigious, and the overwhelming majority of species are far smaller and far less noticeable than the species most of us recognize easily. Insects—in particular beetles and ants—predominate. A single tree can harbor more than 10,000 beetle species. The relative paucity of undergrowth in lowland rain forests is such that by far the greatest diversity and concentration—some 90 percent of the fauna—exists unseen in the treetops. The forest floor is a relatively stagnant world by comparison. The sunlit canopy is a factory of fecundity teeming with animals, birds, and insects—most species being unique to their lofty realm. This universe of the canopy is a final frontier of scientific research, one of the last outposts of relative obscurity, what the 19th-century naturalist William Beebe described as an "undiscovered continent." Only in recent years have scientists begun to study life in these cathedral-like ceilings—an experience

Lowland Rain Forest

now made easy for lay visitors with canopy tours by suspended walkways or in harnesses.

Countless animal species spend their lives in the canopy and have evolved to avoid the need to come down to the ground. Humus accumulates so thickly on high branches that subspecies of arboreal earthworms have evolved, while arboreal snakes that can stiffen their elongated bodies to bridge gaps between trees have developed. Many mammal species have also adapted for climbing and leaping: The spider monkey's muscular tail, which can support the animal's whole weight, has a sensitive fingertip-like pad that makes it good for grasping. And tailless sloths move lethargically from branch to branch using hooked claws perfectly adapted for a life in the trees. Frogs, mice, scorpions, and even a species of crab are among the many terrestrial creatures that have adapted to a life high above the ground.

Although it may not be obvious, animals tend to move on known, well-worn routes through the canopy, rather like traffic streaming along major highways. Where howler monkeys and anteaters might pass by day, a kinkajou makes nightly forays, followed perhaps by a chocolate brown tayra prowling silently, with its teeth bared in a toothy grimace. Well-camouflaged snakes such as the green tree viper lie patiently in wait for prey such as opossums or mice.

Ironically, the voluptuousness of this fecund realm is not derived from the soil, which is nutritionally barren. Whereas in deciduous forests, leaves drop simultaneously, accumulate, and build up a rich layer of humus, leaf fall in tropical forests occurs throughout the year. The leaves that drop decompose quickly as a result of the constant heat and daily rains, so that their nutrients are swiftly reabsorbed into the canopy without allowing any buildup in the soil. Over millions of years, tropical soils have been leached so efficiently that only aluminum and iron oxides remain in quantity. This rust red earth is acidic, further adding to the destruction of nutrients. Homesteaders convinced of the richness of tropical soils are swiftly brought down to Earth. Within two or three years, the land they clear and plant for farming is usually left sterile.

A harpy eagle perches in the treetops, its sharp eyes searching for prey below.

Spider monkeys live among canopy plants that enfold the boughs of the forest ceiling.

Relatively sparse foliage at lower levels lets the tanager and the tayra move freely.

Tapirs roam the light-starved forest floor.

A macaw soars over the emergent layer, where scattered giants top the canopy.

Toucans and howler monkeys live high in the canopy.

Branching out at low level, under-story trees form a sub-canopy.

A katydid and a mantis rest in the thin leaf litter.

Parque Nacional Corcovado

This crown jewel of rain forest biology forms a mini-Amazon whose appeals are worth the discomforts of sodden humidity and rains—up to 25 feet (8 m) per year at higher elevations. In the tropics, water (and lots of it) spells life. From crocodiles in the marshy wetlands to sleek jaguars on the prowl, Corcovado has earned a reputation for some of the nation's best wildlife viewing.

Fording rivers is part of hiking in Corcovado National Park—but only try it at low tide!

Parque Nacional Corcovado

🗺 Map pp. 172–173

✉ 30 miles (48 km) SW of Puerto Jiménez

☎ 2735-5036

💲 $$

corcovadoguide.com

Corcovado was established in 1975 to protect 103,259 acres (41,787 ha) of tropical rain forest in addition to seven other distinct habitats—rare jolillo palm forest, freshwater swamp, mangrove swamp, alluvial plains forest, prairie forest, cloud forest, and areas of montane forest on the upper slopes of **Cerro Rincón** (2,444 feet/745 m).

You can enter the park either from the northwest via the **San Pedrillo Ranger Station,** from the northeast via the **Los Patos Ranger Station,** or from the southeast via the **La Leona Ranger Station.** The park headquarters is at **Sirena,** in the heart of the park. Basic dorm rooms are available at Sirena; you can camp at any of the ranger stations. You also can easily visit the park from any of a half dozen or so ecolodges that fringe the shore just outside the park boundaries.

Abundant Wildlife

This lush ecological Eden boasts wildlife in astonishing abundance.

Around one-tenth of all mammal species in the Americas live in the park. You are certain to see howler and capuchin monkeys, and possibly even endangered squirrel monkeys. Anteaters are common, as are peccaries and tapirs. One of the best places for viewing tapirs is **Laguna Corcovado,** where the timid, strange-looking creatures commonly come to drink at dawn and dusk. After dark you can watch bats swoop down to pluck fish from the water. And Corcovado is one of the few places in the country where sightings of jaguars and other big cats are common. These cats also hang out around the lagoon, as do large, fast, toothy crocodiles.

Corcovado's forests vibrate with the squawking and chirrups of countless birds. Of the nearly 400 bird species, 1 species and 17 subspecies are endemic—found only here. Egrets, herons, and ibises pick among the sedge wetlands, where jacanas can be seen walking across water, tiptoeing across the lily pads by using the ultrawide span of their toes to disperse their weight. Even the harpy eagle, recently considered locally extinct, has been seen with increasing frequency. And nowhere else in Central America has such a large population of scarlet macaws—about 1,200 birds. You are sure to see them feeding on almond trees as you walk along the beach, or flying overhead in pairs.

There are in excess of 115 reptile species, including poison dart frogs that hop about the jungle floor like enameled porcelain figurines. You may even spot the diminutive red-eyed tree frog or a species with transparent skin, appropriately called the glass frog. Do not be surprised to come across female marine turtles as you walk along the miles of beaches: Hawksbills, leatherbacks, olive Ridleys, and Pacific greens all lay their eggs above the high-water mark. ■

Hiking

Though Corcovado can only be seen on foot, no place in Costa Rica will more richly reward your effort with magnificent wildlife. Arm yourself with the very helpful Instituto Geográfica Nacional 1:50,000 map, as trails are poorly marked. You can go it alone, or hire guides in Puerto Jiménez. You will need good walking shoes, bug spray, and water. Watch out for venomous snakes, especially fer-de-lances, pit vipers with yellow-brown backs and pink bellies; their bite can be fatal in minutes.

The 24-mile-long (39 km) main trail from La Leona to San Pedrillo mostly follows the beaches. Allow two days, including a side trip to Laguna Corcovado from Sirena, 9 miles (15 km) northwest of La Leona. Midway between Sirena and San Pedrillo, cool off beneath Catarata La Llorona, which plunges 100 feet (30 m) onto the beach. You can also hike from Los Patos to Sirena (13 miles/21 km). Rivers must be forded on all trails; tackle these at low tide, not the least to avoid tangling with crocodiles.

Golfito & Golfo Dulce

The erstwhile "banana capital" Golfito, capital of Zona Sur, is long on authentic character. It makes a perfect base for sportfishing in the gulf, hiking in nearby rain forests, boating along the mangrove-lined shores, and snorkeling at remote beaches where both surfers and marine turtles come ashore.

Explore the Esquinas estuary mangroves and wetlands in a kayak.

Golfito

 Map p. 173

Visitor Information

✉ Land-Sea Services, Km 2, Pueblo Civil

☎ 2775-1614

✉ Institute of Costa Rican Tourism, 100 yards (4 km) E of fire station, Rio Claro

☎ 2789-7739

Golfito

Highway 14 dead-ends in Golfito, connecting it to the Inter-American Highway, 16 miles (26 km) away. The town itself sprawls along 5 miles (8 km) of shoreline paralleled inland by steep jungle-clad mountains. Its sultry setting midway down the eastern shore of Golfo Dulce is not ideal, as the hills enclosing the gulf preclude breezes from reaching Golfito, which stews.

The town was born in 1938, when the United Fruit Company established its plantations nearby and built the town from scratch in a unique plantation style. Golfito swiftly became the main banana shipping port in Costa Rica. World

War II injected new vigor when the U.S. military arrived. The good times ended abruptly in 1985 when "Big Fruit" pulled out. To offset the decline, the government created a duty-free zone, the Depósito de Golfito, where tax-free merchandise is sold within a walled compound. The many basic hotels here cater to this itinerant trade. A considerable expatriate population includes a good number of yachters who arrived and succumbed to a spell from which they have never escaped. Others have washed up in more ways than one.

The **Pueblo Civil,** to the east, is a bedraggled section where the main bars and services are located. Highway 14 meanders north past

INSIDER TIP:

The word "ecotourism" can be used to attract business, but some places build roads through the rain forest and cut down trees to build lodges. Do a little research beforehand.

—BEN HORTON
National Geographic field researcher

the Muelle de Golfito banana-loading dock and into the tranquil **Zona Americana,** once the administrative center of the United Fruit Company, with colorful, two-story clapboard houses atop stilts. The airstrip and duty-free shopping compound are located here.

A stiff hike uphill leads to the **Refugio Nacional de Vida Silvestre Golfito,** which protects 3,235 acres (1,310 ha) of forested hills boasting all four species of monkeys plus scarlet macaws. Water taxis depart from Muelle de Golfito for **Playa Cacao,** a ten-minute trip to a small beach with idyllic views across the bay.

Around the Gulf

North of Golfito, steep mountains flank the gulf shores and emerald forests spill down to lonesome brown-sand beaches—**Playa Cativo, Punta Encantado,** and **Playa San Josecito**—where eco-lodges offer hiking, horseback riding, snorkeling, and kayaking just a quick water taxi ride from Golfito. Not to be missed is a visit to the **Casa Orquídeas,** at Playa San Josecito, where guided tours

lead through a botanical fantasia of orchids and ornamentals two decades in the making.

Mountains compose the **Esquinas** part of Parque Nacional Corcovado, a park that embraces **Parque Nacional Piedras Blancas,** funded by the Austrian government. **Esquinas Rain Forest Lodge** (see Travelwise p. 253), which is run as a local cooperative, offers guided nature hikes.

A 10-mile (16 km) water-taxi trip southeast from Golfito, (44 miles/71 km by road) lands at **Zancudo,** a charmingly funky hamlet—popular with sportfishers—sprawling along a sand spit that separates the **Coto Swamps** from the sea. You can explore mangrove and wetland ecosystems by kayak or on guided boat excursions (see Travelwise p. 264)—a chance to photograph river otters and crocodiles.

A dusty track leads south from Zancudo to the fishing community of **Pavones,** legendary for what is ostensibly the longest surf ride in the world. Rocky outcrops puncture the dramatic shore, where marine turtles also pop up out of the surf, mainly from August to December. The road dead-ends at **Punta Banco,** 5 miles (8 km) south of Pavones, at the gateway to the **Reserva Indígena Guaymí de Conte–Burica** *(closed to the public)* and the **Península de Burica.**

Stop at **Tiskita Lodge** (see Travelwise p. 253), a fruit farm with a rustic lodge set on a mountain ridge. It is backed by a private 370-acre (150 ha) rain forest that awaits exploration. Well-maintained trails lead to waterfalls and plunge pools. The birding is stupendous, assisted by a booklet for self-guided tours. ∎

Refugio Nacional de Vida Silvestre Golfito
- ⚠ Map p. 173
- ✉ 0.5 mile (0.8 km) E of Golfito
- ☎ 2775-2620
- 💲 $$

Casa Orquídeas
- ⚠ Map p. 173
- ✉ Playa San Josecito
- ☎ 8829-1247
- 🕐 Guided tours Sun.–Thurs.
- 💲 $$$ (self-guided tour)

Parque Nacional Piedras Blancas
- ⚠ Map p. 173
- ✉ Within Esquinas sector of Parque Nacional Corcovado
- ☎ 2741-8001
- 💲 $$$ (guided tour)

Costa Rica's Unique Lodges

Costa Rica is home to two members of National Geographic Lodges of the World, a collection of properties handpicked by National Geographic's sustainability experts. These lodges offer travelers an intimate encounter with local cultures and habitats and a chance to be part of protecting them for future generations.

A private deck at Lapa Rios offers sunset views over the waters where the Golfo Dulce and the Pacific Ocean meet.

Lapa Rios Eco-Lodge

More than 20 years ago, former Peace Corps volunteers Karen and John Lewis purchased a 1,000-acre (405 ha) tract of rain forest on the tip of the Osa Peninsula. Their initial goal was simply to protect the jungle in the buffer zone around **Parque Nacional Corcovado** (see pp. 182–183), one of the planet's top biodiversity hot spots. "A standing forest is more valuable than one cut down," was—and still is—their mantra. However, in the longer term, tourism—the sustainable kind—has turned out to be a key part of the conservation equation. The Lewises built and staffed **Lapa Rios Eco-Lodge** (see Travelwise p. 253) with the help of the local community and, in turn, helped build and improve the community's schools and infrastructure.

Today Lapa Rios Eco-Lodge comprises a total of 17 thatched bungalows with private decks and garden showers and a main lodge, built along a high ridge above a sea of trees. Just down the hill, wild beaches line the coast and the waters of the Golfo Dulce meet the Pacific Ocean. This prime location means guests can go for a horseback ride on the beach and learn to surf, or venture into the rain forest with a naturalist to discover all kinds of fascinating creatures—and take a dip in a waterfall pool along the way.

A range of naturalist-led excursions are available to visitors, from birding walks to medicinal plant tours, or you can sit by the pool or enjoy a massage as scarlet macaws glide past noisily and howler monkeys offer reveille calls.

Pacuare Lodge

East of the Osa Peninsula, in the thick tropical forests of Limón Province, another National Geographic Lodge offers a different kind of jungle experience. The thatched yet sumptuous **Pacuare Lodge** (see Travelwise p. 246) is nestled in the trees on the banks of Pacuare River, and getting there is part of the adventure: It is only accessible by raft. The property is in a fitting spot for its owner, Roberto Fernández. He started rafting the rivers near his home with friends when he was a boy, using a flimsy raft meant for a swimming pool, wooden paddles, and lifejackets intended for airplanes.

Set on 840 acres (340 ha), with just 19 suites and bungalows, this is a place to get immersed in the rain forest, tune out the rest of the world, and experience the jungle with all your senses. There is electricity—but only in the main lodge; suites are lit by lanterns and candlelight. Spend your days on jungle hikes or kayak excursions, visiting Cabécar Indian villages, or relaxing on your spacious private

Guests raft the Pacuare River, flanked by pristine rain forest, on the way to Pacuare Lodge.

balcony in the trees. In the evening, ascend to a "nest" built high in the forest canopy for a dinner you'll never forget.

EXPERIENCE: Unexpected Rain Forest Excursions

A favorite activity among guests at Pacuare Lodge is the canopy tour, a thrilling two-hour swing through the treetops on a zip line that gives you a birds-eye perspective on the forest—and a chance to see the unusual ecosystem of the jungle canopy up close. The last length of the course sends you swooping high over the thatched roofs of the lodge, and with a quick rappel down you're at home. Your guide on these tours just may be a once notorious poacher. The owner of Pacuare Lodge sought him out more than 20 years ago when looking for a local well versed in the rain forest flora and fauna to serve as a naturalist guide at the lodge. He has become a supervisor of the canopy tours—and over the years has recruited fellow poachers to work as naturalists with him.

Another great example of sustainable tourism in action can be found at Lapa Rios Eco-Lodge, where, on a break from jungle hikes and beachcombing, you can take the "Twigs, Pigs, and Trash" tour. A naturalist will take you behind the scenes at the lodge to witness the innovative green practices that help the lodge operate, but don't overwhelm the guest experience. This includes a visit to the lodge's famous pigs, who eat food scraps from the restaurant. Methane gas, captured from their manure, is then funneled directly to the stove in the staff kitchen, reducing the lodge's need for fossil fuels. The system has proven such a success that the company that now manages Lapa Rios, Cayuga Collection of Sustainable Luxury Hotels and Lodges, is introducing it at its other properties.

Parque Nacional Isla del Coco

For anyone with the time and resources, Isla del Coco will make a memorable high point of a Costa Rica visit. This island, a geographic oddity 300 miles (480 km) southwest of Costa Rica, receives only a fistful of visitors. Yet it is the nation's prime dive spot—not to mention one of its most important seabird rookeries and a repository for endemic bird species.

A male frigate bird inflates its gular pouch to attract a female.

Parque Nacional Isla del Coco

🅰 Map p. 172

Visitor Information

☎ MINAE, National Parks Service: 2291-1215 or 2542-3290

isladelcoco.go.cr

Geographically part of the Cocos volcanic chain that extends south to the Galápagos Islands, this island is wed to Costa Rica by a purely political link. The youthful 20-square-mile (52 sq km) island pierces the Pacific and reaches 2,080 feet (634 m) atop **Cerro Iglesias.** Relatively young, it owes its genesis to a hot spot—a point in the seabed where molten magma has welled up from deep within the Earth's bowels, giving birth to a chain of submarine volcanoes as the Pacific plate has slowly moved over it (see pp. 118–119).

Feral pigs are the only mammal species, but Isla del Coco shares several bird species with its southerly cousins: a subspecies of Galápagos finch plus blue- and red-footed boobies. Endemic species include the Cocos flycatcher

and Cocos Island cuckoo. Frigate birds use the steep bushy cliffs for launchpads, and the snowy white tern, locally called the Holy Spirit bird *(espiritú santu)*, soars overhead.

Isla del Coco is a UNESCO World Heritage site. Traipsing the island is by permit only, although yachters dock here, as do scuba divers operating from live-aboard dive vessels (see Travelwise p. 264), which provide the only transport to the island. The diving here is daunting—and exhilarating. Swirling currents stir up nutrients upon which fishes thrive, drawing hammerhead and white-tipped sharks in abundance. The thrill of diving amid schooling hammerheads is one of the island's greatest draws. Encounters with harmless whale sharks and giant manta rays are also common. And inshore snorkeling amid the coral reefs reveals a world more beautiful than a casket of gems.

Following its discovery in 1526, the island became a popular stopover for pirates and other mariners. Many a pirate supposedly buried his treasure here, though scores of expeditions have scoured the island to no avail. Today, the Ministry of Natural Resources leases the island to treasure hunters, charging hefty fees. At **Bahía Chatham,** the main anchorage, you can see the etchings carved into the face of the cliff by sailors from centuries past. This is the only secure anchorage. ■

Extreme contrasts of valley and mountain, superb botanical gardens, premier white-water rafting, and the country's highest peak

South Central

San Isidro's striking monumentalist cathedral dominates the city center.

South Central

This region encompasses the nation's most rugged terrain. Much of it is part of the Talamanca Massif, whose igneous and sedimentary rocks (many lifted from the ocean bed) underlie rugged forest and, higher up, wind-scoured alpine grasslands. Few people live in these gargantuan ranges; much of the area remains unexplored, tempting intrepid adventurers.

Most of the vast massif is enshrined as Parque Internacional La Amistad; shared with neighboring Panama, the park covers a whopping 479,000 acres (193,929 ha). It encompasses many indigenous and biological reserves, plus Parque Nacional Chirripó, and is crisscrossed by a network of rarely used trails.

Two fertile valleys are sandwiched between the Talamancas and the Fila Costeña coastal range to the west. The Valle de El General, 60 miles (96 km) long by 20 miles (32 km) wide, is drained by the Río General, which is fed by rivers that thunder down from the massif and provides some of the country's best white-water rafting. To the south, the Río Coto Brus and its tributaries drain a short, eponymous valley. The two rivers merge to form the Río Terraba, which funnels west through a steep gorge in the Fila Costeña and links the region with Golfo Dulce.

The steepled Talamancas reach 12,530 feet (3,819 m) atop Cerro Chirripó, whose summit is usually hidden from view by clouds whipped up by a wind that brings torrential rains from the Caribbean. Yet the valleys are so sheltered that they bask in a balmy Mediterranean climate. This, combined with the richness of alluvial soils washed down from the mountains, lends the Valle de El General great importance as the nation's breadbasket. The sun shines benevolently upon pineapple plantations and other fruit fields here, while the flanks of the Valle de Coto Brus are adorned with dark green coffee bushes.

Despite its agricultural vitality, the region developed late in colonial history and remained sparsely settled until the Inter-American Highway reached it in the late 1950s. Before this, poor farmers hauled their produce to market in Cartago and San José over the inhospitable Cerro de la Muerte. Today the two-lane highway spirals down from it to the regional capital of San Isidro de El General at the valley's head. Nearby, San Gerardo de Rivas nestles high in the Chirripó Valley and makes an exceptional base for quetzal-watching, trout fishing, and soaking in

NOT TO BE MISSED:

Costa Rica
Area of map detail

hot springs. The only other town of consequence—San Vito, unusual for its pervasive Italian heritage—sits on the Fila Costeña's northern flanks, at the head of the Valle de Coto Brus.

The South Central region is also the heartland of indigenous culture. In secluded mountain valleys, members of the Boruca and Guaymís tribes live on indigenous land held in trust. Several reserves are opening to tourism. ■

The Route to San Isidro

Tourism has bypassed this peaceful valley, despite the fact that the all-important town of San Isidro is a gateway to Parque Nacional Chirripó—set in a vale popular with rafters, hikers, and birders. The Valle de El General is devoted to agriculture, mainly fruit plantations and flower farms raising tropical plants for export.

Los Cusingos Neotropical Bird Sanctuary maintains the home of late naturalist Alexander Skutch.

Centro Biológico Las Quebradas

- 🅰 Map p. 190
- ✉ 1.5 miles (2.5 km) N of Quebradas
- ☎ 2771-4131
- 🕐 Closed Mon.
- 💲 $$

fudebiol.com

San Isidro de El General

- 🅰 Map p. 190
- **Visitor Information**
- ✉ Selva Mar, Calle 1 bet Aves. 2 & 4
- ☎ 2771-4582

The descent into the valley from San José via the Cerro de la Muerte is a head-spinner, as the narrow Inter-American Highway (Highway 2) spirals down more than 9,000 feet (2,745 m) in just 20 miles (32 km). On clear days views are sublime, with the valley spilling away below, green and flat as a billiard table. En route, stop at **El Trapiche de Nayo** (tel 2771-7267), a rustic restaurant with a traditional ox-driven sugarcane press, which operates on Saturdays. It stands roadside below the Piedra de Cristo—a giant Christ statue atop a sheer-face cliff—at Km 104.

The **Centro Biológico Las Quebradas,** at the base of Cerro de la Muerte, is a good place to spot quetzals. Accessed by a turnoff north of San Isidro, east of the Inter-American Highway, it has 5,930 acres (2,400 ha) of primary forest, including cloud forest at higher reaches. Trails are difficult.

San Isidro de El General

The main center for the region is this unprepossessing town, known by its municipal name of Pérez Zeledón. The town comes alive during its *fiesta cívica* in late January when families thrill to the rodeos and mariachis, and on May 15, when *boyeros* (oxcart drivers) celebrate with a colorful parade honoring San Isidro, patron saint of farmers.

The town offers few attractions. Nonetheless, the concrete cathedral in modernist style, one block east of the modest plaza at Calle Central and Avenida 0, is worth a peek for the stained-glass windows.

The Valley

South of San Isidro, the warm air is filled with the aroma of *piñas* (pineapples). Soon you are surrounded by fields of pineapples in tidy rows rolling to meet the horizon. The vast commercial enterprise is centered on **Buenos Aires,** 40 miles (64 km) southeast of San Isidro. You can visit Parque Internacional La Amistad (see pp. 200–201) from here, by way of Ujarrás, to see the nation's largest park and adjacent biological and indigenous reserves.

Between Buenos Aires and San Isidro on the western bank of the Río Peñas Blancas is **Los Cusingos Neotropical Bird Sanctuary.** Situated near General Viejo on the lower slopes of the Talamancas, this 350-acre (142 ha) reserve was the longtime home and research site of Alexander Skutch (1904–2004), who co-wrote *Birds of Costa Rica* with Gary Stiles. The Tropical Science Center now manages Los Cusingos for ecological tourism and bird observation. Skutch's home is kept as it was on the day he died.

Finca Tres Semillas *(tel 8512-0234, experiencecostarica .org),* at División, 20 miles (35 km) north of San Isidro, educates about organic farming and sustainable living, and has hikes and horseback rides into the surrounding rain forest. Trails lead past Indian petroglyphs. ■

Los Cusingos Neotropical Bird Sanctuary

🅰 Map p. 190
✉ Quizarrá de Pérez Zeledón
☎ 2253-3267
🕐 Reservations required
💲 $$$

cct.or.cr

Considering a Move to Costa Rica?

According to the Departamento de Migración y Extranjería, almost 400,000 foreigners live permanently in Costa Rica. Many are Europeans and North Americans who came to vacation and discovered a "calling." They followed their heart or gut, inspired by the country's physical beauty, easy pace, and salubrious climate. Others are drawn by its benefits as a retirement destination: Costa Rica has a stable democratic government, a well-educated workforce, excellent telecommunications, and a relatively high standard of living. It's also remarkably inexpensive.

Foreigners can even start a business while on a tourist visa. Three principal options for residency allow foreigners to own a business but not to work for wages. *Pensionado* (pensioner) status requires you to prove that you have at least $1,000 a month in pension income and spend at least four months in Costa Rica. *Rentista* (small investor) status, for non-retirees, also requires a four-month residency, plus proof of a guaranteed monthly income of $2,500. An *Inversionista* (large investor) must invest a minimum of $200,000 in tourism or another "priority sector," and a six-month residency is required.

Non-resident foreigners enjoy most of the same property rights as Costa Ricans, but they can only own up to 49 percent of beach property. Be aware that anyone can be a real estate agent: No license or exam is required, and the field is full of scam artists. The **Association of Residents of Costa Rica** *(tel 4052-4052, arcr.net)* is a good starting point for information.

A Walk in the Clouds

Cerro Chirripó (12,530 feet/3,819 m) lures intrepid hikers seeking the satisfaction of hiking to the top of Central America's highest peak. This nontechnical ascent demands no more of you than stamina, determination, good hiking shoes, and a sleeping bag to guard against the cold during an overnight stop at cloud-hung heights.

A sun-kissed Cerro Chirripó beckons hikers.

The peak crowns a 123,920-acre (50,150 ha) national park that is a high-mountain refuge of pristine, rugged splendor. When hiking this forbidding terrain, it's easy to appreciate why pre-Columbian Indians believed the mountain was sacred. The park remains a sanctum of a different sort: Endangered wildlife—including tapirs and jaguars—are numerous. A side trek to the Savannah of the Lions gives you a good chance of spotting pumas. And because you ascend through three distinct life zones, the birding is excellent.

Before setting off, visit park headquarters in the hamlet of **San Gerardo de Rivas ❶**, 1 mile (1.6 km) south of San Gerardo, to register and pick up a trail map; inquire here about hiring an *arriero* (guide/porter; *tel 2742-5225, $$$ per day*). No camping is permitted. The 9-mile (15 km) ascent covers 7,500 feet (3,035 m), so dress to foil the rain and the wind. The National Parks Service (*tel 2771-3155, in San Isidro*) allows

no more than 40 people on the trail at one time. Hikers must register for two-day stints in the park, so book ahead (*reservations accepted Mon.–Fri.*); payment should be made at the San Gerardo ranger station (*tel 2742-5083 or 2742-5097, $$$$ two days, $$ per extra day*) or prepaid through Banco Nacional.

The Trek

Begin your two- or three-day round-trip trek at San Gerardo de Rivas, where the **Sendero Termometro trailhead ❷** is well marked. Begin at dawn, as the first day's haul takes six to twelve hours, depending on the weather and personal fitness. Rains frequently deluge the mountain in the afternoons.

From here, follow the dirt road east. Go right at each of two Y-forks, until you see a fence marked Sendero al Cerro Chirripó. The 1-mile (1.6 km) track crosses mostly open pasture, good for birding, then another sign points to the official

NOT TO BE MISSED:

San Gerardo de Rivas
• Monte Sin Fé • Los Crestones
• Valle de los Conejos

trail. The route becomes steeper (notably so beyond the **Llano Bonito ❸** marker), and you begin a tough uphill climb along **La Cuesta del Agua.** Fill up on water (which you should boil or treat with chlorine tablets) from the trailside stream. After about two hours on this "staircase" you will crest at **Monte Sin Fé ❹** (Mountain Without Faith), where you can rest and listen to the sounds of the forest: birds, howler monkeys, and the wind in the trees. A *refugio natural—* wooden shelter—marks the halfway point.

Mists swirl overhead as you enter the cloud forest at 7,500 feet (2,300 m)—a haunting world of gnarled trees festooned with epiphytes and old man's beard. The 2-mile (3.2 km) ascent is known as **La Cuesta de los Arrepentidos** (Repentants' Hill), ending in the salvation of the **Centro Ambientalista El Paramó ❺**, a simple

albergue (hostel) beside the **Río Talari** in the saddle between **Cerro Crestones** and **Cerro Paramó.** The hostel has a self-serve kitchen, but cooks will prepare meals by advance request. The hut sits beneath unusual rock formations called **Los Crestones ❻**.

After a chilly night at Centro Ambientalista El Páramo (bring a warm sleeping bag), you should be back on the trail at dawn to beat the fog that shrouds the peak by mid-morning. The 3-mile (5 km) hike leads past waterfalls and through the **Valle de los Conejos ❼** (Valley of the Rabbits), amid alpine grasslands. After about 90 minutes you will reach the summit. With luck, the sun will shine and you can enjoy the views. The peak is surrounded by lakes good for a dip.

Expect clouds to appear soon and the wind to whip around the summit—head back to San Gerardo de Rivas, to make it by late afternoon.

> 🅰 Also see area map p. 190
> ▶ San Gerardo de Rivas
> 🕑 2–3 days (1 night on mountain)
> ↔ 11.5 miles (18.4 km)
> ▶ The summit

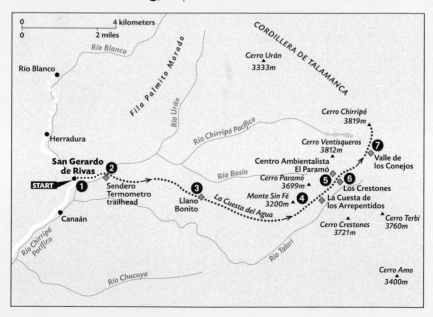

Valle de Chirripó

Due east of San Isidro, a deep valley cleaves the Talamancas; the rock-strewn Río Chirripó tumbles between its steep flanks. The secluded valley is popular with fly fishermen, whitewater enthusiasts, and birders on the trail of quetzals.

San Gerardo basks in the valley's upper reaches.

Valle de Chirripó
🄰 Map p. 190

Cloudbridge Nature Reserve
🄰 Map p. 190
✉ 1 mile (1.6 km) NE of San Gerardo de Rivas
☎ 917/494-5408
💲 Donation

cloudbridge.org

Talamanca Reserve
🄰 Map p. 190
✉ 2.5 miles (4 km) NE of San Gerardo de Rivas
☎ 2742-5080

talamancareserve .com

Several interesting sites lie on the road leading through the valley, whose balmy microclimate is perfect for growing fruits. You can buy apples, citrus, peaches, and other treats from roadside stalls.

Four miles (6.5 km) into the valley is **Rivas,** a rustic hamlet and the setting for **Rancho La Botija** *(tel 2770-2146, rancholabotija.com, closed Mon., $),* a farm famous for its traditional hand-operated *trapiche* (sugarcane press) and a boulder etched with pre-Columbian petroglyphs. It also has a charming restaurant, horseback riding, and a swimming pool.

Beyond Rivas, the road narrows and becomes dirt as it scrambles into the upper reaches of the valley.

Around San Gerardo de Rivas

About 14 miles (22 km) east of San Isidro, **San Gerardo de Rivas**—headquarters for Parque Nacional Chirripó—is an alpine village above the Río Chirripó, which runs wild and effervescent as champagne in the lee of the Talamancas. The aroma of pine trees and log fires scents the crystal clear air. The nearby hamlet of **Canaán,** immediately south, is a center for coffee production. Together these villages offer a selection of rustic *albergues,* including **Albergue Montaña El Pelícano** *(tel 2742-5050, hotelpelicano.net),* a hostel that includes the **Museo El Pelicano,** whose owner—Rafael Elizondo Basulto—crafts sculptures from wood and stone. The upscale **Monte Azul** mountain retreat (see Travelwise p. 254), at Chimirol de Rivas, combines sublime accommodations with art classes, cooking workshops, and trails in its own 125-acre (48 ha) nature reserve.

A dirt road leads northwest from San Gerardo de Rivas and follows the **Río Blanco** to the trail for **Aguas Termales** (hot springs), which you can reach via a 20-minute uphill trail.

Cloudbridge Nature Reserve, at the end of the dirt road east of San Gerardo, offers forest hikes on the mid-level slopes of Chirripó. This 430-acre (174 ha) private cloud forest has trails and guides. Don't be surprised to see spider monkeys and tayra here. Nearby, **Talamanca Reserve** also has trails, including for ATVs. ∎

EXPERIENCE: Learn Spanish in Costa Rica

Costa Rica is renowned as a center for Spanish-language instruction. There are dozens of schools to choose from in San José. Heredia and Alajuela have also evolved as centers for learning Spanish. And there's no shortage of dedicated language schools in the beach resorts of Nicoya and in other key tourist resorts, such as La Fortuna and Monteverde. You can choose from a one-week quick immersion class to month-long (or longer) intensives.

It helps that Ticos enunciate with very clear diction and that the country offers so much to see and do when class is out. Spanish-language courses are also a tremendous way to immerse yourself in local culture, not least because most schools have their students room with local families. And many combine language instruction with classes in local dance and cultural mores. Some combine excursions.

Rarely do classes take up more than 20 hours per week; the norm is 4 hours daily, Monday to Friday. Check to ensure that classes are small—the more personal attention you can get, the better. If you seek one-on-one tutoring, make sure it's available before signing up. Costa Ricans are very patient, so don't be afraid to practice what you are learning outside of the classroom.

Here are a few reputable schools:

The **Costa Rican Language Academy** (tel 2280-1685, spanishandmore.com), in San José's university district, is owned and operated by Costa Ricans, and all of the teaching staff are native Spanish speakers. It also has Latin dance and cooking classes, and contributes 3 percent of tuition funds to conservation.

The **Forester Instituto Internacional** (tel 2225-3155 or 727-230-0563, www.fores.com), in San José, was founded in 1979 and offers beginner to advanced classes, including short-term immersion classes of one to four weeks and longer-term sessions. This school is used by several foreign universities for their study abroad Spanish programs.

The **Institute for Central American Development Studies** (tel 2225-0508, icads.org), in the San Pedro suburb of San José, provides Spanish instruction while emphasizing knowledge about political, social, and environmental issues. ICADS supplements intensive conversation, grammar, and practice with guest lectures and discussions on culture, the environment, political processes, women's issues, and development, as well as site visits that create opportunities for additional total immersion learning.

Intensa (tel 2281-1818, intensa.com) has campuses in San José, Alajuela, Escazú, and Heredia. Founded in 1980 by North American linguist Robert Patterson, it was a pioneer in Spanish-language instruction in Costa Rica. The approach combines classroom learning with interactive excursions.

Intercultura (tel 2260-8480, interculturacostarica.com) offers instruction in Heredia and by the beach in Sámara, and provides options for homestays or hotel accommodation. It has activities from cooking to yoga, and you can volunteer to teach local children.

Spanish Abroad (tel 888/722-7623, spanishabroad.com) is the largest language school in Costa Rica, with nine locations that include La Fortuna (Arenal), Manuel Antonio, Monteverde, and Tamarindo. You can mix and match locations, with classes starting every Monday of the year.

Spanish for Success (tel 866/310-7600, spanish forsuccess.com) represents seven Spanish-language schools throughout Costa Rica. In addition to regular Spanish classes, it offers special-interest language instruction, such as for teens, families, and medical staff.

White-Water Rafting

Costa Rica is a white-water paradise, and rafting is a popular outdoor activity. As you plunge like a log down a flume through a no-man's land of dark, brooding rain forest, rafting provides the ultimate combination of thrills and natural beauty. Below the mountains, the rivers settle down, flowing for mile after mile in solitude and peace. The country's combination of high mountains and plentiful rain produces scores of runnable rivers—enough to keep even experienced rafters occupied for weeks.

Rafters on the Río Savegre enjoying Class II rapids

The country boasts some of the most diverse and spectacular river runs on the continent. Depending on the river chosen, you'll pass through several life zones as you tumble through canyons overhung with tropical foliage. You are sure to find something that appeals to you. Travelers have gotten more adventurous in their demands, taking up paddles with gusto; river trips are now also available for the physically challenged.

Whatever the time of year, you'll find a river trip being offered. Major rivers such as the Pacuare, the Reventazón, and the Corobicí are run year-round. Others are seasonal, depending on water levels. In general, the best times are May to June and September to October, when water levels are high and the rainy season serves up more potent excitement. The Río General and the Río Chirripó—two mammoth rivers in the South Central that tumble out of the Talamancas and cascade through great gorges—are often compared with California's Tuolumne and Idaho's Middle Fork of the Salmon.

Choose Your Adventure

Río Reventazón in the Central Highlands is the intoxicating Dom Perignon of white water, a river that will have you laughing with sheer delight. It and the adjacent Río Pacuare are considered the quintessential rivers on which to experience an immersion in the rain forest environment. Both rivers pour down through mountain gorges and spill onto the Caribbean plains. Monkeys and toucans screech in the canopies en route, and there are waterfalls and tranquil stretches that allow quiet contemplation of nature.

In Guanacaste, the lazy Río Corobicí offers an entirely different experience, perfect for children. This short, relatively calm river flows through a dry forest environment. Its waters—controlled by a dam and released year-round—draw to its banks all manner of wildlife, from howler monkeys and giant iguanas to herons and snakes.

Prepare to Get Wet

Rivers are rated from Class I (flat water, considered a "float" trip) to Class V (high waves, deemed suitable for experts only). No prior experience is necessary for Class I to III runs; some companies accept beginners on Class IV runs as well. Life vests and helmets are mandatory, but the tour operator will supply all equipment (plus expert guidance). The industry was established by North American experts and is operated to strict professional standards. More than 20 established companies operate rafting trips, although there is no government regulation. Most companies offer paddle trips, where you and your raft-mates do the work of powering through a rock-pocked slalom course while your guide controls things from the rear.

On some rivers, all you need to wear is a swimsuit, a T-shirt, and river sandals or sneakers that you don't mind getting wet. Expect to get drenched on Class III to V rivers—that's half the fun! A wet suit is recommended for the upper reaches of such high-mountain rivers as the Río General and Río Chirripó. Remember to take plenty of sunscreen—you'll be out in the sun all day—as well as a set of dry clothes and shoes to change into at float's end. On overnight trips you will sleep in tents or jungle lodges, where the day's rafting guides often rematerialize as the evening's chefs.

EXPERIENCE: Down the River

Outfitters offer river rafting throughout Costa Rica. The best seasons are May to June and September to October. Trips vary from half-day to four- and five-day excursions. Here are what the different regions offer and some of the the best outfitters:

In the Central Highlands, Ríos Reventazón and Pacuare offer one- or three-day runs with Class III or IV rapids year-round. In Guanacaste, the Río Corobicí is a calm float, with short rapids year-round.

In the Central Pacific, Ríos Naranjo and Savegre offer Class III and IV rapids. In South Central, Ríos General and Chirripó are Class III or IV experiences. In the Northern Lowlands, Ríos Peñas Blancas and Sarapiquí offer Class II and III rapids.

Aguas Bravas
(Puerto Viejo, de Sarapiquí, tel 2761-1645, aguasbravascr *.com)* runs trips in the Northern Lowlands.

Amigos del Río
(tel 2777-0082, amigosdelrio .net) offers rafting in the Central Pacific.

Costa Rica Expeditions
(San José, tel 2521-6099, costaricaexpeditions.com) is the oldest and most reputable company, with trips in the Central Highlands.

Costa Sol Rafting
(tel 4031-4914, costasol rafting.com) costasolrafting .com) offers trips in the Central Highlands and the Northern Lowlands.

Desafío Adventure Company
(tel 2479-0020, desafiocostarica .com) offers rafting trips in the Northern Lowlands.

Ríos Tropicales
(San José: tel 2233-6455, riostropicales.com) runs trips throughout the country, including floats on the Corobicí in Guanacaste. It's Costa Rica's largest whitewater specialist.

Parque Internacional La Amistad

Beyond the pale of human incursion, the vast Talamanca Massif is a last frontier for tourism. Here Costa Rica's wildest terrain has been enshrined for posterity in a mammoth park—the nation's largest—that the country shares with its southern neighbor, Panama.

The 479,200-acre (193,920 ha) Parque Internacional La Amistad girdles the Talamancas, a great tectonic massif thrust from the ocean over several million years and twisted into a number of ranges. Unlike the mountains in the northern part of Costa Rica, the Talamancas are not volcanic, but instead are composed of sedimentary rock and igneous intrusions; these mountains span a width of 50 miles (80 km) and make up a fifth of the national territory.

La Amistad

La Amistad, which extends south into Panama, begins at barely 450 feet (137 m) above sea level along the southern Caribbean shore and rises to the dizzying heights of Cerro Chirripó. The park spans eight of Costa Rica's twelve life zones, encompasses other national parks, and shelters the largest repository of animals, birds, and tropical forest in the nation. On the Caribbean slopes, La Amistad protects the largest area of montane rain forest in Central America, rising above 3,500 feet (1,060 m) to a prodigious expanse of cloud forest—home to the largest concentrations of quetzals in the country. The mountain is a last refuge for several endangered species. Tapirs thrive in the isolation, as do pumas and jaguars, and harpy eagles

Relatively few travelers venture into Parque Internacional La Amistad to enjoy its serene beauty.

still soar above the southern Talamancas.

Hiking is a true adventure and should only be undertaken with adequate preparation. The park has scant facilities, but the park office in San Isidro provides information, as does the CONAI (National Commission for Indigenous Affairs) office at **Ujarrás** *(tel 2257-6465, conai.go.cr)*.

Reserva Indígena Ujarrás (7.5 miles/12 km NE of Buenos Aires) protects lands of the Cabécares indigenous people, who are opening up to ecotourism. At **Durika Biological Reserve**, a farm and reforestation area on a 21,000-acre (8,500 ha) private reserve, you can assist the community's efforts to conserve the land. The mountain road is a challenge; consider a jeep-taxi from Buenos Aires.

INSIDER TIP:

Hire nature guides, even if you are an experienced naturalist. Their eyes are better than yours, and they know the habits of the local fauna.

—JOHN LONGINO
National Geographic field researcher

The central section is accessed from above the village of Biolley (13 miles/21 km E of Hwy. 237 at Guácimo), where the **Estación Altamira** *(tel 2730-9846)*—the park headquarters and main access point—has a small museum and camping facilities. Just below the ranger station, **Finca Coffea Diversa**

EXPERIENCE: Kibbutz-Like Living in Costa Rica

In search of a communal living experience? Costa Rica has a couple of options: **Durika Biological Reserve** *(tel 2730-0657, durika.org)*, high in South Central's Talamanca mountains and accessed by a daunting 4WD track, is a 21,000-acre (8,500 ha) reserve centered on a self-sufficient, ecologically focused commune with about 30 permanent members. It offers accommodations to visitors who can help milk the goats, or with reforestation and conservation projects. Guided excursions are offered.

PachaMama *(tel 8785-8949, pachamama .com)* may be perfect for those on a spiritual quest. Led by a quasi-guru named Tyohar, this Nicoya eco-sensitive commune for transient free spirits is inspired by Eastern mysticism. It offers art and movement classes, meditation, and has a kindergarten for families with children.

(tel 8722-3642) has the world's largest collection of coffee species.

Explore the southern zone from **Hacienda La Amistad** *(tel 2228-0405, haciendalaamistad .com)*, a coffee estate and forest reserve at Las Mellizas, accessed from San Vito by four-wheel drive. Trails lead to two basic high-mountain camps at 6,000-feet (1,830 m) elevation.

A local guide is a prerequisite for a trans-Talamanca journey; you must register in advance with CONAI. The trek is best begun on the Caribbean side, from where the **Talamanca Association of Ecotourism & Conservation** *(tel 2750-0398, ateccr.org)* offers guided hikes. ∎

Parque Internacional La Amistad
🅐 Map pp. 190–191
☎ 2771-3155 in San Isidro
💲 $$
www.sinac.go.cr

Reserva Indígena Ujarrás
🅐 Map p. 191

Durika Biological Reserve
🅐 Map p. 191
✉ 13 miles (21 km) NE of Buenos Aires
☎ 2730-0657
durika.org

A Drive Around Valle de Coto Brus

Superbly scenic yet forsaken by tourists, the Valle de Coto Brus carves a deep gorge between the Talamancas and Fila Costeña. Highway 237 runs the length of the valley along the flank of coastal mountains, offering elevated vistas over the vale; in the distance, the Talamancas rise grandly to mauve-colored, cloud-shrouded heights.

Your journey begins at the community of **Paso Real ❶,** at the eastern end of the Valle de El General, where the Río General and Río Coto Brus merge to form the **Río Terraba,** which flows south and carves a deep gorge in the Fila Costeña. About a half mile (0.8 km) south of Paso Real, turn off the Inter-American Highway and span the wide Río Terraba via a bridge that replaced the ferry, taking the fun out of the crossing. The wiry bare-chested ferrymen who operated the motor looked, thought local ecologist Gail Hewson de Gómez, "as if they were born in the reeds with the crocodiles" (which once waited for scraps thrown from the ferry).

Highway 237, intermittently paved, runs east from here along the valley floor. The soaring peak of **Cerro Kámuk** (11,660 feet/3,554 m) reaches to the sky in the northeast, shadowing the valley, which is grazed by hardy hump-backed cattle. You will pass the sign indicating **Estación Tres Colinas** (17 miles/27 km), a gateway to Parque Internacional La Amistad (see pp. 200–201). At the hamlet of **Guácimo** (10 miles/16 km from Paso Real) turn left and follow the dirt road uphill via El Carmen to **Biolley ❷.** Gaudiesque road markers point the way. The hills hereabouts are corduroyed with glossy green coffee bushes. Finca Coffee Diversa (see p. 201) can be reached by hiking or with a 4WD; the steep, rugged track ends at **Estación Altamira ❸,** the main entrance to Parque Internacional La Amistad. The road has risen above the valley and sidles east along the ridge crest of the **Fila Guácimo,** giving

---

NOT TO BE MISSED:

Finca Cántaros • Las Cruces Biological Station

---

you a grandstand view of **Cerro Echandi** (10,374 feet/3,162 m), a hulking mass veiled in forest and cloud.

About 30 miles (48 km) southeast of Paso Real, the road coils steeply up toward the regional capital of **San Vito ❹** (see p. 204). Follow the main road—Highway 16—south as it snakes uphill past coffee farms including **Finca Cántaros ❺** *(tel 2773-3760, fincacantaros.com, $),* where you should stop for a nature walk along the trails that wind through the 15-acre (6 ha) reserve. Sit on a bench beside **Laguna Julia** and delight in the herons, grebes, and other waterfowl feeding on fish and frogs. It also has a splendid fine art gallery and an educational center for local children.

Four miles (6.4 km) south of San Vito you will pass **Las Cruces Biological Station ❻** (see p. 204) and shortly thereafter you will crest the mountain ridge. The world seems to drop away in front of you, as you stare down over the Valle de Coto Colorado, the Golfo Dulce, and the emerald forested carpet of the Península de Osa beyond. The view is truly awe-inspiring. Drive with utmost care as you descend the steep switchback that claws its way downhill—a drop of some 3,000 feet (915 m)— to the town of **Ciudad Neily,** the end of your scenic drive.

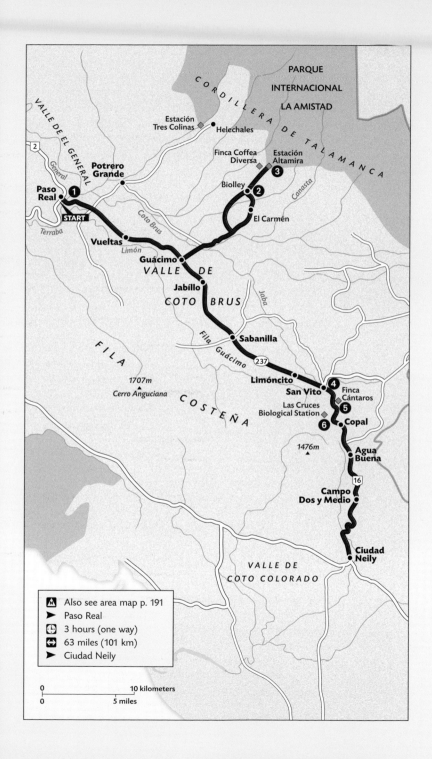

PARQUE
INTERNACIONAL
LA AMISTAD

CORDILLERA DE TALAMANCA

VALLE DE EL GENERAL

2

General

Estación
Tres Colinas   Helechales

Finca Coffea
Diversa   Estación
Altamira
3

Potrero
Grande

Biolley   2

Paso
Real   1

Canasta

START

Terraba   Coto Brus

El Carmén

Vueltas

Limón

Guácimo   VALLE   DE

Jabíllo

COTO   BRUS   Jaba

Sabanilla

FILA   Fila Guácimo   237

Limóncito

1707m
Cerro Anguciana

COSTEÑA   San Vito   4   Finca
Cántaros

Las Cruces
Biological Station   5

6   Copal

1476m   Agua
Buena

16

Campo
Dos y Medio

Ciudad
Neily

VALLE DE
COTO COLORADO

Also see area map p. 191
Paso Real
3 hours (one way)
63 miles (101 km)
Ciudad Neily

0   10 kilometers
0   5 miles

San Vito & Las Cruces Biological Station

The regional capital of San Vito is a jumping-off point for Las Cruces—one of the world's leading research centers for the study of tropical biota. A bonus is its cultivated botanical garden, which ranks among the most complete in the tropical world.

**Las Cruces
Biological
Station**
- 🗺 Map p. 191
- ✉ 4 miles (6.4 km) S of San Vito
- ☎ 2773-4004 or 2524-0607
- 💲 Garden entrance: $$ Guided tours: from $$$$$

ots.ac.cr

In the mid-19th century, Italian farmers founded the compact hill town of San Vito, at about 3,250 feet (990 m). Unlike most Costa Rican towns, San Vito lacks a main plaza. The *plazuela* at the southern end of the main street contains an intriguing verdigris-covered statue of two children who symbolize Italian–Costa Rican brotherhood. You may see Guaymi Indian women in colorful traditional clothing.

Las Cruces Biological Station

Las Cruces, situated a mere 4 miles (6.4 km) south of San Vito, protects a 583-acre (236 ha) reserve of montane tropical rain forest on a ridge of the Fila Zapote range of mountains. It is owned and run by the Organization for Tropical Studies (see p. 112), with whom you can arrange educational stays.

The lush forest, which is often veiled with the mists that nourish a profusion of bromeliads, epiphytes, and other air plants, is a veritable Garden of Eden in a region that has suffered significant deforestation. Birding is especially rewarding—more than 400 species have been recorded. And anteaters, armadillos, deer, kinkajous, monkeys, ocelots, sloths, and tayras are among the many large mammal species that visitors have a good chance of seeing while walking the miles of well-maintained trails.

The best time to visit is from mid-December through mid-April, when the persistent sopping rains diminish. The biological station offers a limited range of accommodations to nonscientific visitors by reservation (see Travelwise p. 254).

Wilson Botanical Garden: The real highlight of a visit to Las Cruces, however, is this 25-acre (10 ha) garden laid out in 1963 under the genius inspiration of Brazilian gardener Roberto Burle-Marx (1909–1994) using a theme of gardens within a garden. Some 6 miles (10 km) of trails dip and rise through lily beds, heliconia groves, a fern grove, an orchid grotto, and the world's largest collection of palms. Make sure that you allow time to stop at the greenhouses, where you'll find spectacular assemblages of anthuriums, cactuses, ferns, and other tropical plants composing a veritable hothouse fantasia. ∎

Superb birding, fishing, and other adventures in a lush world of lagoons, rivers, and rain forest

Northern Lowlands

Costa Rican cowboys take great pride in their *paso fino* horses.

Northern Lowlands

Like a vast green sea, the *llanuras*—flatlands—span northern Costa Rica, sweeping across the nation from east to west. Silt-laden rivers wind lazily across the rolling plains, slicing sinuous paths through the dense carpet of emerald rain forest that grows more lush to the east. The sparkling streams and rivers that rush down from the vaulting mountains leave indelible impressions on those who venture into the Northern Lowlands.

The plains were formed over millions of years by alluvial sediments washing into Lago de Nicaragua and pushing its southern shore north. The llanuras form an elongated triangle with the Río San Juan—the Nicaraguan border—as its northern perimeter, the Caribbean Lowlands to the east as the right-angled side, and the central cordillera, or mountain range, as the hypotenuse. The volcano-studded cordillera rises from the grass-lands in tiers of receding jungle, adding drama to an otherwise monotonously level landscape. The plains are divided into the Llanuras de los Guatusos to the west and the Llanura de San Carlos to the east. Dozens of rivers cascade from the mountains and merge into the Río Frío, the Río San Carlos, and the Río Sarapiquí; the three rivers merge into the Río San Juan, which drains into the Caribbean Sea. In the west, rivers flow into a vast swamp that drains into Lago de Nicaragua.

Rivers served as arteries for colonization during the 16th and 17th centuries and gained prominence two centuries ago during the early coffee boom, when a trail was cut from Heredia to today's Puerto Viejo de Sarapiquí, and the Río Sarapiquí became the major highway to the Caribbean Sea. Yet the region remained virtually unsettled until the mid-20th century, when the Costa Rican government encouraged

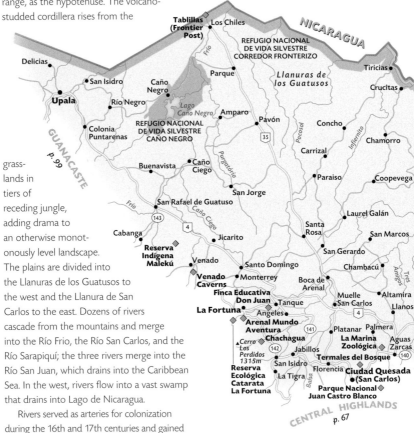

homesteading for cattle (subsidized by the World Bank). At the same time, large-scale banana plantations began to encroach from the east. Precious hardwoods continue to fall as homesteaders and loggers pick over the remnants of rain forests close to the Nicaraguan border. And much of the Llanuras de los Guatusos have been claimed in recent years for large-scale citrus operations.

The area remained isolated from mainstream Costa Rica until 1957, when Highway 126 linked Puerto Viejo to San José. Highway 4, which runs east–west along the base of the mountains and links lowland settlements, is a more recent development; from this road, minor roads wind among the volcanoes, tethering the lowlands to

the highlands and to Guanacaste. A third highway runs north through the region's center to the border town of Los Chiles, site of cross-border subterfuge during the days of the Contra conflict. The regional capital and agricultural center of Ciudad Quesada is perched above the flatlands, on the northern flanks of Volcán Platanar. La Fortuna, gateway to Tabacón hot springs and Parque Nacional Volcán Arenal (see p. 116), is the main tourist center.

Despite their east–west expanse, climatically the Northern Lowlands lie fully within the aegis of the Caribbean. Be prepared for hot, humid weather and relatively ill-defined seasonal differences. Much of the region is prone to floods during the rainy season (May–Jan.), which draws migratory waterfowl in astonishing numbers. As elsewhere in Costa Rica, wildlife is abundant here. Caño Negro is a vast wetland ecosystem and a prime choice for birding, viewing crocodiles, and sportfishing. Private reserves protect huge bands of montane rain forest on the cordilleras' lower slopes. Selva Verde is laced with boardwalks and well-maintained trails on the flatlands, while nearby Rara Avis offers a more rugged option with trails leading up the rain-soaked mountains. Several butterfly farms and a crocodile farm guarantee close-up encounters with wildlife. At La Fortuna, explore caverns, soak in mineral hot springs, or enjoy therapeutic spa treatments. ■

A suspended swing bridge is part of the commute for researchers at La Selva Biological Station.

Llanura de San Carlos

This broad plain, drained by the Ríos San Carlos, Sucio, and Sarapiquí, is a patchwork of banana plantations and rain forests; the latter sweep down the northern flanks of Volcanes Barva and Cacho Negro and extend north in billowy green waves to the Río San Juan. The lush rain forests and riverbanks provide birding nonpareil—including a unique opportunity to spot the endangered green macaw (*Lapa verde buffon*).

Rara Avis

- Map p. 207
- 9 miles (14.5 km) SW of Las Horquetas
- 2764-1111
- $$$$ (guided hikes including canopy tour)

rara-avis.com

Heliconia Island

- Map p. 207
- 3 miles (4.8 km) N of Las Horquetas
- 2764-5220
- $$$

heliconiaisland.com

One of the region's key attractions is **Rara Avis,** a private reserve protecting 3,163 acres (1,280 ha) of montane rain forest abutting Parque Nacional Braulio Carrillo (see p. 85), on Volcán Cacho Negro's eastern flank. As the rain forest is fed by 200 inches (500 cm) of rainfall annually, visitors are almost sure to be deluged. Rara Avis was created to explore ways to derive income from harvesting the rain forest ecosystem without felling trees. The rustic complex includes a biological research station. Rara Avis is also famous as the site for Donald Perry's pioneering canopy research, described in his biographical *Life Above the Jungle Floor* (1986).

The reserve's economic mainstay, however, is ecotourism. Guests eschew all luxuries, and access is via a rugged horseback and tractor-pulled trailer ride through the mud. Visitors can also tramp miles of trails, and treetop platforms put you at eye level with monkeys and other canopy species. One platform overlooks a thunderous waterfall—one of dozens that spill through the forest, forming invigorating swimming pools at their bases. Close-up sightings of monkeys, sloths, and toucans are virtually guaranteed. Poison dart frogs are easy to spy in the leaf litter. Endangered green macaws and umbrella birds are among the 390-plus species of birds found here. The reserve's remoteness and inaccessibility make day visits impossible.; rustic lodges provide accommodations (see Travelwise p. 255).

Nearby, **Heliconia Island** is ablaze with blooms in riotous color. Manicured to near perfection, this

Snakes of Costa Rica

Snakes—*culebras* or *serpientes*—are a fact of life in Costa Rica, which is home to 162 species. The ubiquitous creatures, which are much maligned and little understood, are found in every one of the country's environments. The majority of serpientes are rarely seen, since they are nocturnal.

The highly venomous eyelash or palm viper (*bocaracá*) comes in fluorescent green or yellow.

Many species are painted in magnificent colors and patterns, with a beauty that belies their fearsome reputations. In fact, only 22 species are venomous, of which 9 are potentially fatal to humans (except for the coral snakes, which produce a unique venom, the species all produce the same venom, which varies only in degree of toxicity). Most snakebites happen when people step too close to hidden snakes. When walking, keep your eyes on the ground. Also, look carefully before reaching for a branch, as many snakes are arboreal. While most species are camouflaged in greens and browns the better to catch passing prey, many species—such as the coral snakes—boast gaudy colors meant to advertise their highly venomous nature.

Snakes range in size from diminutive species such as the foot-long (30 cm), pencil-thin bright green vine snake (*bejuquillo*), with its beaked nose, to the 10-foot (3 m) boa constrictor (*boa*), which coils around its prey and squeezes it to death. The boa, which gives birth to live young, is normally benign and retiring, but will strike if you approach too closely; though they are non-venomous, their fangs can inflict a nasty bite.

The much-feared bushmaster (*matabuey*) is a giant among the venomous snakes and highly aggressive—it has even been known to chase people. The bushmaster is restricted to densely forested mountain terrain. Its equally lethal cousin, the terrestrial fer-de-lance—colloquially called the *terciopelo* (velvet)—is far more ubiquitous and accounts for four-fifths of snakebites in Costa Rica, as well as most fatalities. Rather than slink away at the approach of humans, the fer-de-lance holds its ground and will strike with little provocation. Although found in every major life zone, it prefers wet habitats such as tall grassland and along riverbanks.

Costa Rica also has four species of coral snakes, identified by their bands of carmine red, white or yellow, and black. If threatened, they typically flatten their backs and perform a balletic dance meant to intimidate aggressors. Pelagic sea snakes—black-backed and yellow-bellied—are common off the Pacific shore, where they use their spatula-like tails to sidle through the warm water. One commonly seen species, the chunk-headed snake, evolved its extraordinarily slender I-beam shape to bridge gaps between branches. It hides, then ambushes lizards and frogs.

Puerto Viejo de Sarapiquí

ⓜ Map p. 207

Visitor Information

☎ 2766-6768

sarapiqui.cr

Sarapiquís Rainforest Lodge

ⓜ Map p. 207

✉ 1 mile (1.6 km) N of La Virgen

☎ 2761-1004

💲 $$–$$$$

sarapiquis.com

5-acre (2 ha) garden displays more than 80 species of heliconia from around the world, as well as scores of bamboo, orchid, and other species. Birding is stupendous; the air thrums with the wings of hummingbirds. For an unusual experience, request a nighttime tour.

Freshwater Sharks?

For centuries, the sharks in Lake Nicaragua have baffled observers. Scientists once believed that the lake had begun as part of the ocean, and its sharks had adapted to freshwater; we now know, however, that it was formed by tectonic subsidence. The lake is linked to the Caribbean Sea by the 106-mile-long (170 km) Río San Juan. Electronic tagging has shown that sharks, a species able to tolerate both fresh and salt water, migrate between the lake and the sea via the river's rapids.

Serious birders should consider following the **Costa Rican Bird Route** (costaricanbirdroute.com), with four distinct itineraries that connect 18 sites where the great green macaw and other key bird species might be seen.

Puerto Viejo de Sarapiquí

Puerto Viejo, the region's only notable town, huddles at the confluence of the Río Puerto Viejo and Río Sarapiquí, at the foot of the Cordillera Central, whose eastern slopes bear the brunt of damp air masses moving in from the Caribbean. Puerto Viejo long ago relinquished its importance as the country's main shipping port for coffee brought down from the Meseta Central by mule. It now supports the banana plantations unfurling eastward for miles. It also caters to ecotourism. Several lodges highlight the superb nature viewing and offer guided hikes and horseback rides along trails amid the primary rain forest.

The stupendous variety of wildlife can also be seen on boat rides from the *muelle* (dock) at the eastern end of town. Water taxis ply the Ríos Sarapiquí and San Juan as far as Barra del Colorado; you can charter motorized canoes and canopied tour boats with **Oasis Nature Tours** (tel 2766-6108, oasisnaturetours.com, $$$ per hour per person). Expect to see caimans, monkeys, sloths, and even crocodiles as you cruise along the wide waterways. Bring binoculars and plenty of wet-weather clothing.

From San José, the quickest way to reach Puerto Viejo is Highway 4, which branches north from the Guápiles Highway (Highway 32) at **Santa Clara.** A more scenic but challenging route is Highway 126, which crawls down the western flanks of Volcán Barva to the lowland hamlet of **La Virgen.**

Nearby, on the Río Sarapiquí, the **Sarapiquís Rainforest Lodge** (see p. 255) draws visitors. Here the state-of-the-art **Museo de Cultura Indígena** celebrates the extant indigenous cultures of Costa Rica through an impressive collection of artifacts, masks, decorations, and shamanic objects, plus a

An owl butterfly's "gaze" deters hungry songbirds at La Selva Biological Station.

documentary. An archaeological site features a pre-Columbian burial ground and a reconstruction of an Indian village. It's also an experimental farm with a fruit orchard and botanical garden displaying a vivid palette of native species. Trails lead into 330-acre (133 ha) **Tirimbina Biological Reserve,** where a canopy walkway gets you close to monkeys. Tirimbina also has themed guided walks, including a nocturnal "World of Bats" walk.

Dave & Dave's Nature Park, overlooking the Tirimbina rain forest, is a birders' nirvana, with observation decks and camouflaged screens for close-up photography. Guided birding and photography walks are also offered. A stone's throw away, the **Snake Garden** (tel 2761-1059, $$) displays dozens of culebra species, alongside frogs, caimans, and more.

La Selva Biological Station

This research center, immediately south of Puerto Viejo, abuts Parque Nacional Braulio Carrillo. It is owned by the Organization for Tropical Studies (see p. 112), an international body of 50 or so universities that share research facilities, an arboretum, and experimental lots surrounded by 3,700 acres (1,500 ha) of virgin premontane rain forest. Board-walks offer easy hikes by the educational center, but the 38 miles (61 km) of trails are muddy going (Feb.–March is driest). Twice-daily guided hikes are by reservation only. More than 420 bird species have been recorded here, as have more than half of Costa Rica's butterfly species, two-thirds of its mammal species, and 55 of its 162 species of snakes.

Selva Verde

At Chilamate, 4 miles (6.4 km) west of Puerto Viejo, this private reserve protects 475 acres (192 ha) of lowland rain forest bordering Parque Nacional Braulio Carrillo. Trails and boardwalks penetrate the dark forests, where snakes and poison dart frogs abound. Blue-and-gold tanagers, jacamars, motmots, parrots, and toucans are numerous, but they're most easily identified in the company of a trained guide. Selva Verde also offers a netted butterfly garden plus canoe and horseback trips as well as some nice lodgings. ∎

Dave & Dave's Nature Park
- Map p. 207
- La Virgen
- 2761-0801
- $$$$$

eco-observatory.com

La Selva Biological Station
- Map p. 207
- 2 miles (3.2 km) S of Puerto Viejo de Sarapiquí
- 2766-6565
- Guided hikes from $$$$

ots.ac.cr

Selva Verde
- Map p. 207
- 6 miles (9.7 km) W of Puerto Viejo de Sarapiquí
- 2761-1800
- $$$$$ (guided hikes)

selvaverde.com

Around Ciudad Quesada

The capital of the region is not actually in the Northern Lowlands; instead, it perches loftily at 2,145 feet (654 m) on the slopes of the Cordillera Tilarán, while the *llanuras* (lowlands) unfurl majestically below. The town is a major transportation hub.

Ciudad Quesada
- Map p. 206

Visitor Information
- ITC 330 yards (300 m) E & 110 yards (100 m) N of the plaza
- 2461-9102
- Closed Sat. & Sun.

Termales del Bosque
- Map p. 206
- Aguas Zarcas
- 2460-4740
- $$

hoteltermalesdel bosque.com

La Marina Zoológica
- Map p. 206
- 8 miles (13 km) NE of Ciudad Quesada
- 2474-2202
- $

zoocostarica.com

Proyecto Asis
- 13 miles (20 km) W of Ciudad Quesada
- 2475-9121

institutoasis.com

La Marina Zoológica breeds tapirs for release to the wild.

The bustling market town of Ciudad Quesada, which slopes sharply northward and is known colloquially as San Carlos, is surrounded by emerald green pastures that are munched by brown Swiss cattle and black-and-white Holsteins. *Talabarterias* —saddle makers' shops—are a curiosity as you browse the town center, laid out in a grid around a tree-shaded square. If possible, time your visit for April, when a **Fería del Ganado** (cattle fair) is held. Ciudad Quesada is the main gateway to Parque Nacional Juan Castro Blanco (see pp. 77–78).

From the main plaza, Highway 140 sidles down the northern flank of Volcán Platanar, from which gush forth thermal waters. At **Termales del Bosque** visitors can bathe in the mineral springs after hiking or riding horses through lush forest. Spa treatments are offered at **Thermae Spa** (tel 2460-6000, eltucano resort.com), which enjoys a splendid setting beside a deep ravine of steaming springs.

The road descends to **Aguas Zarcas**, setting for **La Marina Zoológica**, a private zoo caring for orphaned and confiscated birds and animals, including dozens of monkeys and such treasures as tapirs, jaguars, and a Bengal tiger.

Farther west, at Florencia, **Proyecto Asis** also functions as an animal rescue center open to tours. It has critters from caimans and coyotes to monkeys and macaws. Visitors can volunteer to assist with animal care, and it even has a special family volunteer program including environmental education and Spanish tuition. ■

Around La Fortuna

The prosperous tourist center of La Fortuna de San Carlos nestles against the Cordillera de Tilarán in the lee of smoldering Volcán Arenal. La Fortuna is the main gateway to the volcano, enshrined within Parque Nacional Volcán Arenal (see p. 116), which is the primary draw for tourists. The attention has fostered a blossoming of local ecotour attractions.

The compact town of La Fortuna bustles with visitors to Volcán Arenal, 4 miles (6.4 km) west of town. Despite the tourists, La Fortuna still serves as a regional agricultural center and retains its strong ties to the local beef cattle economy. *Sabaneros* (cowboys) with lassoes and machetes are a local feature. Horseback riding is popular, and tour operators such as **Desafio Adventure Company** *(tel 2479-0020 or 855/818-0020, desafio costarica.com)* offers rides as far as Monteverde, atop the Cordillera de Tilarán. The most popular ride is to the **Catarata La Fortuna** *(tel 2479-8338, cataratalafor tuna.com),* 1 mile (1.6 km) south of Highway 142, 3 miles (5 km) southeast of town. Here, you can follow a narrow trail and steep staircase downhill to a waterfall, which has pools good for swimming, though this is unsafe in rainy weather due to flash floods.

Nearby at **Finca Educative Don Juan,** ebullient and erudite farmer "Don" Juan Bautista leads fascinating educational tours of his sustainable farm, ending with a delicious lunch prepared on a wood-burning stove. You even get to press your own sugarcane juice in a traditional *trapiche.*

Tour operators offer local adventure travels, from mountain biking, kayaking, and floating on

A swim rewards a scramble down to Catarata La Fortuna.

the **Río Peñas Blancas,** fishing on **Laguna de Arenal** (see pp. 114–115), and spelunking at **Venado Caverns** (see p. 216) to bungee jumping from a bridge over the Río Peñas Blancas.

Highway 142 runs through town and continues toward the volcano and Tabacón Resort (see p. 116). En route you will pass

La Fortuna
 Map p. 206
Visitor Information
✉ Cámara de Turismo Zona Norte (CATUZON)
☎ 2479-7512

Arenal Mundo Aventura
- Map p. 206
- 1.5 miles (2.4 km) S of La Fortuna
- 2479-9762
- $$–$$$$$

arenalmundo
aventura.com

Chachagua
- Map p. 206
- Hwy. 142, 6 miles (9.7 km) SE of La Fortuna
- 4000-2026

chachaguarainforest
hotel.com

Baldi Hot Springs *(tel 2479-2190, baldihotsprings.cr, $$$$)*, with soothing hot springs set in landscaped gardens; one has a swim-up bar and a restaurant. Nearby, **Arenal Natura** *(tel 2479-1616, arenalnatura.com, $$$$)* brings you up close to poison dart frogs and venomous snakes—all safely behind glass—and crocodiles that slosh around in a lagoon.

South of La Fortuna, **Arenal Mundo Aventura** has enough attractions to fill a day: rain forest hiking, riding horses, zip-lining, or even rappelling down a waterfall. Tamer options here include snake and frog exhibits. A nocturnal guided walk in search of insects is a highlight.

Chachagua

At Chachagua, 6 miles (10 km) southeast of La Fortuna, the private **Chachagua Rainforest** reserve protects 124 acres (50 ha) of montane rain forest that melds into the Bosque Eterno de los Niños at the base of the Cordillera de Tilarán. Naturalist guides lead hikes in search of birds and wildlife, such as the large populations of poison dart frogs, ocelots, toucans, and howler and white-faced monkeys. The facility centers around a working cattle hacienda where visitors can watch rodeos. Guests stay in cabins at the forest's edge. Nearby, you can hike and ride horses at **Finca Luna Nueva** *(tel 2468-4006, fincaluna nuevalodge.com)*, a biodynamic herbal farm with a spa, farm tours, and its own rain forest reserve. A stone's throw away, don't miss **Coco Loco Art Gallery** *(tel 2468-0990, artedk.com)* for its superb art and indigenous crafts. ■

EXPERIENCE: Learn to Appreciate the Indigenous Way of Life

The Spanish occupation proved devastating to indigenous cultures, which retreated to valleys where their descendants still live. Today, eight indigenous tribes live in scattered villages on 22 reserves under the jurisdiction of the National Commission for Indigenous Affairs.

Until recently, the reserves were off-limits to visitors, except by permit. Tourism is now being promoted as a way of fostering a renewed pride in traditional beliefs, crafts, and customs. Permits are no longer required to visit the reserves. The most accessible reserves can be reached by 4WD vehicles over trails. The **Museo de Cultura Indígena** *(tel 2761-1004, sarapiquis.com)*, at La Virgen de Sarapiquí, is a superb museum profiling Costa Rica's pre-Columbian and extant indigenous cultures. A visit will give you a sound appreciation as a prelude to visiting one or more reserves. Here are some that welcome visitors:

Reserva Indígena Boruca *(tel 2514-0045, boruca.org)*, in Puntarenas, is known for its carved balsa masks and its Fiesta de los Diablitos, a three-day festival at the end of December. The community has a small museum.

Reserva Indígena Malekú *(tel 8888-4250 or 8839-0540; see p. 216)*, in the Northern Lowlands, has a small museum plus re-creations of traditional life, with performances of music and dance.

Reserva Indígena Yorkín *(tel 2750-3031, costaricaway.info)*, on the Panamanian border, is reached by boat and dug-out canoe. Lodging and facilities at this location are basic.

Refugio Nacional de Vida Silvestre Caño Negro

This 24,633-acre (9,968 ha) reserve is a watery world of swampy bayous. At its heart is a vast lake, which draws migratory waterfowl in such numbers that their rushing wings may be mistaken for the muffled roar of a distant jet aircraft. The waters also teem with plump, olive green crocodiles, grown fat on the local fish.

Keep an eye peeled for spectacled caimans lurking in the waters.

The vast swamp occupies a large basin. **Lago Caño Negro,** at its heart, is filled by the **Río Frío** and other rivers that wash down from the Cordillera de Tilarán. In May the lake begins to swell, and vast lagoons form in the basin. Then, thousands of waterbirds flock here: anhingas, cormorants, ducks, egrets, grackles, and grebes, as well as ibises, wood storks, and roseate spoonbills ladling the black waters with their long, spatulate bills. In the relatively short dry season from February to April, many of the lagoons dry out; the lake shrinks, and much of the waterfowl departs for other climes.

Jaguars, ocelots, deer, tapirs, monkeys, sloths, and other large mammals inhabit the vast carpets of sedge and jolillo palm groves. Caimans are abundant, as are freshwater turtles. Pugnacious crocodiles the size of Peterbilt trucks can be seen sunning in saurian splendor on the banks of muddy sloughs.

Caño Negro is an angler's dream, with tarpon the ultimate prize during fishing season (July–March, license required). Fishing trips and boat tours leave from the small border town of **Los Chiles,** about 60 miles (96 km) northwest of Ciudad Quesada, on the banks of the Río Frío. Canopied boats make the 16-mile (25 km) journey to Caño Negro. Boat trips also depart the hamlet of Caño Negro, on the western shore of the lake. ■

Refugio Nacional de Vida Silvestre Caño Negro

🅰 Map p. 206

✉ Off Hwy. 35, 40 miles (64.4 km) NW of Ciudad Quesada

☎ 2471-1309

💲 $

www.sinac.go.cr

More Places to Visit in the Northern Lowlands

Costa Rican farmers in the Northern Lowlands raise zebu cattle for beef.

Hacienda Pozo Azul

Horseback rides are a specialty at this working cattle ranch, and so are white-water trips on the Río Sarapiquí, rappelling in the river canyon, and mountain biking. A zip line canopy tour will whisk you through the rain forest treetops. Guests can stay in a riverside tent camp or at the Magsasay Lodge on the border of Parque Nacional Braulio Carrillo (see p. 85).
pozoazul.com 🅰 Map p. 207 ✉ La Virgen de Sarapiquí ☎ 2438-2616 💲 $$$–$$$$$ (guided tours)

Laguna del Lagarto Lodge

This private reserve *(4WD access only)* protects 1,200 acres (485 ha) of virgin rain forest and crocodile-rich swamps near the Nicaraguan border. Animals teem around this all-hardwood lodge with a wraparound porch for easy wildlife viewing. Visitors can see two-toed sloths, which spend most of their lives hanging upside down, and crocodiles. The nature lodge overlooks the Río San Carlos, which is good for exploring by canoe or on canopied boat trips. Kayaks are available for exploring the rain forest lagoons.
lagarto-lodge-costa-rica.com ✉ 28 miles (45 km) NE of Aguas Zarcas ☎ 2289-8163 💲 $$ (guided tours)

Refugio Nacional de Vida Silvestre Corredor Fronterizo

Stretching the width of the country, the slender 230-square-mile (59,570 ha) wildlife refuge guards the forests along the Nicaraguan border. Much of the refuge fringes the broad Río San Juan, which can be explored by boat from the community of Boca San Carlos; at El Castillo, 25 miles (40.2 km) upstream, the **Fortaleza de la Immaculada Concepción** has been restored and has a museum on colonial history. Wildlife viewing along the banks is terrific.
🅰 Map p. 206 ✉ Bahía Salinas to Punta Castillo ☎ 2460-0055 or 2460-1412 💲 $$ (Nicaraguan border fee)

Reserva Indígena Malekú

Until recently, the Malekú indigenous culture was relatively unknown. Today the community of about 650 individuals, who speak their own language, promotes themselves to ecotourists who want to learn about their heritage and customs. **Centro Ecológico Malekú Araraf** *(tel 8888-4250, $$$$)*, on the northern slopes of Volcán Tenorio, offers traditional dance performances, and the nearby **Eco-Adventure Tafa Malekú** *(tel 2464-0443, $)* has a museum.
🅰 Map p. 206 ✉ 2 miles (3.2 km) E of San Rafael de Guatuso ☎ 8839-0540

Venado Caverns

These limestone caverns extend for almost 2 miles (3.2 km) beneath the foothills of the Cordillera de Tilarán. They are filled with underground streams and stalactites and stalagmites in fascinating formations. Bats roost on the ceiling, transparent frogs hop about, and a blind species of fish swims in streams. Guides lead two-hour tours *(safety helmets and flashlights provided, bring waterproof footwear)*. The caverns are on the Solis family farm 1 mile (1.6 km) south of Venado, about 22 miles (35 km) northwest of La Fortuna. *cavernasdelvenadocr .com* 🅰 Map p. 206 ✉ 5 miles (8 km) S of Jicarito on Hwy. 4 ☎ 2478-8008 💲 $$$$$

Beaches washed by pounding waves, superb fishing and surfing, coral reefs, wildlife refuges, and unique local culture

The Caribbean

Clear Carribbean waters and a coral reef welcome visitors to Parque Nacional Cahuita.

The Caribbean

Running for 125 miles (193 km) between the Nicaraguan and Panamanian borders, Costa Rica's palm-fringed, surf-pounded Caribbean coast is as wild as the nation's towering interior. Primeval rain forest spreads inland from the sandy littoral, melding into swampy lagoons to the north and rising into the spiraling, cloud-draped heights of the Talamancas to the south.

The entire coast varies little in its hot, humid climate. Rain cascades year-round but peaks from May to August and December to January, when storms bow the palms and turn dirt roads into quagmires. When the sun shines, surfers take to the waves and the wildlife bursts into song and dance.

The Guápiles Highway (Highway 32) links San José with the former banana port of Puerto Limón, which lends its name to the province encompassing the Caribbean north to south. This colorful terminus of the now defunct Atlantic Railroad idles with a languor typical of down-at-the-heels tropical ports, except during Carnival and when cruise ships call.

North of Limón, gray-sand beaches line the wave-washed shore. The rain-sodden hinterland (rains increase northward along the Caribbean) is backed by a broad alluvial plain—the Llanura de Tortuguero and Llanura de Santa Clara—that extends far inland, smothered in banana

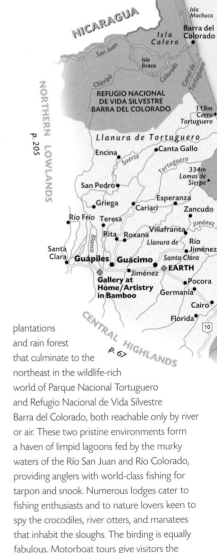

plantations and rain forest that culminate to the northeast in the wildlife-rich world of Parque Nacional Tortuguero and Refugio Nacional de Vida Silvestre Barra del Colorado, both reachable only by river or air. These two pristine environments form a haven of limpid lagoons fed by the murky waters of the Río San Juan and Río Colorado, providing anglers with world-class fishing for tarpon and snook. Numerous lodges cater to fishing enthusiasts and to nature lovers keen to spy the crocodiles, river otters, and manatees that inhabit the sloughs. The birding is equally fabulous. Motorboat tours give visitors the chance to glimpse a wealth of arboreal and terrestrial mammals.

South of Limón, the alluvial plain tapers sharply as the Talamancas crowd the shore. Year-round rains on the steep slopes nourish the virtually impenetrable montane rain forest. Reserva Biológica Hitoy-Cerere, albeit dauntingly rugged, is the most accessible of the reserves tucked into valleys deep in the mountains.

A coral reef is a highlight at Parque Nacional Cahuita, where snorkelers and scuba divers can mingle with reef fish streaming through aquamarine waters. Cahuita and Puerto Viejo—the epicenter of tourism—draw surfers. South of Puerto Viejo, the broad valley of the Río Sixaola opens inland, a portal to the indigenous reserves. This southern zone is known as Talamanca, a Native American word that refers to the slaughter of turtles. Marine turtles still nest up and down the coast: Tortuguero is the prime nesting site in the Caribbean for green turtles; and hawksbill and leatherback turtles nest here and at Refugio Nacional de Vida Silvestre Gandoca-Manzanillo, which extends to the Panamanian border.

Hernán Cortés, who mapped the region in 1522, recorded trade between local Indians and Aztecs from Mexico. Cacao was an important export in the 18th century, shipped from the now defunct port of Matina. The inhospitable Caribbean coast was largely ignored by Spanish colonists; however, pirates and illicit traders filled the void. The region thus evolved apart from the rest of the nation. Its isolation ended in the 1880s, when the Atlantic Railroad was built and Puerto Limón became the chief coffee port. The era saw the arrival of Jamaican laborers, who stayed to work the burgeoning banana fields.

Today, about 50 percent of the culturally distinct Caribbean region's population is of West Indian extraction. The beat of reggae and highly spiced cuisine show their enduring presence. While the area's economy is inextricably linked to the vicissitudes of the banana trade, tourism is now the economic mainstay. Accommodations from budget mountain retreats to chic beach cottages cater to this upsurge in popularity. ∎

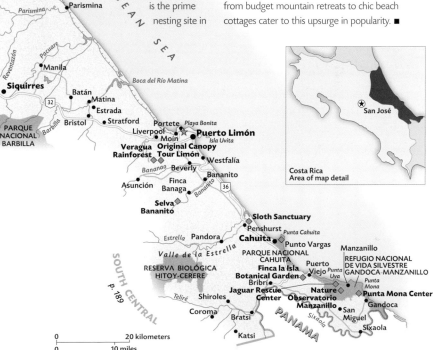

Llanura de Santa Clara

These undulating alluvial plains extend eastward from the foot of Volcán Irazú, forming a vast green sea of banana plantations that meld into swamplands—which, in turn, push up to the ocean. The plains are walled to the south by the steep slopes of the Volcanes Irazú and Turrialba and, farther east, by the soaring Talamancas. Highway 32 runs along the base of this mountain chain, hopscotching scores of rivers that cascade from the high peaks above.

The days of plantation strife past, banana trade today is an important part of Caribbean culture.

Three main towns along Highway 32—**Guápiles, Guácimo,** and **Siquirres**—are service centers for the Río Frío banana region that dominates the western plains, accessed by a maze of dirt roads that extend to the border of Parque Nacional Tortuguero. The towns are rather dirty, disheveled affairs, but they offer notable attractions in their hinterlands. For example, 4 miles (6.4 km) west of Guápiles, one of Costa Rica's most acclaimed artists, North American Patricia Erickson, has a studio—**Gallery at Home** *(tel 2710-1958, by appt.)*—in her house beside the Río Blanco. Her husband, Brian, makes and sells bamboo furniture at **Artistry in Bamboo** *(tel 2710-1958, brieri.com, closed Sun).*

From Highway 32, it's easy to access small private reserves that protect premontane rain forest on the flanks of Volcán Irazú and Volcán Turrialba. They share a wealth of the wildlife for which Costa Rica is known—coatimundis,

INSIDER TIP:

A tour of a banana plantation is fascinating and provides insight into this staple of the local economy, even if you are opposed to large-scale agriculture.

—JOHN LONGINO
National Geographic field researcher

howler and white-faced monkeys, ocelots, sloths, snakes, and birds such as aracarias, hummingbirds, motmots, oropendolas, and toucans. Colorful poison dart frogs are easily spotted on the damp forest floor.

Visitors are welcome at **EARTH,** a university dedicated to tropical agricultural sciences and preserving a 990-acre (400 ha) swath of lowland rain forest with nature trails.

Just east of **Siquirres,** signs point south via dirt road to **Parque Nacional Barbilla,** which protects 29,400 acres (11,900 ha) of lowland tropical rain forest up the northern flank of Cerro Tigre. The rugged trails will appeal to hardy hikers. The ranger station here has facilities.

Well worth the detour off Highway 32, **Veragua Rainforest** is a private reserve with superb exhibits on snakes, frogs, and insects. A National Biodiversity Institute research station is open to view. It has trails and an aerial tram down to a ravine where poison dart frogs hop underfoot. The adjoining **Original Canopy Tour** *(tel 2291-4465, canopytour.com)* whizzes you through treetops on a zip line, with nine platforms and traverses. ∎

EARTH
- 🅰 Map p. 218
- ✉ 800 yards (731.5 m) E of Guácimo
- ☎ 2713-0000
- 🅢 $$$$$ (guided tours)

earth.ac.cr

Parque Nacional Barbilla
- 🅰 Map p. 219
- ✉ 11 miles (17 km) S of Hwy. 32 (junction 3 miles/5 km E of Siquerres)
- ☎ 8396-7611
- 🅢 $$

costarica-national parks.com

Veragua Rainforest
- 🅰 Map p. 219
- ✉ 23 miles (37 km) E of Siquerres
- ☎ 4000-0949
- 🅢 $$$$$

veraguarainforest .com

Bananas' Cost

The Llanura de Santa Clara is awash with banana plantations. Costa Rica exported $835 million of bananas in 2015 (up from $640 million in 2011). Around 128,000 acres (51,800 ha) are planted, mostly in the Caribbean, employing about 8 percent of the nation's workers. U.S.-based Standard Fruit Company is the major producer. The resulting monoculture is blamed for many ecological ills, including the felling of rain forest for plantations. Fertilizer runoff has led reeds and water hyacinths to blossom, filling in habitats and channels, while silt washing out to sea has destroyed much of the coral reefs. Pesticides such as DBCP, banned in North America, have poisoned plantation workers. When plastic bags used to protect fruit stems end up in the ocean, marine turtles mistake them for jellyfish and choke. In a bid to secure an Eco-OK seal of approval, Costa Rica's banana industry is adopting more ecologically responsible methods, although the transnational corporations continue to be accused of maltreating workers.

Refugio Nacional de Vida Silvestre Barra del Colorado

The Río San Juan forms the border with Nicaragua. Between it and Laguna de Tortuguero lie 225,365 acres (91,200 ha) of swampland and rain forest teeming with exotic wildlife. The labyrinthine lagoons and rivers boil with tarpon, snook, and antediluvian garfish, making the refuge the premier sportfishing center in Costa Rica.

A water taxi cuts a wake between raffia palms.

Refugio Nacional de Vida Silvestre Barra del Colorado

 Map p. 218

 40 miles (64 km) N of Guápiles

☎ 2709-8086

💲 $$

The sluggish rivers deposit vast amounts of silt that shift the watercourses yearly in a mosaic of deltas. Endless green rain forest fills the horizon; the forests are gnawed at by loggers, and banana plantations push up against the park's southern borders. The wet, hilly, lowlands are bordered to the west by 1,096-foot-high (334 m) hills, the **Lomas de Sierpe.**

Swampy sloughs meander from lagoon to lagoon. Most backwaters are inaccessible; here manatees breed in relative isolation. Jabiru storks, orpendolas, and green macaws are among the numerous intriguing bird species. Crocodiles bask on mudbanks. And caimans, monkeys, sloths, river otters, and terrapins are sure-bet sightings.

The tumble-down village of **Barra del Colorado**—served by an airstrip—straddles the **Río Colorado,** a branch of the Río San Juan. Anglers set out from sportfishing lodges for colossal fights with record-setting tarpon and snook. The **Caño de Penitencia,** clogged by silt and water hyacinths, links Barra to Tortuguero (see pp. 224–225).

All along the riverbanks are dilapidated shacks on stilts. The river is entirely within Nicaraguan territory; you will need a passport and be prepared to pay a fee. ■

Parque Nacional Tortuguero

This 47,000-acre (19,000 ha) park encompasses diverse wetlands penetrating inland for 9 miles (15 km), a 14-mile-long (23 km) section of shoreline that is the Caribbean's premier nesting site for green turtles, and ocean waters that stretch 18 miles (29 km) offshore. Tortuguero, which is deluged by up to 200 inches (500 cm) of rain a year, comprises coastal rain forest and several distinct wetland ecosystems that are astonishingly rich in wildlife.

This popular, but remote, park is pinned by the funky hamlet of **Tortuguero,** sprawling along a 4-mile-long (6.4 km) sandy peninsula between a lagoon and the sea. At the northern end of the promontory, aircraft swoop down to the grass strip, from which boats ferry travelers to lodges or to the isolated village that offers budget accommodations, canoes, and guides for hire.

The park's maze of waterways guarantees superb wildlife viewing. You are not likely to spot jaguars, tapirs, or other endangered mammal species, but you can expect to see monkeys, giant iguanas, and sloths. Of Tortuguero's 300 bird species (which include rare green macaws), you are most likely to see aracarias, oropendolas, parrots, and toucans. Caimans and river otters frequent the canals. Exploring with an experienced local guide is recommended. **Tortuga Lodge** (see Travelwise p. 256), a prominent nature and sportfishing lodge, offers excellent guided tours, as does **Karla Taylor** *(tel 8527-7620 or 2262-9384)*, perhaps the preeminent local guide.

A well-timed visit may coincide with leatherback, hawksbill, or green turtles coming ashore to lay eggs *(Feb.–Oct.)*. Tortuguero is the Caribbean's primary green turtle hatchery. Guides from a local cooperative

escort nocturnal hikes on the beach *($$$)*, which is otherwise off-limits after 6 p.m. *(only 400 people permitted nightly)*. Report any guides who illegally dig up nests to show you the eggs of hatchlings. To learn more, stop at the **John H. Phipps Biological Station,** north of the village, where the **Natural History Visitor Center** has exhibits. At the village's south end, the **Cuatro Esquinas Ranger Station** also has exhibits; a trail leads into the rain forest, but rubber boots *(available for rent)* are compulsory in the wet season. ■

Parque Nacional Tortuguero

- ⛰ Map p. 219
- ✉ 10 miles (16 km) NE of Zancudo
- ☎ 2710-2929 or 2709-8086
- 💲 $$

John H. Phipps Biological Station

- ⛰ Map p. 219
- ✉ Tortuguero
- ☎ 2709-8125
- 💲 $

conserveturtles.org

Not-So-Tiny Bubbles

Endangered manatees inhabit lagoons in the remote western parts of the park. This herbivorous, heavily wrinkled mammal resembles a tuskless walrus with a spatulate tail. It grows to 12 feet (3.7 m) in length and can weigh a ton (907 kg). It spends most of its time submerged, foraging on water hyacinths and other aquatic fodder that produce flatulence. Bubbles rising to the surface of the water are therefore a good indication that a healthy manatee is expressing itself below.

A Ride on the Canal de Tortuguero

Until the 1960s, travel along the Caribbean coast was nearly impossible. Rough waves and the lack of bays precluded safe passage and anchorage, while the swamps that extend far inland thwarted the construction of roads. During the Trejos administration (1966–1970), a canal was dredged parallel to the shore, linking the remote hamlets of Barra del Colorado and Tortuguero with Puerto Limón and the port of Moín.

Today a journey along the Tortuguero Canal is one of Costa Rica's most rewarding activities—thrilling, too, as your boatman canes your craft with the throttle wide open.

The narrow, 70-mile-long (113 km) Canal de Tortuguero links the various lagoons and major rivers along the northern Caribbean plains and runs a few hundred yards inland of the surf-pounded shore. The canal is a liquid highway of commerce, and the throbbing of weary engines is its mantra. Most of the lodges at Tortuguero and Barra provide their own watercraft for guests opting for the slow, scenic route. Watch for *cayucos*—motorized dugout canoes carved from a single log and traditionally used for ferrying bananas and other agricultural produce—and public water taxis, usually fast-paced *lanchas*. These small riverboats are not built for comfort; a waterproof poncho is recommended.

This boat ride can be done in either direction. It is a 3.5-hour trip from **Moín ❶**, 3 miles (4.8 km) north of Limón. Private boats leave from the JAPDEVA dock *(tel 2709-8005, $$$$$ round-trip)*. Within minutes you are enveloped in the deepest verdure, with patches of rain forest towering over the river. Egrets and numerous other waders stalk the grassy banks in search of tasty tidbits while kingfishers skim over black waters.

Twelve miles (19 km) from Moín, the canal opens into the **Boca del Río Matina ❷**, a broad estuary whose brown-sand beaches are formed by silt desposited by the sluggish river. Female green, hawksbill, and leatherback turtles favor these warm sands for their nests, as well as at Playa Barra de Matina, where 4 miles (6.4 km) of shoreline backing the beach are protected within

NOT TO BE MISSED:

Parque Nacional Tortuguero
• Refugio Nacional de Vida Silvestre Barra del Colorado

the **Pacuare Nature Reserve ❸** *(tel 2798-2220, parisminaturtles.org)*, where scientists conduct turtle research; trails run parallel to the beach and to an inland lagoon.

Tour company charter boats depart for Tortuguero from Caño Blanco marina, at **Barra del Matina Sur,** 2 miles (3 km) upriver.

In all these miles there are no settlements to speak of, although occasionally you will pass a ramshackle hut made of wood and bamboo, raised on stilts to guard against flooding and snakes. The *cimaronnes* (literally, "wild ones" in reference to people of mixed blood), who live along the riverbank, subsist on fishing, the sale of bananas, and cattle that graze in clearings cut from the grasslands and sedge.

The canal opens into the wide estuary of the **Río Parismina ❹**, a popular sportfishing location, particularly during the spring run of tarpon, which can be hauled in from the surf; and for snook, notably mid-August through November. Three sportfishing lodges cater to anglers. Silt from the river often clogs the canal—do not be surprised if your boat grounds. Beyond the river, the canal penetrates **Parque Nacional Tortuguero** (see p. 223), indicated by a sign beside the **Jaloba Ranger Station ❺**—a good place to spot crocodiles on the mudbanks. No fee is charged for passage via the canal.

In places the rain forest canopy merges overhead, forming dark glades that echo with the roar of howler monkeys. Great stands of bamboo rise in feathery clusters. Freshwater turtles and caimans sunning themselves on logs will plop into the waters as you pass. Toucans are noisy and numerous. With good luck, you might even spot an endangered green macaw.

After 49 miles (79 km) you will arrive at the village of **Tortuguero** ⑥, facing a broad lagoon that opens northward to the azure waters of the Caribbean. Most passengers end their journey here.

West of the village, the canal cuts inland and zigzags through the wetlands of **Refugio Nacional de Vida Silvestre Barra del Colorado** ⑦ (see p. 222). Playful river otters are often seen along this 21-mile-long (34 km) section that slices through the aquatic wilderness, where raffia palms hang over the waters. Farther north, water hyacinths clog the channel. Eventually you come to a broad reach near the mouth of the **Río Colorado,** where crocodiles bask on the mudflats.

Three and a half hours from Moín, the village of **Barra del Colorado** ⑧ marks the end of your journey.

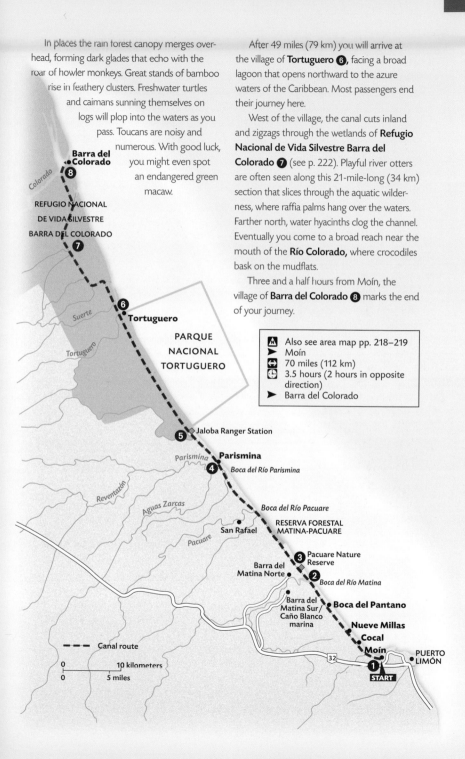

🄰	Also see area map pp. 218–219
►	Moín
🔁	70 miles (112 km)
🕙	3.5 hours (2 hours in opposite direction)
►	Barra del Colorado

Canal route

| 0 | 10 kilometers |
| 0 | 5 miles |

Puerto Limón

Puerto Limón is a sultry town that is more a place to pass through than linger in. The only town along the Caribbean coast, Limón is the main service center for the eponymous region and is the country's main commercial port; it is also the gateway to both Tortuguero and Cahuita National Parks (see pp. 223 & 230), both of which are sea turtle nesting grounds. Puerto Limón hosts the country's main cruise dock and bursts to life during the annual Carnival. A brief visit reveals some minor attractions, including lovely beaches on the outskirts of town.

An old fishing *lancha* rests on Playa Bonita.

Puerto Limón
🗺 Map p. 219

Visitor Information

✉ Institute of Costa Rican Tourism, Edificio COPAZA, Calle 7 bet. Aves. 6 & 7

☎ 2758-0983 or 2758-1008

The port evolved as a center for exporting hardwoods and, during the early colonial era, cacao, but soon fell beyond the pale of Spanish authority. It emerged as a refuge for buccaneers. Puerto Limón blossomed in the late 19th century, when the Atlantic Railroad was built and the banana trade followed. When blights scythed through the plantations from the 1930s on, the port suffered a decline from which it has only recently begun to recover. City leaders have

pulled the city up by its bootstraps in recent years: Streets are well paved, and cruise ships now arrive at the new port facility.

Despite its somewhat forlorn aspect, the city boasts some fine clapboard colonial buildings adorned with filigreed ironwork balconies. The town's oldest and most famous building, the **Black Star Line** (*Ave. 5, Calle 6*), was declared an Architectural Heritage site in 2000. Although it burned down in April 2016, President Solís has vowed to rebuild it. The most appealing building is the **town hall,** or *alcadia,* on the north side of the town plaza, **Parque Vargas,** which lies at the east end of Avenida 1. At its heart is a small bandstand surrounded by promenades shaded by tousled palms and by vine-draped strangler fig trees. Note the bronze busts of Columbus and his son Fernando on the northeast corner. They were dedicated in 1992 in celebration of the 500th anniversary of the Genoese explorer's landing in Mesoamerica. Facing it is a

INSIDER TIP:

Some of the greatest rewards in travel come from what you give rather than receive. Volunteering to protect marine turtle nesting sites is a perfect example and easily arranged through entities such as the Sea Turtle Conservancy [see sidebar p. 144].

—CHRISTOPHER P. BAKER
National Geographic author

faded mural paying homage to Columbus, pre-Columbian Indians, and the immigrant workers who put down roots locally. Completed in 2010, the concrete, post-modernist **Catedral del Sagrado Corazón** *(Calle 7, Ave. 3)* soars over the city center; its choir is acclaimed.

An uninspired seafront boulevard overlooks a coral reef thrust

Carnival

When Día de las Culturas (Carnival) comes around in mid-October, Limón explodes in a bacchanal in which the Limoneses let down their hair and succumb to a promiscuous delirium. Rum, beer, and *guaro* (local grog of fermented sugarcane) flow freely. As many as 100,000 Ticos come to witness (and participate in) costume parades, beauty contests, and general revelry.

from the sea on April 22, 1991, by an earthquake that razed several buildings and compounded the city's ill fortunes. The small isle of **La Uvita** lies 800 yards (730 m) offshore. On September 18, 1502, Christopher Columbus anchored here and became the first European to set foot on the land he called La Huerta–The Garden.

The enclosed, art deco **Mercado Municipal** *(Calle 4, Ave. 3)* is worth a peek for the colorful stalls tucked into narrow alleys. Many restaurants and other businesses are run by Chinese, offspring of indentured laborers who helped build the railroad then stayed on, incorporating their culture into the city's fabric. The community has its own cemetery—**La Colonita China**—on Highway 32 west of town.

North of town, surfers ride the waves off **Playa Bonita,** a handsome beach that is excellent for sunning with occasional breaks for ceviche and grilled fish (washed down by homemade cashew wine) from thatch-roofed *ranchitas.* ■

Valle de la Estrella & the Talamancas

Shaded by coconut palms, a string of beaches leads the eye south from Limón. Highway 36 hugs the shore and makes brief forays inland, seeking narrow necks by which to cross the wide rivers—the Ríos Bananao, Bananito, and Estrella—that flood down from the Talamancas and seasonally inundate the narrow coastal plain and broad valleys.

Sloth Sanctuary
- Map p. 219
- 2 miles (3 km) N of Penshurst
- 2750-0775
- Closed Mon.
- $$$$$

slothsanctuary.com

Reserva Biológica Hitoy-Cerere
- Map p. 219
- Off Hwy. 36, 15 miles (24 km) W of Penshurst
- 2795-1446 or 2206-5516
- $$

costarica-national parks.com

Selva Bananito
- Map p. 219
- 9 miles (14.5 km) W of Bananito
- 2253-8118

selvabananito.com

Twelve miles (19 km) south of Puerto Limón, the road meets the mouth of the wide **Río Estrella,** where lagoons and channels abound with wildlife, including flocks of cattle egrets. The wetlands extend south along the shore to the **Sloth Sanctuary,** which serves as a refuge and research center for orphaned and confiscated sloths. A guided two-hour visit is fascinating, and includes a one-hour canoe trip through the estuary, which teems with wildlife.

Half a mile (0.8 km) south of the river, at **Penshurst,** a side road snakes inland into the Valle de la Estrella. Guided hikes go into the nearby forest. Upriver, the valley opens into a wide basin carpeted with banana plantations and crisscrossed with dirt roads serving processing plants.

The Talamancas soar westward, clad in some of the densest montane rain forest in the isthmus. Some 22,363 acres (9,050 ha) is protected within **Reserva Biológica Hitoy-Cerere,** an undeveloped reserve accessed by four-wheel drive. Trails from the ranger station follow the valley of the Río Hitoy-Cerere to small waterfalls, and across the mountains into Valle de El General.

To the north of Hitoy-Cerere is **Selva Bananito,** a 2,350-acre (950 ha) cattle ranch and reserve with rustic cabins and a nature lodge in premontane rain forest, accessed by horseback or hiking trails. Expect to see sublime wildlife here, from monkeys to toucans. Tree climbing and rappelling tours, including rappels down a waterfall, are specialties. To reach it by road, you will need a four-wheel-drive vehicle. ■

EXPERIENCE: Horseback Riding

Horseback riding is available nationwide in Costa Rica, offering a joyous way to see the country. These are among the best places to saddle up (see also listings by region, Travelwise pp. 260–265): **Rancho San Miguel** (La Guácima, Central Highlands,

tel 2439-0003; see p. 73) **Hotel Hacienda Guachipelín** (Curubandé, Guanacaste, tel 2690-2900, guachipelin.com) **Sabine's Smiling Horses** (Monteverde, Guanacaste, tel 8385-2424, smilinghorses.com) **Discovery Horseback Tours** (Jacó, Central Pacific,

tel 8838-7550, horseride costarica.com) **Rancho La Merced** (Uvita, Central Pacific, tel 2743-8032, ranchola merced.com) **Seahorse Stables** (Punta Cocles, The Caribbean, tel 8859-6435, horsebackriding incostarica.com)

Cahuita

Colorful Cahuita—named from *cawi*, the Native American word for the mahogany used to make dugout canoes—offers a taste of zesty culture and a laid-back lifestyle that draws a hip, unpretentious crowd keen to let down its hair. The rustic hamlet, gateway to Parque Nacional Cahuita (see p. 230), offers fine beaches, simple accommodations, some of the country's best regional cuisine, and activities that range from horseback riding to scuba diving to glass-bottom boat tours.

The southern Caribbean was once a neglected regional backwater that survived by fishing and by growing cacao; the latter industry was destroyed by the *Monilia* fungus two decades ago, about the same time Highway 36 linked it to the rest of the country. Today, lively, colorful Cahuita boasts an earthy charm.

The main village has no central plaza, merely two dirt roads paralleling the coast, with four dirt roads in between. The main street ends eastward at **Kelly Creek** and the entrance to Parque Nacional Cahuita, with a coral-colored beach curling into the hazy beyond. North of the village, dozens of simple accommodations and eateries line a black-sand beach—**Playa Negra**—sweeping north in a palm-shaded scimitar. (Be cautious of riptides.) Contact **Cahuita Tours** for horseback riding and other local activities. The **Tree of Life Wildlife Rescue Center & Botanical Gardens** *(tel 8317-0325, treeoflifecostarica.com)* provides a close-up look at kinkajous, howler monkeys, and other creatures that roam these wilds.

Cahuita's spicy regional cuisine, dialect, and musical influences reflect longstanding links with Jamaica. Rastafarians are numerous, dressed in their trademark clothing of red, yellow, black, and green. Reggae riffs mingle with the sound

Cahuita's friendly, laid-back culture draws a hip crowd interested in the region's earthy charms and spicy cuisine.

of the surf, while pungent *ganja* (marijuana) hangs in the salt air.

The somewhat negative reputation Cahuita had earned has been combated recently by heightened community policing. ∎

Cahuita
🅰 Map p. 219

Cahuita Tours
☎ 2755-0101
cahuitatours.com

Parque Nacional Cahuita

This 2,711-acre (1,097 ha) park envelops a promontory—Punta Cahuita—clad with rain forests, where beaches curl away north and south around topaz blue bays. A coral reef covers 600 acres (242 ha) and extends around Punta Cahuita to Punta Vargas.

The keel-billed toucan's beak has evolved for eating fruit.

Parque Nacional Cahuita

Map p. 219

✉ S of Cahuita village

☎ 2755-0461 or 2755-0302

💲 Donation (Kelly Creek); $$ (Punta Vargas)

A 4-mile-long (6.4 km) trail traces the shoreline and links the **Kelly Creek Ranger Station** with the **Punta Vargas Ranger Station** about 1 mile (1.6 km) south of Punta Vargas and midway down the park. Much of the wildlife that inhabits the jungle green shore can be experienced without leaving the beach. Bands of inquisitive white-faced Capuchin monkeys often scamper in the treetops; coatis, iguanas, and raccoons poke their noses onto the sands; and the barking of howler monkeys echoes from within the dark forests. Agoutis, anteaters, and armadillos are among the other species to be seen while hiking—watch for snakes underfoot and for harmless caimans cooling off in the lagoons and watercourses. Birdlife is also prolific, including green ibises, herons, toucans, garrulous parrots, and scarlet macaws, magnificent in their imperial cloaks of blue, red, and yellow, which flock here seasonally (Dec.–March).

Green, hawksbill, and leatherback marine turtles nest on the sweeping beach south of **Punta Vargas,** where waves help bring them in at high tide and the tidal pools are good on the ebb.

INSIDER TIP:

Capuchin monkeys have learned to beg for food. Don't feed them! Human food-stuffs are unhealthy for monkeys, which have also been known to bite the hand that feeds them.

—CHRISTOPHER P. BAKER
National Geographic author

More than 125 species of fish, including blue parrotfish, gambol amid the hard and soft corals that lie offshore between Punta Cahuita and Punta Vargas. The wreck of a slave ship with cannon and manacles in 20 feet (6 m) of water is an added highlight. Water clarity and reef ecology suffer from silt washing down from the banana plantations *(Feb.–April best for viewing reef).* ■

Puerto Viejo

Puerto Viejo, the Caribbean coast's beloved surfing capital, emits a centripetal pull on counterculture vacationers; it is Costa Rica's mecca of the offbeat. The legendary Salsa Brava wave pumps ashore in front of restaurants that bear an international imprimatur, and discos come alive at night. It all mixes together surpisingly well, resulting in a hamlet spiced with a funky-meets-cosmopolitan flavor.

No waves today? Take a siesta.

Vultures hop on the unpaved streets of the village, 2 miles (3.2 km) east of Highway 36 and 8 miles (13 km) south of Cahuita at the southern end of Playa Negra, which ends at **Punta Pirikiki.** Native American culture is strong here, and guided trips into indigenous reserves are popular. The **Asociación Talamanca de Ecoturismo y Conservación** (ATEC; see Travelwise p. 265) acts as the local information bureau and arranges visits to the Bribrí, Cabecar, and KeKöLdi reserves. Snorkeling, diving, and dolphin viewing are offered by **Reef Runner Divers** (tel 2750-0480). Or explore via **Caribe Horse Riding Club** (tel 8705-4250, caribehorse .com), inland at Playa Cocles, 1.5 miles (2 km) south of the village.

Puerto Viejo's main attraction is **Finca la Isla Botanical Garden,** which spans 12 acres (5 ha) of rain forest and gardens where spices, exotic fruits, and ornamental plants are grown. A self-guided booklet explains the trails, where monkeys, sloths, and snakes abound. Poison dart frogs live among the bromeliads.

South of Punta Pirikiki, **Playa Cocles, Playa Chiquita,** and **Playa Manzanillo** extend 8 miles (13 km) south to Refugio Nacional de Vida Silvestre Gandoca-Manzanillo (see p. 232). The **Jaguar Rescue Center** rehabilitates sick and injured mammals— among them anteaters, big cats, and monkeys—and has guided tours. At **Chocorart** (tel 2750-0075, $$$, by appointment), a Swiss couple produce delicious chocolate from their farm's organic cocoa. ∎

Finca la Isla Botanical Garden

- 🅐 Map p. 219
- ✉ 800 yards (732 m) W of Puerto Viejo
- ☎ 8829-4929
- 🕐 Closed weekends
- 💲 $ (guided tour $$$$$)

costaricaorganics farm.com

Jaguar Rescue Center

- 🅐 Map p. 219
- ✉ Playa Chiquita
- ☎ 2750-0710
- 🕐 Closed Sun.
- 💲 $$$$

jaguarrescue .foundation

Refugio Nacional de Vida Silvestre Gandoca-Manzanillo

This remote jewel extends from Punta Uva, 3 miles (4.8 km) south of Puerto Viejo, to the Río Sixaola, forming the border with Panama. The refuge (a prime turtle sanctuary) combines lush lowland rain forest with a coral reef and an amalgam of wetland habitats where visitors may spot manatees, crocodiles, and even an endemic species of freshwater dolphin. With more than 360 bird species on hand, don't rule out a sighting of the rare harpy eagle.

Refugio Nacional de Vida Silvestre Gandoca-Manzanillo

🗺 Map p. 219

✉ 12 miles (19.3 km) E of Puerto Viejo

☎ 2759-9001

💲 $

Nature Observatorio

✉ Manzanillo

☎ 8628-2663

natureobservatorio .com

Punta Mona Center

🗺 Map p. 219

✉ 4 miles (6.4 km) S of Manzanillo

🕐 Visits by reservation only

💲 $$$$$

puntamona.org

The 23,348-acre (9,450 ha) refuge protects the only mangrove system along Costa Rica's Caribbean coast—as well as the nation's only remaining orey swamp and two equally rare jolillo palm swamps where tapirs find safe haven. These labyrinthine ecosystems extend along the estuary of the **Río Gandoca** and **Laguna Gandoca,** where they provide a breeding place for sea life, including tarpon.

You might catch a glimpse of endangered manatees and rare pink-skinned estuarine dolphins—the *tucuxí*—as they come to the surface, snuffling and snorting, to breathe. The endemic tucuxí can also be seen swimming in the mouth of the **Río Sixaola;** these dolphins are found in coastal lagoons as far north as Nicaragua. .

The wetlands back beautiful palm-lined **Playa Gandoca;** four species of marine turtles deposit their eggs here. To safeguard their nests, the sanctuary encompasses more than 10,961 acres (4,435 ha) of sea, which also protect a live coral reef. The **Gandoca Development Association** *(asvocr.org/ gandoca)* welcomes volunteers to assist in turtle conservation.

Access is from the hamlets of **Manzanillo** or **Gandoca,** which

are linked by a trail that skirts Laguna Gandoca inland and provides fantastic wildlife viewing. Another trail follows the coast to **Punta Mona** ("Monkey Point"). Scuba diving and kayaking are available. **Guias MANT** *(tel 2759-9043),* the local guide association, offers hiking, birding, snorkeling, and turtle-watching tours. For a birds-eye view of the refuge, haul yourself up to the **Nature Observatorio,** a lookout platform high in a nispero tree. The two-story tree house can be rented, and guided nature hikes are offered.

Between Punta Uva and Manzanillo, the 8,765-acre (3,547 ha) **KéKöLdi Indian Reserve** meets the shore. Much of the reserve lies in the Gandoca-Manzanillo refuge; this safeguards the lands of the Bribrí and Cabecar tribes, who are exploring ecotourism and experimental income sources such as iguana farms. Visits can be arranged in Puerto Viejo and Manzanillo through ATEC (see Travelwise p. 265), as well as with **ANAI** *(tel 2756-8120, anaicr.org),* an organization that fosters ecotourism among local communities. Counterculture types might enjoy **Punta Mona Center,** a community that practices and teaches about restorative agriculture. ∎

Travelwise

Bike your way around Nicoya's sleepy towns.

TRAVELWISE

PLANNING YOUR TRIP
When to Go

Time your visit according to where you wish to go, as the country's climate varies by region. In general, the dry season (*verano*, or summer) is November to April, and the wet season (*invierno*, or winter) is May to October. The tourist board calls winter the "green season."

The Central Highlands enjoy a year-round springlike climate, with clear skies and warm weather. The wet season means clear mornings and afternoon showers, although prolonged rain is possible. Upper mountain slopes have alpine climates, with persistent fog and high winds.

Guanacaste sizzles during the dry season, when temperatures soar. Trees explode into bloom, and stiff northwesterly winds whip the Pacific—fun for surfers but puts a damper on fishing.

Rainfall increases progressively southward in Nicoya and along the Pacific coast. Though Golfo Dulce and the Osa Peninsula have torrential rainfall throughout the year, clear skies are also frequent. Be prepared for stifling humidity. The same is true year-round of the Northern Highlands and Caribbean coast, where rainfall increases northward (almost 200 inches/ 500 cm annually in the Barra del Colorado and Tortuguero regions). January through April are the driest months, although heavy rain can fall at any time.

Most tourists visit in the dry season, when the more popular hotels may be booked solid. During green season, many hotels and car rental agencies lower their rates. This is a good time to visit, as many national parks and attractions are less crowded and the foliage is at its best.

What to Take

Costa Rica has a tropical climate, so dress accordingly. Expect hot days with warm evenings, except in mountain areas, where nights can be chilly. On higher slopes, cold winds bring fog and driving rain, so wind- and rainproof gear is essential. A sweater is useful, and a poncho works well against downpours in lowland areas. Loose-fitting cotton shorts and T-shirts are fine, as is clothing made of quick-drying, wicking fabrics. Avoid tight-fitting clothes (which promote fungal growth in the hot, humid climate) and bright colors (if you want to get close to wildlife). Informal wear is fine almost everywhere, but you might want an elegant outfit for smarter restaurants in San José.

You'll want a comfortable pair of shoes for hiking, but be prepared to get them wet. Pack a spare pair.

You will need insect repellent, particularly for wilderness excursions. Mosquitoes and other biting insects can be ferocious in Costa Rica, although they are not such a problem in the highlands.

Do not underestimate the tropical sun's strength. Sunglasses are important, and sunscreen is mandatory, even for brief periods outdoors. Wearing a hat or cap will keep you cooler and block the sun.

BEFORE YOU GO
Customs

Check with customs before bringing culture orchids and plants in sealed vials into the United States. For details contact the U.S. Customs Service, 1300 Pennsylvania Ave., NW, Washington, D.C. 20229, tel 877/227-5511, cbp.gov.

Passports

A passport is mandatory for entry into Costa Rica. U.S. citizens do not need a visa to visit Costa Rica if they are traveling as tourists with a U.S. passport valid for at least 30 days, and if they will be staying for no more than 90 days.

If traveling with children under 18, remember that they become subject to local child welfare laws after 30 days, and you must request permission to take them out of the country. Contact the National Child Protection Agency (*Patronato Nacional de Infancia, Ave. 10 e 12B, Calle 21, San José, tel 2523-0700, pani.go.cr*).

HOW TO GET TO COSTA RICA
By Air

Most flights arrive at Juan Santamaría International Airport (*tel 2437-2400, fly2sanjose.com*) 11 miles (18 km) west of San José. An increasing number of flights arrive at Daniel Oduber International Airport (*tel 2666-9600, liberiacostaricaairport.net*) 8 miles (13 km) west of Liberia, the provincial capital of Guanacaste.

The national carrier, **Avianca Costa Rica** (*tel 2299-8222 or 800/284-2622 in the U.S., avianca .com*), serves nine countries throughout the Americas, including flights from Los Angeles and New York.

The following North American airlines offer regular flights to Costa Rica: **Air Canada** (*tel 888/247-2262, aircanada.com*), **Alaska Airlines** (*tel 800/252-7522, alaskaair.com*), **American Airlines** (*tel 800/433-7300, aa.com*), **Delta** (*tel 800/241-4141, delta.com*), **JetBlue** (*tel 800/ 538-2583, jetblue.com*), **Southwest Airlines** (*tel 800/435-9792, south west.com*), **Spirit** (*tel 801/401-2222, spirit.com*), and **United Airlines** (*tel 800/864-8331, united.com*).

The following airlines fly from Europe to Costa Rica: **British Airways** (*tel 0844/493-0787, britishairways.com*), **Condor** (tel *180/676-7767, condor.com/de*), and **Iberia** *(tel 901/111-500, iberia .com/es*).

By Car

The 2,000-mile (3,220 km) trip from the U.S.-Mexican border takes around two weeks. Preparation, and a four-wheel-drive vehicle, are essential. Arrange all documentation in advance and check your insurance. For advice, contact Sanborn's *(tel 800/222-0158, sanbornsinsurance.com)*.

Group Tours

Around one-third of travelers to Costa Rica choose a package tour. Most such tours are nature related, though sightseeing tours are also available. **National Geographic Expeditions** *(tel 888/966-8687, natgeoexpeditions .com)* offers several. Or contact the **Institute of Costa Rican Tourism** (ICT; see p. 239) for a list of recommended tour companies, or try CANATUR (see p. 239).

GETTING AROUND

By Air

Major destinations are linked to each other, to Juan Santamaría International Airport, and to Tobias Bolaños international airport *(tel 2232-2820)*.

Two domestic carriers serve regional airstrips with a network of scheduled flights. Both use 20- to 35-passenger aircraft. **SANSA** *(tel 2290-4100, flysansa.com)* operates from Juan Santamaría International Airport. **NatureAir** *(tel 2299-6000 or 800/235-9272 in North America, natureair.com)* operates from Tobias Bolaños Airport and Juan Santamaría International Airport. Groups can charter small airplanes to airstrips throughout Costa Rica.

By Bus

There is no national bus network. Dozens of private companies offer fast *(directo)* and slower *(normal* or *corriente)* service. Trips should cost less than $10. Standards vary, with comfortable, modern buses on major routes. Rural areas are often served by retired U.S. school buses. Some lines sell tickets in advance; on others you pay when boarding. Be prepared for crowded conditions, avoid travel on weekends, and guard against pickpockets and luggage theft.

Two shuttle bus services can take you almost anywhere in Costa Rica; fares start at around $21. **Interbus** *(tel 4100-0888, interbus online.com)* serves Cahuita, Fortuna, Manuel Antonio, Tamarindo, and other major destinations. **Grayline Fantasy Bus** *(tel 2220-2126, graylinecostarica.com)* transfers passengers between major tourist destinations. Several bus companies also operate regular service from San José to destinations throughout Central America. Fares are cheap, but trips are time consuming.

San José's bus terminals are widely spread throughout the district called Coca Cola. It is a high-crime area; caution is advised. The bus lines in Costa Rica are privately operated by myriad companies, so determining route information can be difficult, but the ICT does publish a bus schedule, available locally and on visitcostarica.com.

Bus fares are extremely low—from around 140–360 colones (35–70 cents) to travel from the suburbs to central San José, to $3–$12.50 for cross-country trips.

Car Rental

To rent a car, you must be over 21, hold a passport, and have a valid driver's license (a U.S. license is fine) that has been held for at least one year. You will also need a credit card and have to leave a hefty deposit (about $500). Beware of additional charges that might appear on your bill when you return the car or get your credit card statement. Check that the rental includes unlimited mileage. Insurance is mandatory, and most rental companies, including U.S. franchises, refuse to honor insurance issued abroad. Rates vary from about $45 daily for the smallest vehicles, and $70 for mid-size cars, to between $80 and $110 for four-wheel-drive vehicles (recommended, as the road network is in appalling shape). For off-road exploration, a rugged vehicle is essential.

In addition to U-Save, a reputable local company, most major international car rental companies are represented:
Avis, tel 2509-5950, avis.co.cr
Budget, tel 2436-2007, budget.co.cr
Dollar, tel 2443-2950, dollarcostarica.com
Hertz, tel 2221-1818, hertzcostarica.com
U-Save, tel 2430-4647, usavecr.com

These agencies provide 24-hour breakdown assistance, but it can take hours to reach you in outlying areas.

Roads throughout the country are poor, with only one quarter of the 18,000-mile (29,000 km) highway network paved. In the wet season many roads are quagmires, while Nicoya and Guanacaste are thick with dust during the dry season. Many Tico (Costa Rican) drivers are inconsiderate and reckless—there is a high auto fatality rate. Drive slowly and be on your guard. Stray cattle, pedestrians in the road, and potholes are additional hazards.

PRACTICAL ADVICE

Communications

Mail

Postal rates for letters start at 600 colones ($1.10) to North America and 650 colones ($1.19) to Europe. Never mail anything of value, as theft is endemic within the postal service. Allow two weeks for air mail between Costa Rica and North America.

Most mail is delivered to shared postal boxes *(apartados,* abbreviated *Apdo.).* Most major settlements have a post office, usually open Monday to Friday, 7 a.m. to 6 p.m., and Saturday 7 a.m. to noon. In smaller towns, the Correo may close as early as 4:30 and not open on Saturdays. Many gift stores and hotels sell postage stamps.

Faster, more reliable service is offered by private express mail services, such as DHL *(tel 2209-6000, dhl.co.cr),* Federal Express *(tel 800/463-3339, fedex.com/cr),* and UPS *(tel 2290-2828, ups.com).*

Telephones

In remote areas public phones are usually located at the local *pulpería* (grocery store and bar). Service is generally efficient. Have a stack of coins ready: They do not accept credit cards or foreign calling cards. Calls to the U.S. start at 65 cents per minute. Prepaid Viajera Internacional *199* phone cards are sold nationwide in increments of $10 and $20 for international direct-dial calls. Insert the card into the phone, and the cost of your call is deducted.

You can also buy a prepaid phone, or a refillable SIM card ($5–20) for your unlocked phone, upon arrival in Costa Rica. And most major U.S. telecommunications companies offer special travel plans to avoid roaming charges when using your cellphone. Or use your mobile phone in Wi-Fi hot spots to use VOIP video-phone services, such as FaceTime and Skype for free. Hotels often charge a high fee for calls from in-room phones.

For direct-dial international calls, dial 00, then the country code and area code, then the number. For information, dial 113. Dial 116 for assistance in placing international calls or to call collect.

Calling from the U.S., dial 011 plus Costa Rica's country code, 506. There are no area codes. All noncellular numbers now begin

with 2, while cellular numbers now begin with 8.

E-mail

Internet cafés are available throughout Costa Rica. Rates vary from about 350 to 1,500 colones (70 cents–$3) per hour, depending on the venue.

Conversions

Costa Rica uses the metric system of measurement. Useful conversions are:

1 mile = 1.61 kilometers
1 kilometer = 0.62 mile
1 meter = 39.37 inches
1 liter = 0.277 U.S. gallon
10 liters = 2.8 U.S. gallons
1 U.S. gallon = 3.61 liters
1 kilogram = 2.2 pounds
1 pound = 0.45 kilogram

Weather reports use Celsius. To convert quickly (but roughly) from Fahrenheit to Celsius, subtract 30 and divide by two. From Celsius to Fahrenheit, multiply by two and add 30.

0°C	= 32°F
10°C	= 50°F
30°C	= 86°F
100°C	= 212°F

Etiquette & Customs

Costa Rican society is more formal than most. Ticos rarely address individuals by their first names without an invitation to do so. They are class conscious, with campesinos (peasant farmers) and the urban working classes deferring to people considered of a higher status. Black visitors may experience some aloofness.

Costa Ricans use the formal *usted* for you, while the informal *tu* is reserved for intimates. You may also hear the term *vos* used instead of *tu.* They respect professional titles and use them when addressing title holders, such as engineers (e.g., Ingeniero

Rodríguez) and architects (Arquitecto García). Adults are addressed as Señor (Mr.), Señora (Mrs.), or Señorita (Miss). The terms Don (for men) and Doña (for women) are used for high-ranking or respected individuals and senior citizens.

Behavior is dictated by *quedar bien*–a desire to leave a good impression. Ticos are courteous and easily offended. They prefer to use hidden cues rather than state forthright opinions that might disappoint. Thus they will often conceal the truth to create an immediate good impression as, for example, when visitors ask directions. Society operates on "Tico time"; punctuality is not a national trait. Verbal commitments are not necessarily meant to be taken at face value. Costa Ricans tend to be fatalistic about events. *Si Díos quiere*– God willing—is a standard refrain for life's ups and downs.

Bathing suits are frowned on away from the beach. Carry a cover-up or shorts and T-shirt to change into after swimming.

Life revolves around the family. Personal contacts are the key to success, particularly in business and politics. Individualism is frowned upon; team spirit and cooperation take precedence. Costa Ricans tend to be guarded about their family life and rarely extend invitations to their homes.

Outside the main tourist areas you may not be understood in English, so it is advisable to learn a few Spanish phrases. Most restaurants in tourist areas have menus in English but you may have to ask for them.

Health

The national service, Seguro Social (also known as the "Caja"), offers medical treatment for tourists for minimal fees. However, the service is not up to North American standards, and visitors are advised to seek treatment at private facilities, such as **Clínica Biblica** *(tel 2522-1000, clinicabiblica.com)*

in San José or **Hospital CIMA**
(tel 2208-1000, www.hospitalsanjose
.net) in Escazú. Most towns have
private physicians and clinics.

Take out full travel insurance,
which should cover all medical
costs—hospitalization, nursing services, doctors' fees, etc. A medical
evacuation clause is also important
in case sufficient care is not available and you need to return home.

If you require medical help,
consult your hotel. Most maintain a
list of doctors and medical centers,
which can save time. Otherwise,
consult the Yellow Pages of the
telephone book. Keep any receipts
or paperwork for insurance claims.
Make a note of the generic name
of any prescription medications you
take before you leave home. They
may be sold by a different trade
name in Costa Rica.

The main health hazards relate to
Costa Rica's tropical climate, where
bacteria and germs breed profusely.
Wash all cuts and scrapes with warm
water and rubbing alcohol. Although
most water is potable, it is wise to
regard it as suspect: Drink and brush
your teeth with bottled water. Boil
water when camping to eliminate
giardia, a parasite that thrives in
warm water. Avoid uncooked
seafood and vegetables, unwashed
salads, and unpeeled fruits.

Be liberal with the application
of sunscreens and build up your
tan gradually, as the tropical sun
is intense and severe sunburn or
sunstroke can effectively ruin a
vacation. Drink plenty of water to
guard against dehydration.

Biting insects are common,
particularly in the humid lowlands.
Malaria is present in the southern
Caribbean zone and is spread by
mosquitoes: Consult your physician
for a suitable malaria prophylaxis.
Dengue fever is also spread by mosquitoes, and occasional outbreaks
are reported in the Caribbean and
Pacific Lowlands. There is no pre-
ventative medication, so it is wise to
try to avoid being bitten.

Use insect repellents liberally,
and wear earth-colored clothing
with long sleeves and full-length
pants. Be aware that no-see-ums,
tiny biting fleas, strike on the
beaches at dawn and dusk.

Wear long pants when hiking
in grasslands, particularly in Guanacaste, to guard against chiggers
(coloradillos) and ticks *(garrapatas).*

Hunting & Fishing
Hunting is prohibited for foreign
visitors, and firearms cannot be
brought into the country. Fishing
is also regulated, and visitors must
obtain a nonresident permit ($30)
for offshore sportfishing. No license
is required for freshwater fishing.
This is usually arranged by specialist
sportfishing outfitters and lodges,
but can also be purchased at mari-
nas from the Capitania del Puerto.

Media
Newspapers
Costa Rica has three national
newspapers (each of which offers
a conservative view), published in
Spanish: *La Nación, La República,*
and *La Prensa Libre,* available at
newsstands throughout the
country. The English-language
weekly *Tico Times* is available
online *(ticotimes.net)* and offers a
well-rounded and often critical
perspective of the nation.

A number of other English-
language publications also
circulate, including the monthly
magazine *Costa Rica Traveler.*
Major U.S. daily newspapers, such
as the *New York Times* and *USA Today,* and weekly magazines, such
as *Time* and *Newsweek,* are usually
available at leading hotel gift
shops and at select newsstands
in major towns and beach resorts.

Television & Radio
Television reaches almost everyone, although service is inter-
mittent in remote areas. Most
upscale hotels offer cable TV

with European and U.S. programs.
Costa Rica has about 120 radio
stations. All but a few broadcast local and Latin music. The BBC World
Service and Voice of America offer
English-language news. The granddaddy of English-language stations
is Radio 2 (99.5 FM), which plays
hits from the 1960s on, as does
SuperRadio (102.3 FM).

Money Matters
Currency
The national currency is the
colón. U.S. currency is widely
accepted throughout the country.
Most stores, shops, restaurants,
and tour companies will accept it,
including those in smaller towns.
Elsewhere you'll need colones.
Exchange rates are notoriously
fickle, so check the rate before
leaving for your trip.

New bills were introduced in
2012 and come in denominations
of 1,000, 2,000, 5,000, 10,000,
20,000 and 50,000 colones. Coins
are issued in denominations of 5,
10, 25, 50, and 100 colones.

Banks in larger towns usually
have foreign exchange counters.
Most hotels exchange currency,
as do foreign exchange bureaus
(cambios) in the major towns and
tourist centers. Check for high
commission fees. In remote areas,
expect long lines at banks. Limit
the amount of U.S. currency you
exchange, as only $50 worth of
colones can be exchanged for
dollars on leaving.

Visitors may experience trouble
cashing traveler's checks anywhere
but banks, due to widespread fraud.
Many shops will simply refuse to
accept them.

Automated Teller Machines
Many banks now have 24-hour
automated teller machines
(ATMs) for cash advances using
credit cards or withdrawals from
your account using a bank card.

This means your own bank does the exchange. There is usually a small charge for using the ATM.

You will need your personal identification number, or PIN, to withdraw cash. Before leaving home, it is wise to check how much you can withdraw at one time or on any one day. Using ATMs during regular banking hours is advisable, in case of problems (e.g., machines not returning cards).

Credit Cards

Credit cards (tarjetas de crédito) are widely accepted. Visa is the most commonly accepted credit card, followed by MasterCard and American Express.

National Holidays

In addition to Christmas, New Year's Day, and Easter, the following national holidays are observed:
March 19, St. Joseph's Day
April 11, Juan Santamaría Day
May 1, Labor Day
July 25, Guanacaste Day
August 2, Feast of the Virgin of Los Angeles
August 15, Feast of the Assumption
October 12, Columbus Day
December 8, Feast of the Immaculate Conception

Most tourist sites and services, and many stores, stay open for these holidays, but banks and government offices close. Except for tourist services, the country closes down for Easter week (Wed.–Sun.), when fiestas and religious processions occur nationwide; few buses operate on Holy Thursday and Good Friday.

Opening Times

Most stores in Costa Rica are open from 8 a.m. to 6 p.m., Monday through Saturday, with a one- or two-hour lunch break. Malls, supermarkets, and souvenir stores tend to have longer hours and are also open on Sunday.

Bank hours vary, with most opening around 8:15 to 9 a.m. and closing between 3 and 3:45 p.m. Some banks have Saturday morning hours. Most businesses and government offices are open Monday to Friday, 8 a.m. to 5 p.m., often with a two-hour lunch break. Some are open on Saturdays from 9 a.m. to noon.

Most restaurants and other tourist-oriented businesses do not close for lunch.

Places of Worship

Every community has at least one Roman Catholic church, and often a Protestant church as well. Local tourist information offices and leading hotels can usually supply a list of places of worship.

Smoking

Many Costa Ricans smoke. Smoking is banned on public transportation, in taxis, and, since May 2012, in all enclosed public places including restaurants and bars. However, many bars and even restaurants choose to disregard the law.

Taxes

A minimal sales tax is applied to many, but not all, purchases. Only full-service restaurants add taxes to your bill, not sodas or snack bars. There is a 23 percent sales tax at restaurants and for most service industries. Hotels levy a 16.39 percent tourist tax. Be prepared to pay an exit tax of around $29 (payable in colones or U.S. dollars) when leaving the country via air, but check. Since 2014 this should now be prepaid in the price of your airline ticket.

Time Zones

Costa Rican time is the same as U.S. Central Standard Time (CST), one hour behind Eastern Standard Time (EST) and 6 hours behind Greenwich Mean Time (GMT). Costa Rica does not observe daylight savings time, during which the country is 2 hours behind EST, and 7 hours behind British Summer Time.

Tipping

Tipping is not a fact of life in Costa Rica, except in tourist areas, where many people in service jobs depend on tips to make ends meet. However, a tip is an acknowledgment of good service: If the service is not satisfactory, do not tip.

Although a 10 to 15 percent service charge is often added onto restaurant bills, an additional tip should be given for good service. Tour guides should be tipped about $2 per person per day for group tours, and more for personalized services and private tours.

Hotel porters should be given 50 cents per bag and room service staff 10 percent of the bill before taxes. Taxi drivers do not expect tips, although those serving the airport generally expect $1 or so.

Travelers With Disabilities

Costa Rica does not display great sensitivity to the needs of visitors with disabilities, although this situation is changing. Few buildings have wheelchair access or provide accessible toilets. Buses are not adapted for wheelchairs, and curb cuts are rare. In fact, most sidewalks are major obstacle courses, with deep fissures, open gutters, and so forth.

Some modern, upscale hotels have wheelchair access and a few provide specially equipped suites. However, older accommodations and restaurants may present some difficulties. Fortunately, new compliance codes are coming into effect. Outside San José, there are few handicapped-accessible services. New codes are not widely enforced yet.

The following agencies provide information on tour operators, special guides, and other aspects of traveling abroad for visitors with disabilities:

Flying Wheels Travel *(143 W. Bridge St., Owatanna, MN 55060, tel 507/451-5005, flyingwheelstravel.com)*
Independent Living Institute *(Storforsplan 36, 123 47 Farsta, Sweden, tel 8/506 22 179, independentliving.org)*
Society for Accessible Travel & Hospitality *(347 Fifth Ave., Ste. 610, New York, NY 10016, tel 212/447-7284, sath.org)*
Wheelchair Traveling *(wheelchairtraveling.com)* offers a general forum to empower people with limited mobility.

Visitor Information
The Costa Rican government's **Institute of Costa Rican Tourism** (ICT, *tel 866/COSTA-RICA, visitcostarica.com*) has several regional tourism bureaus, including in the baggage-claim area at San José's Juan Santamaría International Airport and at Daniel Oduber International Airport, in Liberia.

The **Costa Rican National Chamber of Tourism,** (CANATUR, *tel 2234-6222, canatur.org*) represents the private tourism sector and publishes brochures and tourist information.

The following locations all have chambers of tourism:

Alajuela, tel 2441-8118
Caribe Sur, tel 8392-3861
Cartago, tel 2551-0396
Costa Bellena, tel 2200-9265
Golfito, tel 8647-6570
Guanacaste, tel 2668-1160
Heredia, tel 2237-2620
Limón, tel 2798-3000
Malpaís & Santa Teresa, tel 2642-1204
Monteverde, tel 8349-5248
Nosara, tel 2682-0161

Osa, tel 8829-2828
Pacífico Central, tel 2643-2853
Puntarenas, tel 2661-2980
Quepos–Manuel Antonio, tel 2777-0749
Sarapiquí, tel 2766-6768
Sarchí, tel 8848-3866
Tenorio–Miravalles, tel 2466-7010
Tortuguero, tel 2257-3887
Turrialba, tel 2556-1200
Zona Norte, tel 2479-7512

Individual tour operators have websites. Costa Rican travel agencies and tour operators are represented by the **Asociación Costarricense de Operadores de Turismo** *(tel 2280-1025, acot.co.cr).*

The following conservation groups can provide information on environmental issues:
Fundación Neotrópica *(tel 2253-2130, neotropica.org)*
Monteverde Conservation League *(tel 2645-5003, monteverde info.com/monteverde_conservation _league)*
Organization for Tropical Studies *(tel 919/684-5774, ots.ac.cr)*
Rainforest Alliance *(tel 212/677-1900, rainforestalliance.org).*

EMERGENCIES
Crime & Police
Crime in Costa Rica is on the increase. Burglary and petty theft are more prevalent than in most North American cities. Caution should be exercised at all times. In major towns, avoid parks, back streets, and unlit areas after dark. In towns there is a danger of pickpockets, so be wary in crowded areas. Highway robbers target tourists. If you get a flat tire, keep driving to a public place to change the tire.

Never leave anything in cars, especially at surfing beaches, where car break-ins are endemic. Don't carry lots of cash or wear expensive-looking jewelry, and keep passports and credit cards out of sight. If anything is stolen, report it

immediately to the police and/or your hotel.

For police, fire, and ambulance, call 911. In most areas you can also call 127 for police or 117 for traffic police; call 128 for the Red Cross and 118 for the fire department. The ICT (see this page) maintains a 24-hour tourist hotline *(tel 800/868-7416).*

Report crimes to the Judicial Police (OIJ) at Calle 17, Ave. 16/18, San José, tel 800/800-3000 or 800/800-0645. Visitors from the U.S. can request a representative of the U.S. Embassy be present.

The traffic police patrol the highways, and a new professionalism belies their reputation for corruption. However, dishonest officials still exist. Never pay a policeman; report any attempts at extortion to the OIJ *(tel 800/800-0645).*

Embassies
U.S. Embassy, in front of Centro Comercial, road to Pavas, Rohrmoser, San José, tel 2519-2000, costarica.usembassy.gov
Canadian Embassy, Oficentro Ejecutivo La Sábana, Edificio 5, Tercer Piso, Sábana Sur, San José, tel 2242-4400, costarica.gc.ca
British Embassy, Centro Colón, Paseo Colón, Calles 38/40, San José, tel 2258-2025, ukincostarica .fco.gov.uk

Snakebites
If a venomous snake bites you, get immediate medical help. Give snakes a wide berth and wear ankle-high shoes when hiking.

Hotels & Restaurants

Accommodations in Costa Rica are varied and reasonably priced, although standards vary widely. There are great differences between the types of facilities available, and it will help you to understand these differences when deciding where to stay. Remember that large areas of the country are remote, so the available or more desirable accommodations may fill quickly during the busy winter months, particularly during Christmas and Easter holidays.

Eating out can be a great pleasure in San José, which offers wide variety. Elsewhere menus are typically restricted to traditional fare and seafood, with more cosmopolitan options in tourist destinations and upscale hotels.

Accommodations

There are several types of accommodations. While these terms are sometimes used interchangeably, *albergues* (hostels), *hospedajes* (boardinghouses), and *cabinas* (cheap hotels) are among the budget options. Mid-range hotels are widely available, offering minimal service and no frills; standards vary. Top-of-the-range city and resort hotels offer international standards. These range from small, family-run boutique hotels, often in superb settings, that combine intimacy with charm, to large beachside resorts and city hotels owned by international chains. Some of these chains have toll-free numbers:

Best Western International, tel 800/780-7234, www.bestwestern.com

Choice Hotels International, tel 877/424-6423, choicehotels.com

Marriott Hotels & Resorts, tel 888/236-2427, marriott.com

Radisson Hotels & Resorts, tel 800/967-9033, radisson.com

Nine superb boutique hotels compose the **Small Distinctive Hotels of Costa Rica** *(tel 2258-0150, distinctivehotels.com).*

Principally for nature lovers, hikers, and anglers, wilderness lodges range from tent camps

and no-frills wooden lodges with basic family-style meals to more sophisticated options with fine dining, spa pools, and saunas.

Avoid "motels," usually used for short-term sexual trysts. *Apartotels* are self-catering units, popular in San José. In budget hotels, sink plugs may be missing, and showers are often cold. Warm (tepid) water may be provided by an electric element above the shower. Electric elements (aka "suicide showers") are common throughout the country; unless wiring is damaged, electrocution is no worry. Ensure windows and doors are secure.

Bed-and-breakfast homestays are increasingly popular. Look for advertisements in the *Tico Times,* or try agencies such as **Bells' Home Hospitality** *(tel 2225-4752, homestay-thebells.com).*

The ICT rating system for hotels uses a Sustainable Tourism ranking, taking into account factors such as the retention of natural ecosystems, the use of recyclables, and the application of energy-saving devices. A 13 percent sales tax and 3.9 percent ICT tax are added to most bills.

Unless otherwise stated:
1. All hotels have dining rooms and private bathrooms.
2. Hotels are open year-round.
3. All numbers over eight digits are dialed direct from the U.S.

Restaurants

The vast majority of Costa Rican restaurants serve *comida típica* (see p. 22) and are open from 11 a.m. to 2 p.m., and 6 p.m. to 11 p.m. Make reservations for the more expensive restaurants,

particularly on weekends. Service is slow; you may have to ask for your bill. As of 2012, restaurants in Costa Rica are nonsmoking.

A selection of good quality restaurants is given below. These are both individual and typical, with notable local associations wherever possible.

Credit Cards

Giving a card number is often the only way to reserve rooms in upscale hotels. Many hotels add a fee of up to 6 percent for credit card payments, however.

Making Reservations

Although we have tried to give comprehensive information, please check details before making reservations. This applies particularly to the availability of

---

PRICES

HOTELS
An indication of the cost of a double room in the high season is given by **$** signs.

$$$$$	Over $240
$$$$	$160–$240
$$$	$110–$160
$$	$70–$110
$	Under $70

RESTAURANTS
An indication of the cost of a three-course meal without drinks is given by **$** signs.

$$$$$	Over $65
$$$$	$50–$65
$$$	$30–$50
$$	$20–$30
$	Under $20

🏨 Hotel   🍴 Restaurant   🛈 No. of Guest Rooms   🅿 Parking   🕒 Closed   🛗 Elevator   🚭 Nonsmoking

facilities for disabled guests or nonsmoking rooms, acceptance of credit cards, and rates. Do not rely on booking by mail: E-mail your reservation. **Please note that U.S. 800 numbers listed do not work within Costa Rica.**

■ SAN JOSÉ

Hotels

🏨 AUROLA HOLIDAY INN
🍴 $$$$
AVE. 5, CALLE 5
TEL 2523-1000
aurolahotels.com
High-rise elegance overlooking Parque Morazán. Full complement of services including a casino, bars, and restaurant with great views.
ℹ️ 201 🔀 🄲 🅰 📺 📶 Free
🅰 All major cards

🏨 BARCELÓ SAN JOSÉ
🍴 PALACIO
$$$$
AUTOPISTA GENERAL CAÑAS,
1 MILE (1.6 KM) NW OF
PARQUE SÁBANA
TEL 2220-2034
barcelo.com
Elegant, modern high-rise with full services. The upscale casino, sports facilities, and spa are highlights, but the betwixt location is unappealing.
ℹ️ 254 🅿️ 🔀 🄲 🄲 🅰 📺
📶 Free 🅰 All major cards

🏨 COSTA RICA
🍴 MARRIOTT
$$$$
1 MILE (1.6 KM) NW OF CIUDAD
CARIARI, 800 YARDS (732 M)
W OF SAN ANTONIO DE BELÉN
TEL 2298-0000 OR 800/228-9290
marriott.com
A rural location on a coffee farm west of town with views to distant mountains. The hacienda-style building has elegant decor, shops, ballroom, golf practice range, and restaurants.
ℹ️ 299 🅿️ 🔀 🄲 🄲 🅰 🅰
📺 📶 Free 🅰 All major cards

🏨 DOUBLETREE BY
🍴 HILTON HOTEL CARIARI
$$$$
CIUDAD CARIARI, 5 MILES (8 KM)
NW OF SAN JOSÉ
TEL 2239-0022
doubletree.com
Full-service resort with modern decor and in-room services, midway between the city and the airport. Popular with groups. Tennis courts, two pools, golf course, casino, lively bar, and choice of restaurants. Children's activities.
ℹ️ 220 🅿️ 🄲 🅰 📺 📶 Free in
public areas 🅰 All major cards

🏨 WYNDHAM SAN JOSÉ
🍴 HERRADURA
$$$$
CIUDAD CARIARI, 5 MILES (8 KM)
NW OF SAN JOSÉ
TEL 2209-9800
wyndhamherradura.com
Several very good restaurants (including Mediterranean and Japanese), a casino, spa, and golf and country club complement the large conference center of this hotel, refurbished with elegant styling.
ℹ️ 230 🔀 🄲 🅰 📺 Free
🅰 All major cards

🏨 AUTÉNTICO HOTEL
🍴 $$$
AVE. 5, CALLE 40
TEL 2222-5266
autenticohotel.com
This well-appointed hotel with new ownership, refurbished in a hip contemporary style—a minimalist interpretation of Costa Rican traditional decor. It is situated near Parque Sábana. Courtesy bus to city center. Italian restaurant.
ℹ️ 92 🅿️ 🄲 🅰
📶 Free 🅰 AE, MC, V

🏨 BALMORAL
🍴 $$$
AVE. CENTRAL, CALLES 7/9
TEL 2222-5022 OR 800/691-4865
balmoral.co.cr
Modern decor, an in-house casino, and an on-site car

rental and tour desk highlight this modest downtown hotel. Rooms are small and rather noisy, but the location is good for exploring the city core. The modern café-style restaurant opens to the street.
ℹ️ 112 🔀 🄲 📺 📶 Free
🅰 All major cards

🏨 CROWNE PLAZA
COROBICÍ
$$$
CALLE 42, 50 YARDS (46 M) N OF
BULEVAR LAS AMÉRICAS
TEL 2543-6000
crowneplaza.com
This high-rise hotel stands on the northeast corner of Parque Sábana. Arranged around a steepled atrium, it has modern facilities including a casino, nightclub, and spa.
ℹ️ 202 🅿️ 🔀 🄲 🄲 🅰 🅰 📺
📶 Free 🅰 AE, MC, V

SOMETHING SPECIAL

🏨 GRANO DE ORO
🍴 $$$
CALLE 30, AVES. 2/4
TEL 2255-3322
hotelgranodeoro.com
A Canadian-run hotel off Paseo Colón in a leafy district a 20-minute walk from downtown, this is indisputably the best hotel in town. Elegant decor includes gleaming white bathrooms. Tasteful artwork abounds, and soothing music wafts through the narrow skylit corridors. Impeccable service and a top-notch restaurant, where Costa Rican fusion cuisine draws the city's elite for gourmet French-inspired dishes using Costa Rican ingredients.
ℹ️ 37 rooms, 3 suites 🅿️ 🄲
📶 Free 🅰 All major cards

🏨 PALMA REAL
🍴 $$$
2 BLOCKS N OF THE I.C.E. BLDG.
TEL 2290-5060
hotelpalmareal.com
This stylish business hotel west of downtown has

🄲 Air-conditioning 🏊 Outdoor Pool 🏊 Indoor Pool 📺 Health Club 📶 Wi-Fi 🅰 Credit Cards amenities such as wireless and high-speed Internet, business center, conference rooms, fitness room, a bar, and two restaurants. There are king-size beds and spa pools in suites.

🏦 65 🅿 🔄 🔲 📺 📶 Free 📵 AE, MC, V

🏨 DON CARLOS
🍴 $$

CALLE 9, AVE. 9
TEL 2221-6707 OR 866/675-9259
doncarloshotel.com
A rambling converted colonial mansion with a homey ambience, in the heart of Barrio Amón. Stained glass, sculptures, and pre-Columbian treasures abound in public areas. Small restaurant.

🏦 36 📶 Free in public areas 📵 All major cards

🏨 GRAN HOTEL
🍴 $$

AVE. 2, CALLES 1/3
TEL 8319-6073
curiocollection3.hilton.com
This hotel, a historical and architectural landmark, has a superb location on Plaza de la Cultura (among several dining options), and a 24-hour casino.

🏦 110 🅿 🔄 📶 Free 📵 AE, MC, V

🏨 HOTEL FLEUR DE LYS
🍴 $$

CALLE 13, AVES. 2/6
TEL 2223-1206
hotelfleurdelys.com
Swiss-owned hotel in restored Victorian mansion with wicker and wrought-iron beds. Rates include tropical breakfast. French restaurant on-site.

🏦 30 📶 Free 📵 AE, MC, V

🏨 HOTEL 1492 JADE Y ORO
$$

AVE. 1, CALLES 31/33
TEL 2280-6265
hotel1492.com
A quaint hotel in a charming colonial home in quiet Barrio

Escalante. The decor features tile mosaics. Evening wine and cheese on a garden patio.

🏦 10 🅿 🔲 📶 Free 📵 MC, V

🏨 HOTEL PRESIDENTE
🍴 $$

AVE. CENTRAL, CALLES 7/9
TEL 2010-0000
hotel-presidente.com
Modern amenities in this heart-of-downtown hotel complement comfortable rooms recently refurbished in smart contemporary style. Appealing restaurant. Casino.

🏦 110 🅿 🔄 🔲 📶 Free 📵 All major cards

🏨 HOTEL VILLA TOURNON
🍴 $$

N BANK OF RÍO TORRES, 200 YARDS (183 M) E OF CALLE 3
TEL 2233-6622
hotelvillatournon.com
This modern hotel near the El Pueblo complex has contemporary art and pools in the garden. Two excellent restaurants include fireside dining.

🏦 80 🔄 🔲 🛏 📶 Free 📵 AE, MC, V

🏨 LE BERGERAC
🍴 $$

CALLE 35, 50 YARDS (46 M) S OF AVE. CENTRAL, LOS YOSES
TEL 2234-7850
bergerachotel.com
This family-run charmer, set in a quiet eastern suburb, has a French provincial style. Antique furnishings and modern art, plus business facilities and gourmet dining on a terrace.

🏦 19 🅿 📵 AE, MC, V 📶 Free

Restaurants

SOMETHING SPECIAL

🍴 PARK CAFE
$$$$

CALLE 44, SÁBANA NORTE
TEL 2290-6324
parkcafecostarica.blogspot.com
This exclusive restaurant inside an antique store combines a one-of-a-kind

setting with stupendous nouvelle cuisine by eccentric Michelin-starred chef Richard Neat. His artful gourmet treats might include roasted tuna fillet with ginger chutney and artichoke salad. You can dine by candlelight in the grassy courtyard with fountain and stone Buddhas.

🅿 🕐 Closed Sun. & Mon. 📵 MC, V

🍴 CAFÉ KALÚ
$$$

CALLE 31, AVE. 5
TEL 2253-8426
kalu.co.cr
Patrons enjoy a triptych—art gallery, boutique store, and restaurant with outdoor deck and hip lounge decor—all at a chic new location. Chef-owner Camille Ratton prepares gourmet fusion dishes using Costa Rican ingredients and meticulous presentation.

🕐 Closed Mon. 🔲 📵 All major cards

🍴 JÜRGEN'S
$$

CALLE 41, 219 YARDS (200 M) N OF AVE. CENTRAL, SAN PEDRO
TEL 2224-2455
hotelboutiquejade.com
Hip comes to San José in this upscale, contemporary eatery with a bold aesthetic and splendid nouvelle cuisine. Finish your fine dining with a nightcap at the cigar bar.

🕐 Closed Sun. 🔲 📵 AE, MC, V

🍴 LA BASTILLE
$$

PASEO COLÓN AT CALLE 22
TEL 2255-4994
This French restaurant is popular with San José's social elite. Elegant ambience and dependable food.

🅿 🕐 Closed Sun. 🔲 📵 MC, V

🍴 LA ESQUINA DE BUENOS AIRES
$$

🏨 Hotel 🍴 Restaurant 🏦 No. of Guest Rooms 🅿 Parking 🕐 Closed 🔄 Elevator 📵 Nonsmoking

CALLE 11, AVE. 4
TEL 2223-1909
laesquinadebuenosaires.net
An Argentinian restaurant with warm bohemian decor, plus superbly executed nouvelle Latin cuisine. Excellent wine list and gourmet beers.
⌖ All major cards

🍴 **LE CHANDELIER**
$$
100 YARDS (91 M) W & 100 YARDS (91 M) S OF THE I.C.E. BLDG., SAN PEDRO
TEL 2225-3980
lechandeliercr.com
Choose from ten dining areas in this colonial mansion turned gourmet restaurant. Nouvelle Costa Rican cuisine is inspired by French classics. Superb art decorates the walls.
🅿 ⊕ Closed Sun. 🅢 ⌖ MC, V

🍴 **LUBNAN**
$$
PASEO COLÓN, CALLES 22/24
TEL 2257-6071
Lebanese specialties such as *kafta naie* (marinated ground beef), kabobs, and falafel. Elegant decor, modest prices. Belly dancing, hookahs, and DJs provide entertainment.
🅿 ⊕ Closed Sun. 🅢 ⌖ MC, V

🍴 **MACHU PICCHU**
$$
CALLE 32, AVES. 1/3
TEL 2255-1717
Peruvian seafood such as garlic octopus, ceviches, and *picante de mariscos* (spicy seafood casserole); try the house Pisco sour.
🅿 ⊕ Closed Sun. ⌖ AE, MC, V

🍴 **NUESTRA TIERRA**
$$
AVE. 2, CALLE 15
TEL 2258-6500
Spacious, airy, and charmingly rustic restaurant specializing in traditional Costa Rican dishes, some with a contemporary twist, like the sea bass *(corvine)* in mango sauce. Open 24/7.
⌖ All major cards

🍴 **TIN JO**
$$
CALLE 11, AVE 6/8
TEL 2221-7605
tinjo.com
Unpretentious ambience and filling meals at fair prices for Asian fare from sushi and Szechuan to Indian and Thai. Live music in the Salón Bambú.
🅢 ⌖ MC, V

🍴 **FLOR DE LOTO**
$
CALLE LOISA, 50 YARDS (46 M) E OF I.C.E. BLDG., SÁBANA NORTE
TEL 2232-4652
This unpretentious restaurant serves up a selection of spicy Hunan and Szechuan fare.
🅿 🅢 ⌖ MC, V

🍴 **SPOON**
$
PLAZA DE LA CULTURA
TEL 2222-5172
spooncr.com
A bargain with various outlets. Salads, submarine sandwiches, plus delicious baked goods make this a favorite of Costa Ricans on the go.
🅢 ⌖ None

■ **CENTRAL HIGHLANDS**

ALAJUELA

SOMETHING SPECIAL

🏨 **XANDARI RESORT & SPA VILLAGE**
$$$$
TACACORI, 3 MILES (4.8 KM) N OF ALAJUELA
TEL 2443-2020 OR 866/363-3212
xandari.com
Contemporary boutique hotel with villas and an innovative tropical spa complex sits atop a ridge overlooking coffee fields and the Central Valley. Stunning architecture and stylish furnishings. Trails lead to waterfalls. TV/video lounge. Macrobiotic nouvelle Costa Rican meals served on the dining terrace. The spa complex includes five hot tubs, treatment rooms, yoga, and physical fitness room.
🛏 24 villas 🅿 🛋 🎽 🛜 Free ⌖ AE, MC, V

🏨 **PURA VIDA BED & BREAKFAST**
$$$
TUETAL NORTE, 3 MILES (4.8 KM) N OF ALAJUELA
TEL 2430-2630
puravidahotel.com
Surrounded by lush gardens, this intimate inn has individually themed cottages. Run by a nice North American couple, who serve gourmet meals.
🛏 6 🅿 🅢 🛋 🛜 Free ⌖ MC, V

🍴 **JAULARES**
$
4 MILES (6.4 KM) N OF ALAJUELA
TEL 2482-2155
jaulares.com
Traditional country atmosphere in an alpine setting. Hearty campesino fare is prepared on an open wood-burning stove, and *refrescos* are created from fresh locally grown fruits.
🅿 ⌖ None

BAJOS DEL TORO

🏨 **EL SILENCIO LODGE**
🍴 $$$$$
BAJOS DEL TORO
TEL 2231-6122
elsilenciolodge.com
Set in a deep mountain vale and surrounded by cloud forest, this luxury ecolodge has gorgeous villas with avant-garde styling; a glass-walled restaurant serves gourmet Costa Rican fare. Full-service spa plus trails to waterfalls.
🛏 15 🅿 🅢 🎽 🛜 Free ⌖ All major cards

ESCAZÚ

🏨 **THE ALTA HOTEL**
🍴 $$$$$
ALTO LAS PALOMAS, 2 MILES (3.2

KM) W OF SAN RAFAEL DE ESCAZÚ
TEL 2282-4160 OR 800/242-0500
thealtahotel.com
A tasteful Mediterranean-style hotel with stunning hillside views and sumptuous contemporary furnishings. La Luz Restaurant serves stylish continental/Costa Rican cuisine.

🛈 23 🅿 ⇅ 🚫 ⬙ 🏊 ⛵ 🔲
📶 Free 🅂 AE, MC, V

🏨 🍴 INTERCONTINENTAL COSTA RICA AT MULTIPLAZA MALL
$$$$

AUTOPISTA PROSPERO FERNÁN-DEZ, 2 MILES (3.2 KM) NW OF SAN RAFAEL DE ESCAZÚ
TEL 2208-2100
ihg.com/intercontinental
Deluxe hotel with huge rooms and warm, charming decor. Executive floor, business center, travel agency, and upscale shops. Three restaurants include Italian gourmet option.

🛈 261 🅿 ⇅ 🚫 ⬙ 🏊 🔲
📶 Free 🅂 AE, MC, V

🏨 CASA DE LAS TÍAS
$$

SAN RAFAEL DE ESCAZÚ
TEL 2289-5517
casadelastias.com
Endearing and colorful family-run bed-and-breakfast in a wood-paneled, plantation-style home close to central Escazú. Breakfast is served on patio.

🛈 5 🅿 📶 Free 🅂 All major cards

🍴 SAGA
$$$$

AVE. ESCAZÚ
TEL 2289-6615
sagarestaurant.com
Sophisticated restaurant with minimalist decor. Chef Evelyn Leff is renowned for her fusion cuisine and desserts. Bakery.

🅿 🅂 All major cards

🍴 PRODUCT C
$$$

EDIFICIO IMAX, AVE. ESCAZÚ
TEL 2288-5570
Fresh seafood is the hallmark

at this hyper-clean restaurant. Menu treats include baked oyster Rockefeller and steamed clams, plus baked smoked trout with leek gratin and grilled ahi tuna burger. Totally sustainable product.

🅿 🚫 🅂 MC, V

🍴 CHEZ CHRISTOPHE
$$

PLAZA DE LA PACO
TEL 2228-2512
In a town renowned for gourmet restaurants, this bakery-café is immensely popular for its omelets, quiches, sandwiches, and delicious pastries. It is packed for Sunday brunch.

🕐 Closed Mon. 🅂 MC, V

LA GARITA

🍴 DELICIAS DEL MAÍZ
$

TEL 2433-7206
lasdeliciasdelmaiz.com
Traditional corn-based dishes, such as tamales and *chorreadas* (corn fritters) from the open grill, are served in atmospheric surroundings.

🅿 🅂 None

LOS ANGELES CLOUD FOREST RESERVE

🏨 🍴 VILLABLANCA CLOUD FOREST HOTEL & SPA
$$$$

6 MILES (9.7 KM) NE OF LOS ANGELES NORTE
TEL 2461-0300
villablanca-costarica.com
An enchanting ecolodge on the Continental Divide, at the edge of a cloud forest. Graciously appointed cottages have fireplaces. Wedding chapel and spa; nature activities include horseback riding and guided hikes.

🛈 35 cottages 🅿 🚫 📶 Free 🅂 All major cards

MONTE DE LA CRUZ

🏨 🍴 HOTEL CHALET TIROL
$$

TEL 2267-6222
hotelchaleteltirol.com
A cozy Tyrolean lodge situated on the edge of cloud forest. Choose from modern rooms or rustic cabins. The French restaurant serves dishes such as shrimp in a fennel Pernod sauce. Full-service spa.

🛈 36 rooms, 10 chalets 🅿 🏊 🔲 📶 Free 🅂 AE, MC, V

🍴 BAALBEK BAR & GRILL
$

LOS ANGELES DE SAN RAFAEL
TEL 2267-6683
Lebanese restaurant with hookahs, belly dancing, and genuine Levantine fare. Tremendous views.

🅿 🅂 All major cards

OROSÍ

🏨 🍴 LA CASONA DE CAFETAL
$$$

5 MILES (8 KM) E OF OROSÍ
TEL 2577-1414
lacasonadelcafetal.com
Elegant lakeside hotel on a coffee estate, offering deluxe comfort and splendid views. The Restaurante Exquisito is known for its Sunday buffets. Spa.

🛈 7 🅿 📶 Free 🅂 AE, MC, V

PIEDADES

🏨 🍴 POSADA CANAL GRANDE
$$

TEL 2282-4089
hotelcanalgrande.com
A luxurious place, with parquet floors in the guest rooms, antiques, leather sofas, and flowers in the lounge. The hotel is surrounded by coffee fields and has an Italian restaurant. Breakfast included.

🛈 12 🅿 🏊 📶 Free 🅂 AE, MC, V

POÁS

SOMETHING SPECIAL

🏨 PEACE LODGE

🏨 Hotel   🍴 Restaurant   🛈 No. of Guest Rooms   🅿 Parking   🕐 Closed   ⇅ Elevator   🚫 Nonsmoking

$$$$$

MONTAÑA AZUL, 3 MILES
(4.8 KM) N OF VARA BLANCA
TEL 2482-2720
waterfallgardens.com
Stunning, one-of-a-kind
decor combines sensually
rustic elements with luxury in
cavernous rooms on the edge
of Braulio Carrillo National
Park. Natural stone hot tubs
and cave-like bathrooms evoke
the Flintstones, but the effect
is quite romantic enhanced by
canopy beds. The amenities
and activities of La Paz Waterfall Gardens are at hand.
⬦ 18 🅿 🄲 🛜 Free 🄰 AE,
MC, V

▦ POÁS VOLCANO LODGE
$$

VARA BLANCA DE HEREDIA
TEL 2482-2194
poasvolcanolodge.com
Set in a superb location
between Barva and Poás
volcanoes, this classy mountain
lodge on a cattle farm com-
bines cozy charm with modern
furnishings. Basic meals; rates
include farmhouse breakfast.
Trail network leads through
cloud forest.
⬦ 11 🅿 🛜 Free 🄰 AE, MC, V

▯ RESTAURANT COLBERT
$$$

VARA BLANCA DE HEREDIA
TEL 2482-2776
Straddling the Continental
Divide, with fine views, this
airy modern restaurant-bakery
serves croissants, pastries, plus
nouvelle Costa Rican fare and
local cheeses.
🅿 🄰 MC, V

SALISPUEDES

▦ MIRADOR
▯ DE QUETZALES
$$

PAN-AM HWY. KM 70
TEL 2200-4185
miradorquetzalescr.com
Ideal for spotting quetzals—
birding is a specialty—this rustic

lodge with cabins sits on the
edge of a cloud forest. Simple
meals and fabulous views.
⬦ 11 cabins 🅿 🛜 Free
🄰 None

SAN GERARDO DE DOTA

▦ TROGON LODGE
$$$

TEL 2293-8181
trogonlodge.com
Nestled in a deep mountain
valley, this gracious lodge
provides a perfect base for
both birding and trout fishing.
Rustic hardwood cabins sit
over a brook and trout pond.
Simple meals are provided.
⬦ 23 🅿 🛜 Free in public
areas 🄰 DC, MC, V

▦ DANTICA CLOUD
▯ FOREST LODGE
$$

2 MILES (3.2 KM) E OF SAN
GERARDO DE DOTA
TEL 2740-1067
dantica.com
IKEA furnishings and walls
of glass in charming two-
bedroom cottages on a
magnificent hillside. Its glass-
enclosed Restaurant El Tapir
serves gourmet dishes using
organic herbs and veggies
from its own garden. First-rate
gallery of indigenous art.
⬦ 9 cottages 🅿 🛜 Free
🄰 AE, MC, V

SANTA ANA

▯ BACCHUS
$$$

200 YARDS (183 M) E & 100 (91 M)
YARDS N OF PLAZA SANTA ANA
TEL 2282-5441
enjoyrestaurants.net/bacchus
Converted colonial home with
tasteful contemporary touches.
Gourmet Mediterranean
nouvelle dishes such as baked
mushroom-and-polenta ragout
draw the monied cognoscenti.
🅿 🄯 Closed Mon.
🄰 All major cards

▯ LE MONASTÈRE
$$$

IN THE HILLS ABOVE SANTA ANA
TEL 2228-8515
monastere-restaurant.com
The waiters dress as monks in
this converted chapel offering
French-inspired cuisine such as
grilled lamb chops, together with
a big wine list. Enjoy the fine
views over the valley.
🅿 🄯 Closed L & Sun.
🄰 All major cards

SANTA BARBARA DE HEREDIA

SOMETHING SPECIAL

▦ FINCA ROSA BLANCA
▯ COUNTRY INN
$$$$

0.75 MILE (1.2 KM) NE OF SANTA
BARBARA DE HEREDIA
TEL 2269-9392
fincarosablanca.com
Designed as a private home and
inspired by Gaudí and the Santa
Fe style, this exquisite boutique
hotel offers eclectic decor. Set
on a working coffee farm, it
has spectacular views over the
valley and its own stable. The
El Tigre Vestido restaurant's
inventive gourmet cuisine uses
local ingredients. Reservations
required. Full breakfast included.
⬦ 9 suites, 6 cottages
🅿 🏊 🛜 Free 🄰 AE, MC, V

▯ LA LLUNA DE VALENCIA
$$$

SAN PEDRO DE BARVA, 1.5 MILES
(2 KM) E OF SANTA BARBARA DE
HEREDIA
TEL 2269-6665
lallunadevalencia.com
Extrovert Catalan owner Vicente
Aguilar presides with ebullient
style at this Spanish restaurant:
Expect him to pour wine down
your throat from a wine sack. Go
for paellas, cooked in an open
kitchen. Live music, including
flamenco each first Sunday of
the month.
🅿 🄯 Closed Mon. & Tues.
🄰 All major cards

🄲 Air-conditioning 🏊 Outdoor Pool 🏊 Indoor Pool 🏋 Health Club 🛜 Wi-Fi 🄰 Credit Cards

SANTO DOMINGO DE HEREDIA

🏨 BOUGAINVILLEA
🍴 $$
0.6 MILE (1 KM) E OF SANTO DOMINGO
TEL 2244-1414
hb.co.cr
On landscaped grounds containing tennis courts, this modern hotel boasts engaging modern art. Elegant restaurant serves popular Sunday brunch.
🛏 80 🅿 ⬍ 🚫 🏊 📶 Free
🚍 AE, MC, V

TURRIALBA

🏨 CASA TURIRE
$$$$
8 MILES (13 KM) SE OF TURRIALBA
TEL 2531-1111
hotelcasaturire.com
Large comfortable rooms in an award-winning modern hotel with classical hints. Situated lakeside on a working plantation, it offers horseback riding, biking, and rafting. Edwardian bar. Excellent cuisine.
🛏 16 🅿 🚫 🏊 📶 Free
🚍 AE, MC, V

SOMETHING SPECIAL
🏨 PACUARE LODGE
🍴 $$$$
BAJO TIGRE, 22 MILES (35 KM) NE OF TURRIALBA
TEL 4033-0060 OR 800/963-1195
pacuarelodge.com
The very definition of a deluxe nature lodge—and perhaps Costa Rica's finest ecolodge—this sublime all-suite rain forest retreat is one of only 24 National Geographic Unique Lodges of the World. Thatched rusticity blends with divine comforts and exquisite furnishings, while inspired architecture integrates imperceptibly with the lush surroundings. Most guests arrive on white-water packages. Option for private treetop dining! Spa.

🛏 16 🅿 🚫 🏊 📶 Free in public areas 🚍 All major cards

■ GUANACASTE

CAÑAS

SOMETHING SPECIAL
🏨 RÍO PERDIDO
🍴 $$$$
SAN BERNARDO DE BAGACES, 15 MILES (24 KM) NE OF BAGACES
TEL 2673-3600
rioperdido.com
A modernist architectural masterpiece, this divinely inspired hotel and restaurant—part of a new adventure activity center with full-service spa and swimming pools—overlooks the Río Blanco canyon on the lower flank of Miravalles volcano. Sensational modernist villas stand atop stilts with balconies amid the dry forest. Chef Andrés Flores delivers gourmet health-conscious fusion dishes with a Guanacastecan twist.
🛏 20 🅿 🏊 📶 Free
🚍 All major cards

🍴 RESTAURANTE RINCÓN COROBICÍ
$
INTER-AMERICAN HWY., 4.5 MILES (7 KM) N OF CAÑAS
TEL 2669-6161
raftingguanacaste.com/restaurant
Diners can watch rafters far below floating on the Río Corobicí. Seafood specialties include *corvina ajillo* (sea bass in garlic), and *comida típica* is also served. Renowned for its refreshing lemonades.
🅿 🚫 🚍 MC, V

LAGUNA DE ARENAL

🏨 LA MANSION
🍴 INN ARENAL
$$$$
5 MILES (8 KM) N OF NUEVO ARENAL

TEL 2692-8018
lamansionarenal.com
A magnificent hillside setting overlooking the lake plus exquisite decor in 16 *cabinas*. The inn has a horizon swimming pool and a charming bar/restaurant. Offers horseback riding, rowboats, and canoes.
🛏 16 🅿 🚫 🏊 📶 Free
🚍 MC, V

🏨 GINGERBREAD
🍴 $$$
1 MILE (1.6 KM) E OF NUEVO ARENAL
TEL 2694-0039
gingerbreadarenal.com
Considered one of the country's finest regional restaurants, it exemplifies the best of fusion fare with such dishes as jumbo shrimp with couscous and lentils. The Israeli chef-owner presides at the pub-like bar and also rents rooms.
🛏 4 🅿 🕐 Closed Mon.
📶 Free 🚍 MC, V

🏨 TOAD HALL
🍴 $$$
HWY. 142, 3 MILES (4.8 KM) E OF NUEVO ARENAL
toadhallhotel.com
Reopened in 2012 by new U.S. owners, this delicatessen, gift store, and café perches above the lake. Views and gourmet health-conscious fare can be enjoyed from a terrace. Villas and rooms feature endearingly eclectic decor.
🛏 5 🅿 🏊 📶 Free
🚍 All major cards

🏨 VILLA DECARY
$$$
HWY. 142, 1.5 MILES (2.4 KM) E OF NUEVO ARENAL
TEL 2694-4330 OR 800/556-0505
villadecary.com
Charming country inn backed by rain forest accessed by trails. Large guest rooms have Guatemalan covers, balconies, and lake views. Gracious North American hosts serve breakfasts, included in rates.
🛏 5 rooms, 3 bungalows
🅿 📶 Free 🚍 MC, V

ARENAL OBSERVATORY LODGE & SPA
$$
1.5 MILES (2.4 KM) SE OF
VOLCÁN ARENAL
TEL 2479-1070
arenal-observatory.com
Mountainside lodge offers
up-close views of Volcán Arenal.
Accommodations vary from
cozy volcano-view rooms to
spacious and elegant suites, plus
a farmhouse villa. Some rooms
are handicapped accessible.
Horseback riding, free volcano
tour, pool and hot tub, and
trails. Family-style meals.
🛏 48 🅿 🏊 🎐 Free 🗠 AE,
MC, V

CHALET NICHOLAS
$$
HWY. 142, 1.5 MILES (2.4 KM) W
OF NUEVO ARENAL
TEL 2694-4041
chaletnicholas.com
Charming guesthouse run by
North American hosts. Rooms
boast a winning combination
of orthopedic mattresses and
volcano views. Hiking and
horseback rides are offered.
Healthy meals are a treat.
🛏 3 🅿 🗠 🎐 Free 🗠 None

RESTAURANT CABALLO NEGRO
$$
1 MILE (1.6 KM) W OF
NUEVO ARENAL
TEL 2694-4515
luckybugcr.net
This German-run bakery and
restaurant sits over a pond. Its
European menu runs from sau-
sages and schnitzel to veal, plus
some vegetarian options.
🅿 🗠 None

LIBERIA

HOTEL LIBERIA
$
CALLE REAL BET. AVE. CENTRAL
& AVE. 2
TEL 2666-0161
hotelliberiacr.com
This elegant newcomer in a

converted 1918 mansion
brings boutique sophistication
to town. Small yet tastefully
decorated rooms.
🛏 14 plus dorm 🎐 🎐 Free
🗠 Most major cards

MONTEVERDE

BELMAR
$$$
400 YARDS (0.4 KM) NE OF GAS
STATION
TEL 2645-5201
hotelbelmar.net
This alpine lodge set on a hillside has clean, wood-paneled
rooms with wide balconies
providing superb sunset views.
Dine in or out at the popular
continental restaurant.
🛏 34 🅿 🎐 🎐 Free 🗠 V

MONTEVERDE LODGE AND GARDENS
$$$
600 YARDS (0.5 KM) SE OF
SANTA ELENA
TEL 2257-0766
monteverdelodge.com
An eccentric design maximizes
light in this upscale brick-and-
timber nature lodge. The
mezzanine bar, which has a fire-
place and a view of the glass-
enclosed spa pool, is a lively
social center. Spacious guest
rooms offer fine vistas. Birds
abound on the landscaped
grounds. Rates include meals.
🛏 27 🅿 🎐 Free 🗠 AE,
MC, V

HELICONIA ECOLODGE
$$
CERRO PLANO, 0.6 MILE (1 KM) E
OF SANTA ELENA
TEL 2645-5109
hotelheliconia.com
This lodge has modern fixtures
in modestly furnished rooms
with balconies. Spa pool.
Trails into a private reserve.
Continental and local favorites
in the restaurant.
🛏 33 🅿 🎐 Free
🗠 All major cards

SOFIA
$$$$
CERRO PLANO, 0.6 MILE (1 KM) E
OF SANTA ELENA
TEL 2645-7017
With large windows overlooking the cloud forest, Sofia
serves Nuevo Latino dishes
using fresh organic ingredients. A perfect meal? Black
bean soup and seafood chi-
michanga. The house mango
ginger mojito is renown.
🅿 🗠 All major cards

CAFÉ CABURÉ
$$
450 YARDS (0.4 KM) E OF GAS
STATION
TEL 2645-5020
cabure.net
Health-conscious salads, tacos,
wraps, and international dishes
such as cannelloni, plus signa-
ture homemade pastries and
chocolate desserts including
artisanal gourmet truffles made
on-site. Shaded terrace dining.
🅿 🗠 MC, V

RINCÓN DE LA VIEJA

HOTEL BORINQUEN MOUNTAIN RESORT & SPA
$$$$
8 MILES (13 KM) NE OF
CAÑAS DULCES
TEL 2690-1900
borinquenresort.com
Mountain resort with huge
rooms furnished in neocolonial
style. A spa offers mud and
thermal treatments, plus
plunge pools. Horseback rides,
ATV safaris, and hikes lead into
surrounding forest.
🛏 30 🅿 🎐 🏊 🎐 🎐 Free
🗠 MC, V

HACIENDA LODGE GUACHIPELÍN
$$$
CURUBANDÉ, 15 MILES (22 KM)
NE OF LIBERIA
TEL 2690-2900
guachipelin.com

🎐 Air-conditioning 🏊 Outdoor Pool 🏊 Indoor Pool 🎐 Health Club 🎐 Wi-Fi 🗠 Credit Cards

A working cattle ranch and adventure center with older (rustic) plus newer rooms with glass walls and shady balconies. Activities from horseback riding and mountain biking to waterfall rappelling.

[i] 64 [P] [S] [≈] [≈] Free [S] All major cards

[H] BUENA VISTA LODGE
[R] $$

8 MILES (13 KM) NE OF CAÑAS DULCES
TEL 2690-1414
buenavistalodgecr.com
A real mountain hideaway on the slopes of Rincón. Stone-and-timber cabins amid lawns, with horseback rides, hikes, a canopy tour, thermal steam bath, and rustic restaurant.

[i] 77 [P] [≈] Free [S] None

■ NICOYA

BAHÍA CULEBRA

SOMETHING SPECIAL

[H] FOUR SEASONS RESORT
[R] AT PAPAGAYO
PENINSULA
$$$$$

PUNTA MALA
TEL 2696-0000
fourseasons.com/costarica
This large-scale deluxe hotel enjoys a dramatic location with spectacular coastline views from the northwestern tip of the bay. Sumptuous tropical-themed decor graces public areas and spacious rooms with balcony views. A championship golf course is a major draw, as is the posh spa. Four restaurants and a lounge.

[i] 145 [P] [S] [≈] [TV] [≈] Free [S] All major cards

MONTEZUMA

[H] YLANG YLANG BEACH
RESORT
$$$$

0.5 MILE (0.8 KM) E OF MONTEZUMA
TEL 2642-0636
ylangylangbeachresort.com
Enjoying a secluded beachfront location, this eclectic place has bungalows, "jungalows" (safari-style tents on decks), and three-story units set amid landscaped foliage.

[i] 21 [S] [≈] [≈] Free [S] All major cards

[H] HOTEL HORIZONTES DE
MONTEZUMA
$$$

1 MILE (1.6 KM) N OF MONTEZUMA
TEL 2642-0625
hotel-horizontes-montezuma.com
Clinical whites bathe this well-run and recently renovated hilltop plantation-style hotel with hammocks on broad verandas around an atrium court. Meals are served on the patio. Specializes in yoga and wellness treatments. Spa.

[i] 7 [P] [S] [≈] [TV] [≈] Free [S] MC, V

■ NOSARA

[H] HARMONY HOTEL
[R] $$$

PLAYA GUIONES
TEL 2682-4114
harmonynosara.com
The classiest hotel in Nosara, this eco-sensitive resort has one- and two-bedroom bungalows around a landscaped pool. Tennis court, yoga dojo, and an outdoor restaurant serving health-conscious dishes.

[i] 24 [P] [S] [≈] [TV] [≈] Free [S] All major cards

[H] LAGARTA LODGE
$$

TEL 2682-0035
lagarta.com
Recently expanded and upgraded German-run hilltop lodge with views north over the wetlands and along Ostional beach. Relaxed, no-frills ambience. Several

trails lead to the estuary, with maps and tree lists available for self-guided tours. Spa.

[i] 26 [P] [≈] [TV] [≈] Free [S] V

[R] BEACH DOG CAFÉ
$

TEL 2682-1293
The place to start your day or break from sunning, this casual close-to-the-beach option offers American breakfasts, plus burritos, sandwiches, and delicious smoothies and juices.

[P] [C] Closed Sun. [S] None

[R] MARLIN BILL'S
$

TEL 2682-0458
This unpretentious hillside eatery serves international favorites, from French onion soup to New York strip steak.

[P] [C] Closed Sun. [S] None

PLAYA COCO

[H] CAFÉ DE PLAYA
[R] $$$$

TEL 2670-1621
cafedeplaya.com
The hippest option for miles, this small boutique beach resort offers classy modernist decor in individually themed rooms. Gourmet restaurant plus alfresco sushi bar. Water sports.

[i] 5 [P] [S] [≈] [≈] Free [S] All major cards

[H] RANCHO ARMADILLO
$$$

TEL 2670-0108
ranchoarmadillo.com
Gracious Texan-run colonial hacienda with timber-beamed bungalows. Meals prepared on request by a former culinary arts instructor.

[i] 7 [P] [S] [S] [≈] [≈] Free [S] MC, V

[H] PUERTA DEL SOL
[R] $

TEL 2670-0195
lapuertadelsolcostarica.com
A small, simple option with fashionably contemporary decor.

Inventive cuisine in an open-air restaurant/café.
 10 **P** 🛋 🏊 🐋 🛜 Free 🅰 AE, MC, V

PLAYA CONCHAL

🏨 WESTIN GOLF RESORT
🍴 & SPA PLAYA CONCHAL
$$$$$
TEL 2654-3500
westinplayaconchal.com
This huge deluxe property backs a white-sand beach and is enfolded by a championship golf course. Spacious rooms boast chic contemporary decor and up-to-the-minute amenities. Choice of restaurants, plus full-service spa, entertainment, tour services, and water sports.
🛏 310 **P** 🛋 🏊 🛜 Free 🅰 All major cards

PLAYA FLAMINGO

🏨 FLAMINGO BEACH RESORT
$$$$
TEL 2654-4444
resortflamingobeach.com
With a magnificent beach setting, this upgraded full-service resort is centered around a vast swimming pool. Car rental and tour services.
🛏 120 **P** 🔄 🅂 🏊 🛜 Free 🅰 AE, MC, V

PLAYA GRANDE

🏨 HOTEL BULA BULA
🍴 $$$
TEL 2653-0975
hotelbulabula.com
Trendily yet simply furnished, this boutique hotel nestles between the beach and estuary. Gourmet fusion cuisine served at the Great Waltini restaurant.
🛏 10 **P** 🏊 🛜 Free 🅰 All major cards

PLAYA HERMOSA

🏨 BOSQUE DEL MAR
🍴 $$$

TEL 2672-0046
bosquedelmar.com
A class act, this exquisite beach resort combines a fine setting with tastefully furnished bi-level suites centered around a pool. Gourmet restaurant is also the best around and specializes in fresh seafood, including sushi.
🛏 38 **P** 🏊 🛜 Free 🅰 MC, V

🏨 VILLA DEL SUEÑO
🍴 $$$
TEL 2672-0026
villadelsueno.com
Set amid lush manicured gardens, this Canadian-run hotel offers six room types, including self-catering condos. Gourmet open-air restaurant hosts live music.
🛏 14 **P** 🛋 🏊 🛜 Free 🅰 All major cards

PLAYA OCOTAL

🍴 FATHER ROOSTER RESTAURANT
$
TEL 2670-1246
fatherrooster.com
This rustic shorefront eatery serves seafood, burgers, and similar dishes. It has an appealing, offbeat ambience, and its beach volleyball court gets lively. Beach BBQs and occasional live bands and parties.
P 🅰 None

PLAYA TAMBOR

🏨 TANGO MAR
$$$$
HWY. 160, 3 MILES (4.8 KM) SW OF TAMBOR
TEL 2683-0001
tangomar.com
Set splendidly on the water, Tango Mar boasts stilt-legged hardwood cabins, spacious rooms, or three types of beachfront villas. There's a nine-hole golf course. Kundalini, Hatha, and Kripalu yoga and breathing workshops are taught on-site.
🛏 18 rooms, 4 villas **P** 🅂 🅂 🏊 🛜 Free 🅰 All major cards

PUNTA ISLITA

🏨 HOTEL PUNTA ISLITA
🍴 $$$$
TEL 2231-6122
hotelpuntaislita.com
Santa Fe–style architecture and luxurious furnishings in individual casitas, which have a commanding hilltop setting. Cliff-face pool, activities, and restaurant serving nouvelle Costa Rican dishes. More than 30 spa treatments available.
🛏 20 bungalows, 9 suites, 5 villas **P** 🅂 🏊 🐋 🛜 Free 🅰 All major cards

SAMARÁ

🏨 SÁMARA TREEHOUSE INN
$$
TEL 2656-0733
samaratreehouse.com
For a touch of Polynesia, reserve one of these delightful beachfront cabins on stilts. Shaded patios with hammocks. Secure parking.
🛏 4 **P** 🏊 🛜 Free 🅰 None

SAN FRANCISCO DE COYOTE

🏨 CASA CALETAS BOUTIQUE HOTEL
$$$
5 MILES (8 KM) W OF SAN FRANCISCO DE COYOTE
TEL 2655-1271
casacaletas.com
This off-the-beaten-path hotel has a spectacular location at the mouth of the Río Jabillo. Deluxe lodgings with tasteful contemporary furnishings. It doubles as a working cattle ranch.
🛏 7 **P** 🏊 🛜 Free 🅰 V

SAN JUANILLO

SOMETHING SPECIAL

🏨 TREE TOPS BED &
🍴 BREAKFAST
$$$
2 MILES (3 KM) N OF OSTIONAL
TEL 2682-1335

costaricatreetopsinn.com
A special treat awaits at the Tarzan-like home of Jack and Karen Hunter, raised on stilts, with views over a magnificent cove ideal for swimming with turtles. A guest room with Wi-Fi is basically furnished and you shower outside in the garden, or choose a simply furnished yet delightful beach-front bungalow. Scintillating conversation is part of the package. Karen is a gourmet chef and serves divine meals by reservation to nonguests.

🛈 2 🅿 🛜 Free 🚭 None

SANTA TERESA

SOMETHING SPECIAL

🏨 **HOTEL FLOR BLANCA**
🍴 **$$$$$**

3 MILES (4.8 KM) N OF MALPAÍS
TEL 2640-0232
florblanca.com
Infused with a Balinese motif, this calming resort sprawls over 7 acres (2.8 ha) of beachfront. Spacious, romantic villas feature outdoor showers and sumptuous furnishings. The gourmet outdoor Nectar Bar & Restaurant serves Pacific fusion cuisine. Large-screen TV lounge is good for rainy days. A spa has been added; yoga is offered in an open-air dojo.

🛈 11 🅿 🆂 ⛱ 🛜 Free
🚭 All major cards

🏨 **LATITUDE 10**
$$$$$

3 MILES (4.8 KM) N OF MALPAÍS
TEL 4001-0667
latitude10resort.com
For the ultimate in intimate exclusive retreats, this takes some beating. Five Balinese-themed villas are tucked amid effusive tropical foliage steps from the beach. The vast open-air bathrooms are set in walled gardens. Sleep beneath gauzy drapes on four-poster king beds with

luxe linens. A personal chef prepares meals.

🛈 6 🅿 ⛱ 🛜 Free
🚭 All major cards

TAMARINDO

🏨 **CAPITÁN SUIZO**
🍴 **$$$$**

TEL 2653-0075
hotelcapitansuizo.com
An elegant beachfront resort with rooms and bungalows set around a pool. Howler monkeys live in the treetops. The open-air beachfront restaurant serves gourmet fusion dishes.

🛈 29 rooms, 6 bungalows 🅿
🆂 ⛱ 🛜 Free 🚭 AE, MC, V

🏨 **JARDÍN DEL EDÉN**
🍴 **$$$$**

TEL 2653-0137
jardindeleden.com
Stylish, European-run hotel with landscaped gardens studded with artistic pools and a floodlit spa pool. Seafood specialties are served in a thatched-roof restaurant.

🛈 20 🅿 🆂 ⛱ 🆅 🛜 Free
🚭 AE, MC

🏨 **HOTEL TAMARINDO DIRÍA**
$$$

TEL 4032-0032
tamarindodiria.com
Large upscale beach resort with tasteful rooms in various types. Four pools, including children's pool. Wide range of amenities includes golf-driving range, casino, and spa.

🛈 239 🅿 🆂 ⛱ 🛜 Free
🚭 All major cards

🍴 **DRAGONFLY BAR & GRILL**
$$$

TEL 2653-1506
dragonflybarandgrill.com
New owners maintain this restaurant's fame for the very

best of fine dining. Fusion cuisine makes the most of local ingredients, such as Thai-style crispy fish cake with curried sweet corn. Airy and romantic setting. Hip music.

🅿 🚭 None

■ CENTRAL PACIFIC

DOMINICAL

🏨 **HACIENDA BARÚ**
🍴 **NATIONAL WILDLIFE REFUGE & ECOLODGE**
$$

1.2 MILES (2 KM) N OF RÍO BARÚ BRIDGE, COASTAL HWY.
TEL 2787-0003
haciendabaru.com
Renowned for its nature reserve, this hacienda is ideal for wildlife viewing. Choose between simple original two-bedroom cabins or newer, nicer ones. The restaurant serves Italian and local fare. A variety of tours can be arranged.

🛈 12 🅿 🛜 Free in public areas 🚭 AE, MC, V

JACÓ

🏨 BEST WESTERN JACÓ
🍴 BEACH RESORT
$$$

AVE. PASTOR DIAZ
TEL 2643-1000 OR 800/780-7234
bestwesternjacobeach.com
Large rooms with modern
furnishings are situated on the
edge of the beach. Full range
of services and activities,
and adequate fare is served in
El Puerto restaurant.

ⓘ 125 🅿 🔄 🆂 🏊 🛜 Free
🆂 All major cards

🍴 TACOBAR
$

20 YARDS (18 M) E OF POPS,
DOWNTOWN JACÓ
TEL 2643-0222
This Israeli-owned open-
air restaurant has hearty
granola, fruit, and yogurt
breakfasts; a buffet taco
bar; gourmet dishes, from
tacos to sushi; plus huge
fresh-fruit shakes.
🆂 None

MANUEL ANTONIO

🏨 ARENAS DEL MAR
🍴 $$$$$

1 MILE (1.6 KM) W OF
LA MARIPOSA
TEL 2777-0576
arenasdelmar.com
This deluxe, eco-sensitive
hotel takes the prize for its
exclusive beachfront locale.
Gorgeous villa-suites and
apartments rise over treetops.
Two gourmet restaurants
incorporate local ingredients
in their menus.

ⓘ 38 🅿 🆂 🎽 🛜 Free
🆂 All major cards

🏨 LA MARIPOSA
🍴 $$$$

2.5 MILES (4 KM) S OF QUEPOS
TEL 2777-0355
hotelmariposa.com
Unsurpassed coastal vistas.
Accommodations range
from cottages that hug

the cliff's face to junior
suites with spa pools, plus
contemporary suites and
penthouses. Creative
French cuisine is served.
Swim-up bar. Free park
shuttle available.

ⓘ 60 🅿 🆂 🏊 🛜 Free
🆂 MC, V

🏨 MAKANDA BY THE SEA
🍴 $$$$

3.5 MILES (5.6 KM) S OF QUEPOS
TEL 2777-0442
makanda.com
Deluxe Japanese-inspired
studios and villas tucked into
Japanese gardens. Cliffside
pool. The nouvelle cuisine
is among the region's best.
Extensive wine list. Reservations required.

ⓘ 6 villas, 4 studios 🏊
🛜 Free 🆂 AE, MC, V

🏨 SI COMO NO
🍴 $$$$

2 MILES (3.2 KM) S OF QUEPOS
TEL 2777-0777 OR 888-742-6667
sicomono.com
Avant-garde design and
decor, with split-level, all-
suite villas around a dramatic
pool and cascade. Theater
shows first-run movies
and camp classics. Shops,
a conference center, and two
acclaimed eateries.

ⓘ 70 🅿 🆂 🏊 🛜 Free
🆂 AE, MC, V

🏨 TULEMAR BUNGALOWS
$$$$

2.5 MILES (4 KM) S OF QUEPOS
TEL 2777-0580
tulemarresort.com
A villa, deluxe rooms, and
octagonal bungalows with
picture windows and modern
furnishings in a secluded
setting with trails. Poolside
restaurant, plus private chefs
can be arranged.

ⓘ 34 rooms, 9 villas 🅿 🏊
🛜 Free 🆂 AE, MC, V

OJOCHAL

🏨 VILLAS GAIA
$$

PLAYA TORTUGA
TEL 2786-5044
villasgaia.com
Wooden bungalows feature
attractive contemporary decor.
Trails lead to rain forest and
mangroves. Kayaking, snorkeling, and scuba-diving trips;
fishing and hiking. Spa.

ⓘ 14 bungalows 🅿 🏊
🛜 Free 🆂 AE, MC, V

🍴 CITRUS
$$$

OJOCHAL
TEL 2786-5175
Now in French hands, this restaurant continues to wow patrons
with Balinese-inspired decor and
mouthwatering fusion fare. Belly
dancers sometimes perform.

🅿 🕐 Closed Sun. 🆂
🆂 All major cards

🍴 EXÓTICA CAFÉ
$$

2 MILES (3.2 KM) E OF
PLAYA TORTUGA
TEL 2786-5050
Tiny, open-air eatery serving sur-
prisingly accomplished and exotic
tropical nouvelle cuisine.

🕐 Closed L & Sun. 🆂 None

PLAYA ESTERILLOS

SOMETHING SPECIAL

🏨 ALMA DEL PACIFICO
🍴 $$$$

PLAYA ESTERILLOS ESTE
TEL 2778-7070
almadelpacifico.com
An architectural masterpiece,
this contemporary stunner
offers colorful and dramatically
designed villas adorned with
the former owners' art and
every conceivable convenience.
Private gardens and full-service
spa. Serves health-conscious
gourmet cuisine.

ⓘ 15 villas 🅿 🆂 🏊 🎽
🛜 Free 🆂 All major cards

🆂 Air-conditioning 🏊 Outdoor Pool 🏊 Indoor Pool 🎽 Health Club 🛜 Wi-Fi 🆂 Credit Cards

PLAYA HERMOSA

🏨 **TERRAZA DEL PACIFICO**

🍽 **$$**

HWY. 34, 1 MILE (1.6 KM)
S OF JACÓ
TEL 2643-3222
terrazadelpacifico.com
This specialized surf hotel and restaurant is tucked beneath cliffs, with miles of black-sand beach to the south. It offers genteel decor combined with a modicum of facilities, including a small casino plus surfing lessons and horseback riding. Two swimming pools.

ⓘ 62 Ⓟ 🛗 🏊 🛜 Free
🚭 AE, MC, V

PLAYA HERRADURA

🏨 **LOS SUEÑOS MARRIOTT**
🍽 **OCEAN & GOLF RESORT**
$$$$$

TEL 2630-9000
marriott.com
This deluxe beachfront resort provides access to an 18-hole golf course, spa, tennis courts, watersports, 250-slip marina, and choice of restaurants, bars, and lounges.

ⓘ 201 Ⓟ 🛗 🔇 🛗 🏊 🖥
🛜 Fee 🚭 All major cards

SOMETHING SPECIAL

🏨 **VILLA CALETAS &**
🍽 **ZEPHYR PALACE**
$$$$–$$$$$

HWY. 34, 3 MILES (4.8 KM)
N OF JACÓ
TEL 2630-3000
hotelvillacaletas.com
Lavishly furnished rooms and hillside villas inspired by "tropical Victorian" architecture in a stunning clifftop setting. The two restaurants serve Costa Rican fare with a French twist. Horizon pool and classical amphitheater for concerts. Poolside bar. For the ultimate luxury, check into Zephyr Palace, with seven mammoth suites inspired by Imperial Rome.

ⓘ 25 rooms, 11 villas Ⓟ 🛗
🏊 🛜 Free 🚭 AE, MC, V

QUEPOS

🏨 **SANTA JUANA**
MOUNTAIN LODGE
$$$

SANTA JUANA, 12 MILES (19 KM)
NE OF QUEPOS
TEL 2777-0777
santajuanalodge.com
Nestling atop a mountain ridge overlooking the Pacific, this rustic lodge features elegant furnishings and slate showers. Wholesome farm fare is served. Community and adventure activities.

ⓘ 6 Ⓟ 🛜 None 🚭 All major cards

🍽 **EL GRAN ESCAPE**
RESTAURANT &
FISHHEAD BAR
$

TEL 2777-7850
elgranescapequepos.com
Burgers, tuna melts, surf-and-turf, and local seafood dishes in this open-air restaurant. Sushi offered upstairs.

🕐 Closed Tues. 🚭 None

SAVEGRE

🏨 **RAFIKI SAFARI LODGE**
$$$

20 MILES (32.2 KM)
SE OF QUEPOS
TEL 8368-9944
rafikisafari.com
African-style lodge specializing in nature activities and white-water adventures, set amid 842 acres (341 ha) of jungle. Accommodation is in fully furnished tents with en suite bathrooms and porches with rocking chairs. Rafiki, which is South African–run, has a traditional *braai* (barbecue) in the Lecker Bar.

ⓘ 9 Ⓟ 🏊 🛜 Free but limited to some areas 🚭 MC, V

UVITA

SOMETHING SPECIAL

🏨 **KURÀ DESIGN VILLAS**
🍽 **$$$$$**

2 MILES (3 KM) E OF UVITA
TEL 8521-3407
kuracostarica.com
This sensational and environmentally sensitive boutique hotel sets a new standard for architectural design in Costa Rica. Its six all-glass cubist villas have en suite glass showers that open to broad glass-framed terraces; bamboo ceilings add a tropical touch. The lounge-restaurant overlooks a travertine sundeck with loungers and an L-shaped infinity pool. Perched atop the coast mountain range, it offers stunning views along the Pacific shore.

ⓘ 6 Ⓟ 🛗 🏊 🛜 Free
🚭 All major cards

▪ ZONA SUR

BAHÍA DRAKE

🏨 **AGUILA DE OSA INN**
$$$$$

MOUTH OF RÍO AGUJITAS, 0.5 MILE
(0.8 KM) S OF AGUJITAS
TEL 2296-2190 OR 8840-2929
aguiladeosa.com
An upscale nature lodge decorated with a native theme, tucked in a canyon. Good for scuba diving and sportfishing. Package rates include inventive meals with free-flowing wine.

ⓘ 4 rooms, 7 bungalows 🛜 Free
🚭 AE, MC, V

🏨 **VILLAS LA PALOMA**
LODGE
$$

0.5 MILES (0.8 KM) S OF AGUJITAS
TEL 2293-7502
lapalomalodge.com
Cozy and graciously appointed hardwood cabins and spacious villas in landscaped grounds facing the Pacific. Family-style meals, tours, and activities.

ⓘ 4 rooms, 7 bungalows 🏊 🛜
Free in public areas 🚭 MC, V

CORCOVADO

SOMETHING SPECIAL

🏨 LAPA RIOS ECO-LODGE
🍽 $$$$$
CABO MATOPALO
TEL 2735-5130
laparios.com
Lauded for its environmental excellence, this deluxe and recently upgraded rain forest eco-lodge is a National Geographic Unique Lodges of the World member. Villa-suites perch atop a ridge with fabulous ocean views on one side and the luxuriant forest within finger-tip reach on the other. Offers nature tours, horseback riding, and kayaking. Rates include meals, served in a thatched restaurant with spiraling mirador. Superb wildlife viewing.
🛈 17 bungalows 🏊 📶 Free in public areas 💳 AE, MC, V

🏨 BOSQUE DEL CABO
$$$$
CABO MATOPALO
TEL 2735-5206 OR 8389-2846
bosquedelcabo.com
Casa Blanca, a clifftop villa on this serene oceanfront property, is the epitome of luxury. Also bungalows and simple meals in a thatched restaurant.
🛈 8 bungalows, 1 house 🅿 🏊 📶 Fee 💳 V

🏨 CASA CORCOVADO JUNGLE LODGE
$$$$
N BORDER OF CORCOVADO NATIONAL PARK
TEL 2256-3181 OR 888/896-6097
casacorcovado.com
This former cacao plantation provides accommodation in graciously appointed thatched *cabinas*. Water sports, guided hikes, and horseback riding offered. Bar and family-style dining. Two-night minimum.
🛈 10 bungalows 🏊 📶 Free in public areas 💳 AE, MC, V

🏨 LUNA LODGE
$$$$
CARATE
TEL 4070-0010 OR 888/760-0760
lunalodge.com
A dramatic hillside setting and tastefully decorated thatched cabins with views into the rain forest. Safari-style tents also available. A dojo is used for yoga. Reached only by four-wheel-drive vehicles.
🛈 8 cabins, 7 tents 🅿 🏊 📶 Free in public areas 💳 MC, V

GOLFITO

🏨 BANANA BAY MARINA
🍽 $$$
TEL 2775-0255
bananabaymarinagolfito.com
This small hotel and sportfishing resort adjoins its namesake marina. Contemporary rooms. American and nouvelle cuisine served in the Bilge Bar & Grill.
🛈 4 🅿 🅂 🏊 📶 Free 💳 MC, V

PAVONES

🏨 TISKITA LODGE
$$
TEL 2296-8125
tiskita.com
Surrounded by rain forest and fruit orchards, this property centers on an old farmhouse where meals are served family style. Accommodation is in wooden cabins with private alfresco showers and toilets. Horseback riding, nature tours, and birding trips.
🛈 17 🅿 🅂 🏊 📶 Free 💳 AE, MC, V

PIEDRAS BLANCAS

🏨 ESQUINAS RAIN FOREST LODGE
$$$
LAS GAMBAS
TEL 2741-8001
esquinaslodge.com
A comfortable, simply appointed nature lodge on the edge of Piedras Blancas National Park. Locals lead nature treks, among other activities. Part of a model project combining research, conservation, and community development.
🛈 14 🅿 🏊 💳 AE, MC, V

🏨 PLAYA NICUESA RAIN FOREST LODGE
$$$
PLAYA NICUESA, 9 MILES (14.5 KM) NW OF GOLFITO
TEL 2258-8250 OR 866/504-8116
nicuesalodge.com
This rain forest lodge enjoys a beachfront location, with trails into a private reserve. Delightfully furnished accommodations have open-air bathrooms. Hammocks abound on broad balconies. Kayaking and windsurfing.
🛈 4 cabins, 4 rooms, 1 house 📶 Free 💳 None

PUERTO JIMÉNEZ

🏨 IGUANA LODGE &
🍽 PEARL OF THE OSA
$$$
PLAYA PLATANARES
TEL 8829-5865 OR 800/259-9123
iguanalodge.com
A jungly beachside setting adds allure to this reclusive no-frills lodge with four thatched stilt cabins. The adjoining Pearl of the Osa lodge has eight airy budget rooms with private bathrooms. Two open-air restaurants offer snacks to gourmet meals. Live music.
🛈 4 cabins, 8 rooms 🅿 📶 Free 💳 None

🏨 LAPA'S NEST TREE HOUSE
$$$
BARRIO BONITO, 8 MILES (13 KM) N OF PUERTO JIMÉNEZ
TEL 2714-0622 OR 8372-3529
treehouseincostarica.com
You can't get a more intimate live-among-the-wildlife experience than at this six-story rain forest tree house wrapped around a huge mahogany tree. Monkeys, scarlet macaws, and more frolic eye-to-eye. Nearby villa offers eight rooms.
🛈 8 rooms, 1 tree house 🅿 🅂 in villa 📶 Free 💳 None

ZANCUDO

🏨 CABINAS SOL Y MAR
🍴 $$
TEL 2776-0014
zancudo.com
This beachfront property has attractive cabins with skylit bathrooms. The outdoor bar and grill serves dishes such as tuna with capers and burgers.
🛏 5 cabins, 1 house 🅿 📶 Free
🚫 None

■ SOUTH CENTRAL

SAN GERARDO DE RIVAS

SOMETHING SPECIAL

🏨 MONTE AZUL
$$$$$
CHIMIROL DE RIVAS
TEL 2742-5222
macastudios.org
Owners and art aficionados Carlos Rojas and Randall Langendorfer host art workshops at this boutique hotel. Contemporary pieces adorn spacious villas set apart in lush riverside gardens surrounded by forest. Enthusiastic local staff prepare gourmet dishes. Hiking trails lace the nature reserve. Phase 2 is under way and will add a theater. Functions as a hotel only when its Artists in Residency program permits.
🛏 4 🅿 🚭 📶 Free
🚫 All major cards

🏨 RÍO CHIRRIPÓ YOGA RETREAT & LODGE
$$
CANAAN
TEL 2742-5109
riochirripo.com
Inspired by Santa Fe style, this handsome lodge has homey yet tastefully decorated cabins with balconies overhanging the gorge. Roofed platforms accommodate campers. Airy rancho dining area. Offers yoga classes and workshops.

🛏 8 room, 2 cabins 🅿 🚹
📶 Free in public areas 🚫 MC, V

🏨 TALAMANCA RESERVE
$$
0.5 MILE (0.8 KM) N OF
SAN GERARDO DE RIVAS
TEL 2742-5080
talamancareserve.com
Modestly furnished cabins, plus a sunlit two-story café-restaurant with 21st-century styling. Hiking and ATV trails. Perfectly positioned close to both the village and the Cerro Chirripó trailhead.
🛏 10 cabins 🅿 📶 Free
🚫 MC, V

SAN VITO

🏨 LAS CRUCES BIOLOGICAL STATION
$$
HWY. 16, 4 MILES (6.4 KM) S OF
SAN VITO
TEL 2773-4004 OR 2524-0607
ots.ac.cr
Attractive contemporary rooms boast verandas, picture windows, and modern amenities in the heart of a forest reserve. The station is set amid the Wilson Botanical Garden, a collection of more than 1,000 genera in 212 plant families, considered the most important Central American plant collection.
🛏 12 🅿 🚭 📶 Free
🚫 AE, MC, V

■ NORTHERN LOWLANDS

CHACHAGUA

🏨 CHACHAGUA RAIN FOREST ECOLODGE
$$
4 MILES (6.4 KM) S OF
CHACHAGUA
TEL 4000-2026
chachaguarainforesthotel.com
A working cattle and fruit farm with a private nature reserve at the foot of the Cordillera de Tilarán is the setting for

this simple yet gracious rustic wilderness lodge.
🛏 23 🅿 📶 Free
🚫 AE, MC, V

LA FORTUNA

🏨 ARENAL KIORO
🍴 $$$$$
12 MILES (19.3 KM) W OF
LA FORTUNA
TEL 2461-1700
hotelarenalkioro.com
This deluxe hotel offers stupendous views through walls of glass in expansive suites, all with hot tubs by the verandas. First-rate restaurant, full-service spa, modern gym, and two thermal swimming pools, plus hot springs nearby.
🛏 53 suites 🅿 🚹 🚭 📶 Free
🚫 All major cards

SOMETHING SPECIAL

🏨 THE SPRINGS RESORT
🍴 & SPA
$$$$$
7 MILES (11 KM) W OF
LA FORTUNA
TEL 2401-3313
thespringscostarica.com
This romantic hilltop retreat offers magnificent volcano views from every angle. The main six-story building and sumptuous guest rooms (in separate units) gleam with marble and glazed hardwoods. Thermal pools abound, including landscaped water cascades. A wildlife refuge displays five species of big cat, plus monkeys. A riverside activity center offers rock climbing, kayaking, and tubing. Restaurants include a sushi bar and the gourmet Las Ventas.
🛏 46 🅿 🚭 🚹 🔳 📶 Free
🚫 All major cards

🏨 ARENAL LODGE
$$$$
13 MILES (21 KM) W OF
LA FORTUNA
TEL 2479-1881 OR 800/716-2698
arenallodge.com
Atmospheric mountain lodge with volcano views. Lounge

bar with stone hearth offers the most impressive vistas. Sportfishing and tours offered. Rates include buffet breakfast, plus use of mountain bikes, hot tub, library, and trails.

🛈 50 🅿 🛜 Free 🚫 AE, MC, V

🏨 NAYARA
🍽 $$$$

6 MILES (10 KM) W OF
LA FORTUNA
TEL 2479-1600 OR 888/332-2961
arenalnayara.com
One of Costa Rica's premier boutique hotels, it exudes a Balinese aesthetic, including its tranquil gardens. Romantic and spacious guest *casitas* (bungalows) in two styles with canopied king beds plus 21st-century amenities; most have indoor and garden showers. Sushi bar and open-air restaurant.

🛈 50 🅿 🔧 🏊 🛜 Free
🚫 All major cards

🏨 TABACÓN HOT
🍽 SPRINGS RESORT & SPA
$$$

TABACÓN, 8 MILES (13 KM) W OF
LA FORTUNA
TEL 2479-2000 OR 855/822-2266
tabacon.com
This modern lodge with views of Volcán Arenal offers guests direct access to the adjacent spa. Rooms are tastefully furnished. A choice of restaurants includes an eatery directly above the thermal pools.

🛈 114 🅿 🔧 🎩 🚫 DC, MC, V

LA VIRGEN

🏨 SARAPIQUÍS
🍽 RAINFOREST LODGE
$$$$

1 MILE (1.6 KM) N OF LA VIRGEN
TEL 2761-1004
sarapiquis.com
This upscale option is in the heart of an ecotourism project next to a rain forest reserve. Architecture and decor blend contemporary and pre-Columbian styles. The elegant restaurant offers à la carte and buffet options, plus forest views

over the canopy. Botanical garden, archaeological site, and museum nearby.

🛈 40 🅿 🔧 🏊 🛜 Free
🚫 MC, V

LAS HORQUETAS

🏨 HACIENDA
LA ISLA LODGE
$$$

6 MILES (10 KM) S OF
LAS HORQUETAS
TEL 2764-2576
haciendalaisla.com
This colonial-built hacienda at the base of Barva volcano has been tastefully converted into a boutique hotel furnished in period fashion. The grounds include an orchard good for birding, and poison dart frogs hop about the forest reserve.

🛈 15 🅿 🔧 🛜 Free in public
areas 🚫 MC, V

🏨 RARA AVIS
$$

9 MILES (14.5 KM) SW OF
LAS HORQUETAS
TEL 2764-1111
rara-avis.com
A remote, rustic, and hard-to-reach wilderness lodge located on a private reserve with swimming holes, canopy platforms, butterfly and orchid houses, naturalist guides, hiking trails, and horseback riding. Two-night minimum stay; reservations required. Rates include simple meals.

🛈 5 cabins, 10 rooms 🅿
🛜 None 🚫 AE, MC, V

MUELLE

🏨 TILAJARI RESORT HOTEL
🍽 $$$

1 MILE (1.6 KM) W OF
MUELLE CROSSROADS
TEL 2462-1212
tilajari.com
Spacious, modestly furnished rooms on the banks of the Río San Carlos. Adequate meals in a large restaurant. Spot crocodiles on the riverbanks. Butterfly

garden, squash courts, disco, sauna, and sports facilities. Tours offered.

🛈 76 🅿 🔧 🏊 🛜 Free
🚫 All major cards

PUERTO VIEJO

🏨 SELVA VERDE
$$$

CHILAMATE DE SARAPIQUÍ,
6 MILES (9.7 KM) W OF
PUERTO VIEJO
TEL 2761-1800
selvaverde.com
Nature lodge set on the edge of rain forest with a choice between rustic rooms, upscale cabins, or bungalows. Library, lecture room, and communal dining room. Guided hikes and canoe trips can be arranged.

🛈 40 rooms, 5 bungalows
🅿 🛜 Free in public areas
🚫 MC, V

■ THE CARIBBEAN

BARRA DEL COLORADO

🏨 SILVER KING LODGE
🍽 $$$

BARRA DEL COLORADO SUR
TEL 8447-5988 OR 877/335-0755
silverkinglodge.net
Well-furnished wooden cabins on the banks of the river from which a fleet of sportfishing boats put out. Tackle shop, TV and video room, indoor spa pool, bar, and restaurant.

🛈 20 🔧 🏊 🛜 Free
🚫 AE, MC, V

CAHUITA

🏨 LA DIOSA
$$

PLAYA NEGRA, 2 MILES (3.2 KM)
N OF CAHUITA
TEL 2755-0055
hotelladiosa.net
Squatting on its own little beach, this quaint and colorful hotel has charming cabins featuring riverstone walls and batik spreads. Delightful

gardens with yoga dojo and Oriental adornments.

(i) 6 rooms, 2 cabins **P** ⛱ **⌂** Free **⊗** None

PASSION FRUIT LODGE
$$

2 MILES (5 KM) NW OF CAHUITA
TEL 8939-9823
passionfruitlodge.com
Off the highway away from the village, this French-run property has four rustic casas with simple yet charming furnishings, plus terraces.

(i) 4 villas **P** **⌂** Free **⊗**

COCORICO
$$

CAHUITA
TEL 2755-0409
Bohemian café-restaurant in Arabian style. Italian gourmet fare including superb pizzas and homemade ice cream. Occasional live music plus films.

P **⊗** None

MISS EDITH'S
$$

CAHUITA
TEL 2755-0248
A long-time heart-of-the-village staple this is *the* place to try authentic Caribbean cuisine such as *rondón* and curried lobster in coconut milk. Family-run, laid-back, and open-air.

P **⊗** None

ESTRELLA

SELVA BANANITO LODGE
$$

9 MILES (14.5 KM) W OF BANANITO
TEL 2253-8118
selvabananito.com
A simple, atmospheric lodge on the edge of the rain forest. Stilt-legged cabins with solar-heated water. No electricity. Hiking, horseback rides, and family-style dining. Four-wheel-drive access.

(i) 11 **P** **⌂** None **⊗** None

PUERTO VIEJO

ALMONDS & CORALS LODGE TENT CAMP
$$$$

PUNTA MANZANILLO, 5 MILES (8 KM) SE OF PUERTO VIEJO
TEL 2271-3000 OR 2759-9056
almondsandcorals.com
A minimalist yet deluxe eco-sensitive wilderness lodge with tents on roofed wooden platforms, situated in shorefront jungle. Private bathrooms nearby. Communal restaurant. Tours and outdoor activities.

(i) 24 **P** **⌂** Free **⊗** AE, D, MC

SHAWANDHA LODGE
$$$

PLAYA CHIQUITA, 4 MILES (6.4 KM) SE OF PUERTO VIEJO
TEL 2750-0018
shawandha.com
Splendid setting for thatched cabins close to the beach. Tasteful furnishings include four-poster beds. Open-air lounge offers similarly contemporary grace. Rates include breakfast.

(i) 12 **P** **⌂** Free **⊗** AE, MC, V

COCO LOCO
$

400 YARDS (366 M) SW OF PUERTO VIEJO
TEL 2750-0281
cocolocolodge.com
A back-to-basics retreat amid lawns surrounded by forest. Small Tahitian-style cabins have few frills but plenty of charm. Mosquito nets over beds.

(i) 4 cottages, 1 bungalow **P** **⌂** Free **⊗** AE, MC, V

LA PECORA NERA
$$$

PLAYA COCLES
TEL 2750-0490
Delicious Italian fare of world-class standard at this unpretentious, thatched open-air restaurant. Calzones, gnocchi, and pizzas are supplemented by superlative daily specials.

P ⊕ Closed Mon. & low season **⊗** AE, MC, V

CAFÉ RICO
$

PUERTO VIEJO
TEL 2750-0510
This simple wooden café-restaurant serves alfresco breakfasts. Book exchange, hammocks, and bike rental.

P **⊗** None

TORTUGUERO

TORTUGA LODGE & GARDENS
$$$

2 MILES (3.2 KM) N OF TORTUGUERO
TEL 2257-0766
tortugalodge.com
Comfortable wilderness lodge with walk-in swimming pool on Tortuguero Lagoon, close to the airstrip. Enjoy hearty family-style meals on the airy riverside terrace. Superb guides lead hikes, sportfishing outings, and boat tours of Parque Nacional Tortuguero.

(i) 24 **P** ⛱ **⌂** Free **⊗** AE, MC, V

CASA MARBELLA B&B
$

TORTUGUERO VILLAGE
TEL 8833-0827 OR 2709-8011
casamarbella.tripod.com
Simple Canadian-run B&B in the heart of Tortuguero. Owner is a font of local knowledge. Community kitchen.

(i) 5 **⌂** Free in public areas **⊗** None

MISS JUNIE'S LODGE
$

TEL 2709-8029
iguanaverdetours.com/lodge
Cozy all-hardwood rooms on the edge of the village. Down-home cooking by a village elder. Fish platter special with beans and rice simmered in coconut milk; ginger cookies, and *pan bon,* bread laced in caramelized sugar.

(i) 16 **⊗** None

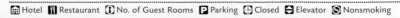

Shopping

The tourist boom has spawned an outpouring of quality crafts, from beautiful pottery, wooden bowls, and carvings to exquisite gold jewelry and colorful wooden *carretas* (traditional oxcarts). San José is filled with crafts stores and art galleries; the latter reflects an explosion of energy in the art world.

Many crafts use hardwoods, such as lignum vitae, purpleheart, rosewood, satinwood, and tigerwood. Larger items include carved headboards, lathe-turned rockers with leather seats, and decorative mini-carretas for use as liquor bars or garden ornaments that can be shipped home with relative ease.

Costa Rica's renowned coffee is available nationwide. Buy prepackaged, premium export-grade coffee; domestic coffee is notably inferior. Juan Santamaría International Airport has several quality gift stores, including those of Café Britt where you can buy coffee. Most upscale hotels have stores selling arts and crafts, as does the airport, which also has duty-free stores.

Opening Times

See p. 238.

■ SAN JOSÉ

West of Avenida 2, between Calles 4 and 9 are art and craft stores. Centro Comercial El Pueblo, to the northeast of the city center, has alleys lined with galleries, stores, and restaurants. The suburb of Moravia (San Vincente) is known for art, crafts, jewelry, local leatherwork, and wicker furniture.

Arts & Antiques

Andrómeda Gallery *(Calle 9, Ave. 9, tel 2223-3529)*. Paintings by Costa Rican and Central American artists, including top local names. Works cost as much as $10,000.
Andrómeda Contemporáneo *(Ave. 9, Calle 9, tel 2223-3529)*. Broad representation of works by leading artists.
Galería Valanti *(Ave. 11, Calles 33/35, tel 2253-1659)*. This compact gallery specializes in works from throughout the Americas, with a focus on local artists of note.

Books & Maps

Librería Internacional *(Ave. Central, Calles 3/5, tel 800/542-7374, libreriainternacional.com)*. Costa Rica's preeminent book chain has six outlets in San José.
Mora Books Mora Books *(Calle 5, Ave. 5/7, tel 8383-8385, mora books.com)*. Used bookstore and popular expat hangout.

Clothes & Accessories

Artesanías Malety *(Ave. 1, Calles 1/3, tel 2221-1670)*. Pick up a pair of stylish cowboy boots, including alligator skin.
Mercado Central *(Ave. 1, Calles 6/8)*. Local clothing, including *guayaberas*, cowboy boots, leather belts, and embroidered blouses.
Mundo Aventura *(Ave. 3, Calle 36, tel 2221-6934, maventura.com)*. Outdoor wear and accessories for activities from mountain biking to rock-climbing.

Crafts & Jewelry

Boutique Annemarie *(Don Carlos hotel; see p. 242)*. Arts and crafts, from carved walking sticks to balsawood masks.
Boutique Kiosko Kalú *(Calle 31 & Ave. 5, Barrio Escalante, tel 2253-8426)*. Sells exquisite Costa Rican–made crafts and jewelry, including indigenous and designer clothes.
Chietón Morén *(Calle 17, Aves. 2/6, tel 2221-0145, chietonmoren .org)*. Operated by a Boruca indigenous association, sells indigenous crafts direct from the artists.
Dantica Gallery *(Lincoln Plaza, Local 306, Moravia, tel 2519-9306, danticagallery.com)*. Highest quality indigenous crafts from throughout Costa Rica and Latin America.

Esmeraldas & Diseños *(Sábana Norte, tel 2231-4808, esmeraldas ydisenos.com)*. Jewelry includes pre-Columbian-style gold.
Galería Namú *(Ave. 7, Calles 5/7, tel 2256-3412, galerianamu.com)*. High-quality indigenous arts and crafts and paintings from Costa Rica and Panama.
Museo del Oro Precolombino (see p. 58). Contemporary gold and silver, precious stones. Superb pre-Columbian reproductions.

Gifts

Don Benigno Cigars *(Commercial Center Plaza Mayor, Pavas, tel 2296-8111, benignocigars.com)*. Sells its own brand of hand-rolled cigars.
Guitarras Guzmán, Ltd. *(Cinco Esquinas de Tibas, tel 2223-0682, aristidesguzman.com)*. Sells classical guitars carved from precious woods.

Malls

Plaza San Pedro *(Ave. Central Circunvalación, tel 2280-1701)*. The city's largest mall, with dozens of upscale stores. Everything from jewelry and fashion to leathers and books. Also a bank, movie theater, and two-story food court.

Markets

Mercado de Artesanía *(Plaza de las Artes. Calle 11 & Aves. 4/6, closed Sun)*. Around 30 craft stores under a single roof.
Mercado Central *(Bet. Calles 6/8 & Aves. Central/Calle 1)*. A maze of tight alleyways where street stalls and shops sell everything from medicinal herbs and flowers to cowboy boots and guayabero shirts. Closed Sundays. Beware of pickpockets.

CENTRAL HIGHLANDS

Santa Ana is famous for ceramics. Sarchí is the nation's undisputed center of crafts, with furniture workshops, and fine leatherworkers. It also is the sole remaining production center in the country for carretas (traditional oxcarts). Workshops and craft stores line the main street.

Crafts & Jewelry

Biesanz Woodworks (Biesanz; see p. 70). Costa Rica's premier wood-carver oversees 20 master carvers in his workshop. Exquisite bowls, boxes, and humidors.
Casa del Soñador (see p. 86). Buy primitive-style pieces carved from coffee wood.
Cerámica Las Palomas (Alto de las Palomas, Santa Ana, tel 2282-7001). Exquisite contemporary ceramics plus earthenware bowls, vases, and urns are made on old-fashioned kick wheels and fired in an outdoor kiln.
Creaciones Santos (Ave. 3, Calles 1/3, San Miguel de Escazú, tel 2228-6747). Exotic stained glass made on-site.
Fábrica de Carretas Eloy Alfaro (Sarchí Norte, tel 2454-4131, souvenirscostarica.com). Costa Rica's only remaining workshop making traditional oxcarts. A huge store sells miniatures, plus crafts of every kind.
Fábrica de Carretas Joaquín Chaverrí (Sarchí Sur, tel 2454-4411). A huge selection of arts and crafts from hardwood to kitchenware. In the family-run workshop, you can see miniature carretas being made.
Molas & Coffee Gift Shop (Atenas, tel 2446-5155). A fine array of native arts and crafts, plus jewelry. Indigenous craftspeople employed on-site.
Señor y Señora Ese (Barrio Villa Bonita, Alajuela, tel 2441-8333, srysraese.com). This factory produces hand-crafted hardwood items, from jewelry to sculptures. Factory tours offered.

Gifts

Café Britt (see p. 83). Offers premium prepackaged coffees at wholesale prices, handcrafted wooden kitchen utensils, bowls, and other items with Costa Rican themes. Café Britt outlets are in many hotels plus the José Santamaría International Airport.

Malls

Avenida Escazú (Escazú, tel 2288-0101, avenidaescazu.com). Boutiques and specialty stores.
Multiplaza (Autopista Prospero Fernández, Escazú, tel 2288-1178, multiplaza.com). Costa Rica's largest mall has specialty stores that range from books to fashion to jewelry.

Markets

Mercado Central (Bet. Calle 4/6 & Aves. Central/1, Alajuela). An entire block of stalls selling fresh farm produce, meats, fish, spices, leatherwork, and household goods. Be alert for pickpockets and thieves.
Mercado Central (Bet. Calle 2/4 & Aves. 6/8, Heredia). A tight warren of stores offering farm produce, crafts, and general wares. As with all markets, guard your valuables.

GUANACASTE

Monteverde has galleries and gift stores selling some of the most creative works in the country.

Crafts & Jewelry

Committee of Artisans of Santa Elena & Monteverde (CASEM; Monteverde, tel 2645-5190). Works by more than one hundred local artists, from paintings to ceramics. Sales benefit the local community.
Gallery Artes Tulio (Monteverde, tel 2645-5547). Works by gifted local artist Marco Tulio Brenes include jewelry, paintings, and sculptures.

Hummingbird Gallery (Monteverde, tel 2645-5030). Wildlife posters and prints, Guatemalan textiles, and crafts from throughout the isthmus, including prints and slides by local photographers Michael and Patricia Fogden.
Souvenirs La Gran Nicoya (Hwy. 21, near Daniel Oduber International Airport, tel 2667-0062). A vast range of souvenirs, including ceramics, beachwear, and cigars.
Toad Hall (see p. 246). Quality arts and crafts, books, postcards, and Cuban cigars.

Gifts

La Lechería (see p. 109). Various cheeses and ice creams made on site, plus meats.

Markets

Mercado Central (Ave. 3, Calle 2, Puntarenas). Waterfront market crammed with seafood and fresh produce stalls.

NICOYA

Guaitíl is the center of the Indian pottery tradition. Matriarchs work clay into bowls, plates, and vases painted in traditional animal motifs. Ask for a tour. A trademark three-legged vase in the form of a cow costs between $15 and $50.

Crafts & Jewelry

Azul Profundo Boutique (Centro Comercial Plaza Tamarindo, Tamarindo, tel 2653-0395, azulprofundo boutique.com). Fine clothes and accessories, including swimwear.
Oven Store (Guaitíl, tel 2681-1696). This family workshop produces quality pottery, from plates and vases to animal figurines.

CENTRAL PACIFIC

Quepos has numerous souvenir stores and art galleries, and Manuel Antonio has beachfront stalls; several hotels have excellent gift stores. Boruca produces Indian crafts. The men make balsawood masks and decorate gourds.

Crafts & Jewelry

The Captain's Booty (Bet. Quepos & Manuel Antonio, tel 2777-1907). Wide range of crafts and artwork, from Chorotega pottery to jewelry and T-shirts.

Dantica Gallery (Plaza Herradura, Playa Herradura, tel 2637-7572, danticagallery.com). Top-quality indigenous art and crafts from throughout the Americas.

Galería Yara (Plaza Yara, Manuel Antonio, tel 2777-4846). Paintings and sculptures by local artists.

Regalame (Si Como No hotel, Manuel Antonio; see p. 251). First-class paintings, sculptures, and handicrafts by local artisans.

Villa Caletas (see p. 252). Sells juried gold items and quality crafts.

Gifts

House of Cigars (Quepos, tel 2777-2208, closed Sun.). A Cuban exile rolls quality smokes on-site.

■ ZONA SUR

Golfito draws Costa Ricans from afar to its duty-free Depósito Libre zone, but there are few items of interest for tourists. Puerto Jiménez has several souvenir shops; many hotel gift shops sell local crafts, including balsawood masks.

Crafts & Jewelry

Jagua Arts & Crafts (Puerto Jiménez, tel 2735-5267). Beside the airstrip, this small store's fine collection includes Boruca masks, wooden carvings, jewelry, and owner Karen Herrera's own blown-glass items.

Reserva Indígena Boruca. Mileny González (tel 2730-5178) runs the local cooperative; members make colorful animal masks and figures, plus hammocks and woven goods.

Taller Familiar de Artesanías Independiente Boruca (tel 8941-6349). Workshop of a local cooperative making and selling Boruca masks and other carvings, plus handwoven bags and skirts.

■ SOUTH CENTRAL

Shopping is not this region's strong suit. However, San Isidro and San Vito have many shops selling cowboy boots and other leather goods. The indigenous communities of the Talamancas produce crafts, including colorful molas.

Crafts & Jewelry

Finca Cántaros (Hwy. 16 at Linda Vista, 2 miles S of San Vito, tel 2773-3760). Quality arts and crafts; ceramics, jewelry, and clothing.

Gifts

Quesos Canaan (Canaan, Río Chirripó Valley, tel 2742-5125). A tiny family farm that produces quality artisanal cheeses.

■ NORTHERN LOWLANDS

Ciudad Quesada has several talabarterías (saddle shops) selling cowboy boots, decorated saddles, and other leather goods. La Fortuna has souvenir shops selling crafts from throughout the nation.

Crafts & Jewelry

Coco Loco Art Gallery (Chachagua, tel 2468-0990, artedk.com). Fabulous selection of arts and crafts includes indigenous masks and contemporary ceramics.

Galería Onirica (La Fortuna, tel 2479-7589, galeriaoniricacr.com). Represents about a dozen top-ranked Costa Rican artists.

Reserva Indígena Malekú (2 miles E of San Rafael de Guatuso). Naïve native crafts, including masks.

Markets

Mercado Central (Calle 2, Ave. Central, Ciudad Quesada). Bustling hive offering produce, plus arts and crafts from the local artisans' cooperative.

■ THE CARIBBEAN

Puerto Viejo's entrepreneurial expatriate population produces and sells a wide selection of jewelry, batiks, and tourist trinkets.

Art & Antiques

Francisco Ureña (Siquirres). Vividly naïve paintings sold at his home gallery.

Gallery at Home (Río Blanco, tel 2711-0823 or 8489-5672). Studio of acclaimed North American artist Patricia Erickson. Call for appointment.

Clothes & Accessories

Color Caribe (Puerto Viejo, tel 2750-0403). One of the country's best-stocked souvenir stores offers jewelry, plus hand-painted and silk-screened T-shirts and other clothing.

Reggaeland (Puerto Viejo, tel 2750-2096). Quintessentially Caribbean store selling everything from flip-flops and skateboards to all things Bob Marley.

Crafts & Jewelry

LuluBerlu (Puerto Viejo, tel 2750-0394). Splendid range of souvenirs, including hammocks, jewelry, embroidered Guatemalan vests, and sandals.

Paraíso Tropical (Tortuguero, tel 2709-8095). Diverse array of arts and crafts, plus hammocks, swimwear, and more. Donates 10 percent of proceeds to the local school.

Markets

Mercado Municipal (Bet. Calles 3/4 & Aves. 2/3, Limón). A small, intriguing market with stalls that sell everything from household goods and crafts to fresh meats and fish. Be on guard for thieves.

Entertainment & Activities

San José has everything from classical concerts to discos. Casinos are here and in a few resort hotels; though most are small, classier ones have opened. *TicoTimes.net* and the "Viva" section of *La Nación* list festivals and events. The entertainment scene is supplemented by activities highlighting Costa Rica's natural diversity. The companies listed may cover additional activities and other areas.

Activities & Tours

Cheesemans' Ecology Safaris, tel 408/741-5330 or 800/527-5330, cheesemans.com

Costa Rica Expeditions, tel 2521-6099, costaricaexpeditions.com

Holbrook Travel, tel 352/377-7111 or 800/451-7111, holbrook travel.com

Horizontes Nature Tours, tel 2222-2022, or 888/786-8748, horizontes.com

Canoeing & Kayaking

Costa Rica's rivers offer a range of experiences. Contact:

Canoa Aventura, tel 2479-8200, canoa-aventura.com

Desafío Adventure Company, tel 2479-0020 or 855/818-0020, desafiocostarica.com

Karla Taylor's Experience, tel 8915-2386 or 2262-9384. Guided nature trips in Tortuguero.

Canopy Touring

Get close-up views of wildlife from narrow walkways between trees or zip lines that whisk through the treetops. See regional entries.

Fishing

See feature pp. 164–165 for details on the types of fishing available. Boat charters for up to four people cost $400–$600 for a half day and $650–$1,000 for a full day:

Eddie Brown Sportfishing, Tortuguero, tel 2252-4426, captaineddiebrown.com

JP Sportfishing Tours, Quepos, tel 2244-6361 or 866/620-4188, jpsportfishing.com

Tamarindo Sportfishing, Tamarindo, tel 2653-0090, tamarindosportfishing.com

Golfing

The Central Highlands and Pacific Northwest have six premier golf courses. See regional entries.

Horseback Riding

Horseback riding is available nationwide; in Guanacaste, working cattle farms cater to visitors.

Equitour USA, tel 307/455-3363 or 800/545-0019, ridingtours.com

Hidden Trails, tel 888-987-2457, hiddentrails.com

Motorcycling

Costa Rica's back roads are ideal for motorcycle touring for those who know how to ride.

Costa Rica Motorcycle Tours & Rental, tel 2527-6700, costaricamotorcycletours.com

Costa Rican Trails, tel 2527-6700, costaricantrails.com

Mountain Biking

Many hotels rent bikes. Most tours are one or two days; a van carries luggage and equipment.

Backroads, tel 510/527-1555 or 800/462-2848, backroads.com

Coast to Coast Adventures, tel 2280-8054, ctocadventures.com

Experience Plus! Specialty Tours, tel 800/685-4565, experienceplus.com

Nature Cruising

Travel at night; spend days at wilderness sights. Guides lead hikes. May offer diving and snorkeling.

National Geographic Expeditions, 1145 17th St NW, Washington, D.C., tel 888/966-8687, national geographicexpeditions.com

Un-Cruise Adventures, tel 206/284-0300 or 888/862-8881, un-cruise.com

Windstar Cruises, 2401 Fourth Ave., Ste. 1150, Seattle, WA, tel 206/292-9606 or 877/827-7245, windstarcruises.com

Rafting

The industry (see feature pp. 198–199) is not regulated by the government, so book only with a reputable company. Large operators include:

Costa Sol Rafting, tel 4031-4914, costasolrafting.com

Ríos Tropicales, tel 2233-6455 or 866/722-8273, riostropicales.com

Scuba Diving

On the Pacific coast, see groupers, manta rays, and sharks. Catalinas, Isla del Coco, and Islas Murciélagos (Bat Islands) are popular trips. Caribbean diving focuses on coral reefs, best Feb.–April. Visibility is poor by international standards. Temperatures are above 75°F (24°C) year-round. See regional entries.

Surfing

The Pacific coast has some of the world's longest rides. Rent boards at surf camps such as Tamarindo in Nicoya. **Costa Rican Surf Report** *(crsurf.com)* and **Surf Costa Rica** *(tel 866/502-0817, surfcostarica.com)* give local information. **Costa Rica Surfing Company,** tel 805/669-7873, costaricasurfingcompany.com

Windsurfing

Laguna de Arenal (see pp. 114–115) and Bahía Salinas (see p. 128) are the two major sites. Contact: **Costa Rica Kite,** tel 8907-9889, costakite.com

■ SAN JOSÉ
The Arts
Little Theater Group (Centro Cultural Eugene O'Neill, tel 8858-1446, littletheatregroup.org). English-language theater.
National Symphony Orchestra (Teatro Nacional, tel 2240-0333, osn.go.cr; see p. 59). Weekly, April–Dec.
North American Cultural Center (San Pedro, tel 2225-9433, centrocultural.cr). Movies, lectures and more for North American expatriates.
Teatro Popular Melico Salazar (tel 2295-6000, teatromelico.go.cr, see p. 60). Performances June–Aug.

Festivals
Festival de la Carretas, Nov., Paseo Colón & Parque Central. Parade with oxcarts (carretas) and traditional dress. Musicians play the cimarronas.
Festival de la Luz, Christmas. A nocturnal parade of dozens of floats decorated with lights, from Parque Sábana straight to downtown.

Nightlife
Club Vertigo (Centro Colón, tel 2257-8424, vertigocr.com). Head-spinningly hip nightclub. DJs spin hip-hop to techno.
Discoteque Infinito (Centro Comercial, El Pueblo, tel 2223-2195). Three disco areas under one roof.
El Cuartel de la Boca del Monte (Ave. 1, Calles 21/23, tel 2221-0327). Live music and dancing.
Hoxton Pub (TBlvd. Los Yoses, tel 6105-5926). Off-the-hook popular (and crowded) nightspot with dancing. Closed Sun. & Mon.
Jazz Café (Ave. Central, Los Yoses, tel 2253-8933, jazzcafecostarica.com). The best spot for live jazz and blues.
Río (Ave. Central, San Pedro, tel 2225-8371). Packs in chic hipsters; live music and music videos.

Other Activities
Bowling
Boliche, Calle 37, San Pedro, tel 2253-5745, bolichedent.com

Casinos
Casino Club Colonial, Ave. 1, Calles 9/11, tel 2258-2807, casinoclubcolonial.com
Horseshoe Casino, Ave. 1, Calle 9, tel 2233-4383, horseshoecr.com

Dance Lessons
Merecumbé, S. Pedro, tel 2224-3531
Prodanza, Carretera Vieja a Escazú, Santa Ana, tel 2290-7969

Golf
Cariari Country Club (tel 2293-3211, clubcariari.com) has an 18-hole championship course.

■ CENTRAL HIGHLANDS
Festivals
Día de Boyeros, 2nd Sun. in March, San Rafael de Escazú. Oxcart drivers' (boyeros) parade, music, dancing, and folk tales.
Easter Procession, Easter Sunday, San Isidro de Heredia. Solemn religious festival, a celebratory theme.
Juan Santamaría Day, April 11, Alajuela. Week of festivities honoring the boy hero (see p. 29). Music, parades, and street fairs all week.
La Negrita Pilgrimage, Aug. 2, see p. 89.

Nightlife
Casino Real at the Intercontinental Costa Rica, see p. 244.
La Planta Brewpub (Ciudad Colón, tel 2249-0919, beer.cr). The country's premier brewpub serves three super suds.
Rouge (Centro Comercial, Escazú, tel 2201-8517, rougecr.com). Chic cocktail lounge and nightclub with live events.

Other Activities
Bungee Jumping
Tropical Bungee, Rosario, tel 2203-0449, bungee.co.cr

Casinos
Fiesta Casino, Garden Court Hotel, Río Segundo de Alajuela, tel 2431-1455, fiesta.cr

Fishing
Trout farms offer fishing from pools. Bring your own tackle.
Savegre Hotel Natural Reserve & Spa, San Gerardo de Dota, tel 2740-1028, savegre.com

Golf
Parque Valle del Sol (Santa Ana, tel 2282-9222, vallesol.com). 18-hole course.

Horseback Riding
Club Hípico la Caraña (Santa Ana, tel 2282-6754, lacarana.com). Lessons and tours
Hacienda el Rodeo, Ciudad Colón, tel 2249-1013, haciendaelrodeo.com
Rancho San Miguel, La Guácima, see p. 73

Mountain Biking
Hotel Casa Turire, tel 2531-1111, hotelcasaturire.com
La Angelina Mountain Bike Park, Barrio Ochomogo, Cartago, tel 2279-1335

Rafting
One- or three-day runs with Class III or IV rapids.
Costa Rica Expeditions, San Jose, see p. 260
Ríos Tropicales, San José, see p. 260

■ GUANACASTE
Festivals
Día de Guanacaste, July 25, Liberia. Marimba and mariachi music, parades, and rodeos.
Fiesta Cívica, May, Cañas. Traditional music and dance, rodeos, and topes.
Virgin of the Sea Festival, July, Puntarenas. Gaily decorated boats, including a dragon boat represent-

ing the Chinese community, honor Carmen, the Virgin of the Sea. **Día del Sabanero,** Nov., Liberia. Cowboys whoop it up with *topes* and rodeos.

Nightlife
Monteverde Beer House *(Santa Elena, tel 2645-6943).* Craft beers on tap.

Other Activities
Birding
Esteban Daily Guided Tours, Monteverde, tel 8685-5982, estebandailyguidedtours.com

Canopy Tours
The Original Canopy Tour, Santa Elena, tel 2645-5243, theoriginalcanopy.com
Río Perdido, see p. 117
Selvatura Park, see p. 111
Sky Trek, Santa Elena, tel 2479-4100, skyadventures.travel/skytrek

Diving
See p. 263 for operators to the Islas Murciélagos.

Guided Hikes
Heliconias Lodge, Bijagua, tel 2466-8483, hotelheliconias.co.cr

Horseback Riding
Buena Vista Mountain Lodge & Adventure Center, 8 miles NE of Cañas Dulces, tel 2690-1414, buenavistalodgecr.com
Hotel Hacienda Guachipelín, Curubandé, tel 2690-2900, guachipelin.com
Sabine's Smiling Horses, Monteverde, tel 8385-2424, smilinghorses.com

Mountain Biking
Hotel Hacienda Guachipelín (see Horseback Riding above)
Río Perdido (see Canopy Tours above)

Rafting
Río Corobicí is a calm float, with short rapids and water all year.
Rincón Corobicí Rafting, Hwy. 1, 3 miles (4.6 km) N of Cañas, tel 2669-6162, raftingguanacaste.com

Surfing
From Witch's Rock you can ride to Playa Naranjo. Try Playa Portrero Grande (featured in *Endless Summer II*) and Playa Blanca.

Windsurfing
Winds peak at Laguna de Arenal November to April. Bahía Salinas has high winds November to May.
Blue Dream Kiteboarding Resort, Bahía Salinas, tel 2676-1042, bluedreamhotel.com.
Costa Rica Kite, Bahía Salinas, tel 2676-1042, costaricakite.com.
Tico Wind Surf Center, Hwy. 142, Laguna de Arenal, tel 8283-8694, ticowind.com

◼ NICOYA
Festivals
Fiesta Cívica, late January, Playas del Coco. Beauty pageants, rodeos, and street parties.
Fiesta Cívica, January 15 & July 25, Santa Cruz. Firecrackers, marimba music, dancing, rodeos.
Festival of the Virgén de Guadalupe, December 12, Nicoya. This colorful and often very lively festival combines Catholic and Chorotega traditions with the legend of the Virgin of Guadalupe, or La Yequita (Little Mare). Streets are thronged with crowds who throw fireworks *(bombas),* drink *chicha,* and play traditional music.

Nightlife
Aqua Disco *(Tamarindo, tel 8339-0070).* Nicoya's hottest disco.
Father Rooster *(Playa Ocotal, tel 2670-1246).* Atmospheric beach bar. Theme parties.
Nativo Sports Bar *(Malpaís, tel 2640-0356).* Relaxed open-air bar. Live music.
Sharky's *(Tamarindo, tel 2653-4705, sharkysbars.com).* Party central with draft beers. Theme nights.
Zi Lounge *(Playas del Coco, tel 2670-1978, zilounge.com).* Classy lounge bar with DJ and theme parties.

Other Activities
For a variety of outdoor activities contact:
Arenas Aventuras, Tamarindo, tel 2653-0108, tamarindoaventuras.com
Montezuma Expeditions, Montezuma, tel 2441-3394 or 2642-0919, montezumaexpeditions.com

Canopy Tours
Congo Trail Canopy Tour, 5.6 miles (9 km) W of Sardinal, tel 2666-4422
Montezuma Canopy Tour, Montezuma, tel 2642-0808, montezumatraveladventures.com
Wingnuts, Playa Sámara, tel 2656-0153, wingnutscanopy.com
Witch's Rock Canopy Tour, Bahía Culebra, tel 2696-7101, witchsrockcanopy.com

Cruises
Bay Island Cruises, tel 2258-3536, bayislandcruises.com
Calypso Cruises *(tel 2256-2727 or 855/855-1975, calypsocruises.com).* State-of-the-art catamaran.

Golf
Four Seasons Golf Club, Bahía Culebra, tel 2696-0000, fourseasons.com/costarica
Hacienda Pinilla, Playa Avenallas, tel 2680-3000, haciendapinilla.com
Los Delfines Golf & Country Club, Playa Tambor, tel 2683-0294, delfines.com
Tango Mar, see p. 249
Westin Golf Resort & Spa Playa Conchal, see p. 249

Horseback Riding
Ario Tours *(5 miles/8 km N of Santa Teresa, tel 8777-2319, ario tours.com).* Horseback riding plus cattle round-ups.
Painted Pony Guest Ranch, Tamarindo, tel 2653-8041, paintedponyguestranch.com

Scuba Diving
See eagle rays at Punta Gorda, or visit the Islas Murciélagos.

Agua Rica, Tamarindo, tel 2653-0094, aguarica.net

Bill Beard's Costa Rica, Playa Hermosa, tel 2479-7089 or 877/853-0538, billbeardcostarica.com

Resort Divers de Costa Rica, Playa del Coco, tel 2670-0421, resortdivers-cr.com

Rich Coast Diving, Playa del Coco, tel 4030-7561, richcoastdiving.com

Sea Kayaking

Kayaking grants close-up views of bird colonies and mangroves.

Gulf Islands Kayaking, tel 250/539-2442, seakayak.ca

Seascape Kayak Tours, Tambor, tel 8314-8605, seascapekayaktours.com

Spelunking

Barra Honda's caves are open November to April. Experienced spelunkers can enter without a guide (by permit only).

Asociación de Guías Especializadas de Barra Honda, tel 2659-1551. Guided descents.

Sportfishing

The Golfo de Papagayo delivers record sailfish and blue marlin.

Dream On, Playas del Coco, tel 8735-3121, dreamonsportfishing.com

Flamingo Bay Pacific Charters, tel 2297-3857 or 800/836-7133, fishincostarica.com

Tamarindo Sportfishing, Playa Tamarindo, tel 2653-0090, tamarindosportfishing.com

Surfing

Check out Playa Tamarindo, Santa Teresa, and Malpaís.

Iguana Surf Shop, Playa Tamarindo, tel 2653-0091, iguanasurf.net

Malpaís Surf Camp & Resort, Malpaís, tel 2640-0031, malpaissurfcamp.com

Safari Surf School, Nosara, tel 2682-0113, safarisurfschool.com

Ultralight

Flying Crocodile Flying Center, Sámara, tel 2656-8048, flying-crocodile.com

Yoga

Nosara Retreat, Nosara, tel 2682-0071, nosarayoga.com

■ CENTRAL PACIFIC

Festivals

Envision Festival *(Feb, Dominical, envisionfestival.com)*. Performance artists, music, inspirational speakers. Inspired by Burning Man.

Nightlife

Bambu Jam *(Quepos, tel 2777-3369)*. Sports bar with salsa dancing

Casino Kamuk *(Hotel Best Western Kamuk, Quepos, tel 2777-0811, kamuk.co.cr)*. Unpretentious casino.

Cuban Republik Disco Lounge *(Quepos, tel 8345-9922)*. Party-hearty disco with Ladies Night.

El Gran Escape *(Quepos, tel 2777-0395)*. Lively bar with large-screen TVs and occasional live music.

Hotel Amapola *(Playa Jacó, tel 2643-2255, hotelamapola.com)*. Small casino and disco.

Jaco Blu *(Jacó, tel 2643-4372)*. Beach club with pool parties.

Si Como No Movie Theater, Si Como No Hotel, see p. 251.

Other Activities

Local tours offer cruises, horseback riding, and visits to palm oil plantations.

ATV Tours

AXR Tours, Jacó, tel 2643-3130, axrjaco.com

Canopy Tours

Hacienda Barú, see p. 250

Rainforest Adventures Aerial Tram, Playa Jacó, tel 2257-5961, rainforestadventure.com

Vista Los Sueños, Jacó, tel 2637-6020, canopyvistalossuenos.com

Crocodile Safaris

Crocodiles are prolific.

Ecojungle Cruises, see p. 157

Diving

Mad About Diving, Uvita, tel 2743-8019, madaboutdivingcr.com

Villas Gaia, see p. 251. PADI certification and snorkeling.

Dolphin Safari

Planet Dolphin, Quepos, tel 2777-1647, planetdolphin.com

Golf

Los Sueños Marriott Ocean & Golf Resort, see p. 252

Horseback Riding

Brisas del Nara, Londres, 5 miles (8 km) E of Quepos, tel 2779-1235, horsebacktour.com

Del Pacifico Horseback Riding, Esterillos, tel 2778-7070, delpacifico.net/costa-rica-equestrian

Refugio Nacional de Vida Silvestre Rancho Merced, Uvita, see p. 168

Kayaking

Explore the mangroves of Pacific river mouths silently by kayak to get close to the critters.

Dolphin Tour, Uvita, tel 2743-8013, dolphintourcostarica.com

Kayak Jacó, Punta Leona, tel 2643-1233, kayakjaco.com

Quepoa Expeditions, Manuel Antonio, tel 2777-0058

Rafting

Ríos Naranjo and Savegre.

Amigos del Río, Quepos, tel 2777-0082, amigosdelrio.net

Ríos Tropicales, Quepos, tel 2233-6455 or 2777-4092, riostropicales.com

Sailing & Cruises

Sunset Sails Tours, Quepos, tel 2777-1304, sunsetsailstours.com

Sportfishing

Quepos is one of three key centers on the Pacific coast.

Big Eye Charters, Quepos, tel 8379-1702, fishingcostarica.net

Bluefin Sportfishing, Quepos, tel 2777-0000, bluefinsportfishing.com

Costa Rica Dreams, Los Sueños Marina, Playa Herradura, tel 2637-8516, costaricadreams.com

Surfing

Surfboards and other surfing equipment are available for rent at Playa Jacó and Playa Hermosa. Playas Esterrillos, Oeste, Este, Dominical, and Manuel Antonio are also popular.

■ ZONA SUR

Festivals

Festival de las Artes (Golfito, Ciudad Neily, and others, tel 2248-3240, festivaldelasartes.go.cr). Full spectrum of arts at multiple venues.

Nightlife

Hotel Samoa del Sur (Golfito, tel 2775-0233). Open-air bar with pool, foosball, and darts competitions.
Pearl of the Osa (Playa Platanares, tel 8829-5865, iguanalodge.com/dancing). Hugely popular Friday night dance lessons and party. Craft beer.

Other Activities

Canopy Tours
Original Canopy Tour, Drake Bay, tel 8810-8908, corcovadocanopytour.com
Osa Canopy Tour, Puerto Cortes, tel 2788-7555, osacanopytour.com

Diving
Aggressor Fleet, tel 706-993-2531 or 800/348-2628, aggressor.com/cocos.php
Aguila de Osa Inn, Drake Bay, see p. 252

Hiking
Reserva Biológica Campanario, see p. 175. Treks, ecology courses.

Nature Tours
Aldea del Río Sportfishing (Sierpe, tel 2788-1157, aldeadelrio.com). Tours of the Terraba-Sierpe delta, Corcovado, and more, plus nighttime crocodile tour.
Aventuras Tropicales, Puerto Jiménez, tel 2735-5195, aventurastropicales.com
The "Bug Lady" Tour (Agujitas, tel 8701-7356, thenighttour.com). Fascinating nocturnal insect tour.

Land-Sea Tours, Golfito, tel 2775-1614 or 8886-9360, golfitocostarica.com
PsychoTours, Puerto Jiménez, tel 8353-8619, psychotours.com

Sea Kayaking

Kayaking provides a silent entrée into mangrove swamps.
Aventuras Tropicales. See Nature Tours, this page
Zancudo Boat Tours, Playa Zancudo, tel 2776-0012, loscocos.com/boattours.htm

Sportfishing

Banana Bay Marina, Golfito, tel 2775-0255, bananabaymarina golfito.com
Crocodile Bay Lodge, Puerto Jiménez, tel 800/733-1115, crocodilebay.com
Zancudo Lodge, Zancudo, tel 2776-0008 or 800/854-8791, zancudolodge.com, closed Oct.

Whale-Watching

Aldea del Río Sportfishing, see Nature Tours, this page
The Divine Dolphin, Drake Bay, tel 8818-9784 or 619/784-4444, divinedolphin.com

■ SOUTH CENTRAL

Festivals

Día del Boyeros, May 15, San Isidro de El General. Traditional oxcarts, rodeos, and more.
Festival de los Diablitos, Dec. 30, Boruca. Masked men disguised as animals and devils rush through the village creating harmless mayhem, aided by copious amounts of alcohol. The colorful Native American celebration lasts three days and has an allegorical happy ending.

Nightlife

La Compañía de Danza Folclórica Chirripó (tel 8878-9357). Traditional music and dance.

Other Activities

Birding
Birdwatching Costa Rica, San Isidro, tel 2771-4582, birdwatchingcostarica.com
San Vito Bird Club, San Vito, sanvitobirdclub.org

Hiking up Chirripó
Two-day hike can be done solo (see feature pp. 194–195) or with a guide.
Costa Rica Trekking Adventures, San Isidro, tel 2771-4582, chirripo.com

Rafting
Ríos General and Chirripó are Class III or IV experiences.
Costa Rica Expeditions, see p. 260
Explornatura, tel 2556-0111 or 866/571-2443, explornatura.com
Ríos Tropicales, see p. 260

■ NORTHERN LOWLANDS

Festivals

Expo San Carlos (April, Ciudad Quesada, tel 2475-7010 ext 115). Costa Rica's largest cattle fair, with a parade (tope), rodeos, and festivities.

Nightlife

Club Lava Lounge & Sports Bar (Liberia, tel 2479-7365, lavalounge costarica.com). Chill and colorful open-air bar with live music.
Volcán Look Disco (La Fortuna, tel 2479-9690). The deafeningly loud music and whirling lights on display draw patrons from miles around. Dance classes offered.

Other Activities

Ballooning
Serendipity Adventures, Turrialba, tel 2556-2722 or 888/226-5050, serendipityadventures.com

Canoe Trips
Laguna del Lagarto, Lagarto, tel 2289-8163, lagarto-lodge-costa-rica.com

Selva Verde, see p. 255
Tilajari Resort Hotel, see p. 255

Canopy Tours
Arenal Canopy Tour,
(La Fortuna, tel 2479-8712, arenal
canopy.com). Represents seven
canopy tour operators in the area.

Fishing
Inland fishing at Caño Negro
Lagoon or Laguna de Arenal.
Caño Negro Natural Lodge,
village of Caño Negro, tel 2471-
1426, canonegrolodge.com
Hotel de Campo Caño Negro,
village of Caño Negro, tel 2471-
1012, hoteldecampo.com

Horseback Riding
Alberto's Horses, La Fortuna, tel
2479-9043
**Cinco Ceibas Rainforest Reserve
& Adventure Park,** Sarapiquí, tel
2476-0606, cincoceibas.com
Desafio Adventure Company,
La Fortuna, see p. 260
Tilajari Resort Hotel, see p. 255

Rafting
Ríos Peñas Blancas and Sarapiquí
both offer Class II and III trips.
Aguas Bravas, Puerto Viejo
de Sarapiquí, tel 2761-1645,
aguasbravascr.com
Desafio Adventure Company,
see p. 260

Rain Forest Hiking
Chachagua Rain Forest Lodge,
see p. 254
**Cinco Ceibas Rain Forest
Reserve & Adventure Park,** see
above
Selva Verde, see p. 255

Spelunking
Explore the Venado Caverns.
Aventuras Arenal, La Fortuna,
tel 2479-9133, aventurasarenal
.com
Venado Caverns, see p. 216

■ THE CARIBBEAN
Festivals
Festival Internacional de Calypso
(July, Cahuita). Three-day calypso
festival with local and International artists.
Festival Ák Kuè (Sept., Amubri).
Traditional Bribri-Cabécar indigenous celebration.
Puerto Viejo Chocolate Festival
(Oct., Puerto Viejo, pvchocolate
festival.com).
Carnival, Oct. 12, Puerto Limón.
Traditional Caribbean carnival
with beauty pageants, parades,
and music. Revelers flood the
town to celebrate to the beat of
calypso and reggae.

Nightlife
Cocos Bar (Cahuita, tel 2755-0437).
The most colorful and liveliest bar
in town.
Johnny's Place (Puerto Viejo, tel
2750-0445). Classy cocktail bar
where the party spills onto the
beach.
Maxi (Manzanillo, tel 2759-9086).
Unpretentious bar, with dancing.
Point Bar & Grill (Puerto Viejo, tel
2756-8491, thepointcostarica.com).
Delights sports fans with its pool
table and big screen.

Other Activities
Cahuita Tours, Cahuita, tel 2755-
0101, cahuitatours.com

Canoeing
Rent dugout canoes (cayucas)
and motorized pangas to explore
Tortuguero. Rent kayaks to
visit Río Estrella's wetlands and
Gandoca-Manzanillo.
Karla Taylor's Experience (tel
89815-2386). Guided nature trips.

Diving
Cahuita's small coral reef includes
the remains of a small wreck.
Gandoca-Manzanillo also has a
coral reef.
Aquamor, Manzanillo, tel 8886-
9431

Dolphin Safaris
Wahoo Fishing Tours,
Puerto Viejo, tel 8601-5294,
wahoofishingtours.com

Fishing
Costa Rica Outdoors (tel
800/308-3394, costaricaoutdoors
.com). Offers fishing trips in Costa
Rica's lakes, rivers, sea, and ocean.
Eddy Brown's Sportfishing,
Tortuguero, tel 8834-2221,
captaineddiebrown.com
Jungle Tarpon Lodge, Parismina,
tel 866/411-2327, jungletarpon
.com
Río Parismina Lodge, Parismina,
tel 210/824 4442, riop.com
Silver King Lodge, see p. 255

Hiking
You can hike alone in many places,
but a guide is always recommended.
ATEC (Asociación Talamanca de
Ecoturismo y Conservación), Puerto
Viejo, tel 2750-0398, ateccr.org
Cahuita Tours, see this page

Horseback Riding
Cahuita Tours, see this page
Seahorse Stables, Punta Cocles,
tel 8859-6435, horsebackriding
incostarica.com

Surfing
Puerto Viejo's legendary Salsa
Brava wave kicks up during storm
season. Boards can be rented, and
there are specialized accommoda-
tions. Lesser spots include Playas
Bonita and Portrete, north of
Puerto Limón.
Totem Surf School, Puerto Viejo,
tel 8621-7572

Turtle Research
Sign up as a volunteer, and help
guard hatcheries against poaching
and predation.
**Marine Turtle Conservation Proj-
ect,** c/o ATEC (see Hiking above)
Sea Turtle Conservancy, Tortuguero, tel 2297-5510 or 352-373-6441,
conserveturtles.org
**Wider Caribbean Sea Turtle Con-
servation Network,** tel 2236-0947
or 314-954-8571, widecast.org

INDEX

ILLUSTRATIONS CREDITS

National Geographic

TRAVELER
Costa Rica
FIFTH EDITION

Since 1888, the National Geographic Society has funded more than 12,000 research, exploration, and preservation projects around the world. National Geographic Partners distributes a portion of the funds it receives from your purchase to National Geographic Society to support programs including the conservation of animals and their habitats.

The information in this book has been carefully checked and to the best of our knowledge is accurate. However, details are subject to change, and the National Geographic publisher cannot be responsible for such changes, or for errors or omissions. Assessments of sites, hotels, and restaurants are based on the author's subjective opinions, which do not necessarily reflect the publisher's opinion.

National Geographic Partners
1145 17th Street NW
Washington, DC 20036-4688 USA

Become a member of National Geographic and activate your benefits today at natgeo.com/jointoday.

For information about special discounts for bulk purchases, please contact National Geographic Books Special Sales: specialsales@natgeo.com

For rights or permissions inquiries, please contact National Geographic Books Subsidiary Rights: bookrights@natgeo.com

ISBN: 978-1-4262-1828-6

Printed in Hong Kong

17/THK/1

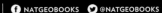